The Transatlantic Indian, 1776–1930

The Transatlantic Indian, 1776–1930

Kate Flint

PRINCETON UNIVERSITY PRESS

PRINCETON AND OXFORD

Published by Princeton University Press, 41 William Street,
Princeton, New Jersey 08540

In the United Kingdom: Princeton University Press, 6 Oxford Street,
Woodstock, Oxfordshire OX20 1TW

Library of Congress Cataloging-in-Publication Data

Flint, Kate.
  The transatlantic Indian, 1776–1930 / Kate Flint.
    p. cm.
  Includes bibliographical references and index.
  ISBN 978-0-691-13120-7 (alk. paper)
1. English literature—History and criticism.   2. Indians in literature.   3. English
literature—American influences.   4. Indigenous peoples in literature.   5. Group identity
in literature.   6. American literature—Indian authors—History and criticism.
7. Indians—Transatlantic influences.   I. Title.

PR151.I53F57 2008
820.9'352997—dc22

                                                                        2008030164

British Library Cataloging-in-Publication Data is available

This book has been composed in Sabon

Printed on acid-free paper. ∞

press.princeton.edu

Printed in the United States of America

10   9   8   7   6   5   4   3   2   1

To Alice

Contents

Illustrations

Preface

My first Indian was on a mug. To be precise, he was on the top row of Eric Ravilious's Alphabet Mug: an iconic noble profile of a warrior wearing a feather headdress. *I* is for Indian, and similar images graced entries in illustrated dictionaries and encyclopedias. Mounted Indians galloped through the pages of the British comics that I read in the early 1960s—*Eagle* and *Wizard* and *Lion*—and they fearlessly and viciously attacked pioneers in the television series that were imported at the time—*Laramie, Bonanza, Rawhide.* Playing cowboys and Indians meant some tough choices. One could make one's own bow and arrows, which was much more satisfactory than wielding a plastic gun from Woolworth's. Scouting, tracking, and building wigwams were all great fun. Nonetheless, to be an Indian always meant, ultimately, to be on the losing side.

The origins of *The Transatlantic Indian* lie in the mid-1990s. In 1994 I had accepted an invitation to teach in Santa Fe, New Mexico, where the Bread Loaf School of English had recently opened a summer campus. I knew next to nothing about the American Southwest, and even less about contemporary Native American life. Yet suddenly I had in my classroom students who came from and/or who taught on the Navajo reservation and several of the local pueblos. Since I had come from England, my knowledge and expectations barely went beyond those of my childhood, and I rapidly started reading—both history and literature—to make up for lost time. My first and deeply heartfelt thanks go to Jim Maddox, whose suggestion that I teach in Santa Fe that summer changed my life in many important ways, and to Lucy Maddox, who generously and graciously gave me the books and reading suggestions that first introduced me to Native American writing and whose own scholarship has been a model and an inspiration.

It was not long, however, before I started to reflect not only on my personal blind spots but on the question of what a British person in the nineteenth century might, or might not, have known and thought about the indigenous inhabitants of North America. This book was initially conceived as part of a project about Victorian views of the United States, but it soon became clear to me that the representation of Native Americans was a huge question in its own right, one that could be used to open up a lot of issues concerning the changing relationships between the two countries, whether at the level of high politics or of popular culture. And then I started to see how very one-sided this approach was: I had initially failed to register the numbers of native people who traversed the Atlantic

Figure 1. Eric Ravilious, Alphabet Mug designed for Wedgwood, 1937.
Photo by Kate Flint.

in their own right and who left accounts of their impressions and responses to the society that they encountered. The fact that many of them,
in their turn, came from Canada rather than from the United States
meant, moreover, that I needed to rethink my ideas about what, precisely,
constituted the "transatlantic." I only wish that I had had the space to
give more weight to the part that needs to be accorded to Central and
South America when considering the ramifications of this word.

I have incurred a huge number of debts while working on this book. I
carried out the first sustained research during a wonderful semester as a
Visiting Fellow at the Humanities Research Center at the Australian
National University. My thanks to Ian Donaldson and all the staff and

fellows there for making my time such a happy and profitable one. A packed couple of weeks as a Visiting Senior Professor at the University of Alberta gave me an opportunity to try out a number of my ideas in lecture form for the first time. Patricia Clements, Isobel Grundy, Juliet McMaster, Julie Rak, and Heather Tapley all contributed to a memorable visit. I worked on the final revisions at the beginning of my stay as a Rockefeller Fellow at the National Humanities Center, North Carolina. The director, Geoffrey Harpham, together with Kent Mullikin, Lois Whittington, and the rest of the staff, provided a superbly comfortable and enabling working environment; Josiah Drewry, Jean Houston, and Eliza Robertson managed to hunt down the volumes that I needed in order to nail the last pesky, elusive footnotes into place.

I am enormously grateful to the Department of English and the School of Arts and Science at Rutgers University and to the Faculty of English at Oxford University for their support in a number of ways, whether in granting leave or providing funds for research that has enabled the writing of this book. At Rutgers, Barry Qualls has been the best of friends and the best and most imaginative of deans; my life would be the poorer without him. Richard Miller has been an extraordinarily resourceful and enabling departmental chair. Cheryl Wall, likewise, contributed greatly, during her period as chair, to fostering conditions in which research can flourish. Other friends and colleagues, especially Ann Fabian, Billy Galperin, John Kucich, George Levine, John McClure, Meredith McGill, Jonah Siegel, and Carolyn Williams, have at one time or another asked searching questions that have allowed me to think harder about what I have been trying to say. In different ways, the cheerfulness and efficiency of Eileen Faherty, Quionne Matchett, and Cheryl Robinson kept me going, as did that of Sarah Barber, Paul Burns, Jenny Houlsby, and Jackie Scott-Mandeville in Oxford. Among my colleagues in Oxford, Paul Slack and the Fellows of Linacre College have been long-term interlocutors of this book from its earliest incarnations, and members of the Faculty of English, past and present, have also contributed a great deal; my warm thanks to Elleke Boehmer, Stephen Gill, Jo McDonagh, Nick Shrimpton, and Robert Young.

This book would not have been possible without the resources of many libraries and the helpfulness and resourcefulness of their staff. Chief among these are the British Library, the Bodleian Library, the Firestone Library of Princeton University, the library of the University of New Mexico, Rutgers University Library, UCLA Library, the National Library of Australia, the London Library, and Cambridge University Library. Special thanks to the people in the Archive Room at the Grey County Museum, Owen Sound, and those working at the Pauline Johnson House, Brantford.

I have given talks based on research for *The Transatlantic Indian* at Kings College, London; Rutgers University; the University of Southern California; the University of New Mexico; Princeton University; the Université de Montréal; Royal Holloway College, London; Reading University; Dartmouth College; the University of Notre Dame; Harvard University; Cambridge University; Oxford University; Yale University; Hull University; the Centre for British Studies, Berlin; the University of Florida; North Carolina State University; the University of Woollongong; the University of Melbourne; the University of Maryland, College Park; the University of North Carolina, Greensboro, and conferences organized by the MLA; the North American Victorian Studies Association; the Royal Historical Society/North American Conference on British Studies/British Association for American Studies; as well as the conference entitled "The Traffic in Poems: Nineteenth Century Poetry and Transatlantic Exchange" (Rutgers University); "Locating the Victorians" (London); "The Great Exhibition and Its Legacies" (CUNY); and "America and England in the Nineteenth Century," (University College, Worcester, UK). My very best thanks to all who invited me, were responsible for making arrangements, and, above all, asked the many stimulating, provocative, and difficult questions that helped me to define and refine my arguments.

Kristie Allen and Megan Ward have, at various times, done sterling work as research assistants. Other graduate students, present and past, have allowed me to try out ideas on them and have in turn posed searching questions; they include Sarah Alexander, Matthew Beaumont, Kirstie Blair, Devin Griffiths, Isobel Hurst, Rick Lee, Pablo Mukherjee, and Muireann O'Cinneide. On a drive between Los Angeles and Santa Fe, Bruce Smith asked some important questions that made me think through some difficult turns in the argument. Isobel Armstrong, Gillian Beer, Eileen Gillooly, Helen Groth, Wendy Jacobson, Laura Jagles, John Jordan, Andrea Lunsford, Peter Mandler, Gabriel Melendez, Tim Morton, Deborah Nord, Donald Pease, Jason Rudy, Kate Thomas, John Warnock, and Tilly Warnock have all helped to make this a better book than it would otherwise have been. The intelligent and enduring friendship of Dinah Birch, Deirdre David, Hermione Lee, and Helen Small means a very great deal to me. I owe more than I can easily say to Clare Pettitt; her intellectual curiosity and enthusiasm for life have been an inspiration to me.

At Princeton University Press, Hanne Winarsky has been the best of editors: both encouraging and steady-handed. Her upbeat efficiency, together with that of her editorial assistant, Adithi Kasturirangan, and the book's production editor, Leslie Grundfest, has made working on this book a great pleasure. Dalia Geffen has been an impeccable and inspired copy editor. I am very much indebted to the comments made by the anonymous readers of the manuscript. All remaining errors and infelicities are entirely my own.

My parents, Joy and Ray Flint, have been exemplary friends to this book. Their careful reading and helpful comments on the manuscript have been invaluable, and their enthusiasm and interest unflagging. They helped to provide me with the many newspaper cuttings and Web links that prove there is still a lively interest in Native Americans within Britain, from the repatriation of artifacts, complete with ceremonies marking the occasion, through build-your-own-tepee days in Midlands urban parks, to the tracing of the Salford descendants of the Lakota chief Charging Thunder, who stayed behind from Buffalo Bill's Wild West in 1903 to marry a local girl, and the refurbishing of a Kwakiutl totem post on the Salford quays, a commemoration of the city's transatlantic trading past. Conversations with Nigel Smith about *The Transatlantic Indian* have invariably been stimulating, and challenging; I owe him a huge debt of gratitude for these and for much more besides.

Finally, but foremost, my deepest thanks go to Alice Echols for all that she has brought to this book and to my life. She has read more drafts of *The Transatlantic Indian* than she and I would want to think about, bringing to them an acutely perceptive eye a keen ear for language, and an unwavering belief in the importance of history's complexities and contradictions. Much more than that, her cheerful enthusiasm, thoughtfulness, and generosity have been unstinting. This book is for her, with all my love.

Parts of chapter 5 have appeared as "Exhibiting America: The Native American and the Crystal Palace," in *Victorian Prism: Refractions of the Crystal Palace*, ed. James Buzard, Joseph W. Childers, and Eileen Gillooly (Charlotte: University of Virginia Press, 2007); and as "Is the Native an American? National Identity and the British Reception of *Hiawatha*," in *The Traffic in Poems: Nineteenth-Century Poetry and Transatlantic Exchange*, ed. Meredith McGill (New Brunswick: Rutgers University Press, 2008). Considerably revised portions of "Dickens and the Native American," in *Dickens and the Children of Empire*, ed. Wendy S. Jacobson (Basingstoke: Palgrave, 2000), appear in chapters 2 and 6.

CHAPTER ONE

Figuring America

The Albert Memorial, completed in 1872 and recently restored to its glistening, gaudy Victorian splendor, stands on the southern edge of London's Hyde Park. It commemorates not only Queen Victoria's late husband, but also national pride in commerce, arts, and science—all of them causes in which Prince Albert had taken an energetic interest. The monument ostentatiously places Britain at the center of the world, at the apex of a ground plan that installs Europe, Asia, Africa, and America at the round Earth's imagined corners. John Bell's sculpture follows European classical tradition by representing the entire American continent as an Indian.[1] Wearing resplendent feathered headwear, she rides on the back of a curly maned bison. Her component lands accompany her. The United States is in the forefront, tickling the bison between the horns with her scepter; a classically draped female figure, she wears a single feather in her hair. On the other side of the bison stands Canada, clasping the Rose of England to her breast, the national maple leaf and Nova Scotia's mayflower woven into her headdress. Slightly behind the United States is a Mexican Indian with an Aztec crest, with the fruit of the cochineal cactus at his feet; apparently on the point of rising, he may very well symbolize the Mexican revolutionary wars of the 1860s and that country's desire for national independence. A fit young man, he certainly has a more lively air than the mestizo who represents South America. Partly clothed with sombrero and poncho and holding a carbine and lasso, he is clearly employed in the ranching industry, with which Britain had strong economic ties.[2] Although the dynamics of the group as a whole are unquestionably forward looking, alert observers were not oblivious to the potential ironies inherent in the iconic figures. At the moment of the monument's erection, the American plains were heaped with the carcasses of dead bison, killed not just by sportsmen but by American troops, who, in their turn, were instruments of a government eager to subdue Indian autonomy, if not to eliminate the race altogether.[3]

This book is, in part, about the place of the Native American in the British cultural imagination from the time of American independence up to the early decades of the twentieth century. As the resonances of Bell's sculptural cluster suggest, the topic stretches beyond the borders of the United States. The iconic image of the Indian is not only inseparable from

Figure 2. *America*, Albert Memorial, London. Sculpted by John Bell, 1872. Photo by Kate Flint.

the expansion and the internal policies of the new nation during the nineteenth century, and from the country's reflections concerning its history and its national identity, but is also central to Britain's conceptualization of the whole American continent. Additionally, the Indian is a figure charged with significance when it comes to Britain's interpretation of her whole imperial role and her responsibility toward indigenous peoples. In other words, the Indian is a touchstone for a whole range of British perceptions concerning America during the long nineteenth century and plays a pivotal role in the understanding and imagining of cultural difference. But transatlantic crossings were not limited to visual and textual representations. A significant number of Native Americans visited Britain in the long nineteenth century, and this book explores their engagement with that country, its people and institutions, and these visitors' perceptions of the development of modern, urban, industrialized life. Their reactions—whether curiosity, shock, resistance, or enthusiasm—show them to have been far from the declining and often degenerate race that popular culture frequently made them out to be. This book examines the centrality of the Indian—both imaged and actual—to our own understanding of that changing transatlantic world.

How did the British come to learn about Native Americans? First, through numerous kinds of publications. These included informed and informative periodical and newspaper articles, news reports of battles between Indians and American troops, accounts of and interviews with Indian visitors to Britain, and sensationalist narratives of captivities and sudden attacks, anthropological studies, works of racial science, and missionary narratives and evangelical tales, quite apart from the many imaginative works of fiction and poetry that foregrounded both idealized and demonized Indian figures, whether contemporary or historical. Some of these materials were produced in, and also circulated widely within, North America, and many common attitudes toward Indians were, as we shall see, readily replicated on each side of the Atlantic. All the same, British travelers, in a large number of accounts, in both book and magazine form, grappled with issues raised by the culture and policies of the United States in order to see what might be learned from that country by way of example or warning. Their authors' attitudes ranged from profound relief at the familiarity created through a shared language and shared assumptions about domestic life—coupled with the disorientation that followed from recognizing that this apparent similarity could be highly delusory—to apprehension generated by the raw primitiveness of conditions the farther one moved away from the eastern seaboard, to expressions of anxiety and alarm at those signs of difference or change that might be equated with the menace of modernity, commercialism, and vulgarity. Native peoples were very frequently mentioned in passing, even if firsthand contact (with the notable exception of those who went on hunting expeditions or who served as missionaries) tended to dwindle as the century wore on. Nonetheless, British administrators in Upper Canada, as well as missionaries there, were also keen to distinguish their activities from those of their counterparts in the United States.

In many of the publications that originated within the United States, which turned curiosity about the country and its original peoples into a commodity and which ensured the rapid transatlantic circulation of stereotypes, we find that tracing British forms of knowledge of the Indian means witnessing the speed with which American popular culture was disseminated within the British Isles. The most obvious case in point here is the fiction of James Fenimore Cooper and its legacy both in the form of imported dime novels and in the British-authored Western, as produced by Charles Murray, Mayne Reid, Arthur Paterson, and others.

Print culture, however, took second place to the real thing, even as it helped to form many of the expectations that greeted actual native peoples. Small groups of Indians, as well as tribal representatives, visited Britain throughout the nineteenth century. On occasion they put on entertainments; more frequently they were political visitors concerned with land rights issues, or they were missionaries or occasionally lecturers. Whatever their role, the press inevitably treated them as objects of public curiosity. Two entrepreneurs were notable for displays that, in their different ways, set out both to inform and to entertain. In the 1840s the American traveler and cultural memorialist George Catlin mounted an exhibition composed of Indian artifacts and his own paintings of Western scenes. Shown first in London and then the provinces, the static objects on show were enlivened, after three years, by actual Indians. Then, at intervals from 1888 onward, Buffalo Bill's Wild West Show, sustained by a highly professionalized publicity machine, vaunted its triumphalist version of the conquest of the West, taking its spectacular performances to London's Earl's Court and on tour around the country.

As a supplemental context to these live Indians, something of the scale of America, at once exhilarating and daunting, was conveyed through panoramas, their painted cloths offering vicarious tourism and surrounding spectators with the force of Niagara or the vastness of the plains. The plains formed the dwelling place of indigenous peoples whose presence guaranteed America's difference from Britain, and they were also the site of their displacement in the name of "civilization." Charles Dickens, writing in late 1848 about "Banvard's Geographical Panorama of the Mississippi and Missouri Rivers," a supposedly three-mile canvas that took two hours to pass before its audience at the Egyptian Hall, Piccadilly, drew a moral from the variety of materials and peoples, representative "of the different states of society, yet in transition," to be found on the banks of these rivers:

> Slaves and free republicans, French and Southerners; immigrants from abroad, and restless Yankees and Down-Easters ever steaming somewhere; alligators, store-boats, show-boats, theatre-boats, Indians, buffaloes, deserted tents of extinct tribes and bodies of dead Braves, with their pale faces turned up to the night sky, lying still and solitary in the wilderness, nearer and nearer to which the outposts of civilisation are approaching with gigantic strides to tread their people down, and erase their very track from the earth's face. . . . We are not disposed to think less kindly of a country when we see so much of it, although our sense of its immense responsibility may be increased.
>
> It would be well to have a panorama, three miles long, of England. There might be places in it worth looking at, a little closer than we see them now; and worth the thinking of, a little more profoundly. It would be hopeful, too, to see some things in England, part and parcel of a *moving* panorama: and not of one that stood still, or had a disposition to go backward.[4]

Dickens moves from a ritualistic melancholia, evoked by the representations of dead and potentially dying Indians, to the broader issue of national responsibility. His themes here—the rhetorical juxtapositioning of America with Britain, while refusing to allow any clear privileging of one country over another, and the use of the past to raise questions about present and future—set the ground for what follows in this book.

The idea that Indians belonged to the past—either to a mythical past or to an anachronistic, atavistic world that needed to be rapidly abolished—was a dominant nineteenth-century trope, on both sides of the Atlantic. At the opening of *Gone Primitive*, Marianna Torgovnick writes of the way that white Western culture perpetuates an "immensely powerful and seductive" set of images of primitive peoples: "They exist for us in a cherished series of dichotomies: by turns gentle, in tune with nature, paradisal, ideal—or violent, in need of control; what we should emulate or, alternately, what we should fear; noble savages or cannibals."[5] These stereotypes began circulating from the time that Columbus, having crossed the Atlantic, had reached the islands of the Indian Ocean and first praised the indigenous people that he met for their liberality, honesty, and generosity, while subsequent Europeans condemned their strange appearance, customs, and hostility. The dichotomies were firmly established by the period that I am writing about, which stretches from the aftermath of the War of Independence, when Indians could be seen alternately as bloodthirsty enemies or noble, if ultimately doomed, allies, through the nineteenth century, when Indians were almost invariably thought of as being in a terminal decline, which stood for the condition of all "primitive" peoples.[6] Contemporary comments on the Albert Memorial's American figures both draw on and recirculate the stereotypes. James Dafforne, in his 1878 book on the memorial complex, describes the presiding figure of America as "mounted on a noble bison, which is bearing her onwards through the long prairie-grass; signifying thereby the rapid progress of the country in the march of civilization," proceeding to remind, or inform, his readers that "the 'red man' has almost vanished from view: he disappeared as the white man advanced, and never became incorporated with him, or grew up into a civilised likeness of him, as have some of the native tribes of other continents." In this context, he directs our attention to the foot of the United States herself, where "lies the Indian's quiver, with but one or two arrows only left in it; showing that the period for using such weapons has almost passed away."[7]

As we shall see, the possibilities for using Indians not as historical beings in their own right but as symbols for a more diffuse sense of loss and melancholy inform numerous literary works. Yet by the early decades of the twentieth century, which conclude the main part of my book, a number of writers, both American and British, came to look at the Indian in a new spirit of idealization, setting up the figure in opposition to a modernity they characterized as artificial, mechanical, and drained of natural, instinctual emotions. As this trajectory suggests, cultural responses to Native Americans can never be divorced from a wider set of concerns relating to national identity and the development, both political and social, of those lands which native peoples originally occupied.

The history of native-white relations in the Americas is a long one, and it has generated a very considerable scholarly literature.[8] The nineteenth century witnessed more systematic disruption and denigration of native peoples than ever before. Live Indians were commonly thought of as better dead (whether through the decay and degeneration of a "primitive" race that many presumed was inevitable or through more violent means), or a more humane alternative of "civilization"—that is, assimilation to the manners and values of Anglo-Christian lifestyles—was projected for them. This is very familiar territory. What distinguishes the period covered by *The Transatlantic Indian* is the fact that within the United States, the interactions that count are no longer between the British and Indians, as was the case before 1776, but between Britain's literal and figurative heirs and the land's original inhabitants.[9]

Throughout the nineteenth century, British commentators were fascinated by the paths the former colony had taken. It was, as it were, a renegade family member. They recurrently invoked the metaphor of the rebellious daughter, setting off powerful resonances of ingratitude and impropriety toward the mother country, resonances that could very handily be played upon with a queen on the throne and the development of a cult of maternity as a keystone value underpinning a successful empire. They also frequently expressed the commonly held view that Canadian First Nations people enjoyed a vastly superior relationship with their white rulers to that experienced by American Indians under the government of the United States. We may gauge the fact that administrators in Canada built upon the familial trope when impressing Victoria's role upon First Nations people by the public expressions of filial loyalty some of the Indians expressed while on Buffalo Bill's tours. For example, in 1887 it was reported that the Lakota Red Shirt, speaking through an interpreter, "said that he and his young men had sat up all night talking about the 'Great White Mother' . . . It pleased all their hearts that she came to them as a mother, and not with all her warriors around her. Her face was kind and pleased them, and every one of his young men resolved that she should be their great white mother."[10] The fact that the rhetoric of British commentators framed the Indians according to whether they came from Canada or the United States is crucial to this book and, indeed, to affirming the point that "the transatlantic" is a greatly weakened term if it is taken to apply to British-American traffic alone.

For many British pundits, the United States offered, or threatened, a model for an expanding democracy. Their anxieties included a concern over what appeared to be a destabilizing dissolution of boundary lines between classes and the knock-on effects of a rapidly growing economy. The responses in political and financial spheres had their counterparts at a more popular level and were translated into worries about, and a fastidious repulsion toward, commercialism, rampant consumerism, the brashness of the moneyed, and a lack of genteel femininity among American women.[11] Even the commodification of Indian artifacts, on which a large number of travelers remarked, could be seen to stand for America's compulsive drive toward money making. Moreover, by the end of the century, the territorial ambitions of the United States increasingly began to look like a form of imperialism that had the potential (unlike earlier westward expansion) to threaten existing British interests—to the point where it became increasingly apparent, in global terms, that Britain had more to gain from treating the United States as an ally than as a rival. The ever closer literary parallelism of British and American modernists in relation to the Indian stands in a synecdochic relationship to the two countries' political positioning: this is the moment when the distinction between British and American attitudes toward Native Americans becomes far less clear cut. But before this point was reached, the following question was frequently posed, both overtly and implicitly: if this is what could happen when a younger branch of the family struck out for independence, what conclusions might be drawn about the futures of other territories and the growing demands for autonomy that were being voiced by settlers, by their dependents, and by indigenous peoples themselves? During the long nineteenth century, these questions surface in relation to a number of such peoples, whether Australian Aborigines or New Zealand Maori, the native inhabitants of India or—rumbling and longer-standing undercurrents much closer to home—the Scottish Highlanders and the population of Ireland.

Given such contexts, British perceptions of how the Americans managed their interactions with Indians had complex resonances. Attitudes toward native land rights—or, rather, dispossession—and their perceived inhumanity, greed, and sustained duplicity in such matters could be taken as symbolizing a whole range of American behaviors and outlooks. Some travelers interpreted the poverty and alcoholism they witnessed among Indians on the fringes of white towns as evidence of the race's innate "degeneracy" and an indication of its inevitable demise. But others saw the same conditions as evidence of a callous willingness to exploit the vulnerable for economic ends, something also observed in the maladministration of a number of Indian agents charged with the distribution of shoddy goods and inadequate resources on the new reservations.[12] The treatment of Indians could easily be juxtaposed with the much vaunted democratic principles of the young nation, and in this respect parallels were drawn with the hypocrisy and lack of attention to human rights on the part of those who supported slavery. As will become apparent, many of those who, in their imaginative poetry and prose, wrote most sympathetically about the Native American also protested forcefully about slavery's inhumanity. But whether one looks at the United States from the point of view of those British people who abhorred the practice—or, for that matter, who supported it on economic and even social grounds—the figure of the African American did not carry with it the same complicated, and often contradictory resonances of national identity.

Some very valuable recent work has demonstrated the place that the Indian holds in what Lauren Berlant has so usefully termed the "national symbolic"[13] and the part the iconic Indian played in the post-Revolutionary conceptualization of national identity has become increasingly apparent. As Philip Deloria points out, the frequency with which Indians appear, in British political prints of the mid-eighteenth century, "to symbolize the colonies as alien and uncivilized and therefore needful of (and deserving) the rule of empire" in fact aided their adoption as a national symbol by republicans wishing to borrow their connotations of willfulness, determination, accomplished oratory, and physical strength. Their images decorated military flags, newspaper mastheads, coins, and a large number of handbills.[14] Werner Sollors, in *Beyond Ethnicity*, helpfully summarizes the Janus-headed situation of the new Americans of the 1770s:

> The American revolutionaries . . . found themselves in a double role as republicans: on the one hand, they overthrew and usurped Indian legitimacy—perceived in European terms as the doomed role of an aristocratic nobility of chieftains—in the name of European republicanism; on the other hand, they defied the parental authority of the mother country by invoking the spirit of the Indian and by symbolically "acting Indian" in clothing and military strategy. The settlers were metaphoric "Indians" in their attempts to define themselves as "non-British," as "Americans" (a term originally applied exclusively to the Indians); but they were emphatically European when they identified with the destined mission of republicanism against aboriginal

legitimacy. Americans could conceive of themselves both as Tammanies following the westward course of empires and as frontiersmen pitted against a savage wilderness.[15]

Some commentators, such as Carroll Smith-Rosenberg and Susan Scheckel, have written of the prominent place the Indian occupied among the range of Others against whom Americans defined themselves, and here, as elsewhere, the resonances of those binary oppositions associated with the Indian—nobility and cruelty—have been extensively explored. "Crowding the pages of political pamphlets, broadsides, sermons, "even dictionaries and geographies," Smith-Rosenberg writes, "a host of negative others worked to solidify the new American subject[:] . . . sybaritic British aristocrats, wild European revolutionaries, deceitful men of credit and commerce, seductive and extravagant women. . . . Shadowing all these negative others, however, was a still more sinister, primeval figure—the savage American Indian warrior."[16] Yet Philip Deloria and Cheryl Walker, among others, have recently observed how during the nineteenth century, the figure of the Indian *did*, in fact, become identified with America—whether it stood symbolically for a powerful connection with the land or for resolution and strength. A figure from the ancient past, it allowed American authenticity to be located within a mythology, within history.[17] Scheckel's invocation of Anne Norton's remarks about liminal figures in Norton's *Reflections on Political Identity* is, in its turn, extremely helpful when it comes to recognizing the flexibility of Indians within the construction of national identity. "Liminars," Norton postulates, "serve as mirrors for nations. At once other and like, they provide the occasion for the nation to constitute itself through reflection upon its identity. Their likeness permits contemplation and recognition, their difference the abstraction of those ideal traits that will henceforth constitute the nation."[18]

But it would be highly erroneous to view this process as one-sided. Walker makes the crucial point that although it had already been noted how during the nineteenth century, the United States was "actively engaged in the process of constructing a sense of 'nationness' through iconography, art, writing, rituals, speeches, institutions, and laws," what had not been adequately perceived prior to her own work was the fact that Native Americans "also participated in this cultural process, sometimes in order to distinguish themselves from the invaders but sometimes in the interests of revising notions of America to include the tribes themselves."[19] The degree to which those Indians who visited Britain in this period possessed agency when it came to determining the impression that they made, and the degree to which this offset the ways in which they were manipulated by others for ideological and commercial purposes, will be a central question for this book. Their presence, moreover, gave a material reality, however mediated by the conditions of performance, to a people far more frequently encountered on the printed page. Lucy Maddox has recently written of the importance of understanding "the extent to which Indian people were performing their histories, their successes and failures, their political appeals, and their individual and collective identities before a largely white American public" in order to make an assessment of the nature and form of American Indian intellectual activity from the 1890s through the early decades of the twentieth century.[20] In this book, I maintain that the capacity of Indians to inhabit British public, intellectual, and social spaces attests to their participation not just on the troubled terrain of the United States and Canada, but within a yet broader transatlantic context of developing modernities.

This argument is dependent, of course, on the adoption of a pan-Indian stance, something that must be balanced against the continual need to be alert to the demands of tribal specificity, for the use of the term "Indians" is inevitably problematic. It may be a pejorative instrument (and in the nineteenth century, it frequently was, albeit often unintentionally), or it may signify the recognition of a homogenizing stereotype; or—more positively—its employment may be a gesture of political and ethnic unity and solidarity.[21] During the nineteenth century, all kinds of difference were subsumed under the generic label, as one might suspect. Yet it is encouraging to find that, throughout the period, the idea of the universal Indian was challenged in a number of ways. At the beginning of the century, the recognition of distinctions between tribes was frequently related to a discrimination between political allies and enemies, whether current or in the recent past. By the midcentury, the development of anthropology as a distinct field of inquiry (aided by the publication in 1841, in London, of George Catlin's *Letters and Notes on the Manners, Customs, and Condition of the North American Indians*) led to an increasing emphasis on recognizing and recording specific customs, beliefs, and legends. This was given urgent and poignant emphasis by the recurrent lament that these peoples were rapidly hastening toward extinction. Such detailed information also animated the pages of some travelers' accounts, especially those who made the journey to the lands west of the Mississippi. The more firsthand contact such travelers had with Indians, the more likely they were to distinguish carefully between tribes, and even between different bands of the same tribe. This gives a compelling edge to the accounts of, for example, sportsmen whose successful hunting depended on working alongside Indian guides and those of missionaries.

Nonetheless, within popular usage, "Indian" almost invariably signified uncouth, untamed, "uncivilized." It was not just employed in relation to the aboriginal inhabitants themselves, but could be casually extended to anyone from over the Atlantic. The English aristocracy in William Thackeray's historical novel *The Virginians* (1857–59) might be able to brandish around the names of various tribes, but this is done only to intensify the unsuitability of their visiting American cousin Harry and to underscore his unfamiliarity with their mid-eighteenth century parochial outlook: a snobbish inwardness that Thackeray himself is at pains to satirize. So in chapter 13, when Fanny is instilling in Harry the basics of the minuet, her boorish brother sneers: " 'Infernal young Choctaw! Is he teaching Fanny the war-dance?' "[22] Nor is their mother any better: " 'You booby!' she begins to her adored Fanny. 'You double idiot! What are you going to do with the Huron? You don't want to marry a creature like that, and be a squaw in a wigwam?' " (122). In chapter 17, she—and Thackeray—are still laboring the joke, calling Harry "the Iroquois" and warning Fanny that if she were to marry him, she would have to live in a country " 'with Indian war-whoops howling all round you: and with a danger of losing your scalp, or of being eat up by a wild beast every time you went to church' " (146). In Anthony Trollope's *The Eustace Diamonds* (1871–73), the American Lucinda Roanoke is critiqued in an even more complex derogatory way, native epithets being blended with African American racist slurs. As Kathy Psomiades has put it: "The black hair, 'broad nose,' and 'thick lips' that Lucinda shares with her aunt; the epithet 'savage' so frequently applied to her; the Native American word that stands as Lucinda's patronym all conspire to racialize, primitivize, and archaize her."[23]

This condescension lasted right through the nineteenth century, and not just in fiction. American women complained that they were customarily thought of as raw and unmannerly by comparison with their British counterparts. Jenny Churchill, the American-born mother of Winston, recollected late in her life that "in England, as on the Continent, the American woman was looked upon as a strange and abnormal creature, with habits and manners something between a Red Indian and a Gaiety Girl. . . . No distinction was ever made among Americans: they were all supposed to be of one uniform type."[24] Or, if the visitors were not categorized as natives themselves, they were popularly presumed to live under constant threat from them, in a way that managed to damn their whole country as backward. In 1897 Consuelo, Duchess of Marlborough, experienced her new mother-in-law, Lady Blandford, making "a number of startling remarks" to her "revealing that she thought we all lived on plantations with Negro slaves and that there were red Indians ready to scalp us just around the corner."[25] Such attitudes are deliberately played upon, and satirized, by Henry James in *The Portrait of a Lady*

(1881), when he has his more mentally agile Americans turn the tables on their English detractors. Lord Warburton initially treats Isabel with considerable social superiority, educating her in "the peculiarities of English life" as though she had no experience or imagination: " 'He thinks I'm a barbarian,' she said, 'and that I've never seen forks and spoons' "; and she asks him artless questions for the pleasure of hearing him answer seriously. Then when he falls into the trap, " 'It's a pity you can't see me in my war-paint and feathers,' she remarked; 'if I had known how kind you are to the poor savages I would have brought over my native costume!' "[26] This extension of the Indian to act as a symbol for all Americans is in part, of course, an indication that its capacity to stand for national identity very readily crossed the Atlantic. But it also points to a crucial difference between British and American appropriations of the figure. In the United States, the Indian was inseparable—whether positive or negative associations came into play—with the nation's sense of itself. But in Britain, the figure was far more protean. The general connotations of nobility, of savagery, and of the nostalgia attendant on immanent extinction could be adopted extremely easily for a number of ends that had nothing whatsoever to do with the self-image of the United States. Instead, this readily malleable icon facilitated, but was secondary to, discussion or amplification of a whole range of issues, from sentimentality to violence, or from democracy to the woman question.

Moreover, even if British writers could borrow the figure of the Indian as a ready-made stand-in for generic American uncouthness—or for other aspects that they believed characterized the United States as a nation—the grouping at the base of the Albert Memorial serves as an important reminder of the contemporary recognition that Indians are not just found within that country, that the associations set in train by the word "Indian" do not just apply to the native inhabitants of the United States, and, implicitly, that the boundaries of Indian nations do not correspond with other international borderlines. Indigenous peoples are found from the northern shores of the continent down to Tierra del Fuego, and at one time or another, all, in undifferentiated fashion, are given the label "Indian." Witness Wordsworth's "Complaint of a Forsaken Indian Woman" (1798), its snowy scenario derived from Samuel Hearne's *Journey from Prince of Wales's Fort in Hudson Bay to the Northern Ocean* (1795), together with the fact that Darwin, and many others, used the term to describe natives throughout South America, right down to the plains of Patagonia and beyond.

Nonetheless—although I will have something more to say about Central and South America in a moment—the main focus of this book falls on the exchange of representations and points of view in the northern hemispheric transatlantic space. As we have seen, the United States increasingly employed the iconic Indian as a signifier of nationhood, and images of indigenous inhabitants were, likewise, called upon by those who wrote about Canada. Some of these authors were immigrants, others—including many administrators—were visitors who did not settle permanently. But there was a remarkable similarity between the views expressed by those who lived permanently in Canada (often recognizing their familial, political, and emotional ties to Britain) and those who spent a shorter spell of time there. The figure of the Indian often acted as shorthand for certain features that were thought to characterize the settler colony. Above all, the ready cooperation of First Nations people in hunting, trapping, transportation, and trading (and in taking action against the French) was emphasized; they thus could be made to appear both in possession of necessary survival and specialist skills and willing to harness these to Britain's economic ends. More symbolically, the figure suggested that the settler colonists themselves shared something of the courage, the hardiness, the endurance, the nobility, and the *manliness* of the land's original occupants.

One should not let the celebratory rhetoric and imagery blind one to the very legitimate grievances borne by First Nation peoples. In 1815 they constituted at least one-fifth of the population; by 1911 their numbers had halved to just over 100,000—at the time, barely 1 percent of Canada's total. As in the United States, disease had devastating effects. Tribes who sold their lands were kept waiting, sometimes indefinitely, for payment.[27] Nonetheless, the dominant and frequently reiterated British viewpoint was that their position was vastly preferable to that of Indians on lands that had passed from British jurisdiction. "A survey of the North American Indian's history brings out a contrast between his treatment at the hands of the white man above and below the forty-ninth parallel so striking as to call for explanation,"[28] writes the Canadian J. Macdonald Oxley in *Macmillan's Magazine* in 1889. He claims that both the French and the activities of the Hudson's Bay Company (trading from around 1677 and bought out by the Canadian government in 1868) had prepared the ground for smooth interracial contact.[29] He argued that initial Indian relations with the British benefited enormously from the administrative wisdom of Sir William Johnson and from his organization in 1764 of a convention of Indian tribes at Niagara. This, combined with his own conciliatory spirit, had laid the foundation— Oxley now falls into rose-tinted prose—"for a friendly feeling towards British authorities, which, thanks to the unswerving good faith practised by them ever since in all dealings with their aboriginal subjects, has been extending and deepening without check or interruption" (195). He does not pause to consider the emotions that may in fact have been precipitated by the confinement of many bands to reservations and then, starting with the 1869 Gradual Enfranchisement Act, by the pressures put on native men to relinquish their lands. Rather, he congratulates Canada on the fact that her Indian subjects "have not yet been made to feel that they are being crowded out by the white man" (197), their freedom for hunting and fishing vastly superior to that of the Indian in the United States.

The belief that Britain's attitude toward "her" Indians was far more accommodating and humane than that expressed through the policies of the United States was revitalized by the episode involving the Sioux war chief Sitting Bull. Sitting Bull crossed into Canada in late May 1877—eleven months after the battle of Little Big Horn and his victory over Custer. Preceded by several bands of Sioux, the arrival of Sitting Bull and his followers brought the number of American Indians in Canada to around five thousand; they attempted to occupy the same area of southern Saskatchewan that was being hunted by indigenous peoples. While Sitting Bull would have preferred to have been recognized as a Canadian subject, John A. Macdonald's government was not prepared to go that far, although it seems that the Sioux leader was told that he could stay in Canada as long as he conducted no border raids and lived according to Canadian law. Eventually, in July 1881, Sitting Bull followed many of his people back over the border into the new reserves of North Dakota, convinced that this was the only viable alternative in the face of dwindling food resources. The Canadian version of events, however, both at the time and subsequently, has tended to attribute this peaceful outcome of a potentially explosive situation to the calm diplomatic handling of the Royal Canadian Mounted Police, putting forward their combination of patience and courage as a far more effective means of handling the Indian than the measures the American military adopted.[30] These tactics—explained in terms of character traits rather than armed strategy—were described in words that emphasized the power of those attributes of tactful understanding and of a gradualist building of trust, which had been seen as distinguishing the successful missionary in Canada since the early decades of the nineteenth century. As Ged Martin has argued, in many ways the real importance of British North America to the British lay not so much in questions of investment, or trade, but in its southern neighbor, the United States, and the ideological challenge which that country lay down to British monarchical institutions—including, by extension, the institution of empire and the assumptions of benevolence, obligation, or duty toward colonized peoples who were commonly considered, at least in theory, to go along with it.[31]

Native peoples did not uniformly share these perspectives, by any means. While some, like the Ojibwa William Wilson in his 1838 poem

"England and British America," could chirpily proclaim, "Hail to thee, Canada! the brightest gem/That decks Victoria's brilliant diadem,"[32] others expressed far more resentment at the fact that they, or their ancestors, had given military support to the British but were now not being treated with reciprocal loyalty, or they voiced outright opposition to the newcomers who brought new social ways with them. The Englishman Gilbert Malcolm Sproat, sent to establish a sawmill on Vancouver Island, recorded his conversation with an unidentified Seshahts Indian about what he saw as an inevitable process:

"We don't care to do as the white men wish."

"Whether or not," said I, "the white man will come. All your people know that they are your superiors; they make the things which you value. You cannot make muskets, blankets, or bread. The white man will teach your children to read printing, and to be like themselves."

"We do not want the white man. He steals what we have. We wish to live as we are."[33]

However, British commentators rarely recorded such oppositional native voices. Far more common were the views expressed by the journalist William Trant, writing in the *Westminster Review* in 1895 in terms as complacent as Johnson's. He stressed both the degree to which the native inhabitants of the provinces had become "civilised"—"they are rapidly reaching the point where the line dividing them from other citizens becomes indistinct and gradually vanishes"[34]—and the success of the government when it came to dealing with the problems of the Plains Indians after the post-1868 western expansion and the decimation of buffalo herds. Trant does acknowledge Indian perspectives—their sense of disorientation when faced with new cultural forms, their understanding of their relationship to the land, and so on—but he nonetheless warmly praises the effectiveness of reservations, the grants of agricultural equipment made to tribal members, and the provision of education and instruction in trades. There is no mention of the establishment of federal power to depose hereditary chiefs and replace them by elected councils—dating from 1876—nor the outlawing of the potlatch and the sun dance. Rather, the tone is one of benevolent paternalism, of pride that the Indians have been "tranquilised" by a country that has been able, as it were, to read their inmost desires: "Not only is there no discontent or disaffection, but the red man has become thoroughly attached to the white man's government. One reason for this is that the Indians had long yearned for what they got, a yearning not the less strong because it was not expressed or formulated" (520). Success is measured by assimilation, manifested in both material terms ("Some of them live in houses equal to any, and superior to many, of those of the British settler. They have organs, melodeons, violins, stocks, sewing machines, pictures, ornaments, and others marks of civilised life" [522]), and ideological ones: the Indian's "course is marked by a manly independence, intelligent enterprise, and unflagging industry" (523). In other words, the Indian has become the epitome of an idealized upper-middle-class Englishman—apart from the fact that he still enjoys a dinner of boiled dog. In all of this, credit is given not only to the Indians themselves, but also to the administrators in the Indian department of the Canadian government, whose activities are sharply contrasted with the bad faith generated by the U.S. government toward Indians: "There the Indian is regarded as we regard rats" (526). "It would have been our fault," Trant concluded,

> if we had looked on the Indians' vast territories merely as outlets for our surplus population, without considering the claims of the occupiers to our aid, our protection, ay! and to our sympathy, as men with souls and as British subjects with rights. . . . Canada has saved the Indians, and in doing so she has profited herself. It is argued by many that, figures notwithstanding, the Indians are dying out. Even if this be so, surely it is better that their last words be words of thankfulness and blessings for the good done to them, rather than imprecations and curses against those whom Destiny has placed to rule over them. (527)

Responses to the native peoples of Central and South America were more diverse and more confused, if, rarely, less condescending. The confusion, in part, stems from the fact that the identification of nationhood with Indian ethnicity—or with policies toward Indians—was nowhere nearly as marked, from a British perspective, as it was in relation to the United States or Canada. As a result, stereotypes were even more frequently invoked. First, at a popular level, an Indian was an Indian: potentially cruel and violent, often a threat, but just possibly supplying the local knowledge and the tools of survival that would prove indispensable to a story's hero when in strange lands. In such plot-driven writing, native peoples readily homogenize. A notable, but by no means atypical, example of this can be found in Wilkie Collins's *Hide and Seek* (1854; revised 1861), when the well-traveled Mat tells his new friend Zack "about the life he had been leading in the wilds of North and South America,"

> Wild, barbarous fragments of narrative they were; mingling together in one darkly-fantastic record, fierce triumphs and deadly dangers; miseries of cold, and hunger, and thirst; glories of hunters' feasts in mighty forests; gold-findings among desolate rocks; gallopings for life from the flames of the blazing prairie; combats with wild beasts and

with men wilder still; weeks of awful solitude in primeval wastes; days and nights of perilous orgies among drunken savages.[35]

With decided incongruity, he claims to have woken up, on one memorable occasion, in an "Indian wigwam" in the Amazon, scalped (152). Such characterization demonstrates all too readily the tendency for a composite Indian to be produced with no reference whatsoever to tribal distinctions; further, in such versions, national and geographic borderlines have ceased to matter.

Yet in other instances, such borders prove crucial. However useful to popular culture as a bloodthirsty figure when found on American soil, the Indian, once encountered or imagined farther south, could often be immediately invested with a more positive set of connotations. To some extent, this derived from a perception that the Incas and the Aztecs, in particular, were much more "civilized," as witnessed by their well-developed (that is, amenable to Western understanding) systems of government and, above all, by their craftsmanship: their skill in jewelry and metalwork and the edifices they constructed. Moreover, the Indians could often be portrayed as victims: victims both of the Spanish, Britain's traditional enemy, and of Catholicism.[36] Much of my book takes as its guiding principle the assumption succinctly voiced by Linda Colley that the British "came to define themselves as a single people not because of any political or cultural consensus at home, but rather in reaction to the Other beyond their shores."[37] The "Other" that she primarily had in mind was Catholic Europe. As I set out to show, the presence of the United States in nineteenth-century political and cultural relations complicates this conception of Otherness considerably.[38] Yet the sense that the American continent as a whole was an arena for working out these European relations was highly pertinent both to British engagements with the French, whether in Lower Canada, on the Canada–United States borderline, or Louisiana—to name the most obvious areas of contestation—and to the Spanish presence in Central and South America. There is a long literary history of the co-option of indigenous peoples—both in relation to the treatment they received and to the sides that they supported—in the dramatization of what were, effectively, European struggles. William Davenant's play *The Cruelty of the Spaniards in Peru*, performed at the Cockpit in 1658, helped to establish the tradition of the so-called Black Legend, with the English appearing as a Protestant foil to the Spanish, their atrocities having been publicized, above all, through translations of writings by Bartolomé de Las Casas.[39] Such anti-Spanish works supplied a rhetorical means of tempering English concern about the violence that was being perpetrated in their own colonies, or, as Roberto Fernández Retamar puts it, "the nascent bourgeoisie of other metropolises who created the Black Legend" did not do so "for the benefit of those people martyred by the Spanish conquest but rather to cover up their own rapacity."[40] The loaded political significance of those Indians who had suffered most notably and had their cultures transformed at the hands of the Spanish (and, in Brazil, of the Portuguese) helped ensure their utility for patriotic adventure fiction. Likewise, the very strangeness and remoteness of Amazonian tribes could form the basis for further speculative fictions that inevitably foregrounded British resourcefulness and bravery, advanced through the familiar combination of surviving the attacks of hostile natives and borrowing from the skills of more amenable ones. Such adventure narrative often bore a suppressed reference to other forms of exploration and writing both about indigenous peoples and about the more prosaic economic realities of Britain's informal empire of trading interests in Central and South America.[41]

Yet it is not just because of a certain nineteenth-century haziness on the importance of borders when it came to imaginative works—or to understanding the nature of the "primitive"—that the indigenous peoples of these lands claim our attention here. The importance of seeing the Americas as a whole was apparent to Victorian commentators as well as to ourselves. Most prominently of all, J. R. Seeley, in *The Expansion of England* (1883), criticized that version of English history that looks at the topic in terms of England alone, rather than of England in relation to her possessions and to "the ten millions of Englishmen who live outside of the British Islands," in Canada, the West Indies, South Africa, Australia and New Zealand, and India.[42] More than this, he bids his readers to consider that the current empire is a second empire. A hundred years earlier, "we had another set of colonies," which broke off from "the mother country," and Seeley's major preoccupation is to ask what we might learn from this: "The greatest English question of the future must be what is to become of our second Empire, and whether or no it may be expected to go the way of the first" (17). He acknowledges that in looking across the Atlantic, one sees that English relations with the United States were but part of a broader transatlantic stage on which the political struggles of Europe had been played. France, Spain, Portugal, and Holland were, alike, seeking economic and territorial possession; internal European animosities were duplicated within the Americas; and in turn, the New World acted upon European communities. "In one word," writes Seeley, "the New World in the seventeenth and eighteenth centuries does not lie outside Europe but exists inside it, as a principle of unlimited political change" (84). What distinguishes the British Empire by 1883 is the fact that despite its shifting terrain, "it is the sole survivor of a whole family of Empires, which arose out of the action of the New World upon the peculiar condition and political ideas of Europe" (47). Seeley acknowledges the differences set in motion by a fact succinctly set out by Walter Mignolo: "The United States constituted itself as an independent nation from a rising empire . . . whereas Latin American countries obtained their independence from two empires in decay."[43]

Seeley's text put forward a set of propositions on which late Victorian expansionist imperialism was to build: the importance of Britain conceiving of itself as a dispersed world power, not an island; the importance of retaining an empire if one was to remain as a national power; and the importance of the right management of colonies so that these did not turn into another rebellious, independent-minded daughter. Although this in itself is relatively well-trodden ground, we need to recognize the importance of Seeley's demand that we understand the Americas as a complex whole. Here, we might usefully move forward eight years from the date of publication of *The Expansion of England* to an essay authored on the other side of the Atlantic, José Martí's "Nuestra América" (Our America), first published in *La revista ilustrada de Nueva York* in 1891. Seeley spoke from a position of institutional authority, as professor of modern history at Cambridge University; Martí, by contrast—I quote José Saldívar's thumbnail biography in *The Dialectics of Our America*—"is an alienated Cuban, exiled in the ghettoes of New York, one of the first Latin American intellectuals of his time audacious enough to confront U.S. imperial history, its imperial ethic, and its imperial psychology."[44] Again, the metaphor of the family, and of the succoring mother in particular, figures in his discourse. But the location of origins is different. Martí berates those inhabitants of the Americas who deny their ethnic parentage: "Those born in America who are ashamed of the mother who reared them, because she wears an Indian apron; and those scoundrels who disown their sick mother, abandoning her on her sickbed!" He deplores the "deserters" who put their mother "to work out of sight, and live[s] at her expense on decadent lands, sporting fancy neckties, cursing the womb that carried him."[45] This attack on the United States' blatant consumerism and dogmatic adherence to ideas of progress brings Martí close to many contemporary English critiques. But the agent of possession, in Martí's formulation of "*our* America," is the "we" not of the original colonizers but of the original inhabitants and their descendants, both pure-blooded and mestizo. To invoke Martí, as well as nineteenth-century British commentators, reminds us, from the start, that examining the transatlantic Indian is a project that involves not only British assessment of America's indigenous people or the views— so far as they may be recuperated—that Native Americans held of the

British. It must also take into account the fact that the end of the nineteenth century witnessed the beginning of a pan-Indian movement that saw cross-tribal and transborder advantages in recognizing some common cause.[46] Oppression has the power to bring together as well as to fragment, and there are times when despite the necessity of recognizing the particularity of individual tribes and their histories, one must acknowledge that the term "Indian" has a political viability that transcends its currency within thoughtless popularizations.

⚡

What follows is organized in a broadly chronological way. I start by looking at the image of the Indian that the nineteenth century inherited from Romantic writing, one that emphasized the trope of the "dying Indian" as a member of a race associated with positive connotations of bravery, loyalty, dignity, and so on, and I show how it provided an opportunity for poets to exploit their fondness for the melancholic or to explore the qualities of supposedly primitive people. I trace the shift from the way in which the Indian was seen as a vehicle of rhetorical eloquence to being a figure of pathos, situating this within the changing situation of actual tribal people during the period. But the Indian carried more ambiguous associations of cruelty during this earlier period as well—an easy polarity of good and bad Indian was readily taken up by contemporary fiction. All such stereotypes were quickly unsettled, however, by contact with actual Indians, and my third chapter examines the impact made by the Ojibwa and Iowa who toured with George Catlin in the 1840s—and the impression that their travels in Britain made upon them. It is clear that they were far from impressed by their encounters with the modern metropolis. The marriage of the half-Ojibwa interpreter to a young London woman provoked considerable debate—and evidence of extreme prejudice—on mixed-race marriage, and questions of prejudice and marriage, slavery and sentiment, are taken up in chapter 4, on the portrayal of Native Americans by British women writers. This treatment was often far more radical, and far more angry—whether focusing on racial issues or on imperial ambitions in general—than that found in the work of many male authors.

Chapter 5 further develops ideas about the way in which the Indian functioned as a figure of American national identity within Britain. By the time of the 1851 Great Exhibition, America was presenting herself as a thoroughly modern country, yet the empty floor spaces within the U.S. section of the exhibition provided plenty of opportunity to assess this claim, as well as to consider the implications of unpopulated—or apparently unpopulated—space. The sculptural figure of the Wounded Indian, which formed part of the American exhibit, was readily seized upon for its ironic potential. In the light of national self-presentation, this chapter asks whether or not the Indian was, in Britain, identified with, or against, American identity in the midcentury, a question that is highly pertinent to the reception of Longfellow's poem *Hiawatha*. The figure of Hiawatha provides an example, moreover—albeit highly fictionalized and idealized—of the ideals of noble masculinity, something that continues the emphasis on the strongly gendered way in which Native Americans were understood. In chapter 6, on British popular writing, I consider some of the means by which stereotypes of Indians that emanated from the United States circulated within Britain and were modified and filtered through domestic concerns. I first consider the influence that James Fenimore Cooper had on transatlantic adventure and historical fiction, and then pass to Charles Dickens's often contradictory treatments of native peoples, before looking at the more complicated case of Mayne Reid. This British writer of popular Westerns employed contemporary American-generated stereotypes of Indians and at times reinforced that country's message of manifest destiny, yet he also managed to question certain political and racial aspects of American life in a way that offered up a warning to his home readership. These stereotypes are read through a consideration of the shifting nuances of the idea of the "savage" in mid-Victorian Britain.

In chapter 7 I continue to explore issues of gender in relation to native peoples—in commentaries by travelers and sportsmen and, more particularly, in the use of Indian themes to comment on contemporary domestic gender debates, as in Elizabeth Gaskell's "Lois the Witch" and Gilbert Parker's 1894 novel *The Translation of a Savage*, which may be read as a reworking of the Pocahontas story. Parker wrote from a Canadian background, and British–First Nations relations come again to the fore in chapter 8, on Indians and missionaries. The missionaries in question, though, are not just the British who worked in Canada, but First Nations men who toured Britain as preachers and spokespeople. I extend the category to include George Copway, whose account of his 1850 visit to Britain, en route to the third World Peace Conference, provides an extended example of native engagement with, and enthusiasm for, modernity. This was very much at variance with the image of the Indian put across by William Cody in his Wild West Show, of course, and I address this in chapter 9. But what interests me the most, in my treatment of this spectacular show, is the resonances that the Wild West could be made to have for a number of domestic concerns—about mass culture, about gender, and, above all, about Britain's position as a world power. The parallels that could be drawn between the American frontier and various frontiers in the British Empire, together with the apparent lessons that might be taken on board from America's treatment of her native peoples, occupy the first part of chapter 10, after which I move to a discussion of how the visits to London of Catherine Sutton, a Credit Indian, and then of the poet and performer Pauline Johnson illuminate Britain's attitudes toward First Nations people from an Indian perspective. Finally, I examine how such attitudes started to shift at the beginning of the twentieth century—partly under the influence of Western movies, partly as modernist writers and artists started to idealize the Indian for their own ends, and as other wannabe Indians, most notably Grey Owl, began to develop the association of Indianness with environmental preservation. By way of conclusion, I look briefly at some contemporary writing by native peoples—especially James Welch and Leslie Marmon Silko—that aims to reappropriate nineteenth-century transatlantic history in a range of imaginative ways.

This chapter opened by invoking a monument to mid-Victorian confidence in Britain's global centrality. It now closes with a description of a visit made to nineteenth-century America's most potent symbol of state by the most notable transatlantic writer of that century. Both the America of Henry James's fiction and the country he revisited after twenty years of living abroad and described in *The American Scene* (1907) seem to have expelled almost all consciousness of native inhabitants from the comfortable, secure bourgeois world. Yet *The American Scene* contains one particularly telling passage. James recounts going to Washington, and walking around the elegant architecture of the Capitol. He makes no direct allusion to the bas-reliefs *Preservation of Captain John Smith* (by Antonio Capellano), *Penn's Treaty with the Indians* (by Nicholas Grevelot), or *Landing of the Pilgrims* or *Conflict of Daniel Boone and the Indians* (Enrico Causici), which stand above the doors of the Rotunda.[47] Rather, his attention is drawn to the living covisitors to the city whom he encounters:

> I met one morning a trio of Indian braves, braves dispossessed of forest and prairie, but as free of the builded labyrinth as they had ever been of these; also arrayed in neat pot-hats, shoddy suits and light overcoats, with their pockets, I am sure, full of photographs and cigarettes: circumstances all that quickened their resemblance, on the much bigger scale, to Japanese celebrities, or to specimens, on show, of what the Government can do with people with whom it is supposed able to do nothing. They seemed just then and there, for a mind fed betimes on the Leatherstocking Tales, to project as in a flash an image in itself immense, but foreshortened and simplified—reducing to a single smooth stride the bloody footsteps of time. One rubbed one's eyes, but there, at its highest polish, shining in the beautiful day, was the

brazen face of history, and there, all about one, immaculate, the print-less pavements of the State.[48]

James writes with the customary compression of his later prose, which allows for the simultaneous presence of contradictory motifs. He employs the inflections of someone whose viewpoint, like that of so many of his contemporaries on either side of the Atlantic, is self-confessedly modulated through James Fenimore Cooper: these are "braves" severed from their traditional habitat. But rather than exhibit signs of degeneration, they have assimilated, and they bear the tokens of modern urban life. The Indians are both consumer and curiosity. It is unclear whether the photographs in their pockets are souvenirs they have collected or cartes de visite, the fin-de-siècle equivalent of the visiting card that the Indian chief Pitchlynne handed to a surprised Dickens aboard a Mississippi river steamer.[49] Opaque, too, is the agency behind the showmanship. Is James suggesting that the Native Americans serve a federal triumphalism, tacitly proclaiming the success of policies that have prevailed in the light of racial and social predictions? Or is he indicating that their appearance acts as a defiant self-advertisement, an ironic gap opening up between their evident survival and adaptation and the principles that have underlain the previous century's administrative decisions? The Indians themselves seem to have taken on the role of photographic illusionists, their presence creating the dramatic chiaroscuro that allows James to see with dazzling clarity the juxtaposition of native inhabitant and the "ark of the American covenant" that is the Capitol.[50] Instantly, he comes to acknowledge a vertiginous sense of historical process, and his prose tilts from the faintly condescending tones familiar from countless descriptions of Indians to something that recognizes the shocking sublimity of what American history has produced. The "brazen face" is at once the burnished skin of the Indian, a monument in living bronze whose contemporary presence ceaselessly invokes lost nobility; it suggests the unabashed continuity of the Indian in contemporary society and his refusal to become extinct; and it also stands for the shameless path that has led to the aloof architectural symbol at the administrative center of the United States. The "printlessness" of pavements, moreover, points to a double irony: the nation's newly built floor is, as it were, virgin, untrodden land once again; nor does it bear any published record of the violence done.

Nineteenth-century transatlantic studies are a huge and complex terrain, and their importance is increasingly being acknowledged, despite the disciplinary binarization that takes place on both sides of the Atlantic. Too frequently, the internal organization of our national academies has meant that British and American studies have been regarded as separate entities, failing to enter into sufficient dialogue with one another. This book adds to the calls that have already been made by Joseph Roach to pay full attention to the "amplitude of circum-Atlantic relations,"[51] and by Paul Giles to acknowledge how "conceptions of national identity on both sides of the Atlantic emerged through engagement with—and, often, deliberate exclusion of—a transatlantic imaginary."[52] Focusing on the figure of the Native American in this context brings a number of advantages with it. In the first place, it grants Indians a part not previously fully acknowledged in relation to the field.[53] They have important roles as subjects of fascination, as figures of dread, and as symbols of a difference that is a complicated and sometimes contradictory amalgam of national and racial components. From a British point of view, the fact that Native Americans were not scripted into any specific sets of national narratives made them particularly malleable figures. As this book seeks to show, the notional Indian could be readily adapted, in a number of disparate contexts, to demonstrate a great range of clichés, presuppositions, considered analyses, and hypotheses about the nature both of the United States and the Americas more broadly. Most frequently, the Indian served the role of an ahistorical Other against which various narratives of modernity could readily be written.

But examining transatlantic relations from this angle forms only a part of my project, for Indians had a varied and significant presence in Britain and were analytical, commentating voices in their own right. They not only provided a particular slant, or slants, on British society, but were living proof that, in their capacity to react and respond to modern life, they refused to be consigned to that role of the mythical and prehistorical that was so frequently assigned them. Despite the frequent and familiar need of the modern to erect ideas of the temporal Other against which it could define itself, this Other was also undergoing a process of transformation. Of course, this is, in broad terms, a point made very familiar through contemporary histories of postcoloniality. But there are some significant differences. Native American contacts with British culture in the Victorian period demonstrate not only transformation on the part of Indians, but also well-articulated resistance to the processes of appropriation and assimilation that equate with cultural genocide. These Indians are quite definitely not allowing themselves to be consigned to oblivion, nor to occupy the mythical status of the timeless, but see themselves as members of a race that has every intention of surviving. Engagement in this transatlantic contact zone is unequivocally a two-way process, unfolding in a way that disrupts those apparently neat binaries of "traditional" and "modern" on which conventional narratives of national progress have depended. Paul Gilroy, in *The Black Atlantic*,[54] explores how, at a slightly later date, and in the context of African American culture, we see modernities evolving on several fronts simultaneously and at several, nonsynchronic speeds.[54] Looking at the Victorian period, we see how, in what we may call the space of the *Red Atlantic*, the process is already well under way.

CHAPTER TWO

The Romantic Indian

Joseph Wright's painting of 1785, *The Widow of an Indian Chief Watching the Arms of Her Deceased Husband,* depicts a woman—feather in her hair, yet classically draped—seated in a conventional position of grief.[1] She may be gazing into the distance, or she may be wrapped in retrospective contemplation; either way, the spectator is denied immediate access to her person and feelings. Rather, the Indian Widow—whether encountered in the original painting or in the 1789 mezzotint engraving by John Raphael Smith—is a figure onto which the late-eighteenth-century spectator could project a range of compassionate emotions, generated both through the sentimental associations that were growing up around the idea of the American Indian and through knowledge of the conditions in which they lived. When Wright exhibited the painting in Mr. Robins's Rooms, in London's Covent Garden, his notes for the catalogue amplified his subject.

> This picture is founded on a custom which prevails among the savage tribes of America, where the widow of an eminent warrior is used to sit the whole day, during the first moon after his death, under a rude kind of trophy, formed by a tree lopped and painted; on which the weapons and martial habiliments of the dead are suspended. She remains in this situation without shelter, and perseveres in her mournful duty at the hazard of her own life from the inclemencies of the weather.[2]

If her garments seem somewhat incongruous, the accoutrements at least appear genuine, as one might expect from an artist who has paid as much attention to authenticity as Wright habitually did.

More mystifying, given the paucity of live volcanoes on the North American mainland, is the smoking cone on the right-hand side of the picture. While this may signify nothing beyond Wright's fascination with this particular geological phenomenon—he painted a number of works showing Vesuvius in full eruption in the mid-1770s—the cone here is not erupting in the spectacular show of fiery pyrotechnics that usually most intrigued Wright. Rather, it is smouldering in a subdued and sultry manner, and it is tempting to draw on this landscape feature

Figure 3. John Raphael Smith, *The Widow of an Indian Chief Watching the Arms of Her Deceased Husband,* 1789. Founders Society Purchase, Lee and Tina Hills Graphic Arts Fund. Photograph © 2000 The Detroit Institute of Arts. Mezzotint after Joseph Wright, *The Widow of an Indian Chief Watching the Arms of Her Deceased Husband,* 1785.

to make some allegorical parallels with the more central figure of the Indian Widow. First, one might say, the painting hints at the possibility for hidden and unpredictable destructive violence even within that which is apparently quiescent. Second, just as the volcano provides the foundation for a nation's soil, so one may understand the Indian as crucial to the formation of the country's prehistory, yet now becoming, like a volcano, potentially extinct. Additionally, the geographic anachronism of the landscape may be seen as metonymic of that familiar tendency to group all native peoples as one. Wright's topic had been proposed to him by the poet William Hayley two years previously, and in Hayley's own translation of parts of Ilonso de Ercilla y Zuniga's *La Araucana* (1569–90), which he had published in his 1782 *Essay on Epic Poetry,* the bloodiness of the Spanish-Indian conflict in Central America is underscored by the timeliness of a natural eruption: "The vext air feels the thunder of the fight,/ And smoke and flame involve the mountain's height;/Earth seems to open as the flames aspire,/And new volcano's spout destructive fire.[3]

Neither Wright's choice of subject nor the details of its execution would have been likely without a preexisting interest in Native Americans as peoples with distinct and intriguing traditions and lifestyles, to be found in exotic, remote, or challengingly inhospitable landscapes. Wright's treatment draws on a number of further features that were adapted and modified as a result both of changing political and social circumstances and of cultural models during the post-Revolutionary period. At this time, the idea of the Indian as in some way exotic coexisted with a growing number of accounts—from soldiers, traders, and others—of firsthand interaction and cooperation with native peoples, especially in the border area between the United States and British Canada. Direct observation combined with motifs of disappearance and degeneration, of stoic endurance and latent violence, in order to establish both the dominant themes and the paradoxes that were to remain at the center of nineteenth-century transatlantic stereotypes.

The specific moment Wright depicts seems to have been developed from James Adair's *History of the American Indians*, published in 1775.[4] The Anglo-Irish Adair, born around 1709, emigrated to America in 1735 and worked as a trader to the Indians, first principally the Cherokee, and then the Chickasaw and Choctaw.[5] Describing the Chickasaw mourning rituals, Adair wrote: "Their law compels the widow, through the long term of her weeds, to refrain all public company and diversions. . . . And if he is a war-leader, she is obliged for the first moon, to sit in the daytime under his mourning war-pole, which is decked with all his martial trophies, and must be heard to cry with bewailing notes." In a footnote to this passage, Adair added that "the war-pole is a small peeled tree painted red, the top and boughs cut off short: it is fixt in the ground opposite to his door, and all his implements of war, are hung on the short boughs of it, till they rot."[6] Adair's book was not illustrated, and while it seems that Hayley had nothing helpful to offer when Wright wrote to him inquiring about what an Indian widow might have worn by way of mourning dress, the painter was clearly able to lay his hands on some genuine Indian artifacts.

The availability of Indian weapons and accessories testified to a long tradition of collecting Indian paraphernalia in Britain.[7] Such items came back with those who had served in the army in America who had been administrators there (a practice that Canadian officials were to continue throughout the nineteenth century), who had been traders on the continent, or who visited as inquisitive travelers. The next century would witness, of course, an increasing production of Indian goods aimed specifically at the rapidly expanding tourist market, but in the later eighteenth century, their possession still frequently signified a degree of firsthand experience with Indian societies. It is worth noting, moreover, that the traffic in goods was not just one way. England also produced commodities that were exported to Indians: "Knives and hatchets, kettles and spoons, woollens and linens, needles and scissors, earrings and glass beads, liquor and tobacco, firearms and gunpowder"—indeed, tomahawks and scalping knives.[8]

What is particularly notable about Wright's picture, however, is not its inclusion of picturesque props, but its dramatization of the theme of mourning, on the part both of the widow and, vicariously, of the spectator. The idea of the "dying Indian," with the demise of one individual standing for the oblivion that was supposedly coming to the race as a whole, was yet to consolidate on either side of the Atlantic, although it was to become a dominant—perhaps *the* dominant—theme in discussions of Indian-white relations in the century to follow. Within cultural history, interest in "dying Indians" has, until recently, tended to preclude studies of their continuance and survival. But the theme of the extinction of a race that could readily be invested with all kinds of positive connotations of bravery, loyalty, impressive oratory, dignity, and—as in the case of Wright's widow—strong family ties was a potent one. Moreover, Indian deaths could be given a positive Christian spin and interpreted as a sign of God's favor toward settlers, since their demise was seen as freeing up land that had not previously been properly cultivated.[9] And, not least because the eighteenth century had witnessed an appalling loss of Indian life from diseases originating in Europe—a decimation that was to continue into the century to come—the inevitability of Indian extinction was very frequently put forward as a given fact, its claim to truth deepening with each successive reiteration.

In British poetry, the topos of the dying Indian may be traced back at least as far as Joseph Warton's poem of 1756 of that name, although here the speaker is unmistakably from Central America (in his version of heaven, "my forefathers feast/Daily on hearts of Spaniards"),[10] and the overall mood is defiantly anticonquest, rather than elegiac. The association of the Indian death song with stoic indifference to one's imminent death was consolidated by Jonathan Carver's description of an Illinois Indian singing while under torture from his captors, retaining a smile of mingled scorn and triumph to the last.[11] As Tim Fulford has written, "Gentleman-poets, remote from the American frontier, fixed upon the death-song precisely because they could construe it as a heroic triumph of meaning over violence, as a language whose authenticity as primitive poetry seemed vouchsafed by its emergence from bodily suffering."[12] Indeed, the mode could be made to stand for the "agony, the ecstasy, the plenitude of belief," that poetry has the power to produce in those who utter it. "The Greek Rhapsodists, according to Plato"—and according to Thomas Babington Macaulay, in his 1825 essay on John Milton—"could scarcely recite Homer without falling into convulsions," and this is seen to be on a par with "the Mohawk [who] hardly feels the scalping knife while he shouts his death-song."[13] Here the cultural parallel is, of course, highly favorable to the Indian.

Wordsworth's "Complaint of a Forsaken Indian Woman" is the best-known prototype of the British "dying Indian" poem. Published in 1798, it forms part of a cluster that includes Josias Arnold's "The Warrior's Death Song," of the previous year, Thomas Gisborne's "Dying Indian" (peculiarly lurid in the details of torture it includes—he quotes Carver in the preface to the volume in which it appears),[14] and Robert Southey's "Songs of the American Indians": "The Huron's Address to the Dead," "The Peruvian's Dirge over the Body of His Father," "Song of the Araucans," "The Old Chikkasah to His Grandson," and the "Song of the Chikkasah Widow," all of 1799.[15] The last of these, like Wright's painting, draws directly on Adair:

> Ollanahta, all day by thy war-pole I sat,
> Where idly thy hatchet of battle is hung;
> > I gazed on the bow of thy strength
> > As it waved on the stream of the wind.
>
> The scalps that we number'd in triumph were there,
> And the musket that never was levell'd in vain.[16]

In the case of his thematically linked poems, Southey seems to have been prompted more by the idea of the eloquence to be found among primitive peoples than by the pathos of their demise, and again, like Warton and Arnold, he stresses their desire for agency: "Tomorrow the victims shall die,/And I shall have joy in revenge," the widow concludes (144). Such utterances may usefully be read in the light of Philip Fisher's discussion of the place of the "vehement passions" in our lives. If, as he argues, modern Western culture has increasingly come to depend "on a concept of an inner life that is, first and foremost, for one's own consciousness alone," and that "the passions are a domain in which our important modern notion of a private life is impossible,"[17] then a concern with strongly expressed states of being as manifested by "primitive" peoples, accessed through figures who are revengeful, angry, or publicly grief-stricken, may be seen as a form of enablement, allowing for the exploration of a range of powerful emotions that might be hard to utter in an autobiographical voice. Moreover, this particular interest in the forceful expression of emotion relates to the fact that during the later part of the 1790s Southey was a member of a literary community that included Wordsworth and Coleridge, preparing the first edition of the *Lyrical Ballads*, with its concern for the sentiments of socially unsophisticated peoples.[18]

Wordsworth's "Complaint of a Forsaken Indian Woman" is preoccupied with stoicism in the face of abandonment and imminent death, an example of "the fluxes and refluxes of the mind when agitated by the great and simple affections of our nature."[19] Like his other poems of the period, it is more concerned with endurance than extinction. As Fulford has ably shown, though, Wordsworth's sympathy toward Indians demonstrated a clear decline, as he came "to see Indian 'wildness' as being dangerously destructive of the emotional and moral structures that he defined as being naturally British."[20] The irresponsible Youth with Cherokee feathers in his cap who woos, marries, and then abandons Ruth clearly had his flaws mirrored and fed back to him by roaming around "with vagrant bands/Of Indians in the West";[21] but these "savages" were doing no more than exacerbating the man's innate tendencies. By the time of *The Excursion* (published in 1814 and written between 1797 and 1814), the Solitary goes so far as to suggest that it is precisely those characteristics that have contributed toward the Indian's dispossession (he is a "creature weak/In combination . . . (wherefore else driven back/So far, and of his old inheritance/So easily deprived?)" (3:919–22) that in theory fit him out for a dignified, self-sufficient, and enviably contemplative existence. But theory and reality are two different things. In the event, when this incorrigible pessimist reaches the "unviolated woods" (3:944) of the west,

> that pure archetype of human greatness,
> I found him not. There, in his stead, appeared
> A creature, squalid, vengeful, and impure;
> Remorseless, and submissive to no law
> But superstitious fear, and abject sloth.
>
> (3:951–55)

Such a pattern of disappointment—squalid reality replacing the nobility that had been projected onto the idea of the Indian—was to become a very well worn commonplace in nineteenth-century travel writing.

Southey's treatment of the Indian, outside of the "dying Indian" poems, also proved decidedly ambivalent. The compositional history of his long, two-part poem *Madoc* brings this home very well. The poem was eventually published in 1805 but begun more than fifteen years earlier and revised in ways that illustrate something one finds frequently during the nineteenth century: that in the writing of transatlantic history involving native peoples, the major concern is not so much the interpretation of an earlier historical moment as the reworking of the past in a way that comments on contemporary social and political concerns. The starting point of *Madoc* lay in the idea of a group of twelfth-century Welsh people under the leadership of Prince Madoc who had supposedly founded a colony in Mexico.[22] The legend had been recycled by a number of seventeenth-century historians because it offered an alternative to Spanish claims, and the theory that there were Indians descended from Madoc persisted for at least the first half of the nineteenth century, not least because Catlin was convinced of the Mandan tribe's Welsh ancestry.[23] Southey began his treatment as a prose project in 1789; it grew to a book and a half of verse by 1794, when it was set aside until early 1797, its first draft finished during 1798–99.

Almost immediately, he was dissatisfied with it. His original choice of a Peruvian location seemed overused.[24] So Southey relocated the action of his poem to the southern branches of the Missouri. Here, he has the Welsh emigrants encounter the Aztecs (or Aztecas, as they are called in the poem), who—Southey explains in the preface to his first edition, in a manner that does nothing to clarify geography—had abandoned Aztlan, their own country, and founded the Mexican empire. At the opening of part 1, "Madoc in Wales," the Welsh become acquainted with the Hoamen, one of their tributary peoples, whose major value to the Aztecs is to provide them with a regular supply of sacrificial victims—a tradition that Madoc successfully calls upon them to resist, before returning to Wales in an attempt to gather support for his new colony. In part 2, "Madoc in Aztlan," he crosses the Atlantic again, to find that the Aztecs are returning to their old practices and that relations with these Indians are becoming somewhat strained. In the struggles that follow, the Welsh slowly gain the upper hand; the Aztecs come to believe that their only hope lies in the renewal of the sun, which their calendar promises will happen providing they make a human sacrifice on top of a sacred mountain after sunset. The multitude watch the sun sink beneath the plain.

> Such sinking at the heart
> They feel, as he who hopeless of return,
> From his dear home departs. Still on the light,
> The last green light that lingers in the West,
> Their looks are fasten'd, till the clouds of night
> Roll on, and close in darkness the whole heaven.
>
> (2:4821–26).

They wait for the sacred spark to be applied to the pyre on the summit, but fire of a different kind erupts on the mountain top: "The liquid fire boils out,/It streams in torrents down" (2:4878–79). Once again, a volcano has served its purpose, naturalizing the poet's ideological stance and sending a message—one articulated by a conveniently croaking bird—

of "Depart! depart!" (2:4936). Madoc and the Welsh are thus left in possession of the colony, with those Aztecs who wished to submit to them. The others leave, to spread their "foul idolatry" in new locations, "till Heaven,/Making blind Zeal and bloody Avarice/Its ministers of vengeance, sent among them/The heroic Spaniard's unrelenting sword" (2:5284–87). These final lines manage to damn both native peoples and their eventual Catholic conquerors.

Throughout the poem, natives are moved around both topographically and historically for aesthetic convenience, and, as Southey's notes show, they are shamelessly homogenized. He borrows details from a whole range of tribal practices—those recorded by Carver, in David Brainerd's *Journal,* in Henry Timberlake's *Memoirs* of the time he spent with the Cherokee, and in other sources—including, with extravagant incongruity, accounts of Arab and Chinese customs. However, in the considerable remodeling and expansion that the poem underwent in 1803–4, the most significant reworking occurred in Southey's political position. Initially, *Madoc* was linked to the project of Pantisocracy, a Utopian plan for establishing an ideal colony in America (and, as such, the starting place for Paul Muldoon's 1990 *Madoc: A Mystery,* which imagines what might have happened had Southey and Coleridge succeeded in emigrating—or, rather, which figures how a whole panoply of subsequent nineteenth- and twentieth-century thinkers might have understood their emigration and their subsequent collisions with native peoples). It was also to have acted as a vehicle for Southey's earlier religious opinions; thus, as Mark Storey puts it, "The Welsh bardic 'Unitarians' were to have gone to Peru to escape the Saxon Catholic tyranny at home."[25] The poem is nothing if not ambivalent in its attitude toward colonialism.

But the early political idealism rapidly became subordinated to Southey's desire to write a British epic, emulating Homer and Camoens, an epic that ends up equating missionary work (as was so often the case later in the century) with profitable colonialism. The account is not crudely one-sided. The natives, "of dark-brown colour, tinged/With sunny redness (1:911–12), are initially presented as inhabitants of an Edenic country, although their practices, particularly when it comes to worship, are treated with far more revulsion. Yet while Neolin, an Indian priest and snake-god worshiper, is generally presented in the poem as a fanatic, he nonetheless is not completely reviled but is used as a mouthpiece to assert the importance of cultural difference, claiming that to the Indians "was given/A different skin and speech and land and law" (2:510–11). Erillyab, the woman who rules the Hoamen people (and who appears in the guise, once again, of a Chickasaw widow),[26] is also at times sympathetically depicted. Indeed, in early plot sketches for the poem, Madoc was to have married her. And while Southey's primary sympathy lies with Madoc's mission of colonial expansionism, labor, and cultivation ("More fields reclaim'd, more habitations rear'd/More harvests rising round" [2:104–5]), he also puts some eloquent lamentations into the mouths of the dispossessed.

But however much Southey invests in the importance of Madoc's "civilizing" enterprise, as a figure Madoc fails to carry sufficient emotional or psychological weight to pull the reader along with him, as many contemporary readers were quick to point out. "Often very insipid and contemptible," Wordsworth called him.[27] The poem's conclusion, rather than being dominated by triumphalism, lays far more poetic emphasis on defeat, on the emotive effect of the setting sun, on the valiant melancholia of exile. The Native American has been invested with the pathos of a doomed race, and in fact Southey's apparently careless blending together of all kinds of tribal characteristics has the effect of spreading this destiny across the continent. The dying Indian is no longer primarily a vehicle of inspirational rhetoric, or even of defiantly voiced vows of revenge that showcase his innate cruelty. Rather, his predicament is made to stand for the situation of his peoples as a whole.

How did this transition come about? The answer lies in a combination of factors. Taken together, these illustrate the interdependency of poetic traditions on either side of the Atlantic during this period and the adaptability of the idea of the dying Indian to serve a range of aesthetic, political, and emotional ends. In both Britain and the United States, there was a growing and increasingly compassionately expressed knowledge about what was happening to native peoples. By the time Southey published *Madoc* in 1805, Indians in North America, however numerous they might appear to those who still saw them as formidable military allies or opponents, were becoming increasingly vulnerable: not just to diseases, but to displacement. The Louisiana Purchase of 1803 added around 800,000 square miles between the Mississippi and the Rockies to the territories that the United States counted as its own, and at this time, Thomas Jefferson began to consider the possibility of removing "uncivilized" tribes to these lands, freeing up their former possessions for white farming.

But even before Jefferson's policies started to take effect, the elegiac was becoming established as a mode well suited to, and served by, the figure of the Indian. Probably the best-known prototype of the newly melancholic genre by an American writer was Philip Freneau's "The Dying Indian," published in the *Freeman's Journal* on 17 March 1784, and then far more widely available in England after the two-volume publication of Freneau's poems in 1786. Although ostensibly an individual warrior's valediction to his earthly life, the manner of his leave-taking, bidding adieu to a familiar landscape, takes on the burden of a more archetypal physical displacement.

> Farewell, sweet lake; farewell surrounding woods,
> To other groves, through midnight glooms, I stray,
> Beyond the mountains, and beyond the floods,
>   Beyond the Huron bay![28]

This imagery and tone of lamentation both drew from and fed into certain strands that had been developing in British poetry since the mid-eighteenth century and which, in their turn, were inseparable from issues of culture and national identity. As critic Fiona Stafford has written, in both Thomas Gray's "The Bard," of 1757, and James Macpherson's "translations" of Ossian, of 1760–63, "the principal character is the last bard of an ancient Celtic race, threatened by the expansion of English culture"[29]—a figure, in other words, who bears a decided resemblance to Madoc.[30] Moreover, "contemplation of the last bard, although apparently an antiquarian interest, both reflected and promoted gloomy thoughts of personal transience and the decline of modern Britain."[31] Adding another layer to this motif of racial decimation and displacement was the incorporation of the figure of the eloquent survivor lamenting the depopulation of the English rural landscape, as when the speaker in Oliver Goldsmith's "The Deserted Village" (1770) poses as the last bard of his own race, looking over the ruins of Auburn, victim of a land "where wealth accumulates and men decay" (52): a village whose inhabitants have emigrated halfway across the convex world, to a country filled with thickly matted woods, rank poisonous plants, mad tornadoes, and "savage men" (356).[32]

There is no sense here that the emigrants may, in their turn, be displacing these native inhabitants. But by the time the poet and polymath John Leyden wrote *Scenes of Infancy: Descriptive of Teviotdale* (1803), the Scottish peasant who has been forced into emigration by finding himself in an unacceptable position of servitude and the Indian whom he, in turn, ousts have become almost as one. Both are victims of dispossession. In the fourth section of *Scenes*, given over to emphasizing the importance of one's native land and the emotional pull of the place in which one's forefathers are buried (and prefaced with a quotation from Chateaubriand's tragic story of Indian life, *Atala* [1801]), Leyden writes of the impetus to emigration that occurs in contemporary Roxburghshire:

> The peasant, once a friend, a friend no more,
> Cringes, a slave, before the master's door;
> Or else, too proud, where once he loved, to faun,

For distant climes deserts his native lawn.
And fondly hopes beyond the western main
To find the virtues here belov'd in vain.
So the red Indian, by Ontario's side,
Nurs'd hardy on the brindled panther's hide,
Who, like the bear, delights his woods to roam,
And on the maple finds at eve a home,
As fades his swarthy race, with anguish sees
The white man's cottage rise beneath his trees,
While o'er his vast and undivided lawn
The hedge-row and the bounding trench are drawn,
From their dark beds his aged forests torn,
While round him close long fields of reed-like corn.
He leaves the shelter of his native wood,
He leaves the murmur of Ohio's flood,
And forwards rushing in indignant grief,
Where never foot has trod the falling leaf,
He bends his course. . . .

Long may the Creek, the Cherokee, retain
The desert woodlands of his old domain,
Ere Teviot's sons, far from their homes beguiled,
Expel their wattled wigwams from the wild![33]

A later passage in this section connects the practices of the Indians by Lake Erie who ceremoniously confer with their dead chiefs and the narrator's own graveyard consultation with the spirits of his ancestors, who advise him to hold on to his "home-bred virtues" and to his ancestral land. Very likely, Leyden penned these concluding lines as he himself was leaving for India.

The comparison of both ancient Britons and, indeed, contemporary Celts with Native Americans was a long-standing one, going back at least as far as the early seventeenth century. In her invaluable book *Indians and English: Facing Off in Early America,* historian Karen Ordahl Kupperman remarks that thanks to the influence of Tacitus in fostering in the English a concern with their roots, and with the roots of their institutions, "the assumption that in looking at the Indians English men and women were looking at their own forebears became a commonplace in England: the early inhabitants of both Britain and Germany were, as Nathanael Carpenter wrote, 'little different from the present Americans.'"[34] These comparisons were not always positive ones. John White's portfolio of paintings of Carolinian Algonquians in 1585 finished up with representations of ancient Britons and Picts with garishly painted bodies and holding up the bloody severed heads of their enemies;[35] one might have been tempted to identify with the Roman conquerors of these primitive peoples and the social progressivism for which they could be made to stand, rather than with those whose ancestral claims rested on their original occupancy of the land. But the growing eighteenth-century concern with those who had inhabited the margins of Britain, with the combination of esoteric and enduring cultural formations that they embodied and practiced and with their political standing and rights, helped to change the emphasis. There were, moreover, some telling comparisons to be made with the descendants of these original inhabitants, both in terms of their political marginalization within an increasingly centralized country and in cultural terms. Helen Carr has explored how Indian poetry was an influential component in theorizing the importance of "primitive" poetry: an enthusiasm that fed both into the pre-Romantic cult of sensibility and into Romanticism itself, on both sides of the Atlantic. In particular, Hugh Blair's *Critical Dissertation on the Works of Ossian* (1763) and *Lectures on Rhetoric* (delivered in 1759, published in 1783, but circulated in manuscript form in the intervening period) promote the importance of primitive poetry by foregrounding the characteristics of Indian languages: "Bold, picturesque, and metaphorical; full of strong allusions to sensible qualities, and to such objects as struck them most in their wild and solitary life."[36]

But the location of this "wild and solitary" life was changing. In literal terms, Indians in the United States were being forced westward (hence away from the cultural centers on the East Coast); figuratively, this imagined lifestyle was increasingly a literary construct. Initially conceived of as a splendid orator, the dying Indian—whether seen in individualistic or racial terms—was not just co-opted into the rhetoric of sensibility but became invested with the Romantic tendency to fetishize the ruin, the decayed empire, the passing and crumbling into dust of the formerly great. In Mary Shelley's *Frankenstein*, the Creature vicariously learns of the history of Western civilization by listening to Felix's education of his Arabian friend: "I heard of the discovery of the American hemisphere and wept with Safie over the hapless fate of its original inhabitants."[37] In 1819, the year after Shelley's novel was published, the Moravian missionary John Heckewelder brought out his *Account of the History, Manners, and Customs of the Indian Nations Who Once Inhabited Pennsylvania and the Neighbouring States* (which was to serve as a major source for James Fenimore Cooper), and his elegiac cadences exemplify a prototype that was to be incessantly repeated on both sides of the Atlantic: "Alas! in a few years, perhaps, they will have entirely disappeared from the face of the earth, and all that will be remembered of them will be that they existed and were numbered among the barbarous tribes that once inhabited this vast continent."[38]

Nor were the poetic lamentations from one side of the Atlantic only. Americans also appropriated the figure for apocalyptic ends. William Cullen Bryant, extremely popular in England (particularly after the appearance of the 1832 edition of his work) and a ready furnisher of epigraphs and sonorous quotations to the travel writer, extended his immediate comment on the wrongs of dispossession so as to invoke the longer-term effects of a cyclical version of history.[39] In "An Indian at the Burial-Place of His Fathers" (1816), an Indian returns to his ancestral lands, now tame and cultivated, with moldering bones tossed aside by the plow.

> They waste us—ay—like April snow
>   In the warm noon, we shrink away;
> And fast they follow, as we go
>   Toward the setting day—
> Till they shall fill the land, and we
> Are driven into the Western sea.
> But I behold a fearful sign,
>   To which the white men's eyes are blind;
> Their race may vanish hence, like mine,
>   And leave no trace behind,
> Save ruins o'er the region spread,
> And the white stones above the dead.

"The realm our tribes are crushed to get," the poem concludes, "May be a barren desert yet."[40]

But does the elegy for the Indian, when written by a British person for a predominantly British audience, have the same implications as a poem by William Bryant or Lydia Huntley Sigourney, another writer who followed his elegiac lead and who also had a considerable British readership? Certainly, what writers on both sides of the Atlantic share is an indulgence in the pleasures of melancholia and in using the stylized grief and deprivation of others as an occasion for the acknowledgment, and celebration, of their own capacity for compassionate feeling, both in their individual capacity and as members of society. In this context, Julie Ellison's observation that "much of the literature of sensibility exposes a complicated awareness of the human costs of national and imperial economies, as well as the knowledge that sensibility itself is a privilege," is a highly telling one.[41] She acknowledges that the sentiment, as expressed in imaginative writing, amounts to much more than a taste for pathos. It is "consciously bound up with the social management of sentimental knowledge," and those who employ it are alert to the market for reading about pain, yet troubled by the stirrings of what we come to recognize as liberal guilt. She calls our attention to the inequalities that became inherent in the eighteenth-century writing of sensibility:

> Sensibility increasingly is defined by the consciousness of a power dif-
> ference between the agent and the object of sympathy. The literary
> victim is typically marked by racial, social, or national disadvantages:
> the deep-feeling Moor, the dying Indian, the impoverished veteran, the
> slave, the vagrant. While writings featuring such characters under-
> score the pleasure in global prospects available mostly to white Anglo-
> American authors, they show that the nation also could be criticized
> as a corrupt system from which no one was exempt. The global geog-
> raphy of otherness leads to territories of emotion. North Africa and
> North America become zones in which non-European and European
> men meet in order to be glamorized as troubled sons and lovers expe-
> riencing crises of authority.[42]

But for all of her thoughtful tracing of the culture of sensibility in its transatlantic manifestations prior to 1776, Ellison devotes the later chapters of *Cato's Tears,* to the literature of the new republic and the role the politics of emotion and race played within the new nation. She persuasively argues the importance of writing about the Native American and, indeed, about the African American for such writers as Philip Freneau, Sarah Wentworth Morton, and Ann Eliza Bleeker: "The specific benefit to these poets was the engagement of global histories and spaces. . . . [They] create transatlantic and trans-continental vistas where once and future nations pass in parade. These vistas, in turn, become the correlative of citizenship as understood by the public-spirited intellectual."[43] What falls by the wayside, and what lies at the center of my book, is what it might mean for English writers to continue to write of the Indian. Very frequently, the figure carries resonances that have a bearing on British culture quite different from those held by such home-generated stimuli to sympathy as a widow of the Napoleonic Wars or a solitary leech gatherer.

On both sides of the Atlantic, the motif of the dying Indian remained available for reworking throughout the nineteenth century, a continual prompt to a reader's capacity for sympathetic feeling. Despite the differing national reverberations, the sustained use of the figure had the effect of making history seem prescribed. Its literary presence performed a kind of cultural genocide. The more often a poetic Indian died—and the more frequently, as is invariably the case, he or she died either from old age or from intertribal conflict—the more inevitable the fate of the race as a whole appeared to be. Additionally, a range of supposedly scientific and anthropological theories came to be advanced to reinforce this inevitability. Without a future, the figure, no longer in any lasting sense a threat, could readily be domesticated into an object of compassion.

Two important aspects serve to distinguish the implications of "dying Indian" poetry within Britain from those that it bore within the United States. First, it was associated with the trope of the "dying Negro" and hence with American involvement with slavery. *The Dying Negro* was the title of John Bicknell and Thomas Day's much reprinted abolitionist poem (1773) about a despondent, dispossessed slave, once a brave and energetic Gambian, now a chained victim of greed, who shoots himself on board a ship on the Thames. Day's poetic postscript, in which the spirit of Afric rouses itself and destroys Europe, drives home the political point. Admired by Hannah More and other abolitionists, it inspired further poetry around the same theme.[44] The rising criticism of Americans as slave owners is reflected in the attack on the colonists that Day made in the lengthy prose dedication to Rousseau, which he added to the third edition of *The Dying Negro* in 1775: "Behold the men, whose avarice has been more fatal to the interests of humanity, and has more desolated the world than the ambition of its ancient conquerors!"[45] Such language, in its abstraction, meant that grounds for comparisons between the American treatment of slaves and of their country's native inhabitants became readily available. As we shall see, in Britain anger at the practice of slavery frequently went hand in hand with indignation against the policies toward Indians and a critique of territorial dispossession—particularly after Britain's own antislavery legislation had passed in 1807.

Moreover, from a British perspective, the emotion of mourning could be invested with some highly complex characteristics. The object of regret could well be more than the Indians themselves; it could also include Britain's former colonial possessions. The sense that Americans were deficient guardians of the landscape became a commonplace of British travel writing in the century following the Revolutionary Wars. This represents an inversion of the trope of a collapsed civilization; what takes its place is, rather, the idea of the destruction of nature and, indeed, of a people whose own way of life had, since the earliest transatlantic settlers, frequently been presented as being in harmony with the beauties of the natural world—living "gentle, loving, and faithful" lives, "void of all guile and treason. . . . after the manner of the golden age."[46] Such sentiments lie behind the melancholic tone that pervades Fanny Kemble's September 1832 descriptions of the scenery of the Northeast.

No one, beholding the prosperous and promising state of this fine country, could wish it again untenanted of its enterprising and industrious possessors; yet even while looking with admiration at all that they have achieved, with expectation amounting to certainly all that they will yet accomplish, it is difficult to refrain from bestowing some thoughts of pity and of sadness upon those whose homes have been overturned, whose language has passed away, and whose feet are daily driven further from those territories of which they were once sole and sovereign lords. How strange it is to think, that less than one hundred years ago, these shores, resounding with the voice of populous cities,— these waters, laden with the commerce of the wide world,—were silent wildernesses, where sprang and fell the forest leaves, where ebbed and flowed the ocean tides from day to day, and from year to year in uninterrupted stillness; where the great sun, who looked on the vast empires of the East, its mouldering kingdoms, its lordly palaces, its ancient temples, its swarming cities, came and looked down upon the still dwelling of utter loneliness, where nature sat enthroned in everlasting beauty, undisturbed by the far-off din of worlds "beyond the flood."[47]

Kemble's account, like many other versions of the "dying Indian" topos, is dependent upon a heavy investment of her own values in the figure of the seemingly dispossessed and powerless, as well as demonstrating her personal capacity to perform the role of mourner.[48] Locating loss in a foreign land that is no longer the responsibility of one's nation is a way of sharing in the sentiment of nostalgia with her readers while sidestepping the need to engage with any kind of responsibility for having brought such change about. It produces emotional, but not political, engagement.

The association of the Indian with lands in which the British felt a proprietorial interest was, of course, particularly strong in the thirty years or so that followed the end of the American Revolution. During the period between the 1783 Peace of Paris, which recognized the independence of the thirteen former colonies, and the 1814 Peace of Ghent, the British entered into a number of alliances and treaties with a range of Indian tribes on the American frontier. Although some of the tribes that had inhabited the thirteen states felt understandably betrayed by the peace settlement, many of them recognized that they had common cause with the British against further American expansion, especially after aggressive American campaigns in the later 1770s and early 1780s, particularly waged against the Iroquois, Seneca, Cayuga, Onondaga, and Cherokee.[49] This period saw the last powerful nativist struggles east of the Mississippi, with the Iroquois Joseph Brant, his adopted nephew and successor, the Cherokee Scot John Norton (Teyoninhokarawen), and the Shawnee Tecumseh, all looking—albeit with caution—to the British for help in the defense of their lands. In the case of Brant and Norton, their availability as icons of heroic resistance, and the ease with which they could be portrayed primarily as rugged, determined individualists, may be gauged by the poses in which they were painted on their visits to London. Brant sat for George Romney in 1776, and in 1786, for John Francis Rigaud and Gilbert Stuart; Norton, whom the regimental paymaster Thomas Scott described to his brother Walter as "a man who makes you almost want to be an Indian chief,"[50] for Thomas Phillips in 1816. Viewed from below, with light falling on their faces—and, in the case of Norton, rather ominously on the blade of his tomahawk—their stances, against dark backdrops or wild skies, follow the developing style of Romantic heroic portraiture. All sense of the local environment is effaced. The artists are doing little more than producing studio paintings according to the contemporary conventions of heroic masculinity. Although doubtless invested with a sense of their subjects costumed as exotic curiosities, and hence as exempla of their race, these canvases project, in every case, a defiant singularity. These later Indians are credited with a sense of fortitude and endurance, but, ultimately, they are seen as isolated beings. Their importance is divorced from that of their people and land.

Violent Indians

It would be a major error to think that all the versions of the Indian that the nineteenth century inherited were as benevolent as those found in Wright's painting, in the developing tradition of the dying and displaced Indian, or in the London portraits of handsome, resolute leaders. The Native American whom the nineteenth century inherited was a far more ambiguously coded figure, one who could, most certainly, be regarded as embodying a number of positive values, but who could also be presented as cruel, vengeful, and "uncivilized." This dichotomy was hardly new. Kupperman describes how reactions toward native peoples were expressed in terms of exaggerated extremes from the time of early settlers onward: "The least sign of friendliness was taken for admiration, love, or reverence, and hostility and stealing were expected constantly; when an Indian was too friendly, they expected treachery."[51] However, by the later eighteenth century these binarized attitudes had become inextricably entangled with the representation of other conflicts that were taking place on North American soil, whether Anglo-American or Anglo-French. The Indians who supported the French became a standby in fiction for particularly cruel and inhumane practices. "They are such cruel villains, these French and their painted allies," Thackeray has George write home in *The Virginians*, "that we do not think of showing them mercy";[52] Lismahago in Tobias Smollett's *Humphry Clinker* (1771) has a finger sawed off with a rusty knife, a toe mangled between two stones, splintered reeds stuck up his nostrils, and calves incised with a tomahawk, plugged with gunpowder, and ignited. In political rhetoric—although less frequently in imaginative writing—Whig opponents of the Revolutionary War also played up images of Indian cruelty in order to attack those British commanders who employed native people against the country's own colonists. Edmund Burke, in February 1778, expounded on the Indian's "native cruelty," as demonstrated in their habits of scalping their victims and "the gratifications arising from torturing, mangling, roasting alive by slow fires, and frequently even devouring their captives";[53] and a month later he was stirring up the visceral imagination of Members of Parliament when he spoke against funds' being provided for "hatchets, tomahawks, scalping knives, razors, spurs etc. for the savages to butcher, torture, scalp, and massacre old men, women, children, and infants at the breast."[54] Novelists found it highly useful to perpetuate this crude dichotomy: polarization into good Indians and bad Indians was an easy, even lazy way to enhance the dynamics of a plot.

We may see this if we turn, by way of example, to Charlotte Lennox's epistolary novel of 1790, *Euphemia*. Lennox had firsthand knowledge of British interaction with Indians, and much of this finds its way wholesale into some extremely informative pages, which, in their carefully observed details of community life and commentary concerning native culture, sit rather awkwardly with the more conversational body of the text, which deals with domestic and amatory melodrama. As the daughter of James Ramsay, an army officer, Lennox spent some of her childhood in Albany, New York. She returned to England when she was fifteen, after her father's death around 1744, but used her familiarity with American settings both in her first novel, *The Life of Harriot Stuart* (1750), and in *Euphemia*. The dating of *Euphemia*'s action is somewhat shaky; while it must surely be considered a historical, pre-Revolutionary novel, one of the characters sits at a picnic tea party reading Frances Burney's *Cecilia* (published in 1782), which functions as a suggestion that whatever the supposed time of its action, its moral and racial messages are intended as contemporary ones.[55]

Euphemia Neville accompanies her ill-tempered husband to America, where he is posted first to the garrison at Albany—remarkable for nothing, we are told, besides the volume of its trade with Indians, particularly Mohawk—and then Schenectady, "seldom visited by any strangers, but Indians, who straggle hither, not only from the five nations of the Iroquois, our allies, but the savages of Canada, and other barbarous nations." The last phrase seems to refer to the French, against whom and their Huron allies the British were seeking to establish a dominant presence in the region. While the first two volumes of this four-volume novel, prior to the voyage from Britain to America, are taken up largely with the correspondence between Euphemia and her friend Maria Harley, and crammed with the tensions of marriage, money, and courtship, the letters from Euphemia rapidly switch to a more educational register, informing both Maria and reader alike about the interactions of Indian, Anglo, and Dutch settler life,[56] about the details of trade "with the Indians, who barter furrs for blankets, Osnaburgh shirts, guns, hatchets, knives, kettles, powder and shot";[57] the appearance of the Mohawk, the interiors of their wigwams, their propensity for drinking rum, and the ways in which they combine elements of Christianity with their own religious practices. The register is that of popular contemporary travel narratives.[58] Particularly noteworthy is the way in which Euphemia incorporates passages of more philosophical reflection, stimulated by the views of a new acquaintance, Mr. Euston, who had recently spent a whole year among the "savages."

Euston, drawing his opinions from Abbé Reynal, advances the idea that these people are happy, since the earth provides abundantly for them; the Indian is self-sufficient, working when he needs to and sleeping when weary. " 'War is a matter of choice to him,' " proclaims Euston, ignoring the realities of internal Indian conflicts as well as the part they played in Anglo-French fighting.

> "The savage is serious, but not melancholy; his countenance seldom bears the impression of those passions and disorders, that leave such shocking and fatal traits on ours. He cannot feel the want of what he does not desire; nor can he desire what he is ignorant of. Most of the conveniences of life are remedies for evils he does not feel. He seldom experiences any of that weariness that arises from unsatisfied desires; or that emptiness and uneasiness of mind, that is the offspring of prejudice and vanity. In a word, the savage is subject to none but natural evils."

By contrast, the "civilized man," although

> "his food is more wholesome and delicate than that of the savage; he has softer clothes, and a habitation better secured against the inclemencies of the weather. But should he live under a government, where tyranny must be endured under the name of authority—to what outrages is not the civilized man exposed! If he is possessed of any property, he knows not how far he may call it his own; when he must divide the produce between the courtier, who may attack his estate; the lawyer, who must be paid for teaching him how to preserve it; the soldier, who may lay it waste; and the collector, who comes to levy unlimited taxes."

It must be confessed, this picture, though a little overcharged, is not ill drawn. (3:28–31)

In some ways, this picture is not so much "a little overcharged" as completely obfuscates the realities of life for Indian tribes in upper New York State at the time, who very much depend (as the novel itself shows) on an endless succession of treaties and negotiations with Europeans.

There is another underlying dynamic at work here, however, and that is the lauding of Indian qualities with the implicit aim of criticizing English, or Western, society. This was a repeated trope throughout the eighteenth century, its best-known examples being the satire that Joseph Addison published in Richard Steele's *Spectator* in 1711, putting critical words about high society into the mouths of the Indian "Kings" who had visited the previous year; John Shebbeare's *Lydia; or, Filial Piety* (1755), where the central protagonist, Cannassatego, is shocked by the lifestyle in Europe; and Voltaire's *L'Ingénu* (1767 and appearing in English translations in 1768, 1771, and 1786). It was not entirely to disappear in the decades that followed.[59] Arthur Young's epistolary narrative, *The Adventures of Emmera* (1767) tells of a girl brought up by her father in Arcadian seclusion near Lake Erie, with gentle Indian neighbors. She is horrified when—as a result of one of the twists in a convoluted plot—she visits England and meets a range of falseness, deceitfulness, vanity, and quarrelsomeness: "My blood runs cold to think of the intolerable wickedness in the world, and amongst people that think themselves refined in their understandings and polished in their ideas! These are the people that call the Americans savages! Virtuous and amiable people! I have quitted the neighbourhood of men to become the companion of brutes!"[60] Small wonder that—to the delight of the Indians—she returns to a peaceful farming life in America. In Lennox's novel, Euphemia's remarks may very readily be taken as constituting an indirect critique of the Anglo society about which she is writing, in which women, certainly, have to struggle against prejudice and the "tyranny" that "must be endured under the name of authority," particularly the presumptuous authority of their husbands.[61]

Yet Lennox's novel operates at the level of sensational entertainment as well as serious reflection. Euphemia is startled when a tea party in the woods is violently interrupted by three drunk Indians. Shortly afterward, she gives birth to her son, and as a consequence of the fright she receives, "our little boy bears under his left breast the distinct mark of a bow and arrow, the arms born by one of these savages (3:124–25). It proves to be just as well that he is thus marked by experience, for a couple of years later, on an expedition to the Falls of Cohas, the beloved young Edward, left temporarily in the care of a manservant, disappears, together with his supposed guardian. It is presumed, on the grounds of a misleading report, that he has drowned. But a few years later still, Mrs. Benson, out walking one evening, is approached by a dark-skinned man whom she initially takes to be an Indian and then recognizes as the servant William; he is accompanied by an apparently Indian boy, who is revealed as Edward, instantly identifiable by his curious birthmark. The two had, in fact, been taken captive by Hurons, who, by way of a replacement son, handed over Edward to a recently bereaved mother, a scenario that is doubled when William, on a hunting expedition with the tribe, is in turn captured and adopted by Algonquins, "an idolatrous nation, whose savage custom and manners, filled him with horror and dismay" (3:218). However, all works out well. Edward's foster mother, on her deathbed, expresses deep remorse at having robbed his natural parents of their child and makes the local Catholic missionary promise to try to reunite them. True to British suspicions of Catholicism, the missionary would rather recruit Edward for the church, and he is sent to the Jesuit College in Montreal, where Providence ensures that he is reunited with the escaped William. After a couple of more twists and turns, which result in friendly Mohawk fur traders dressing them as Indians and enabling them to return safely, mother and son are reunited.

These two (very different) strands—using Indians as tools for philosophical postulations about the true nature of humankind and to add excitement and danger within an adventure plot—were staples of the British fiction that engaged with North America during the second half of the eighteenth century. The motif of the Indian who is kind and compassionate to the captured can be found, for example, in Henry Mackenzie's *The Man of the World* (1773); in Susanna Blamire's verse tale "Stoklewath, or the Cumbrian Village" (written around 1776, although not published until 1842), a soldier returns to his native home after a long absence overseas and tells how he had been treated well by the Indians who captured him: "Tho' different in their manners, yet their heart/Was equal mine in every better part./Brave to a fault, if courage fault can be;/Kind to their fellows, doubly kind to me.[62] Orlando, captured by Indians in Charlotte Smith's *The Old Manor House* (1793), seems likely to suffer from their cruel atrocities, until he is befriended by the kindly Wolf-hunter who would happily absorb him into tribal life; as with the material she incorporates in several of her sonnets of this date, Smith appears to be drawing on different aspects of the captivity narrative.[63]

In Thomas Day's *History of Sandford and Merton* (1783–86), much reprinted throughout the nineteenth century as a book for children, we encounter yet another former captive soldier, a Highlander who gives an extended, and mixed, account of the "savage tribes"[64] that he encountered; gentle in peace, "they are more dreadful, when provoked, than all the wildest animals of the forest" (428). However, the clergyman Mr. Barlow, the humane, antiracist moralizer who is Day's primary educational voice throughout the long work, is ready to excuse them, up to a point, and, once again, to use their good features as a point of contrast with English society, claiming: "I see many around me that are disgraced by the vices of uncivilized Americans, without a claim to their virtues" (433–34). What distinguishes Day's figuration of Indians is the emphasis he places on the importance of altruism in the education they receive and in their attitudes toward their fellow beings, something that is completely in keeping with the work in which it is found, yet which, in stressing the virtues of tribal education, also offers something of a challenge to the prevalent tendency of advancing the Indian as an example of "natural man," as found in a precivil state, modified only by various physical, climatic, and historic forces. By the mid-eighteenth century, the numerous differences that could be found between members of different tribes—detailed factual information recorded by missionaries, traders, soldiers, and other travelers in North America—enabled speculation about the operation of such forces with detailed and specific reference to Native Americans. Supposed "barbarians"—whose historical counterparts could be found in Goths, Vandals, Franks, Picts, and others and whose modern-day peers existed in superstition-loving noneducated peoples—were put into the broad context of new modes of social theory, either to prove that moral action bore no relation to the stages of a society's development or, alternatively, that it is inseparable from it. [65] Those who adhered to the former position were the more ready to support the idea of what has commonly been called "the noble savage";[66] those who favored the latter point of view were also those most inclined to see innate depravity in "primitive" peoples, manifesting itself in a disposition for violence and cruelty. This viewpoint could be readily supported by examples derived from observation—or hearsay—and translated into imaginative forms.[67]

What Dr. Johnson called "the contest over the original benevolence or malignity of man"[68] diminished as a philosophical issue in the early decades of the nineteenth century, although the radical dichotomy was soon to be recirculated in ethnology and anthropology. When Thomas Campbell published his narrative poem *Gertrude of Wyoming* in 1809, however, both of these polarized stereotypes were still very much in circulation in their nonscientific form, and both are called upon by Campbell. The eighty-seven Spenserian stanzas of the poem are divided into three parts. From the first stanza, it is clear that this will be a tragedy; it explains why one now finds "ruin'd wall/And roofless homes" in what was once "the lovliest land of all." (1:2–3). The ruins on the banks of the Susquehanna are instantly poignant, drawing on the resonances of the "shapeless ruin" and "mouldering wall" of Goldsmith's Auburn.[69] In part 1, Outalissi, an Oneida chief, brings Henry Waldegrave, a boy orphaned by a Huron attack on a frontier town, to live—at his dying mother's request—with Albert, Gertrude's widowed father. As he leaves the boy, he performs one particular version of noble indigenousness:

> As monumental bronze unchanged his look;
> A soul that pity touch'd, but never shook;
> Train'd from his tree-rock'd cradle to his bier
> The fierce extremes of good and ill to brook
> Impassive—fearing but the shame of fear—
> A stoic of the woods—a man without a tear
>
> (1:202–7)

It is not immediately clear, at the opening of part 2, why Henry appears in Spanish costume. It turns out that he had been sent for by his English relatives when he was twelve, and on returning to the banks of the Susquehanna to look for his former protectors, he decided to wear a disguise and arrive in the district incognito, fearing that Gertrude and Albert might no longer be alive. Everyone seems untroubled by the incongruity, whether sartorial or ideological, and the outcome is inevitable: Gertrude and Henry are rapturously reunited. Yet the romantic and pastoral idyll is shattered in part 3 by the American Revolution. Henry knows that he must leave and fight. Suddenly, Outalissi bursts into their bower and collapses, exhausted, on the floor. Henry recognizes him without difficulty, and they have a touching reunion. But Outalissi has come with a purpose—to warn them of an imminent threat:

> The mammoth comes—the foe—the Monster Brandt—
> With all his howling, desolating band . . .
>   he left of all my tribe
> Nor man, nor child, nor thing of living birth:
> No! not the dog that watch'd my household hearth,
> Escaped that night of blood upon our plains!
> All perish'd!—I alone am left on earth!
>
> (3:139–40, 147–51)

No sooner has he issued his warning than there is the unearthly sound of whoop after whoop. Indian warriors are once again associated with volcanic violence ("Then look'd they to the hills, where fire o'erhung/The bandit groups, in one Vesuvian glare" ([3:173–74]). In the ensuing chaos—syntactical, as well as bellicose—first Albert falls dead, and then Gertrude. Henry and Outalissi—"casting his Indian mantle o'er the youth" (3:304)—are left to mourn them. The poem closes with Outalissi singing a death song, which incorporates all the familiar elements of the dying Indian genre, in its successive stages from the mid-eighteenth century onward. First he vows vengeance, but asks what subsequent destination remains to them. Henry's own, once-loved home is empty and desolate. What if they were to go to the homeland of his own "kindred nation"?

> Ah! there, in desolation cold,
> The desert serpent dwells alone,
> Where grass o'ergrows each mouldering bone
> And stones themselves to ruin grown,
> Like me, are death-like old.
>
> (3:344–48)

He hears "the trump"—whether this is a military instrument somewhere in the valley or the Last Trump calling for him is left obscure—and sees his father's ghost, bidding him to battle, and to

> dry the last—the first—
> The only tears that ever burst
> From Outalissi's soul;
> Because I may not stain with grief
> The death-song of an Indian chief!
>
> (3:358–61)

These concluding lines are heavily ambiguous. On the one hand, Outalissi takes on the responsibility that goes with a vatic role (and as literary historian Astrid Wind has pointed out, this association was underscored by an engraving in the 1822 London edition, depicting him in a long, bardlike robe);[70] on the other, he is undeniably exhorting himself to keep *his* dignity at the moment of his own demise. Campbell simultaneously makes the poem a lament for a version of emigrant life that was shattered by demands for "Transatlantic Liberty . . . wrapt in whirlwinds, and bigirt with woes,/Amidst the strife of fratricidal foes" (3:47–50) and an occasion to mourn the departure of an Indian who—the last of his tribe—stands for the usual panoply of native virtues: loyalty, courage, eloquence, and stoicism,—except when pushed beyond all emotional endurance, at which point he becomes recognizably human, as well.

"Gertrude" bears a curious relation to poetic nationalism. For all that it is set in Pennsylvania, it manages to be nostalgic not only for a utopian version of pastoral settler life there, but also for an English motherland. Racial and familial identity are conflated when Gertrude exclaims:

> And yet, loved England! when thy name I trace
> In many a pilgrim's tale and poet's song,
> How can I choose but wish for one embrace
> Of them, the dear unknown to whom belong
> My mother's looks,—perhaps her likeness strong?
>
> (2:55–59)

It was readily embraced by American readers as an example of what a national poetry might accomplish: Washington Irving epitomized these reactions when he wrote that Campbell's poem "may assist to convince many, who were before slow to believe, that our own country is capable of inspiring the highest poetic feelings."[71] Yet it met with a mixed critical reception in England, one that even called Campbell's own patriotism into question (not least because the violent Indians of the poem were acting under British orders). Walter Scott, in the *Quarterly Review*, expressed "a hope that Mr. Campbell will in his subsequent poems chuse a theme more honourable to our national character, than one in which Britain was disgraced by the atrocities of her pretended adherents."[72] In other words, he was taking a Burkean line, criticizing not just the choice of enlisting Indian military help but also the fact that Campbell had chosen to write about the massacre at Wyoming, an event that was much less creditable to the British than Campbell shows it, since they, under the command of Major John Butler, organized and participated in the attack on the colonists. But Whig reviewers were more enthusiastic, and the broader public warmed to its sentimentalism. Its popularity (it went into three editions within two years) ensured the continued diffusion of polarized images of the Indian, amplified by the poem's reliance on a pattern of Manichaean opposites—or, as William Hazlitt put it, a "systematic alternation of good and evil, of violence and repose."[73]

The legacy of this poem, however, is more complicated than helping to consolidate images of the Indian, both savage and noble. Diminishing the degree of British involvement in the Wyoming massacre helps to intensify the Otherness of the Indian, not only in cultural terms but, for the British reader, in geographic ones as well. The poem both has Gertrude futilely longing for the mother country and depicts settler life as a kind of displaced English pastoral idealism, in which one reads Shakespeare and Milton in exquisitely picturesque, fertile countryside. The Indian enacts—in Campbell's version of history—the central role in the destruction of this idyll, thus playing up a sense of America as still a wild and unpredictable country, the antithesis of the homeland. Throughout the nineteenth century, this sense of America as an elsewhere, however close its symbolic familial relations with England might be, is crucial to British representations of the figure of the Indian, both positive and derogatory. Yet, in the form of Outalissi, the Indian also helps the reader to mourn the loss of a kind of agrarian Englishness. The mourning, moreover, links a lost imagined English national past with the loss of a noble Indian ancestral line, and with tribal lands.

But whatever the implied message of the poem's ending, the Indian was not in the terminal decline that "Gertrude" suggests. While many readers on both sides of the Atlantic may have responded sympathetically to the stereotypes on which it drew, this was certainly not true for one important Indian reader: Joseph Brant's son John (Chief Ahyonwaeghs). John Brant visited London in January 1822, bringing with him documents that proved his father was not in Wyoming at the time of the massacre and protesting against the injustice done by Campbell to his father's memory. In a lengthy letter printed in the *New Monthly Magazine* in February of the same year, Campbell set out to explain himself, saying that he had taken Joseph Brant's character "as I found it in popular history" (primarily Isaac Weld, whom he cites extensively in his notes to the poem).[74] He attempts to redress the balance by writing of Brant's learning and his expressive talents in both written and spoken English; the friends whom he made in England; "the memorials of his moral character" (98) that may be found in Canada; and the high opinion and affectionate regard in which he was held by several eminent British officers in America. Moreover, not only does he acknowledge that "your native tribes may have had a just cause of quarrel with the American colonists" (100), but he also starts to imagine how an Indian, faced with accusations of cruelty, might respond in comparativist terms.

> If I were to preach to you about European humanity, you might ask me how long the ashes of the Inquisition have been cold, and whether the slave-trade be yet abolished? You might demand, how many—no, how few generations have elapsed since our old women were burned for imaginary commerce with the devil. . . . As to warlike customs, I should be exceedingly sorry if you were to press me even on those of my brave old ancestors, the Scottish Highlanders. (101)

This unease about how European practices might look when viewed from the outside was to become a staple of serious writing about Native Americans during the nineteenth century: a deliberate defamiliarization in the interests of suggesting, if not necessarily celebrating, a common humanity.

Yet in many ways, the crux of Campbell's letter lies in its second paragraph, when he writes: "I really knew not, when I wrote my poem, that the son and daughter of an Indian chief were ever likely to peruse it, or be affected by its contents" (97). Campbell's failure was not just one of misinformation about the specifics of Brant's life; his response betrays his lack of imagination at the time he composed the poem. Indians, for him, as surely for most of his British readers, were not real people; they were primarily ciphers. They stood for a range of British—and European—projections about primitive peoples and about what constitutes "natural" humanity. They provided occasions for the display of sensibility, the elaboration of the horrible, or a structuring device so that a novelist could alternate the contemplative with dynamic action.

Certainly, throughout the nineteenth century, Native Americans continued to serve a range of aesthetic and often predictable functions within imaginative literature, recycling stereotypes whose roots were already established by the late eighteenth century. This book goes on to explore the fact that live Indians, like John Brant, continued to interact with the British within the British Isles, as well as across the Atlantic, and expressed their own views on cultural relations and representations, rather than remaining passive—mere objects of representation. In other words, one witnesses a continual movement between the mythical and the material; between native peoples as beings consigned to another age, their narrative already inscribed, and as active participants in contemporary transatlantic history.

CHAPTER THREE

"Brought to the Zenith of Civilization": Indians in England in the 1840s

The family of George Catlin experienced the realities behind the Wyoming Valley massacre at firsthand. His grandfather escaped being killed by swimming the Susquehanna; his grandmother and mother were held prisoner for several weeks. These events helped to determine the direction that the young Catlin was to take. In *Life amongst the Indians* (1861), he recalls how, in 1806, when he was ten years old, he encountered an Oneida man, On-o-gong-way, on the lands around his family's home in this same valley. Although initially terrified, he began to converse with On-o-gong-way and came to see things from a different perspective. The man told the boy tribal stories, taught him how to throw a tomahawk, and described what it was like for an Indian to travel, in contemporary America, "some hundreds of miles over a country partly of forest, and partly inhabited by a desperate set of hunters whose rifles were unerring, and whose deep-rooted hostility to all savages induced them to shoot them down whenever they met them in their hunting grounds."[1] Shortly after this formative meeting, On-o-gong-way, presumably journeying home, was found murdered.

This episode not only laid the foundation for Catlin's interest in the specifics of Indian cultures but also informed his subsequent understanding of the threatened position of the Indian in modern America. During the 1830s, he traveled west five times, painting and recording the life of the Plains Indians on their own lands, as well as witnessing the forced migration of tribes after the passing of the Indian Removal Act in 1830, and seeing the terrible effects of diseases, such as smallpox, on the lives of indigenous peoples. His paintings, extensive collection of native artifacts, and ethnographic writings were all underpinned by the belief that the race was persecuted, facing inevitable extinction, and that the opportunity to commemorate it should not be lost. Although he exhibited, lectured, and demonstrated on the East Coast—sometimes accompanied by Indians, sometimes not—his antagonism toward the way in which the U.S. government was treating its native inhabitants was very likely a major factor in his being unable to persuade them to purchase or support his collection. Short of funds, and led to believe that he would find a sympathetic audience in England, Catlin sailed from New York to

London in late 1839 with his collection of Native American objects, costumes, and some six hundred portraits and other paintings.[2]

CATLIN'S BRITISH SHOW

The artwork illustrated the appearance, habitat, and customs of various tribes; the items on show included men's and women's robes, "garnished and fringed with scalp-locks from their enemies' heads,"[3] bows, quivers, spears, shields, cradles, calumets, tomahawks, scalping knives, war clubs, eagle and raven headdresses, wampum, whistles, rattles, drums, and masks. Catlin rented the Egyptian Hall, in Piccadilly, set up in the center a Crow tepee made of twenty or more ornamented buffalo skins, and proceeded to mount what was initially a highly popular exhibition. This ran for two years before going on tour to Liverpool, Manchester, Sheffield, Leeds, York, Edinburgh, Glasgow, Belfast, and Dublin. Catlin was on the point of returning to the United States when the opportunity arose to add some live Indians to his show: first 9 Ojibwa (in 1843–44), then 14 Iowa, who visited Britain and Paris (1844–55), and then 12 more Ojibwa (1845–46), who, already in London, then traveled to Paris to join with Catlin there and to visit Belgium with him.

In his account of these years, Catlin relates how he and his Irish assistant, Daniel Kavanaugh, found themselves continually answering the questions of an inquisitive audience. Possibly, Catlin exaggerated the naïveté of the inquiries in order to play up the pioneering, and highly necessary, nature of his own enterprise. But as he tells it, the explanations often addressed some rather basic questions. Indeed, Kavanaugh hit on a plan of having a table printed with the answers to the most frequently posed queries. Some of these are culturally specific: the "Indians" are "not cannibals." They do not scalp the living; they never eat the scalps. "There are no tribes that go entirely naked; they are all very decent." But some of the responses are more general and, at the very least, suggestive of the perceived haziness, in the popular culture of the early Victorian period, of the fundamentals of transatlantic social and physical geography. "The Rocky Mountains are in *America*, between New York and the Pacific Ocean, and *not* in the *Indies* at all." "The Americans are *white*, the same colour exactly as the English, and speak the same language, only they speak it a great deal better, in general." Perhaps most surprising of all among these commonly required responses is: "You *can't come overland* from America" (1:48–49). If this represents a considerable degree of ignorance about Catlin's homeland as a whole, it suggests yet more strongly the relatively blank canvas onto which he projected his information and interpretation concerning native peoples.

The one significant source of ideas about the Indian with which a number of his British audience would have been familiar was the fiction of James Fenimore Cooper. First published in London by J. Miller in 1826, Cooper's 1831 edition of *The Last of the Mohicans*—with the author's notes—was brought out the same year by Henry Colburn and Richard Bentley, with new editions appearing in 1834 and 1836. In 1838 Edward Ravenscroft published the novel in parts, which were then brought together in single-volume format. Clearly, Catlin capitalized on Cooper's popularity. The question of "whether Cooper's descriptions of the Red Indians were true" figures in the list of common inquiries (1:148); when the Iowa camped outdoors, he "advertised that for one shilling, 'the public will have an opportunity of witnessing for the first time in Europe illustrations of the stirring descriptions given by Cooper in his celebrated novels, The Last of the Mohicans, Prairie &c.'"[4]

Cooper's dominant elegiac theme built, in both sentiment and cadence, on those tropes of Romantic poetry that sought to commemorate a fast-disappearing race. Early in *The Last of the Mohicans* (1824), Chingachgook famously and formulaically laments: "'Where are the blossoms of those summers!—fallen, one by one, so all of my family departed, each in his turn, to the land of the spirits. I am on the hill-top, and must go down into the valley, and when Uncas follows in my footsteps, there will no longer be any of the blood of the Sagamores, for my boy is the last of the Mohicans.'"[5] Cooper added a footnote to the opening of the second chapter in 1831, establishing a historical context for his readers by informing them of the confederation known as the Six Nations and concluding, "There are remnants of all these people still living on lands secured to them by the state, but they are daily disappearing, either by deaths or by removals to scenes more congenial to their habits. In a short time there will be no more of these extraordinary people, in those regions in which they dwelt for centuries, but their names" (13).

The material exhibits were complemented by the lectures Catlin gave and by the appearance, in 1841, of his *Letters and Notes on the Manners, Customs, and Conditions of the North American Indians*, describing his travels in the United States and his firsthand knowledge of tribal lives. This book, published in London (a decision based on the lack of an international copyright law), was received sympathetically by reviewers. Above all, what they picked up on was that Catlin sought to memorialize what he feared were a people on the edge of oblivion: "(to use their own very beautiful figure)," he writes in Letter 1, "they are fast travelling towards the shades of their fathers, towards the setting sun."[6] Celebrated in such terms, the Native American was unmistakably invested with some of the Romantic fascination with the idea of the Last Man, the possessor of an acute sensibility and capacity to register the beauties of the natural world, but with no fellow being left with whom these sensations can be shared.[7]

In considering the idea of vanishing races, Catlin had, additionally, a political point to make, with implications that stretched far beyond his own country. In a fully attended lecture at the Royal Institution on 14 February 1841, he not only made the case for a preservationist Museum of Mankind but also tied in what he had observed in North America to the dangers that colonizing powers in general presented to the native inhabitants of the lands they sought to rule, whether humans were exterminated through the bayonet through smallpox, or through whiskey and rum. He directly addressed the land that he was visiting and its spirit of expansionist enterprise:

> Great Britain has more than thirty colonies in different quarters of the globe, in which the numbers of civilized men are increasing, and the native tribes are wasting away—that the march of civilization is everywhere, as it is in America, a war of extermination, and that of our own species. For the occupation of a new country, the first enemy that must fall is *man*, and his like cannot be transplanted from any other quarter of the globe.[8]

However, in proposing that artists and men of science should be sent off to make records of disappearing tribes around the world, he did not dissent from the dominant view of his time: that extinction was, in the long run, inevitable. His speech had, indeed, a good deal in common with the essay "On the Extinction of the Human Races," which the influential British ethnologist James Cowles Prichard had published two years previously: his latest version of his much worked-over argument that while all of humanity was descended from the same stock, different races developed and degenerated according to different time scales.[9] And while in his address to the Royal Institution, and in further versions of the speech that he gave to audiences drawn from a range of literary and scientific institutions, Catlin stressed material causes, his theories were underwritten by the primary assumptions of extinction discourse, one founded on the premise of a progressive history of racial development, "with the white, European, Germanic, or Anglo-Saxon race at the pinnacle of progress and civilization, and the 'dark races' ranged beneath it in various degrees of inferiority."[10] As Patrick Brantlinger writes at the opening of his valuable discussion of the dominance of extinction theory in the long nineteenth century, such discourse, like Orientalism and other versions of racism,

> does not respect the boundaries of disciplines or the cultural hierarchies of high and low; instead, it is found wherever and whenever Europeans and white Americans encountered indigenous peoples. A

remarkable feature of extinction discourse is its uniformity over other ideological fault lines: whatever their disagreements, humanitarians, missionaries, scientists, government officials, explorers, colonists, soldiers, journalists, novelists, and poets were in basic agreement about the inevitable disappearance of some or all of the primitive races. (1)

For his Royal Institution lecture, Catlin dressed up a couple of English people in native costumes, weapons in hand, and by 1842 the exhibition was amplified by his decision to introduce a couple of Englishmen in tribal gear so that they might bring the costumes to life, sing an Indian song, and give "the frightful war-whoop"[11]—a gesture straddling the line between educational innovation and publicity gimmick. Nor did Catlin have any qualms about appropriating Indian identity later the same year when attending the fashionable Caledonian Ball at Almack's, together with his nephew Burr and Charles Murray. Murray, a great supporter and facilitator of Catlin's, was a recognized British authority on Indian matters, having published his *Travels in North America, Including a Summer Residence with the Pawnee Tribe of Indians* in 1839.[12] From 1838 to 1844 he was master of the household at Queen Victoria's court, and his family and social connections undoubtedly facilitated Catlin's stay in London. The men dressed in some of Catlin's finest costumes; painted themselves up in red and black and experienced the excited crowd pressing in upon them; their identities were revealed only when they were called upon to dance and their war paint started to run in sweaty streaks. This experience in "redding-up" may have given Catlin some partial insight into what it felt to be the object of intense curiosity, to have one's personal space disregarded, and to be subject to street taunts. But he and his companions could retreat from their masquerade "and deliberately and leisurely . . . scour ourselves back again to our original characters."[13] At first sight, this was hardly an option available to real Indians, although, as we shall see, the potential for masquerade did in fact work in two directions.

The poignancy behind Catlin's overall message was intensified by the arrival in England of actual Indians. When nine Ojibwa, from Canadian territory, arrived in Liverpool in November 1843, they were unquestionably objects of spectacle.[14] They were visiting England under the custodianship of Arthur Rankin, a Canadian who had been brought up on the borders of their lands and had served for six years in the British army. In part they were looking to speak to the queen on a local land issue; more generally, they hoped to earn money to take back to their families. Rankin came to an arrangement with Catlin, and the Ojibwa stayed with him for around seven months, forming a compelling part of his exhibition. As a Canadian, moreover, Rankin could write with some authority when he contextualized the Ojibwa in relation to the country they were visiting; they belong, he wrote, "to a numerous and powerful tribe, which has ever been devotedly attached to the British Government."[15] He emphasized—thus implicitly flattering the nationality of potential spectators—how much more favored these First Nations people were than their counterparts in the United States: "Those Indians who are fortunate enough to be within the British territories receive much better treatment, and the paternal consideration of our Government has led to a strong feeling of attachment on the part of these primitive people towards their 'Great Mother,' as the Queen of England is called by them."(7) Following a falling out with Catlin, which pivoted on the question of the motives that underpinned the public display of these people, Rankin resumed his role as their manager; shortly afterward, when the fourteen Iowa Indians, under the sponsorship of the impresario George H. C. Melody, joined Catlin, they took on much the same role as the Ojibwa had done.[16]

Both groups performed dances and uttered "the dreadful war-whoop" in the same rooms that his canvases and objects were on show, and both groups were, effectively, live exhibits, introduced and explained in lectures and in the question-and-answer sessions Catlin held. Whatever his anthropological motives, they therefore could not escape being regarded by many member of the public in the same light as other shows of supposed freaks and curiosities, from Tom Thumb to African Bushmen to the Norfolk giants, who themselves visited Catlin's show and called on the Iowa in their lodgings, where the Indians—anxious that their reports of these physical anomalies would not be believed on their return home—took the giants' measurements with lengths of string. Yet despite this table-turning moment, one cannot deny that many responders to Catlin's Indians reacted as though they were just one more example of "ethnological show business."[17] Viewing Catlin retrospectively, Cheyenne W. Richard West, director of the National Museum of the American Indian, has written of how he represents an "easy and large target," an "emblematic exploiter of native peoples. . . . Taking his canvases, artefacts, and live Indians on tour to a host of venues, including European cities where the show's 'red men' inspired a familiar combination of awe and condescension, Catlin can be seen today as a cultural P. T. Barnum, a crass huckster trading on other people's lives and lifeways."[18]

Such a comment underrepresents the degree to which Catlin, despite his faults, seems to have been motivated by genuine caring not only for the individuals with whom he toured but for their tribal lifestyles, anxious to achieve an understanding of their ways of life, and not just to present a flashy, superficial stereotype. Nonetheless, he cannot avoid his position in a long line of those who displayed the Indian before the British

Figure 4. "A Group of Iowa." Unattributed photograph, frontispiece to
William Harvey Miner, *The Iowa* (Cedar Rapids, IA: Torch Press, 1911).

people as an object of curiosity, albeit often, as in the case of the 1710
Iroquois visit, in conjunction with political motives.[19] Richard Hakluyt,
in his *Divers Voyages* (1582), quotes from Fabian's chronicle that told of
three Newfoundland men brought to Henry VII's court by John Cabot;
they were wearing skins, eating raw meat, and "spake such speech that
not man coulde understand them"—yet a very early example of assimilation is then recorded, since the account goes on to note that "two
yeeres after, I saw two apparelled after the manner of Englishmen in
Westminster pallace, which that time I could not discerne from Englishmen."[20] In 1609 Walter Cope took some "Virginians" to England, where
they gave a demonstration of canoe handling on the Thames. To be sure,
many visits combined the functional or diplomatic with elements of display. Manteo and Wanchese, Carolinian Algonquians, were brought
back to England in 1584 so that they could teach their language to Thomas Heriot and return with him to Roanoke the next year. When Pocahontas arrived in England in 1616, accompanied by Uttamatomakkin, a
leading man and priest among the Powhatan of the Chesapeake, she
functioned as a kind of living advertisement for the Virginia Company,
being received and entertained both by Queen Anne and the bishop of

London; to quote Frances Mossiker, she was "on the payroll and on parade."[21] But increasingly, as their political usefulness to the British declined, Indians were thought of as entertainers rather than as emissaries. At the same time, their travels became increasingly multifunctional, as often they looked to earn money as well as engage in land rights negotiations. Thus the Seneca chief and six braves who visited England in 1818 appeared in theaters in Liverpool, Manchester, Leeds, and London.

So the Indians who appeared with Catlin's show both were and were not a novelty. Even at the moment of the Ojibwa's arrival, there was a Sac chief, Joe Kosot (Walking Bear), in London.[22] Nor—although one might think so from Catlin's account—did they remain a singular attraction. In May 1845 Maungwudaus, a cousin of the missionary Peter Jones, brought a group of eleven Canadian Indians, from the Ojibwa, Odeauwai, and Missassagee tribes, to London, where they appeared at the Egyptian Hall, before joining Catlin in Europe.[23] Yet both at the time and in his subsequent narrative, Catlin's combination of showmanship and urgent rhetoric led him to present his visitors as creating a startling impact; he played up their visual and aural strangeness, and—a theme that would be insisted upon again in the publicity surrounding Buffalo Bill's Wild West Shows later in the century—the unrepeatability of witnessing at firsthand a people facing extinction. To be sure, their presence in urban centers away from London must have been astonishing, especially to working people who frequently, in the 1840s, had only a hazy sense of the world that lay outside their own environment and origins. As they toured Manchester, the Ojibwa

> were all clad in skins of their own dressing, their head-dresses of eagles' quills and wild turkeys' feathers; their faces daubed and streaked with vermilion and black and green paint. They were armed with their war-clubs, bows and quivers, and tomahawks and scalping knives, just as they roam through the woods in their country; and their yells and war-whoops, which were occasionally sounded in the streets at some sudden occurrence that attracted their attention, gave a new excitement amid the smoke and din of Manchester.[24]

It is impossible to gauge, of course, how far Catlin was encouraging his companions to perform "Indianness." But the Indians' visit was not entirely a matter of their being placed passively on display. Their presence afforded the opportunity for different types of ethnological observation; Mr. Bally, a phrenologist, took casts of their skulls, which were presented to Catlin for his collection, with Bally himself retaining a copy.[25] They had their photographs taken (photographs that, if they surface, would probably be the earliest surviving photographs of Native Americans). "The Indians," reported the *Manchester Guardian*, "were greatly surprised at the 'mystery,' by which portraits were obtained in so very short a time. We understand that the portraits were very good ones, the proverbial immobility of the Indians making them admirable 'sitters.'"[26] What is more, the experience of being in a new country—a modern, industrializing country—was designed to be educational for the Indians. In and around Manchester, they visited cotton mills and wool mills, receiving rolls of flannel and woolen cloth as gifts. We shall return to the problems of assessing the nature of such visits and of interpreting the Indians' responses; what needs to be noted here is that the press continually drew attention to the sensational impact they made on those who encountered them. "Their singular appearance excited much curiosity," reported the *Manchester Courier and Lancashire General Advertiser*, "and the assistance of the police was required to prevent their being obstructed by a crowd of people, who pressed about them to obtain a sight of them. . . . In one large room, where 1,300 power looms were attended by six hundred and fifty girls, the girls were so astonished or affrighted at the appearance of the Indians, that they lost the broken threads for some minutes."[27]

Yet it is also apparent that Catlin's enterprise did not go unchallenged. "Philanthropos," who claimed some firsthand knowledge of Indian tribes in both the United States and Canada, wrote to the *Courier* that while he had been gratified to visit "Mr Catlin's most picturesque and instructive gallery," he also felt "a painful pity, in witnessing human creatures, fellow-men of superior manly form and carriage, with intellect in their eye and feature, and yet behave and act parts that were not above the wild but measured gambols of the rudest of little children." He wondered aloud if they were Christians, believing that if they were, they "would better know the dignity of [their] regenerated nature than thus to exhibit" themselves; if they were not, the blame lay at the hands of those who advised and superintended them.[28] Later, in London, on the second night of the Ojibwa's appearance at the Egyptian Hall, Catlin himself recorded the presence of two protesters, one asking whether he thinks it is right "'to bring those poor ignorant people here to dance for money?'" and one who claims that he thinks "'it is degrading to those poor people to be brought here, Sir, to be shown like wild beasts, for the purpose of making money.'" Making his defense, Catlin pointed out his friendliness toward "these abused and dying people," that he had personally always been opposed to the kind of exhibition described, that these Indians were subjects of the queen who had voluntarily entered into a contractual engagement with the man who had brought them over, and that they were trying by honest means to earn a little money to take back to their children.[29]

The existence of such protests indicates the sensitivity of certain members of the public to the Indians' human rights and to the possibility that

they were being exploited for financial ends. Such concerns about anthropological display were not new in England. They had been voiced
when Saartjie Baartman, the San woman commonly known as the Hot-
tentot Venus, was exhibited in London in 1810–11, and here not just the
fact of display, but the fact that she appeared to be kept in a condition
of servitude was directly linked to Britain's recent abolitionism.[30] It is
significant that humanitarian concerns should again be raised when the
relationship of the Indians to Catlin, and the conditions in which they
lived and traveled, were manifestly not as extreme as those which Baartman suffered. In both cases, however, there is an explicit or implicit connection to the politics of slavery. Indeed, a *Punch* cartoon of October
1842 brings out well the complex resonances of slavery and Indians
when it came to signaling American national identity. Ostensibly, this
cartoon shows a reluctant, somewhat taken-aback Britannia accepting
the cup of peace (while noting the imminent threat of the dagger labeled
"War"). The occasion was the treaty established by American Secretary
of State Daniel Webster and the British foreign minister, Alexander, first
Baron Ashburton, which established a clear borderline between Maine
and New Brunswick in the northeastern United States, as well as settling
some uncertain lines of demarcation in the Great Lakes region; it was
notable as a land dispute settled by diplomatic negotiation, not violence.
The United States, represented as an arrogant aggressor by *Punch*'s artist, is once again figured as a feathered Indian, albeit one with "savage,"
rather than classical, features. However, around his waist—above the
skirt made from the American flag—is a belt of slavery. Slavery is thus
openly equated with the United States, but the drawing simultaneously
conveys, whether deliberately or not, the potential for reading its native
inhabitants as also bound to its national repressive practices.[31]

There was considerable overlap between those who were active in antislavery issues and those who protested against the American government's treatment of the country's native inhabitants. Catlin's Indians—
and indeed Catlin himself—were, as they toured Britain, greeted warmly
by those who had been abolitionists and were sympathetically interested
in the lives of indigenous peoples. Quakers, in particular, with their long
history of amicable relations with and toward Indians, were very keen
on meeting the Ojibwa and the Iowa. What concerns me in the next section, however, is not the responses of those who were relatively well informed and humanitarianly sympathetic, toward the visiting Indians,
but the perception of the general public, as far as this may be estimated
from Catlin's account and from press reports. Above all, this throws
light not just on the ways in which Indians were regarded but on the
popular consciousness of race in the 1840s and, in particular, on the
question of mixed-race liaisons.[32]

Figure 5. "Fair Rosamond; or, The Ashburton Treaty," Punch, October 1842.

INDIANS, SEX, AND INTERRACIAL MARRIAGE

Indian men were seen as sexy. This, at any rate, is the message one receives from the account George Catlin gives. On just the second night of the Ojibwa's first public appearance, in Manchester, the good-looking Sah-mah seems to have made a notably striking impression. One lady tried to kiss him, and then,

> The excitement and screaming and laughing among the women in that part of the room made kissing fashionable, and every one who

laid her hand upon his arm or his naked shoulders (and those not a few) got a kiss, gave a scream, and presented him a brooch, a ring, or some other keepsake, and went home with a streak of red paint on her face, and perhaps with one or two of black or green upon her dress. (1:119)

Similarly, in London,

Many ladies were offering them their hands and trinkets: some were kissing them, and every kiss called forth the war-whoop (as they called it, "a *scalp*"). The women commenced it as *Sah-mah* had dashed into the crowd; and as he was wending his way back, finding it had pleased so well, he took every lady's hand that was laid upon his naked arm or his shoulder as a challenge, and he said that he kissed every woman that he passed. This may or may not be true; but one thing is certain, that many there were in the room that evening who went home to their husbands and mothers with streaks of red and black paint upon their cheeks, which nothing short of soap and water could remove. (1:168–69)

Prominent among the London fans was a woman whom Catlin labels the "jolly fat dame." On her first visit to the Indians when they were appearing at the Egyptian Hall, she affected to be on the point of fainting, sat on the edge of the stage, and realized that she could not see the main attraction from her position (and that the crowd was also looking at her and that she had omitted to put on her stays); her rotund form became wedged in a state of semisuspension as she tried to descend back into the crowd. She was rescued by the chivalric efforts of the interpreter, Note-enaakm ("Strong Wind," more frequently called by his French Canadian father's name, Cadotte, by Catlin), and seated in the shadow of the performers. This gallantry precipitated an extreme infatuation on her part; she was back the next night (in stays and in her best poplin-and-lace dress), admired the young man with "every breath she inhaled, and at every glance that she had of his manly and herculean figure as it moved before her" (1:163), and returned evening after evening. Nor was she the only one. From other women, he received "many precious and sly gifts, and amongst them several little billets of the most sentimental nature, containing enclosures of beautiful little stanzas, and cards of address, &c." (1:181). Despite the intense interest of the "jolly fat dame" in Cadotte—of whom more later—after the departure of the Ojibwa, and the arrival of the Iowa, she had no difficulty in transferring her affections to them. Some of the Iowa, in their turn—especially the Medicine Man Senontiyah—evidently thoroughly enjoyed playing up to the women in the audience (2:25).

Figure 6. "Catlin's Indians in Egyptian Hall," in *Catlin's Notes of Eight Years' Travels and Residence in Europe, with His North American Indian Collection*, 2 vols. (London: published by the author, 1848).

What might we make of these responses? First, they evince a perhaps surprisingly unabashed capacity for the public expression of sexual attraction on the part of these early Victorian women. It is not altogether easy to place the audiences for popular displays such as these in class terms. Certainly, the novelty of live Indians was sufficient to attract inquisitive spectators of all classes. Catlin's accounts suggest that many were not very highly educated, yet clearly they not only had the financial resources to pay the entrance fee of a shilling, but were comfortable giving away money, as well as bangles, pins, and other trinkets. The "jolly fat dame" was accompanied on at least one occasion by two maids. Yet if their behavior could hardly be considered seemly by the increasingly consolidating standards of bourgeois respectability, its public nature ensured that it partook of the carnivalesque: if this is to be seen as a transgressive expression of libido, its arena is a highly artificial one. It has something in common with the twentieth-century phenomenon of the female fan, flirting and squealing with a desire that is focused on an object both immanent and, in practical terms, unattainable.

Interestingly, Catlin's Indians were not the first to excite the longings of British women—at least if one puts any credence in the bawdy ballad that Harry Howard wrote in 1765,[33] on the occasion of the visit of three Cherokee chiefs to London on a mission to complain about the English encroachment on their lands: "Wives, Widows and Matrons, and pert little Misses,/Are pressing and squeezing for Cherokee kisses."[34] Did the London women of the 1840s have any sense of a folk tradition, in which Indian men were somehow thought of as specially attractive? or were they, which is more likely, turned on by the very strangeness and exoticness of the eagle and ostrich plumes, the shields and war clubs, the dances, the half-naked, painted, bronzed male bodies? How, indeed, might one assess their prior knowledge and assumptions concerning Native Americans in general, and is it possible to relate their sexualized responses to such knowledge? What we face here is the problem of going outside literary traditions of representation, or, at the very least, of attempting to gauge the degree of impact such representations might have on these audiences. While these displays undoubtedly were attended by Catlin's friends and acquaintances who had known Indian culture at firsthand and who, like Charles Murray, wrote about it both in travelogue and fiction; and while those who encountered the touring Indians at, say, the breakfast party that Disraeli held for them at his house overlooking Park Lane may very well have been familiar with the literary role of Indians in sentimental and humanitarian poetry; and while the visitors were besieged by members of numerous religious denominations who had varying degrees of knowledge of missionary work among Indians, hypotheses become much more shaky when one tries to weigh up the cultural preconceptions held by visitors to the Egyptian Hall and other venues. As we have seen, the closest hard evidence lies in the notes Catlin took of the questions that were frequently posed during the first London appearance of the Ojibwa, and some of these were unmistakably, if mildly, sexually inflected. "Several ladies were waiting to inquire 'whether the Indians actually had no beards'; and a great number of women after these, some of whom lingered patiently until all other questions had been answered, begged to know 'whether the interpreter and the handsome little fellow *Sah-mah* were married'" (1:148).

The cultural history of white-Indian liaisons was a long one within England, reaching back to Pocahontas's rescue of John Smith and her subsequent marriage to John Rolfe—something that, by the mid-nineteenth century, had become a fable of assimilation and was turned to American nationalistic ends. A version of this narrative was also found in the frequently reworked story of the trader Thomas Inkle's rescue by, and romance with, the beautiful Indian woman Yarico.[35] Felicia Hemans's "The American Forest-Girl" (1826) had more recently offered a poetic version of the Pocahontas story, although the events are sanitized through her making it clear that the "young slight girl—a fawn-like child" is motivated by her love for a lost brother.[36] In 1841 Lydia Sigourney's *Pocahontas* was published in London; first it celebrates the young

Indian girl for having saved the germ of the Saxon race in America through her passionate intercession, and then concludes with stanzas that reinforce neatly Catlin's emphasis on a people in terminal decline while incorporating echoes of Gray's "Elegy," which suggest that the contribution of the "unhonored dead" to a country is perhaps nonetheless worthy of record.[37]

> Forgotten race, farewell! Your haunts we tread,—
>   Our mighty rivers speak your words of yore,
> Our mountains wear them on their misty head,
>   Our sounding cataracts hurl them to the shore;
> But on the lake your flashing oar is still,
> Hush'd is your hunter's cry on dale and hill,
>   Your arrow stays the eagle's flight no more;
> And ye, like troubled shadows, sink to rest
> In unremember'd tombs, unpitied and unbless'd.
>
> The council-fires are quench'd, that erst so red
>   Their midnight volume 'mid the groves entwined;
> King, stately chief, and warrior-host, are dead,—
>   Nor remnant, nor memorial, left behind:
> But thou, O forest-princess, true of heart,
> When o'er our fathers wav'd destruction's dart,
>   Shall in their children's loving hearts be shrin'd;
> Pure, lonely star, o'er dark oblivion's wave,
> It is not meet thy name should moulder in the grave.[38]

In each of these instances, the conventional gender hierarchy mirrors the racial hierarchy: the cultural valence of both whiteness and masculinity is consolidated in the same figure. What happens when the pattern is inverted, and white woman is the subject of the attentions of Indian man? The dominant model here, of course, is the captivity narrative, which customarily works in two directions: white woman as victim—taken away from her family, raped, tortured, even murdered (the paradigm case is Jane McCrea, in Linda Colley's terms "a captive and slaughtered virgin, a war propagandist's dream")[39]—or white woman assimilated, as epitomized by the best-selling *Narrative of the Life of Mrs. Mary Jemison* (1824); Jemison, of Scottish Irish parents, freely chose to live as a Seneca and was happily married to two successive husbands, despite acknowledging, in her terms, "my reduction from a civilized to a savage state."[40] The Quaker Mary Howitt, who published a number of pro-Indian poems in the 1820 and 1830s, offers a version of this pattern in her poem "Elian Gray," in which an escaped British soldier is rescued by someone he takes to be an Indian woman, but as he hears her singing a ballad in her wigwam, he realizes she is English. Yet, despite being happy to pray with him, she has no desire to return, to be "rescued"; she is now completely domiciled among the family who took her in when she was starving and is "an Indian wife" and mother.[41] While neither she nor Howitt is exactly exuberant about her situation, the overall message of the poem is one of Indian kindness, which deserves to be repaid with loyalty, and of the validity and strength of new family bonds. There is no hint of any unease at cross-racial marriage or at miscegenation; on the other hand, nor is there any hint of physical or emotional attraction.

Yet if one moves away from literary representation, or from the sanctioned, artificial space for the carnivalesque that the public display of Native Americans provided, the ways in which sexual attraction between the races was perceived shift dramatically. The infatuation of the "jolly fat dame" with Cadotte may have been serious to her, but the very fact of its seriousness—combined with her physical appearance—allows Catlin to turn the woman, without too much cruelty, into a figure of fun, indeed, to treat her in a similar register of condescension to that in which he periodically writes of the Indian. However, when Cadotte falls in love with an English girl, Catlin is dismayed. Daniel Kavanaugh had to enlighten his employer as to the cause of the symptoms of sickness the interpreter had been manifesting. Next door to the house where the Indians have been lodging, he tells Catlin, "is one of the most beautiful black-eyed little girls that I have seen since I have been in London, and, by putting her head out of the back window to look at the Indians, and by playing in the back yard, she long since showed to everybody who saw her that she was fascinated with Cadotte. She used to kiss her hand to him, and throw him bouquets of flowers, and, at last, letters" (1:179). She and her sisters, and then her father, mother, and brother, come into the lodging house to visit, and Cadotte in turn becomes smitten. The "black-eyed maiden"—Catlin does not name Sarah Haynes (her name is found in newspaper reports) but refers to her only by a balladlike epithet—starts to visit the show nightly and had—at least according to Catlin—a notable somatic effect on her beloved's performance. Catlin acknowledges, coyly and awkwardly, that he has difficulty writing about the episode (having been used to "record the dry realities of Indian life, stripped of the delicious admixture which is sometimes presented when Cupid and civilization open their way into it") (1:175–76), and, indeed, his registers start to slide around in a most unstable fashion. His embarrassment is signaled by the ways in which he deploys racial and gender stereotypes—of the noble Indian, untainted by civilization, being contaminated by the designing siren—almost to the point of parody, as though he is uncertain whether to convey horror or patronizing amusement.

The whole soul of the "*Strong Wind*," which, until now, had been un-chained and free as the mountain breeze, was completely enveloped in the soft and silken web which the languishing black eyes, the cherry and pulpy lips, and rosy cheeks of this devouring little maid had spun and entwined about it. He trembled when he straightened his tall and elegant figure above the platform, not that he was before the gazing world, but because *her* soft black eyes were upon him. His voice fal-tered and his throat was not clear when he brandished his glistening tomahawk and sounded the shrill war-whoop. This was not that the ears of hundreds, but that the ears of ONE, were open to catch the sound (1:181).

Yet Catlin's opinions are entirely clear when he is dealing not, as it were, with romance, but with what he sees as something quite different: the practical implications of the liaison. He discusses the situation with Arthur Rankin and is less than pleased to find that Cadotte has already asked for, and received, Rankin's consent in the matter of marriage: "I told him I thought such a step should be taken with great caution, for the young lady was an exceedingly pretty and interesting girl, and, I had learned, of a respectable family, and certainly no step whatever should be taken in the affair by him or me without the strictest respect to their feelings and wishes." Learning that the father remained opposed to the marriage, Catlin thought it would be cruel to do anything to promote it and that,

> much as I thought of Cadotte, I did not feel authorized to countenance a union of that kind, which would result in his spending his life in London, where his caste and colour would always be against him, and defeat the happiness of his life; or she must follow him to the wilder-ness of America, to be totally lost to the society of her family, and to lead a life of semi-barbarism, which would in all probability be filled with excitement enough for a while, but must result in her distress and misery at last. (1:183–84).

At this point in the narrative, the focus shifts from the imminent mar-riage to Catlin's own wrangles with Rankin about who, effectively, had the stronger claim to exhibit the Indians: Rankin, who was, from Cat-lin's viewpoint, an out-and-out showman, or Catlin, who, despite the accusations that he was using these native peoples for his own financial ends, took pains to stress that his prime motive of anthropological inter-est. What does become clear is that Rankin wanted to make capital out of the nuptials, announcing the hour and day at which the couple were to be married in Saint Martin's Church, sponsoring a wedding proces-sion with four-in-hand coaches and bands and generally drumming up a curious audience for his subsequent show, at which *"the beautiful and interesting bride of the 'Strong Wind,' the interpreter, will make her appearance on the platform with the Indians, and preside at the piano"* (1:187). But Rankin was foiled on two counts. First, the London press turned against this blatant attempt at exploitation; and second, Cadotte himself, not having been consulted about the proposed appearance of his bride, refused to have anything more to do with Rankin. Rankin had to explain himself to an angrily disappointed audience. After a short stay with the Haynes family, the couple returned to Canada.

Sarah Cadotte did not escape from being an object of curious attention, even after she left London. The couple took up residence on a reservation, Walpole Island, at the entrance to the Saint Clair River, which was shared by Ojibwa and Pottawatamie. Visiting in 1853, William Kingston heard of the disappointment of the "poor, poor girl," who had little dreamed, he said, "of the melancholy contrast between the life her romantic imagination had pictured and the reality," as she arrived in a small log hut with her piano, her books, and her elegant furniture.[42] According to him, she—well read in James Fenimore Cooper—had projected all kinds of nobility and virtues onto Cadotte, but he took to drink and abused her. Moving, after two years, to Sault Sainte Marie, she converted to Roman Catholicism and opened a small Catholic school; although Cadotte's conduct toward her improved, and she believed it was her duty to stick by him and help in his reformation,

> the idol she had once adored had proved a hideous monster—her love had fled, and her heart was breaking. Yet to the last she refused to leave him—her sole earthly desire to see him better prepared for the eternity to which she was herself so rapidly hastening. And thus she died and slept at last in peace—another of the many examples of woman's folly, and of woman's constancy, and of severe and bitter punishment for one fault—

that is, falling blindly and extravagantly in love with the wrong man (1:240). The Englishman William Hancock, traveling in the area the year before Kingston, drew similar conclusions. In his travel book of 1860, he noted that Cadotte

> treated her as bad, or worse than any wife-beating Englishman could have done; but, though many attempts were made to induce her to return to England, they all proved unsuccessful, and she died some years since, as she had lived, the faithful loving wife of the degraded savage. Is it so seldom thus with woman's love? Given in all its over-flowing richness, depth and purity where least valued and least deserved; to be, by others, sought, and craved and prayed for—in vain.[43]

To the last, the rhetoric surrounding the romance determinedly expropriated what it wanted from this singular story in order to satisfy its own generalizing ends. Hancock naturalizes the exceptional, making it fit a familiar norm—in this case, one in which, seemingly, sexualized affection is seen, predictably but disastrously, to be stronger than the conventional dictates of racial difference. The specter of woman's desire is made manifest through her apparently irrational enthusiasm for the Indian; this willful emotion is seen as symptomatic of a gendered weakness.

Was Catlin correct? Would Cadotte's "caste and colour" have been against him in London? How was this mixed-race marriage seen? As far as one can tell, popular opinion—apart from being fascinated by the sensational element—saw in these nuptials a form of amalgamation that denigrated the woman, reducing her, and her offspring, to the level of the presumed racial inferior. This was not necessarily a result of her supposed subordinate position in the hierarchy of gender; cross-racial marriage was generally thought of as having a lowering effect. This can be seen by considering something that was rarely picked up on at the time: Cadotte, as his name suggests, was not pure-blood Ojibwa but the son of an Indian mother and a Frenchman "who had long been an interpreter for the English factories in those regions."[44] As H. L. Malchow has explained, in most areas of Canada, "mixed-bloods were treated as Indians rather than being enculturated as whites,"[45] and this enculturation and costuming of Cadotte certainly led him to be treated by the London press as unequivocally Indian, even if some of the more serious papers, in passing, noted his family background accurately.

An interesting parallel may be drawn with the case of Eliza Field, the South London, daughter of the owner of a soap and candle factory, who in September 1833 crossed the Atlantic to marry the Mississauga preacher Kahkewaquonaby. Also known as the Reverend Peter Jones, Kahkewaquonaby, whom she had met while he was on a fund-raising preaching tour of England, was, like Cadotte, the son of a white man and an Indian woman. But the Welsh side of his ancestry seems to have made no difference to the reactions on either side of the Atlantic to this marriage. Despite the fact that Eliza, who came from a devout background, would be working on an Indian mission, friends and relatives opposed the marriage—her brother-in-law looked upon it "in horror."[46] The New York *Commercial Advertiser* emotively attacked the union: "Many people have denounced Shakespeare's Othello, as too unnatural for probability. It can hardly be credited that such a fair, beautiful and accomplished woman, as Desdemona is represented to have been, could have deliberately wedded a black a moor as Othello. But if we ever entertained any incredulity upon the subject, it has all been dissipated by the occurrence of which we speak."[47]

This offensive racism, together with a collapsing of all non-Caucasians into a repellent racial Other, cannot be explained away by transatlantic differences. For even if the serious London press was somewhat more respectful in its terminology, taking pains to emphasize that Sarah Haynes was a woman from a respectable background, the event was seen as an occasion for humor, at the expense of both Indians and women. *Punch*'s sustained piece of sneering manages to incorporate a reference to a growing social concern:

> We have a superabundant female population. This fact is on all hands allowed and deplored. We see an easy remedy for this. Let parties of Indians be imported. Let us have samples of the Chippewas, the Dog-Ribbed, the Sioux, the Chactaws—indeed, a company of every tribe of wild men, from Hottentots to Greenlanders—and let them be let loose in our various towns for the sole purpose of captivating the hearts, and so carrying away in lawful wedlock, our superabundant females.[48]

The laborious humor continued in the next week's number, which contained mock advertisements purporting to be from other Ojibwa looking for wives. The blatant racism of these pieces is the more notable in the light of *Punch*'s sustained opposition to slavery, suggesting that the periodical found something especially ridiculous in the Native American that was not present in the African American. Very probably, the Indians themselves had become tainted in England through being seen as part of what was commonly perceived as a commercial enterprise (and Rankin's attitudes here did not help), with the consequent suspicion that therefore there was something bogus about their ethnicity.

Popular print shared in *Punch*'s deliberately careless racial homogenization. Two contemporary broadsides, in particular, provide vivid evidence of 1840s racial thinking at the level of street culture. In these two ballads, "The Ojibbeway Indians and Love" and "The London Lass and the Ojibbeway Indian," several things stand out. First, there is a complete lack of any concern with the specificity of Native American culture. Racial Others are interchangeable: "His name is Nowka, Jigglem, Ching,/ Busco, Bango, Shy, Strong Wind,/Smitherem, Diego, Jiggle, Jum, Jars."[49] Indeed, the dominant racial characteristics that are called upon are unmistakable African stereotypes: "A nose just like an orange outang"; "Mouths as big as turnpike gates"; "These Injians wear a dirty clout,/ And a great bone ring run through their snout."[50] The overall Africanist—or black-face—impression is cemented by the employment of a stock printer's block showing a crude representation of a dancing black man.

The second notable characteristic of these ballads is their insistent emphasis on the sexual. This is both personal, in the way the verse leers at

Miss Haynes ("married without delay,/Unto a covy black and brown,/ With his jiggem jiggo hanging down,/And in 9 months time will bring to town,/A little ojibbeway indian" [lines 84–88]), and implicates women more generally:

> The lasses all I do declare,
> Around the Hampstead Road and Euston Square
> Wives and daughters gay and smart,
> Deep and wounded to the heart
> In love with those great Indian blacks"
>
> (Lines 5–9)

"The London Lass" goes so far as to prophesy a dismal future for the nation if this tendency should take hold.

Toward the end of *Colonial Desire*, Robert Young's considered analysis of nineteenth-century ideas concerning hybridity, the author writes that "nineteenth-century theories of race did not just consist of essentializing differentiations between self and other: they were also about a fascination with people having sex—interminable, adulterating, aleatory, illicit, inter-racial sex."[51] This fascination passed far beyond the theorizations of such writers of racial science as James Cowles Prichard and Robert Knox. But when we witness it in England in its most vernacular form, the disgust and hatred are leveled not so much against these racial Others (although that certainly underpins the stereotyping) as against the women who dare flirt with them, desire them, even marry them, in a way that bears no resemblance to the decorous versions of interracial romance offered in polite literature. The inferiority—to put it mildly— of the Indian is taken for granted; what is truly shocking to many commentators (and Catlin is not immune from an embarrassed equivocation on the issue) is that the presence of the Ojibwa in London sparked not just public curiosity but public displays of libido on the part of women. The most widely expressed concern that the presence of Catlin's Indians stirred up in London was, ultimately, one about domestic sexual politics.

OJIBWA AND THE SOCIAL CONDITIONS OF BRITAIN

There is plenty of evidence in the British press about how Catlin's show and the Indians who appeared in it were publicly received in the 1840s. But how did these Indians interpret England? Our evidence is somewhat limited, since it must come largely from Catlin's words, in the book he published about his years in England and Europe. To this may be added Maungwudaus's brief but significant account, written "for the benefit of his youngest Son, called Noodinokay, whose Mother died in England."[52] What we hear of Indian voices in Catlin may, of course, fairly be termed an act of ventriloquism.[53] But Catlin spent a great deal of time with them; he talked with them at the end of each day about their impressions of what they had seen—admittedly often through an interpreter, although he had a good working knowledge of their languages—and he set down their views in a manner that one may assume is an approximation to authenticity. This may seem a bold statement, but elsewhere in his narrative Catlin is very careful to record localized speech forms—distinguishing between Manchester and London working-class accents, for example—and my case is strengthened by the fact that he is not a polished, literary writer; he repeats himself, he rambles, and he has little sense of molding his material into an aesthetic, or even a polemical whole. To be sure, a certain condescension creeps into his presentation —he refers to their "rude, uncultivated minds," for example, when describing the impression made on them when they watched the state opening of Parliament (1:173). We should acknowledge, too, the factor of linguistic hierarchy that comes into play precisely because Catlin *does* attempt to differentiate between Indian expression and standard English; in relation to Franz Boas's records of Indian narratives, Charles Briggs and Richard Bauman have recently called our attention to language's use in "legitimating hierarchical relations between 'modern' and 'backward' or 'traditional' groups, societies and nations and in naturalizing social inequality within nation-states through assertions of cultural difference."[54] In conveying Indian voices, Catlin invariably makes them sound as though they think and express themselves in a simpler, more "innocent" way than the—by implication—more sophisticated product of Western civilization. He thus completely obliterates any trace of the verbal subtleties and suppleness of the Ojibwa language, a tongue charged with energy (almost four-fifths of its words are verbs) and full of evocative nuances. In 1850 the Ojibwa speaker and writer George Copway wrote how much more could be conveyed, in a verbally condensed form, in his language by comparison with English: "It would require an almost infinitude of English words to describe a thunder-storm, and after all you would have but a feeble idea of it. In the Ojibway language, we say 'Be-wah-sam-moog.' In this we convey the idea of a continual glare of lightning, noise, confusion—an awful whirl of clouds, and much more."[55] Moreover, sometimes Catlin suppresses information that would have allowed his readers to see that the Indians had already had, in some cases, considerable exposure to cross-cultural contact. Trading patterns had been long established between the French, the English, and the Ojibwa, and the tribe had given military support to the British. One of the party,

Pat-au-a-quot-a-wee-be, had fought on British lines, and been wounded, in the 1812 war. Although Catlin was happy enough to suggest the Ojibwa's primitivism to the British public, he was quick to signal, when the Iowa took their places, that there was something more authentic about these second visitors—a perspective that the public was happy to take at face value.[56] At their first appearance, they were compared with the previous group, and it "was proclaimed in every part of the room, that they were altogether more primitive in their appearance and modes, and decidedly a finer body of men" (2:11). He explained to them "that the position of this tribe being upon the great plains between the Missouri and the Rocky Mountains, 1000 miles farther west than the country from which the Ojibbeways came, their modes and personal appearance were very different, having as yet received no changes from the proximity of civilization" (2:12). Yet such an introduction ignores the fact that Neu-mon-ya, the chief of the Iowa, had visited Saint Louis and Washington D.C., to negotiate over land rights, let alone the fact that this particular group had already performed together publicly in, among other locations, Hoboken, New Jersey.

In reading Catlin's account, one is led to believe that he is introducing both groups of Indians to all aspects of white society for the very first time, and that they translated their impressions directly into their own, unmediated terms. Thus to see the smoke of an industrial city is to think "the prairies were on fire" (1:113, 129); the tunnel that is being excavated under the Thames is "the Great Medicine Cave" (1:152). And we also hear of the enthusiasm of the Ojibwa at the prospect of meeting their "Great Mother," Queen Victoria, and their disappointment at her short stature and the general lack of flamboyance at Windsor; of the Iowa's breakfast with the politician Disraeli and of their responses to such diverse attractions as a fox hunt in Yorkshire; Truman and Hanson's London brewery (where, to the astonishment of the workforce, they performed a medicine dance in an empty vat) and the Surrey Zoological Gardens. When the Iowa encountered "the poor distressed and ragged prisoner, the buffalo from their own wild and free prairies, their spirits were overshadowed with an instant gloom; forebodings, perhaps, of their own approaching destiny," hypothesizes Catlin, milking the moment for all its rhetorical potential (2:88). The Iowa exercised on Lord's Cricket Ground and during the summer moved from the Egyptian Hall to camp in that long-standing entertainment venue, the Vauxhall Gardens. Both groups were skeptical toward many of the well-intentioned clergy who tried to convert them, recollecting the double standards of missionaries whom they had known back home. We can see how Indian views of English sexual conduct were heavily, and unfavorably, inflected by their

Figure 7. Ojibwa dancing for Queen Victoria, *Catlin's Notes of Eight Years' Travels and Residence in Europe, with His North American Indian Collection,* 2 vols. (London: published by the author, 1848).

prior experience of missionaries. As the Ojibwa Gisheegoshegee said on the occasion of a visit from the well-intentioned Reverend Mr. S—:

> My friends—A few years ago a *black-coat* came amongst us in the town where I live, and told us the same words as you have spoken this morning. He said that the religion of the white man was the only good religion; and some began to believe him, and after a while a great many believed him; and then he wanted us to help build him a house; and we did so. We lifted very hard at the logs to put up his house, and when it was done many sent their children to him to learn to read, and some girls got so as to read the "good book," and their fathers were very proud of it; and at last one of these girls had a baby, and not long after it another had a baby, and the *black-coat* then ran away, and we have never seen him since. My friends, we don't think this is right. I believe there is another *black-coat* now in the same house. Some of the Indians send their boys there to learn to read, but they dare not let their girls go. (2:1)

Both the Ojibwas and the Iowa were decidedly more sympathetic toward Quakers. The Iowa frequently met with Thomas Hodgkin in London, and members of the Society of Friends, very visible in their audiences in Birmingham and York, also invited them into their homes.

However tempting it is to recount these many examples of cultural collision, I want, finally, to think a little more closely about two types of response that Catlin records: one of silence, and the other—toward English social conditions—seemingly exceeding the engagement with "civilization" that he himself wished his Indians to experience. When the Ojibwa arrived in Manchester in November 1843, they were taken, among other outings, on a visit to the cotton mill of Mr. Orrell, in the nearby town of Stockport. "With his customary politeness," writes Catlin,

> he showed us through it, and explained it in all its parts, so that the Indians, as well as myself, were able to appreciate its magnitude and its ingenious construction.
>
> Upon this giant machine the Indians looked in perfect amazement; though it is a studied part of their earliest education not to exhibit surprise or emotion at anything, however mysterious or incomprehensible it may be. There was enough, however, in the symmetry of this wonderful construction, when in full operation, to overcome the rules of any education that would subdue the natural impulses of astonishment and admiration. They made no remarks, nor did they ask any questions, but listened closely to all the explanations; and, in their conversation for weeks afterwards, admitted their bewildering astonishment at so wonderful a work of human invention. (1:121)[57]

But how far, we may ask, did the visitors relate the fact that the cotton mill was not "in full operation" to the unemployed whom they also witnessed on the streets of Manchester? Anxiety about the incendiary potential of public gatherings was a major reason, according to Catlin, for the police's dispersal of the crowds who gathered to watch the Indians taking the air on their lodging-house rooftop.[58] How far might this silence also conceal their responses to the fact that, as Friedrich Engels puts it in his *Condition of the Working Class in England in 1844*, "Stockport is renowned throughout the entire district as one of the duskiest, smokiest holes, and looks, indeed . . . excessively repellent"?[59] And how far did these Canadian First Nations people associate the manufacture of cotton with those involved in its cultivation and gathering in the United States? Despite the arguments that I am making both in this chapter and in *The Transatlantic Indian* as a whole for the degree of Indian critical engagement with certain aspects of life in industrialized countries, I am pointing, as well, to the importance of the unrecoverability of some important areas of these encounters: this silence may be read not so much as a dazed, stunned response, or along the lines of Jean-François Lyotard's notion of the "differend," which longs to be put into language, but as affirmation of difference.[60]

The sense of privilege experienced by both groups of Indians who toured with Catlin comes out well in his account of the Ojibwa's first outing in London, where they

"saw a great many fine houses, but nobody in the windows; saw many
men with a large board on the back, and another on the breast, walking in the street—supposed it was some kind of punishment; saw men
carrying bags of coal, their hats on wrong side before; saw fine ladies
and gentlemen riding in the middle of the streets in carriages, but a
great many poor and ragged people on the sides of the roads; saw a
great many men and women drinking in shops where they saw great
barrels and hogsheads; saw several drunk in the streets. They had
passed two *Indians* in the streets with brooms, sweeping away the
mud; they saw them hold out their hands to people going by, as if they
were begging for money: they saw many other poor people begging,
some with brooms in their hands and others with little babies in their
arms, who looked as if they were hungry for food to eat." They had
much to say about the two Indians they had passed. "It could not be
that white people would dress and paint themselves like Indians in
order to beg money, and they could not see how Indians would consent to stand in the streets and sweep the mud away in order to beg
for money." They appealed to me to know whether they were really
Indians, and I said "Yes; they are natives from the East Indies, called
Lascars. They are naturally, most probably like yourselves, too proud
to work or to beg; but they have been left by some cruel fate, to earn
their living in the streets of London, or to starve to death, and, poor
fellows, they have preferred begging to starvation." The Indians
seemed much affected by the degradation that these poor fellows were
driven to, and resolved that they would carry some money with them
when they went out, to throw to them. (1:129)[61]

One might usefully juxtapose these accounts with descriptions given
by British travelers to Indian settlements on the edges of Canadian and
American towns, and the revulsion they expressed at the drunkenness
and degradation that they witnessed: the Indians visiting England are
conspicuously more concerned with learning about the processes of
cause and effect that lie behind poverty and with considering the question of responsibility. The Indians did not routinely give money to beggars and other poor people whom they saw in the streets, but when on
tour, there were occasions when a considerable share of their profits
went to local causes, and they also supported one-off cries for help. In
Birmingham, Catlin recalls, the Indians encountered "a miserably poor
old woman, with her little child, both in rags, and begging for the means
of existence"; they not only offer her money but are "anxious to talk
with her, and find out how it was that she should not be better taken
care of." She had, it emerges, been in the workhouse but was not allowed to live with her husband there, so had taken to the streets to beg.

"The poor Indians, women and all, looked upon this miserable shivering object of pity, in the midst of the wealth and luxuries of civilization, as a mystery they could not expound" (2:135–36). Once again, in suggesting wide-eyed wonder, Catlin is trying to present these native people as naive primitives, distanced from modern society, but he undermines his own rhetoric through the evidence he provides of the Indians' very shrewd social and economic awareness of the society in which they found themselves. Also in Birmingham, handing over £721.16s, Senontiyah, the Medicine Man, speaking publicly, addressed his audience in very direct terms:

> "My Friends,—If we were rich, like many white men in this country, the poor people we see around the streets in this cold weather, with their little children barefooted and begging, would soon get enough to eat, and clothes to keep them warm.
> "My Friends,—It has made us unhappy to see the poor people begging for something to eat since we came to this country. In our country we are all poor, but the poor all have enough to eat, and clothes to keep them warm. We have seen your poorhouses, and been in them, and we think them very good; but we think there should be more of them, and that the rich men should pay for them.
> "My Friends,—It makes us unhappy, in a country where there is so much wealth, to see so many poor and hungry, and so many as we see drunk." (2:143)

The Indians were determined, too, that the British should recognize how the host country was implicated in the causes of the Indian poverty that underlay their reasons for crossing the Atlantic to raise money, including the introduction of smallpox, venereal disease, and the sale of "fire-water."

The urge to document and understand British society, with its hardships and inequalities, is particularly noticeable in the case of one of the Iowa, Jim (Wash-ka-mon-ya), who, profoundly shocked by aspects of what he witnessed, set out to look into these conditions in his own right. He mirrored the techniques of nineteenth-century Anglo social investigators and travelers by donning, with the Medicine Man, Western clothing in order to go out into London unobserved. From Catlin's perspective, this dress—beaver hats, frock-coats, woolen pantaloons, high-heeled boots, wigs, and canes or umbrellas—enabled them to profit "by gazing upon the wonders and glories of civilization, which we never otherwise could have beheld together" (2:65). But in fact, this sartorial disguise allowed its Indian wearers not so much to greet British civilization with awe as to "pass" in order, ultimately, to critique its practices. Jim began to learn to speak and write English so that he could better carry out his inquiries. He had Daniel Kavanaugh, Catlin's assistant, help him make a record book of all he saw; he kept statistics on poorhouses, prisons, breweries. He counted gin shops, keeping the score by notching a tally stick. He noted the annual consumption of spirits in Great Britain, the estimation that 50,000 "drunkards die yearly in England and Ireland," and the attribution of much insanity, pauperism, and crime to alcohol: something that, he said, he looked forward to showing those "black-coats," or missionaries, who were always talking about Indians getting drunk (2:188). He collected newspaper clippings on issues that interested him, such as the petition to the queen, signed by 100,000 women, against white slave-trading; he started to enter into his notebook the number of murders and robberies recorded in the *Times* and took notice of accounts of death from starvation. Amused by *Punch*, he suggested that they take out a subscription and try to pay for it with the numerous Bibles that they were given by well-meaning British Christians. He visited a coal mine in the north east of England, where he saw "six or seven hundred men, women, and children, as black as negroes," living and working underground: he thought that being in the debtors' cells of a prison

> would be far preferable to the slavery they there saw, of "hundreds of women and children drawing out . . . from some narrow places where the horses could not go, little carriages loaded with coal; where the women had to go on their hands and knees through the mud and water, and almost entirely naked, drawing their loads by a strap that was buckled around their waists; their knees and their legs and their feet, which were all naked, were bleeding with cuts from the stones, and their hands also; they drew these loads in the dark, and they had only a little candle to see the way." (2:160)

Jim noted the Crown's expenditure, seeing how the apparatuses of the state functioned, soldiers and police alike being necessary "to keep people at work in the factories, and to make them pay their taxes" (2:186). He "said he thought it was wrong to send missionaries from this country to the Indian country, when there were so many poor creatures here who want their help" (2:71). This was hardly a unique perspective. But the point about missionary work is rather different when made by an Iowa than when Dickens protested in *Bleak House* that missionary effort would be better directed domestically than overseas.

Jim's views were very close to those that Catlin privately held. He wrote at some length to his father on 3 March 1842, saying that he was completely sick of the insolence of wealth and the wretchedness of poverty which belongs to this great polished nation, with its boasted Institutions—its wealth, its refinements, its luxuries—with its vices, with its incongruous mass of loyalty & disloyalty, Republicanism and Despotism—mixed & patched up together, soon to fall & crumble to pieces into the levels of Agrarianism, or the hands of Nations which will stand ready to prey upon the riches of the ruined & falling edifice.[62]

But Catlin's publicly expressed responses to these social investigations were decidedly equivocal. While he started off encouraging Jim in his note taking, pleased that he would be carrying a record of the advanced modern world back to his people, the reportage did not equate with what he originally anticipated.

> They had been brought to the zenith of civilization that they might see and admire it in its best form; but the world who read will *see* with me that they were close critics, and *agree* with me, I think, that it is almost a pity they should be the teachers of such statistics as they are to teach to tens of thousands yet to be taught in the wilderness. . . . I have long since been opposed to parties of Indians being brought to this country, believing that civilization should be a gradual thing, rather than open the eyes of these ignorant people to all its mysteries at a glance, when the mass of its poverty and vices alarms them. . . . (2:187–88)

Quite possibly, he included the Indians' perspectives on urban life because they matched his own, yet he was not running the risk of offending the British by letting the observations appear in his own voice. Rather than his ventriloquizing *them*, he was, when it suited his purpose, letting them speak for *him*.

But we might respond to Jim's investigations somewhat differently. First, we can see readily that Native Americans, viewing England from their cultural and social perspectives, were in a position to challenge its contemporary claims to greatness. More important for my argument, however, and more important for Native American history, is the fact that these peoples were quite definitely not allowing themselves to be consigned to oblivion, nor to the status of the ahistorical and timeless. Their presence affords what Gerald Vizenor has called "an aesthetic, ideological disanalogy" with the idea of a vanishing race.[63] Jim's activities not only contradict the view that Catlin was promulgating about native people's being on the edge of destruction, and the alternative possibility for assimilation that was also being rhetorically and politically allowed for, but also show his engagement, on the part of his people, with the values of various societies in the present and future.

A further native perspective on 1840s Britain is provided by the Ojibwa Maungwudaus (George Henry). After converting to Christianity around 1825, he attended the Methodist mission school at the Credit Mission in the late 1820s and went on to serve at several missions in the 1830s before moving to Walpole Island in 1837. Speaking fluent English, he worked as a government interpreter at the Saint Clair mission in 1840, the year he resigned from the Methodist church.[64] Doubtless inspired by Catlin's example, he organized a dance troupe of Walpole Island Ojibwa that traveled to England in 1844. Like other Indians in London in the early 1840s, he met with Queen Victoria. He was kindly greeted and entertained by members of the Society of Friends, visited the tunnel under the Thames and the Zoological Gardens, attended a public execution, and performed the rites of a literary tourist, going to Shakespeare's house and grave at Stratford, Byron's Newstead Abbey, and "Burns's cottage, small, with straw-roof" (8). He suffered personal tragedy during his visit. Three of his troupe members died from smallpox (they had refused white man's medicine; the Quakers had seen to it that everyone else was vaccinated). Two of his children, and then his wife, also passed away. Joining up with Catlin in France, the overall impressions of the American's venture that he took away with him were not happy ones, either. Frank Little, who met Maungwudaus when he stopped at his family's general store in 1850, recalled that the Ojibwa chief had told him: "The Indians under Catlin did not thrive. They pined for their wigwam homes and native woods. The artificial mode of living, diet, clothing, sleep, etc. preyed upon their health. They sickened, and many died."[65] Little introduced him to Taundoqua, who was to become his second wife; re-forming a troupe, they performed at the Saint Lawrence Hall, Toronto, in 1851.

Maungwudaus is a clear example of a First Nations member preferring to act—and being prepared to act—as an impresario for performers who are his own people; what we know of his life bears witness to the weight he gave to personal, and tribal, autonomy. His capacity to speak on his own behalf is also evinced by the short pamphlet he produced after his European visit. His words, unlike those of the other Ojibwa visitors, are not selected and framed by a white man's account. But many of the rhetorical devices he employs are quite similar to the ways in which their views were recorded, although in his case there is a much more conscious sense that he is translating the culturally unfamiliar into terms that would make his experiences vivid to an Indian audience. He writes of the crowds in London: "Like musketoes in America in the summer season, so are the people in this city, in their numbers, and biting one another to get a living" (3); the guardsmen in Queen Victoria's entourage "do not shave the upper part of their mouths, but let the beards grow long, and this makes them look fierce and savage like our American dogs when carrying black squirrels in their mouths" (4); He conveys the height of Canterbury Cathedral's spire by saying that it was too high for their arrows to reach; explains how women hold their knife and fork at the table, "with the two forefingers and the thumb of each hand; the two last ones are of no use to them, only sticking out like our fish-spears, while eating" (5); and describes his visit to the medical school in Edinburgh: "We went to see about seventy young men, who are to be medicine men. They had thirty dead bodies, and they were skinning and cutting them same as we do with venison" (8). While he did not draw attention to questions of poverty in the same way that Catlin's Indians did, Maungwudaus did note, apropos of his visit to Ireland, that "the country people make fire of turf; many of them are very poor; the British government is over them" (8). Nonetheless, he gives a lively account of what we may take as an encounter with modernity, showing, as it does, the domestication of science and the shifting perspectives on physical existence offered by optical technology. In Ipswich, dining with Quakers, one of their number placed a small cheese on the table at the end of the meal.

When our eating was over, a doctor, whose name is F. W. Johnson, placed over the table, what he calls microscope; it had three brass legs and a small glass to it, and when he had put a very small bit of the cheese we had to eat on a clean plate, he made us look at it through the little glass that was on the three legged brass, and we saw hundred of worms moving in it. This made all our friends laugh, and we tried to laugh too, but we were very much frightened at the same time knowing that we must have swallowed thousands of them. When our friends saw that we were frightened, the medicine man dropped one drop of rain water in a clear glass, and he made us look at it again through the little glass, and we saw hundred of living creatures swimming in it; some like beasts, some like snakes, some like fish, some had horns and some had no horns, some with legs and some had no legs; some had wheels on each side of their bodies, and with these they were moving about like steamboats, hooking, chasing, fighting, killing and eating one another. Then one of our oldest friends said to us, "Now, friends, you must not think that this is the first time you have been eating worms. We swallow thousands of them every day either with food or water. They are floating in the air, and we inhale them, when we draw breath; thousands of them are also floating in our veins. The Great Spirit, who made us and all other beings is wonderful in power and wisdom. We sincerely hope that you will at all times love him, and obey what he tells you in your hearts." We waited two or three days for the worms to bite. Sometimes we would be looking for them, thinking that they might have grown larger while they were in our bodies, but we did not feel their bites nor saw any of them. We have oftentimes been thinking since, that our friends must be something like bears, who loves to eat living worms or maggots. (10–11)

Here, as throughout his account, individual experience gains its importance not through subjective response but as something that may be shared through terms designed to reach a specific readership or audience, with its own familiar frames of reference. Native peoples are not the Other against which modernity is being postulated; rather, the modern world is being presented for them.

 ⚶

Maungwudaus, like the Indians who traveled alongside Catlin, had been affected by a number of the features that we have come to consider characteristic of modernity. These include demographic upheavals and the concomitant severance of people not just from their ancestral habitats but from a sense of their traditional connections to both space and time; the expansion of their relationship to capitalist world markets and industrialization, including the growing tourist industry; their role as subjects, rather than agents, in the formation and development of a huge nation-state and their subjection to externally imposed bureaucracy; their relationship to the growth of the rhetoric of individuality (frequently a bad fit with tribal identity) and to the articulation of various freedoms, whether these involved self-determination, the ownership of property, or freedom of speech; and their incorporation into systems of mass communication—whether we think of accounts of tribal lifestyles and warfare in the press or the ways in which they became the subjects of photographic record.[66] One might fairly argue that since colonization, an increasing number of Native Americans had engaged, voluntarily or otherwise, with these phenomena, but their impact on native life during the nineteenth century involved unprecedented physical and psychic violence. Nonetheless, Maungwudaus's pamphlet is indicative of one particular desire to regain some agency within this changing order of things, producing, as well as being present within, print culture. Moreover, it—like the words of Wash-Ka-Mon-Ya and other Iowa and Ojibwa visitors—shows him, in terms of his engaged interest in the British, to be refusing what Johannes Fabian has famously termed the "denial of coevalness," that "persistent and systematic tendency to place the referent(s) of anthropology in a Time other than the present of the producer of the anthropological discourse."[67] As this chapter indicates, this was hardly a role universally inhabited by

Native Americans of this, or indeed previous, centuries. Despite the importance, then and today, of tradition as both concept and practice within Indian society, identity, and modes of thought, it stands not isolated from modernity but rather in mediation and dialogue with it—a dialogue that takes place both in relation to material practice and to such things as the role of spiritual life and the place of tribal as against the primacy of individual identity. The Other, as has already been noted, was undergoing a process of transformaton.[68]

Yet assertion of the validity, even superiority, of their own ways of life also strongly characterized the reactions of these visiting Indians. They both participated in and critiqued developing forms of modern life, not just within their own nations and in the superpower that surrounded these, but in a broader social and political circum-Atlantic context. The availability of Indian voices brings home the fact that analyzing British responses to Indians in the nineteenth century is not merely a matter of interacting with a set of icons and images. Such an analysis involves taking into account the British engagement with live individuals, who, for their part, had every intention not just of surviving but also of entering into debates about the directions in which various contemporary societies were developing.

CHAPTER FOUR

Sentiment and Anger: British Women Writers and Native Americans

In Charlotte Brontë's *Shirley* (1848), Shirley Keeldar, frustrated with the social demands to which she must submit as mistress of a household, proclaims: "Happy is the slave wife of the Indian chief, in that she has no drawing-room duty to perform, but can sit at ease weaving mats, and stringing beads, and peacefully flattening her pickaninny's head in an unmolested corner of her wigwam. I'll emigrate to the western woods." By way of reply, her timid suitor, Louis Moore, acutely conscious of the difference between them in terms of social and economic power, develops the motif by drawing on yet another stereotype, one that deliberately overturns the wealth and social position Shirley currently enjoys: " 'To marry a White Cloud or a Big Buffalo and after wedlock to devote yourself to the tender task of digging your lord's maize-field while he smokes his pipe or drinks fire-water.' "[1] This misreading of native culture—active woman and lazy man—was a familiar one in travel writing, especially lingered on by male commentators who were quick to condemn Indian men for being insufficiently respectful of the doctrines of bourgeois domesticity.[2] Within the novel itself, the fanciful setting of "the loneliest western wilds" becomes an imaginary site on which Shirley and Louis can perform their own dance of gender relations. She tells him that she readily thinks of him and his brother Robert as hunters there. " 'And any Indian tribe of Blackfeet, or Flatheads, would afford us a bride, perhaps?' " he inquires. " 'No,' " she replies, after some hesitation: " 'I think not. The savage is sordid. I think,—that is, I *hope,*—you would neither of you share your hearth with that to which you could not give your heart' " (570).

Shirley's blunt dismissal of native personhood is unpalatable. But it must be read, at least in part, as a literary gesture by Brontë, a component of Shirley's consistent and forthright disavowal of the sentimental and feminized. The representation and appropriation of Native Americans within imaginative literature by nineteenth-century British women was, at least in the earlier decades of the century, strongly inflected by sentimentalization and idealized projection. It resulted from an amalgamation of the legacy of the idea of the noble savage, awe at the wonders of nature, and the Romantic pathos attaching to the idea of a vanishing people. It was subject, too, to a variety of North American literary influences: the poetry of William Cullen Bryant and Lydia Sigourney, James Fenimore Cooper's novels and, to a lesser extent, Catharine Sedgwick's novel *Hope Leslie*.[3] Until the midcentury at least, the cultural work performed by those women writers who took Indians as their subject oscillated between mourning their imminent and inevitable demise and protesting against the specific political and racist attitudes that lay behind their treatment in America. After the middle of the century, although women's appropriation of the figure of the Indian occurred less frequently within serious imaginative writing, those poets who engaged with these native peoples showed an increasing tendency to extrapolate from the American context and turn their humanitarian gaze toward the workings of the British Empire itself.

Women seem to have been particularly drawn to Indians as a poetic topic, both finding them a suitable object on which to expend the fashionable literary currency of sentimental compassion and, it has been argued (most powerfully and influentially by Julie Ellison), seeing them, in their apparent disempowerment and marginalization, as an analogue for their own condition as women.[4] Nancy Moore Goslee expressly connects Felicia Hemans's treatment of native subjects with her internalization of the contradictory elements she found in contemporary womanhood; the two, in fact, were conflated in her verse so that one finds that the representations

> involve women either as literal and symbolic victims or as mythic redemptive forces such as liberty or nature. Through Hemans's "red Indian" poems, then, we can explore how this already multiply-determined and to some extent already Anglo-American interpretation of "Indians" as simultaneously alien, uncivilizable objects and universally-feeling subjects relates to interpretations of Hemans's own melancholy.[5]

The degree to which Hemans's representations may be regarded as politically charged, and the relationship between domestic and personal politics on the one hand and the transnational implications of her poetry on the other, have resulted in critical disagreement. Tim Fulford maintains that Hemans writes of Indian women in very anachronistic terms, seeing them in the tradition of British maidens who are betrayed by men, with no independent sense of identity and no ability to survive romantic disappointment; her Indian maiden is treated "simply as a cipher in which to encode the anxieties and hopes of the proper British lady."[6] I have more sympathy with Susan Wolfson's observation that in the "Indian Woman's Death-Song," the "political protest is the rhetorical unconscious of the poem,"[7] a comment that throws the onus of interpretation of this, and other works with an Indian subject, onto the reader, and the contexts that some of them would necessarily bring to Hemans's demands on their sympathetic engagement.

Goslee's comments about melancholy open up some further questions about the relationship between gender and the cultural work practiced by these women poets, who, in Lynn Festa's memorable phrase, engage in "the myriad acts of affective piracy that constitute the singularity of the sentimental self."[8] For Sigmund Freud, mourning and melancholia were two distinct but related states of mind. The former occupies a definite period, involves the necessary working through of a "loss of a loved person, or . . . to the loss of some abstraction which has taken the place of one, such as one's country, liberty, an ideal, and so on."[9] The latter, for him, was more of a pathological condition. Although it might be inaugurated by types of loss similar to those that lead to a period of mourning, loss has become something that it is impossible to overcome readily: "The complex of melancholia behaves like an open wound" that refuses to heal (262). In melancholia, the libido is not turned outward and displaced onto other objects; rather, the lost object is internalized. Thus acknowledgment of otherness goes along with its refusal; the subject of melancholy both is and is not the self. About whom, or about what, one might therefore ask, is the poet who laments the disappearing Indian really writing?

The literary critic Juliana Schiesari, who reassesses and opens out Freud's views in *The Gendering of Melancholia*, uses gendered categories of performance to distinguish between mourning, which, she says, has generally been the particular province of women—a part of domestic ritual, with a nameable object of loss—and melancholia, a wider category, in which men elevate and glorify their losses into "signifiers of cultural superiority," above all putting forward their *own* exquisite sensibilities for us to admire. But if we look at writing on the supposedly vanishing Indian *by* women, we soon find that any such neat distinction is complicated. These women's voices have clear objects; they mark the loss of individuals or tribes. But these poems are also expressions of sensibility offered for both stylistic and generic approval. More notably still, their subject matter both draws on a pre-established arena for the display of such sentiments *and* offers an opportunity, albeit a muted one, to enter into a more public cultural debate. In her excellent book *Women against Slavery*, Clare Midgley writes of the "complex picture in which women abolitionists were involved in constructing, reinforcing, utilising, negotiating, subverting or more rarely challenging the distinction between the private-domestic sphere and the public-political sphere which was so central to middle-class prescriptions concerning men's and women's proper role in society."[10] The same, I would argue, is to some degree true of many of the women who took Native Americans as their poetic subjects.[11] Nonetheless, these women poets may also be seen as employing sentiment and compassion as tools of personal, and national, literary advancement.

Women's poetic treatment of Indians in the early decades of the century is thus complicated by issues of distance and proximity—issues that are tied in both to the geographic and political spaces that exist between them and their subjects and to the nature of the relationship that they construct with native peoples—or with the idea of them. On occasion, they seem to be writing in accordance with the principles that Adam Smith had put forward in his *Theory of Moral Sentiments* (1759), with what Nancy Armstrong has termed its "hyperbolic demonstration of the principle that one individual comes to know how another feels by witnessing the spectacle of the other's suffering"—a witnessing that takes place through the exercise of the imagination, so that we place ourselves in the sufferer's situation, entering into her body, and to some measure feeling something not unlike her sensations and emotions.[12] This is a kind of thinking, as Armstrong goes on to explain, that breaks down the dividing line between "spectator and spectacle of grief" and that is, ultimately, anti-individualistic in nature. We can see it at work in Wordsworth's "Complaint of a Forsaken Indian Woman," for example, as she laments the loss of her friends, her tribe, her child: if the setting is the arctic wastes, the tone is recognizably that of people who have been severed from their closest connections, their reason for living. Writing about this poem, Mary Jacobus has drawn our attention to the way in which an "unfamiliar predicament serves to underline a recognizable humanity,"[13] and this emphasis on a shared sense of the human, carrying protagonists and readers across race, across class, and across physical distance, went on to inform the language of many of those who took Native Americans as their subject matter.

This sense of sympathetic bonding did not apply only to Anglo writers and native subjects; it also helps, to some extent, to explain the circum-Atlantic poetic traffic of the 1820s, 1830s, and 1840s, and the literary exchanges that took place between women poets, mediated, in part, through the model of Wordsworth. For example, Felicia Hemans was highly popular in the United States, where her "powerful cultural voice," as Tricia Lootens has explained, had considerable political influence. "Transplanted into the debates of a nation already at war with Indian nations, and soon to be at war with itself, Hemans's familiar—and generally abstract—explorations of feminine patriotic positions could reveal or assume surprising force."[14] Lootens shows how Hemans went on to play "a clear role in nineteenth-century constructions of national poetic mythology," something that "underscores the ways in which American national identity developed through as well as against notions of 'Eng-lishness'" (245). Yet Hemans knew well the writings of Lydia Huntley Sigourney (popularly known as "the American Hemans")—her prose as well as her poetry—and borrowed epigraphs as well as incidents directly from her. There is a further striking similarity between the style, lan-guage, and attitudes of Sigourney and the writings of Eliza Cook, Mary Howitt, and others. Sigourney wrote extensively about a number of dis-enfranchised groups: not just Native Americans, but slaves, the poor, the insane, and, in her later works, women. The record of her travels in England and France, *Pleasant Memories of Pleasant Lands* (1842), shows her firsthand knowledge of, and contact with, English women writers, as well as her visit to Wordsworth; she wrote several narrative poems in imitative homage to the longer *Lyrical Ballads*. Over and be-yond their interest in native subjects, these women shared a concern with experiences of suffering, dispossession, powerlessness, and loss, as well as of honor, loyalty, and a strong attachment to place.

The Wordsworthian influence is particularly notable in Howitt's "Elian Gray," which borrows the unmistakable stanza form of "The Idiot Boy." To make the indebtedness even more unmistakable, the soldier, on hear-ing the woman's story, finds that she is an emigrant "from the vale of Windermere," who had fallen on hard times before compassionate Indi-ans rescued her. Yet here our sympathy is being sought primarily for the resilience and adaptability of the white woman. Other poets attempt to take the reader more directly into the mind of the native, who can by no means rely on white people—particularly white men—to behave with human decency. Eliza Cook's "Song of the Red Man" is spoken by an understandably angry Indian. He rescues and cared for a wounded sol-dier, giving him wine and bread and goat's flesh. The setting seems in-congruously alpine, but the outcome is made specific to the American location: this soldier has repaid the speaker for his nursing and suste-nance by falling in love with his "pure daughter as bright as the prairie in spring." The Indian has previously been content in his self-sufficient surroundings "where the wandering, white man but rarely has come"; now his whole sense of well-being is shattered. "Oh, white man! the blood may well redden your skin,/For the theft you design is the mean-est of sin:/You have shared all I have till you need it no more;/Yet would take from me that which no hand can restore." He advises the in-terloper to flee before he murders him, turning the adopted weapons of an invading race upon its representative: "Away, then, base coward! there's guilt in thine eye,/And there's lead in my barrel,-away! or thou'lt die!"[15] The meter of Walter Scott's "Lochinvar" has been borrowed to ironic effect, the earlier ballad's celebration of the dashing and daring suitor reversed when the courtship is presented from the point of view of parental—and tribal—dispossession. Of course, this is obvious allegory. The shattering of traditional life patterns has been subsumed into domestic melodrama, a melodrama in which, however much the reader may be asked to sympathize with the potential devastation of the older man's family life, there is nonetheless little likelihood that his defiance will achieve a positive outcome. Yet rather than being presented as mindlessly bloodthirsty, this threat of Indian violence is supported by motivation that is fully understandable from an emotional perspective.

Perspective, however, is a matter of distance rather than identification, and what one notices, time and again, is that despite the standardized appeals to the sympathetic imagination, the emotional melding is more rhetorical than anything else. The Indian, in fact, is very often kept at a remove—a remove that, indeed, also provided something of the aura of mystery and potential evanescence, on which the Indian's attractiveness as a subject partly depended. To be sure, the figure also was habitually treated with great dignity, but as with the figure of Wright's Indian Widow, dignity very readily transformed into stasis. The poetic natives, in other words, are very rarely imagined as having any kind of agency or autonomy; their role is prescribed, serving as the stimulus for certain delimited affects. Inevitably, this meant that the stock responses associated with their poetic representation could readily be reappropriated for a variety of ends, which only enhanced their objectification.

But it would be too easy to regard this appropriation solely in a negative light or as signifying, at best, a benevolent condescension. For a start, the repeated use of the sentimentalized stereotype carries the potential to disturb. The sympathetic apostrophizing of a vanishing race and the concomitant celebration of certain values—family feeling, love of home and place, piety—together with responsiveness to nature, fit, to be sure, very comfortably within a domestic and pastoral elegiac tradition. Moreover, these are precisely the values that, as the century wore on, were cherished as lying at the heart of national identity. But the sentimental is not invariably a safe and reassuring space. Bound up with the treatment of public and political issues, it could be used, on occasion, to challenge some of the developing features of imperial power—and at the very least, it afforded readers the opportunity to extrapolate from the imaginary narratives of North American Indians features that, rightly, might give grounds for concern about how native peoples were treated in Britain's imperial possessions.[16] For although critique of transatlantic policies—however muted in its expression—ostensibly played on and flattered the idea of British rectitude and superiority, these writings served to bring out a troubling family similarity between Britain and America.

Moreover, bearing in mind the considerable overlap between antislavery supporters and those who wrote with concern about the treatment of

Native Americans, one may usefully draw here on lines of suggestion that Toni Morrison put out in *Playing in the Dark: Whiteness and the Literary Imagination*. Morrison writes that we need to ask "in what ways does the imaginative encounter with Africanism enable white writers to think about themselves," claiming that we must "analyze the manipulation of the Africanist narrative . . . as a means of meditation—both safe and risky—on one's own humanity. Such analyses will reveal how the representation and appropriation of that narrative provides opportunities to contemplate limitation, suffering, rebellion, and to speculate on fate and destiny."[17] The same categories come into play in relation to nineteenth-century representations of Native Americans, with an additional political edge: the subject matter encouraged British women writers to look critically not only at American practices but also at the dominant policies of their own country's expansionism, and at the particular types of the masculine ethos that lay behind them.

To look at this, we need to turn back to the topic of mourning and melancholia. Whether British women poets speak *in* the voice of the Indian, or whether they speak *for* the native subject, their laments frequently operate on multiple layers simultaneously. When Felicia Hemans's Indian "The Indian with His Dead Child" (1830) carries his burden from lands that now are shared with white settlers, so that he may be buried with his ancestors and his spirit thus returned to a more heroic time and location, he is both suffering individual bereavement and signifying that there is no generation to succeed him: a way of life is at an end.[18] Similarly, the first stanza of Hemans's "Aged Indian" (1818) incorporates the elegiac lines "Amidst my tribe I dwell alone;/The heroes of my youth are fled,/They rest among the warlike dead."[19] Frances Kemble's "The Red Indian" (1844) includes the following stanza:

> Rest, warrior, rest! thy rising sun
> Is set in blood, thy day is done;
> Like lightning flash thy race is run,
>   And thou art sleeping peacefully.[20]

Her play on the word "race," whether conscious or not, manages, like Hemans's verse, to unite the individual and the tribal lifespan.[21] Heroic decline is signed, quite conventionally, through the motif of the sun sinking in the west, an image that suggests both the "naturalness" and the inevitability of white pioneering expansionism and its accompanying violence.

Renato Rosaldo, in *Culture and Truth*, famously identified the "imperialist nostalgia" that he saw as being expressed by the "agents of colonialism . . . who mourn the passing of what they themselves have transformed. . . . The relatively benign character of most nostalgia facilitates imperialist nostalgia's capacity to transform the responsible colonial agent into an innocent bystander." Yet he writes that "mourning the passing of traditional society and imperialist nostalgia cannot neatly be separated from one another. Both attempt to use a mask of innocence to cover their involvement with processes of domination."[22] However, nostalgia over the departing Indian race is complicated when expressed by British women writers, since they cannot be held directly responsible, whether through nationhood or through gender, for the process of social destruction that characterized the post-Revolution United States. Moreover, while these poems are, unmistakably, elegies for what was commonly assumed to be a people in terminal decline, they have a further function, one that affects not so much what was happening across the Atlantic but that looks, rather, to contemporary British society. In lamenting "the heroes of my youth . . . my kindred chiefs . . . the mighty of departed time"—the epithets are all from Hemans's "Aged Indian" (lines 5, 8, 54)—chivalric ideals are displaced onto Native Americans. Here and elsewhere, chivalry is invoked in part to gain extra pathos and grandeur for the "red man" through association. There is something definitely, and defiantly, belated in this amalgamation of very different forms of nobility, a desire to locate the best of the Old World in the supposedly new one. As Alexis de Tocqueville was to note on his visit to the United States in 1831, a strange affinity pertained between European aristocrats and the Indian, at least in the mind of the former. Since the aristocrat "thinks hunting and war the only cares of a man," he believes that "the Indian in the miserable depths of his forests cherishes the same ideas and opinions as the medieval noble in his castle, and he only needs to become a conqueror to complete the resemblance. How odd it is that the ancient prejudices of Europe should reappear, not among the European population among the coast, but in the forests of the New World."[23]

Yet the adoption of a chivalric register surely signifies something that goes beyond a desire to return to a feudal and obsolete past—however popular the rhetoric, imagery, and alleged values of chivalry were to become in mid-Victorian Britain, offering a supposedly stable social model. In the hands of many of these women writers, who made little other investment in feudal values, it becomes, rather, a means of expressing sadness and the regret that it is no longer possible to believe in the enduring powers of chivalric characteristics themselves. As we shall see in the section of this chapter titled "Protests, Indians, and Empire," such values, as understood in the abstract, crumble in the light of their mutation into those practices of triumphalism that went hand in hand with colonialism—practices underpinned, as has been well noted by Mark Girouard, Joseph Kestner, and others, by the rhetoric of European chivalry.[24] To invest Indians with the aura this rhetoric conveyed was to take an ironic position in relation to the modernizing forces ranged against them and other native peoples.

Moreover, the version of chivalry that was projected onto Native Americans was a dignified and honorable one, entirely compatible with an image of them as peace loving and "civilized"—or civilizable. Hemans's "Indian's Revenge" (a dramatic poem that takes as its starting point "Gertrude of Wyoming") and "American Forest Girl" emphasize the enthusiastic willingness of native tribes to embrace Christianity, and in so doing, they show them to be far from untamable savages; her "Cross in the Wilderness" suggests that there is a parallel, which one ought to respect, between native worship of the Great Spirit and Christian faith.

As Frances Kemble's travel journal showed, both British and Native American could be shown as uniting in a love of nature, thus establishing a further bond of true nobility.[25] The Irish novelist, travel writer, and poet Louisa Stuart Costello—strongly under the poetic influence of Southey—wrote in "The Return of the Indians to Niagara" about the compelling force that the Niagara Falls exerted even on the Indian exile. "They cannot lure the Indian to stay / From his woods and his rivers long away," chants the native speaker, praising the natural spectacle that was just emerging as a tourist attraction (and thus often giving visitors a point of contact with self-commodifying Indians selling curios and acting as guides). This identification of Indians with a passionate, ancestral attachment to place necessarily helped to heighten the level of compassion with which their displacement was considered. Once again, it allowed them to be identified with nobility in its most traditional sense. In the early 1850s, Eliza Cook wrote a piece entitled "Flowers and Trees" for her *Journal*, claiming:

> The tawny savage of the backwoods strides over the wide prairie's purple bells, and gazes on the pine giants of his native forests with an exulting, although an indefinite joy. The ducal master of Chatsworth breathes among his choice exotics, and treads daintily beneath the branches of his ancestral oaks and beeches, with infinite pride and pleasure. The same instinct dwells in each bosom—though one is girded with the ribbon of the Bath, and graced with the star of blazing gems; and the other is swathed in the buffalo's skin and chequered with the red tattoo. They both love flowers and trees. The Infinite and the Beautiful erects an altar alike in the hearts of the Indian Pawnee and the English peer.[26]

Those who sought to suppress, or "civilize," the Indian frequently did so in the explicit or implicit name of modernity. But these appeals to enduring values, albeit highly retrogressive in class terms, complicate the customary teleological narrative that was written around the vanishing Indian.

IMPERSONATING THE INDIAN

Precisely what constitutes nobility, savage or otherwise, is central to Frances Trollope's strange novel of 1849, *The Old World and the New*. This work centers on an English family that emigrates, as Trollope had done in 1828, to Ohio. Robert and Mary Stormont and their two children are helped considerably not just by the money but by the resourcefulness and cheerful resilience of Mary's cousin Katherine. Katherine's determined independence comes, in part, from a desire to put a failed love affair back in England behind her; her otherwise promising fiancé, Mr. Warburton, reacted with an apparent callous abruptness when he heard of the Stormonts' financial problems. By far the greater part of the three volumes deals with the building of a house on a bluff overlooking the Ohio River and with the friendship the new immigrants build with their American neighbors, the Wainwrights. This family introduces them to a local Indian leader, Watawanga—handsome and articulate, he bears more than a passing resemblance to the well-known Shawnee leader Tecumseh, of whom Trollope had surely heard during her residency in Ohio, with its recent violent history of Indian-white relations. He carries himself "with a step and mien that might have found favour in the most select salons of Europe,"[27] and it later transpires that he has taken the baptized name of Ferdinand Augustus Fitzclarendon (Trollope provides this absurd arriviste nomenclature without signaling any ironical intent). Watawanga's cousin Oranego—seemingly much wilder, certainly more uncouth in appearance, with a dark reddish skin and "long, lank coal-black hair . . . falling so low over his forehead as to almost conceal his eyes" (2:126)— becomes devoted to Katherine, helping her with her building and horticultural enterprises. He is increasingly infatuated with her, and the fact that an interracial marriage would not be unthinkable but would rather be an example of the assimilation that was, at the time, being advanced as the only possible alternative to extermination is underscored by the Wainwrights' daughter, Aspasia, who is getting engaged to Watawanga— to everyone's delight. As Katherine herself put it, the mingling of hearts as well as intellects, and the Indians' learning of English and imitation of Anglo customs, " 'is the only truly philosophical way of contemplating the change, the mixture of races, rather, which seems intended by providence' " (2:152). In pre–Civil War America, interracial marriages between Indians and those of European origin did not invariably carry the stigma that they would later bear (causing a number of states to seek to ban them in the 1880–1920 period). Rather, they were a fact of life in many frontier communities in both the United States and Canada.[28] Indeed, as historian Rachel F. Moran has noted, "among Native Americans, mixed-blood children often became tribal leaders because of their unique ability to negotiate with whites," although at times full-blooded Indians mistrusted them, thinking them more likely to favor white interests.[29]

Trollope's treatment here, however, has more in common with the more theoretical line taken by the novelist and literary spokesperson William Gilmore Simms, among others, who, as Lucy Maddox has shown, speculated that had the practice of intermarriage begun early enough, "the result would have been an infusion of the best qualities of the Indian character—pride and independence—into the blood of the earlier colonists."[30] These speculations, Maddox goes on to explain, were "thoroughly consistent with the terms of Simms's argument for incorporating the Indians into the literature of America; just as the real Indians could be gradually transformed into white people through the marriage of properly educated Indian women to white men, so the history of the Indians, properly revised, could become the 'body of crude material, virgin and fertile' Simms spoke of."[31] In one notable way, Trollope is far more radical than Simms, reversing the idea that marriage between an Indian woman and a white man is the best (symbolic) way ahead, since in such a case, the conventions of gender and racial hierarchies are in tandem. This aspect of her plot is far closer to that of Lydia Maria Child's *Hobomok* (1824), where the white woman's marriage to an Indian shocked many contemporary reviewers, on both sides of the Atlantic, despite the fact that Hobomok himself eventually retreats to the West, to mimic and foreshadow the sinking of his race. Child's own ambiguity around the question of intermarriage is replicated, however, in the way that Trollope consigns the Aspasia-Watawanga connection to a subplot. Her heroine, Katherine, although certainly intrigued and drawn by Oranego's kindness and by the profound sympathetic understanding that he shows, is not wholeheartedly drawn to him as a potential marital partner—any racial unease, however, is masked by the fact that she still hankers after Warburton.

Very likely, Trollope was building not just on her own American knowledge and experiences when she wrote this novel but, with her customary and commercially driven eye to the topical, on recent British firsthand familiarity with Native Americans as a result of Catlin's exhibitions. Her novel certainly shares his tone of mournful but impotent regret for "the miserable fatality which seemed to follow" this "race, causing it to perish and disappear, with such strange rapidity from the face of the earth" (2:137). But it is a curious novel in many ways, swerving between deploying stock images of the Indian and making some very pertinent points about native rights—a double approach symptomatic of British attitudes more generally in the mid-nineteenth century, although not normally encountered so vertiginously within the same text. These attitudes are foreshadowed in Trollope's 1832 *Domestic Manners of the Americans*. She writes of her reading when she is sick—Timothy Flint's *Francis Berrian*, Catherine Sedgwick's *Hope Leslie* and *Redwood*, and all of James Fenimore Cooper's novels to date. "By the time these American studies were completed," she writes,

> I never closed my eyes without seeing myriads of bloody scalps floating round me; long slender figures of Red Indians crept through my dreams with noiseless tread; panthers glared; forests blazed; and whichever way I fled, a light foot, a keen eye, and a long rifle were sure to be on my trail. An additional ounce of calomel hardly sufficed to neutralize the effect of these raw-head and bloody-bones adventures.[32]

Yet the Indian is desensationalized and turned into a figure through which American hypocrisy can be revealed when Trollope describes how she was in Washington in 1830, "at the time that the measure for chasing the last of several tribes of Indians from their forest homes, was canvassed in congress, and finally decided upon by the *fiat* of the President": in other words, during Jackson's passing of the Cherokee removal act. Trollope writes, with a mixture of anger and revulsion, that

> it is impossible for any mind of common honesty not to be revolted by the contradictions in their principles and practice . . . you will see them with one hand hoisting the cap of liberty, and with the other flogging their slaves. You will see them one hour lecturing their mob on the indefeasible rights of man, and the next driving from their homes the children of the soil, whom they have bound themselves to protect by the most solemn treaties.[33]

In Trollope's semi-autobiographical novel, *The Refugee in America* (1832), the heroine, Caroline Gordon—something of a surrogate for Trollope—links slavery with the condition of the Indians when she asks a roomful of Americans: " 'Will you tell me how you reconcile your theory of freedom with the condition of your negroes? or your treatment of the Indians with your doctrine of equal rights?' "[34] The propensity of the land's new inhabitants to wreck spectacular landscape elements with mills, factories, and engines is remarked on when Caroline visits the Falls of Genesee with her father: " 'What a scene must this have been, papa, when Indians stopped their chase to look upon it!—And these are the improvements of the white men?' " (1:131). In *Jonathan Jefferson*

Whitlaw (1836), her antislavery novel, Trollope introduces the missionary Edward Bligh and his sister, Lucy, who hide runaway slaves. In one scene, Lucy meets some Choctaw in a forest who at first seem savage, but she is swift to realize that Whitlaw, the overseer of a slave plantation, is more threatening, since she finds "something . . . in the general appearance of the *civilized* man which terrified her more than the painted and scarred features of the Indians."[35]

There is no doubt that throughout *The Old World and the New*, Trollope is showing an active, if ultimately assimilationist, sympathy, toward these "noble-looking relics of the aboriginal race, which had so very nearly passed away," and a disdain for congressional refusals to grant "an assured right and tithe to a little portion of the lands that had once, and at no very different date, been all their own, for the purposes of peaceful, civilized agriculture" (2:128). The sense that Watawonga and Oranego are the last of their tribe is intensified by the text's refusal to produce any other natives: despite the rhetoric of allegiance to their people, their affective relations appear oriented toward their white neighbors. In turn, this underscores Trollope's own belief not only in the educability of the native but also in the sympathetic bonds that would constitute a path toward social progress. Moreover, the capacity of the Indian to behave in a courteous (by which she often means deferential) manner reinforces her own drive, apparent in *Domestic Manners* and barely modified by the late 1840s, to criticize the uncouth brashness that she associated with white Americans. In this earlier work, she recounts the insulting way in which a "lady" shoved her way into her family's carriage places, helped by some whiskey drinkers, and wonders "whether the invading white man, in chasing the poor Indians from their forests have done much towards civilizing the land" (392).

Trollope was not alone in putting forward this contrast, favorably juxtaposing Indian manners with what was taken to be crude American incivility. Amelia Murray, traveling in 1854, remarked: "Nature's gentlemen and gentlewomen, the Indians have a true courtesy and a simple politeness, which might be advantageously copied by those who are their superiors in knowledge and power."[36] Taking the train between Syracuse and Albany, she noted that

> while stopping at one of the stations, a tall, handsome Indian girl, with some bead-work in her hand, entered the car; she wore a picturesque dress, with a black hat and feather, and silently presenting her wares without importunity, she glided on. The noisy and reckless, or ungainly, sulky manner of those around contrasted unfavourably with the subdued, unobtrusive, graceful dignity of the squaw.[37]

Murray does, of course, leave completely unexamined the performative element of the Indian woman's appearance, gestures, and gait in this commercial context.

This sense of the deficiencies of white Americans was not simply one-sided. Trollope firmly makes the point that the attitudes of the Indians themselves toward the English differ from those toward their transatlantic descendants. Toward the end of the story, the narrator pronounces:

> However small may be the degree of partial affection felt by the present possessors of North America towards their English ancestors, the coldness towards us is by no means shared by the original possessors of the soil. It is not from us that they have endured that ceaseless process of cruelty, injustice, and delusion, under which they have been suffering and perishing ever since the banner of the Stars and the Stripes has waved over an independent nation.
>
> To any overture of civility from an Englishman, an Indian is always ready to give a cordial reception. (3:301)

Behind what appears to be a sweeping generalization about manners lies, one may well surmise, the local history with which Trollope would have been familiar. In the late eighteenth century, British redcoats supported the Shawnee and the other Cherokees, Mingo, and Delaware members of the intertribal confederacy that was formed in a futile attempt to halt the expansion of the United States into Ohio.

If Trollope continually uses a more than faintly patronizing register in which to apostrophize "this half-tamed son of the forest," the "poor savage," and "poor Oranego" (2:131), she also stresses many projected Indian qualities. These include respect, civility, a capacity for reverence, steadfastness, and, indeed, physical beauty. The native also serves as a subservient adjunct to British female sensibility; the narrator writes of Katherine's attitude toward Oranego: "The very circumstance of the imputed inferiority of race under which the aboriginal warriors of this new commercial continent are so often seen to wince, had given a tinge of pity and almost of tenderness to her feelings for him" (2:213). British and Native American unite, once again, in a love of nature, consolidating that bond of true nobility and celebrating an early version of the idealized sustainer of the natural world that Shepherd Krech has, in his book of the same name, labeled "The Ecological Indian."

As Oranego helps Katherine with improvements to the estate he is used by Trollope to exemplify the Indian's traditional closeness to the land and its secrets. Katherine is amazed that he can transport a forest of flowering shrubs from miles away to complete her garden and asks how he, a self-proclaimed child of an oppressed race, has " 'found the power in so very masterly a way of doing what no horticulturalist that I have ever heard of in this country, has ever attempted to do at all?'" (2:197). Oranego appeals to her sense of honor and integrity, and to her respect for the secrecy and honor that bind him to his race, and asks: "Can you not imagine that a tribe of red men, however thinned by calamity of all kinds, as well as by the scourge of war,—can you not imagine that they still may have some secret preserved among them, which teaches the use of a very sacred power to a few, that perhaps in ages past might fearlessly have been exercised by thousands? Can you not imagine this, white lady?" (2:198). The fact that re-creating an English shrubbery, moving plants where they had never grown before, could be a form of ecological imperialism does not trouble Katherine. Rather, she is disturbed that Oranego might, after all, conform to some shifty type of native behavior: where *could* he have obtained the funds to carry out these horticultural feats? Despite Oranego's laudable characteristics, Katherine becomes apprehensive that he must, at some level, be guilty of the more negative associations of deceit or violence that clustered around the image of the Indian.

Halfway through the third volume, Trollope has a surprise in store for the reader, which makes one reconsider the roots both of Oranego's reticence and of his worshipful devotion to Katherine. On a picnic outing, he falls down a steep ravine while trying to keep the Stormonts' impetuous son out of danger. He is badly injured, so much so that when he is carried back to the Stormont mansion, his cousin Watawanga will not allow any visitors to his room. What emerges, after some anxious pages, is that Watawanga has hurried off to Cincinnatti to stock up on some new dark ocher skin paint and a new wig, for Oranego is no relative of the handsome Indian after all, but none other than Warburton, Katherine's erstwhile English fiancé, come in disguise to try to test her feelings and to prove his devotion. All sorts of things become clear, like his curious shyness on the topic of Indian languages and customs and, indeed, the fact that his lack of Indian sure-footedness meant that he did not keep his foothold when hurrying over rough country, unlike Watawanga, who went up and down "the precipitous crag, as a native goat might have done" (3:120).

What, we might ask, does Trollope gain—beyond a startling plot shift—by turning an English gentleman into a wannabe Indian? Apart from making some political points about land rights and dispossession, which underscore her habitual criticism of American political hypocrisy, the positive qualities with which she seeks to invest the Native American are, in fact, the qualities she would wish to equate with true gentlemanliness. Although very much a contemporary novel in some ways— Trollope crams in some scenes set in 1848 France—its English sections, and indeed Watawanga's mission to Washington, suggest an earlier date. Warburton is an Austen-esque figure, associated with rural continuity, not with the new forces of industrialism; the England to which he returns with Katherine is one of tradition and stability. If the ways of the Native American are changing and passing, the life of an English gentleman, and the values of honor, loyalty and faithfulness, and sensitivity to a woman's tastes and needs—the values that Trollope would most strongly wish to promote on the domestic front—may still endure elsewhere, *may* still endure, because, of course, as the references to revolutionary France suggest, European society was far from stable. Trollope, in other words, may, like some of the poets mentioned earlier in this chapter, be seen, through the figure of Oranego/Warburton, as celebrating ideals of character that one can read as being under threat, as potentially outmoded in a modern world. The elegy for the "dying Indian" is being borrowed for another cause.[38]

Something more than this—something potentially more radical—is going on as well, albeit perhaps unwittingly. Laura Browder, in her book on racial impersonation, *Slippery Characters: Ethnic Impersonators and American Identities*, writes how "when they are successful, impersonators may trap their readers further in essentialist thinking about race and identity"—and this is precisely the trap into which Trollope's readers, as well as her characters, are led. Her plot depends on the readers, like the Anglo characters, approaching Indians through preformed stereotypes. But, Browder goes on, "it is their exposure as impersonators that offers readers the possibility of being liberated from their fixed ideas about the meaning of racial and ethnic identity."[39] If—*The Old World and the New* makes us ask—race can be convincingly *performed*, of what does it consist? After all, this novel makes a racial identification based on skin color alone into something both comic and unreliable. Moreover, it suggests that the performance can work in both directions, which gives an optimistic gloss to the process of assimilation and, once again, intimates that white people may have qualities of character to learn, or relearn, from Indians. To what ends, Trollope seems to be asking, might one wish to appropriate the persona of the Native American?

PROTESTS, INDIANS, AND EMPIRE

If Trollope's answer is fundamentally a conservative one—the Old World may need to be shored up by elements shared with a still older world—another answer to this question lies within rhetorical performance: such appropriation gives a particular directness to expressions of anger at the race's treatment at the hands of the white people who sought to displace them. The Quaker William Howitt, who, like his wife, the poet, historian, and translator Mary Howitt, was very active in the British antislavery movement, pointedly locates the virtues that the new republicans would claim for themselves within the land's *original* inhabitants. It is the latter who—as expressed in "The Adopted Warrior; Suggested by an Incident in 'Hunter's Captivity amongst the North American Indians' "—are "free, lofty-hearted, sternly just;/Deemed by the white-man rude, forlorn."[40] In his long poem of 1827, "Penn and the Indians," Howitt tied in his condemnation of bellicose attitudes toward Native Americans with a broader, Byron-inflected concern with the inhumanity of violence practiced for the sake of national aggrandizement, or out of bigotry. In showing how Penn met native inhabitants in a spirit of love, not hostility, he makes the point that they—unlike, indeed, some of the English at home, who had sent Penn and his followers into exile—

> Were not a brutish race, unknowing
> Evil from good; their fervent souls embraced
> With virtue's proudest homage to o'erflowing
> The mind's inviolate majesty. The past
> To them was not a darkness; but was glowing
> With splendour which all time had not o'ercast.
>
> (219)

Here it is not presumed that the Indian inhabits some mythical, prehistoric past. Rather, against the specific past of Indian culture is posed a different, less sublime version of history, one in which "Europe's mighty states/The brethren of the cross—from age to age,/Have striven to quench in blood their quenchless hates" (220). This spirit, the poem makes clear, may still, damagingly, be found in the United States, where "the vast, the ebbless, the engulphing tide/Of the white population still rolls on!" (223). Nor were the Howitts the only writers to make this point in verse. Eliza Cook's "Song of the Red Indian" does so strongly, opening with "Oh! Why does the white man hang on my path,/Like the hound on the tiger's track?/Does the flush of my dark skin awaken his wrath?"[41] Aggressive extermination is explicitly linked to racial hatred based on skin color; the implications of this clearly reach out beyond North America and have their relevance to British treatment of indigenous people within the expanding empire. At the same time, it reminds one, yet again, of the overlap between those who were concerned with the plight of the Indian and those who opposed slavery. Cook, born in 1818, the daughter of a Southwark tradesman, was a self-educated poet, journalist, and magazine editor; *Eliza Cook's Journal*, in which many of her poems were reprinted or appeared for the first time, flourished between 1849 and 1854. Although her socially concerned verse constitutes a minor strand in her writing, which

overall emphasizes the value of the domestic, the pains of family bereavement, and the moral importance of everyday objects and actions,
she published some energetic protests against the conditions of urban
poverty, praised ragged schools, and, perhaps more surprisingly, wrote
some impassioned poems in support of Native Americans. In this respect, her writing provides an interesting example of a circum-Atlantic
traffic in subject matter and ideas: her "Song of the Red Man"—known
in the United States as the "Song of the Indian Hunter"—was set to
music, first by Henry Russell in 1837 and then by William R. Dempster
in 1848, both of them British composers who spent a significant portion
of their lives in the United States, where these songs were published.[42]

"Did God So Will It?" (circa 1845) is a generalized indictment of the
frequent misuse of selfjustificatory Christian language by those who seek
to impose political rule. In it, Cook brings out the hypocritical nature of
the rhetoric that lay behind such dispossession and extermination. The
third stanza overtly focuses on North America, where

> The red-skinned savage holds his hunting-field
>   As Nature's heritage by human law;
> Content with what the bush and river yield,
>   His rugged wigwam and his tawny squaw.
> But the smooth white-face drives him back and back;
>   Let his voice tell of *Right*, and *Might* shall still it,
> Till his free steps are thrust from their own track—
>   Did **God** so will it?[43]

Cook makes a similar point in "Song of the Red Indian": "Yet, white
man, what has thy good faith done,/And where can its mercy be,/If it
teach thee to hate the hunter one/Who never did harm to thee?"[44] Again,
her pronativist sentiments in this poem are built on the doctrine of natural rights, with her speaker asking about the "cruel, white man,"

> Oh! why does he take our wigwam home,
>   And the jungled hunting-ground?
> The wolf-cub has his lair of rest,
>   The wild horse where to dwell,
> And the Spirit who gave the bird its nest
>   Made me a place as well.

And, as a number of nonfictional prose writers were starting to do, Cook
asks for sympathy and understanding for the Indian on the grounds that
her readers need to acknowledge cultural relativity:

> The painted streak on a warrior's cheek
>   Appears a wondrous thing;

Figure 8. "The Indian Hunter." Lyrics by Eliza Cook, music by Henry Russell, Keffer Collection of Sheet Music, University of Pennsylvania Library.

The white man stares at a wampum belt,
    And a plume from the heron's wing.
But the red man wins the panthers' skins
    To cover his dauntless form;
While the pale-face hides his breast in a garb
    That he takes from the crawling worm.
And your lady fair, with her gems so rare,
    Her ruby, gold, and pearl,
As the bone-decked Indian girl
Would be as strange to other eyes.[45]

Among all other claims on our attention, Cook's "Song of the Red Indian" is notable for the way in which it calls repeated attention *to* whiteness, rather than treating the skin color of the writer, and probable audience, as invisible. It hints—if not at a full awareness of self-implication on the part of producer and consumer—that their own national positioning with regard to racial Others demands consideration. This idea, that the American treatment of America's indigenous inhabitants was not unique to that country but was shared by other nations seeking to expand their power, was to become increasingly pronounced in the later decades of the nineteenth century.

At the same time, the tendency to distance Indians through a sentimental light declined, not least because it had become a tired mode for awakening a humanitarian awareness. As will become clear, this was due to a number of factors (quite apart from shifts in literary taste). For one thing, those who cast themselves in the role of Indian friends and supporters were anxious to present Indians as open to the effects of Westernization and education. Mary Howitt, whose 1859 *Popular History of the United States of America* by no means evades the role that British colonists (with the important exception of Penn and his fellow Quakers) played in treating Indians as less than human, ends on an upbeat note, linking together optimism about the future of the slave and the future of the country's indigenous peoples:

> Politically and morally the republic of the United States has been a grand, successful experiment. While the nation has grown with an unexampled rapidity, it has not overlooked the essential foundations of national greatness—the religious and social advancement of the people. The school-house and the place of worship have sprung up simultaneously with human dwellings in the wilderness. And although anomalies exist in the characters of her institutions, though the blot of slavery darkens the page of her history, and her abundant harvest fields have been watered by the blood of the Indian, still, even for the slave is there hope of the amelioration of his condition, and it may be

of his redemption, through the growing enlightenment of the South. And as regards the Indian, missionary labour is increasing among his people, and where they are capable of receiving the instruction and civilisation of the whites, it is given. . . .

While these facilities are given for education among the Indians, those which are afforded for society at large are on the most ample and liberal scale. Education is indispensable to the man and woman of the New World, and a system of school education is universally established there, which makes moral and intellectual enlightenment common to all, irrespective of creeds and parties.[46]

This line was insistently promoted by missionary organizations operating within both the United States and Canada.

Even allowing for the sympathetic, even radical attitudes that a number of women had toward Native Americans, plenty of other female writers nonetheless participated in the circulation of negative, or at least stereotypical, images, frequently performing the rhetorical equivalent of a superficial glance. For many women travelers, as we shall see, Indians were very frequently encountered as part of a tourist experience, or they were shadowy figures glimpsed from a train or traveling coach. In her *Retrospect of Western Travel* (1838), Harriet Martineau records how, as she and her companions neared Buffalo, "a solitary Indian might be frequently seen standing on a heap of stones by the roadside, or sleeping under a fence. There is something which rivets the eye of the stranger in the grave gaze, the lank hair, the blanket-wrapped form of the savage, as he stands motionless. We were generally to be seen leaning out of every opening in the stage as long as the figure remained in sight."[47] Martineau's description typifies a good many encounters that the reader has with textual Indians, who appear as vignettes: objects of fascination in their strangeness, frequently causing the author of a travelogue or history to pause, describe, engage in a disquisition (about the pathos of imminent extinction, the iniquities of governmental policy, or tattooing or face painting or skin color), and then move on, a rhetorical format that grants mobility to the writer and observer and that leaves the Indian subject frozen in time, space, and silence. No attempt is made to ask what may lie behind the "grave gaze" of Martineau's "solitary Indian." Isabella Bird recorded that when visiting native peoples in Eastern Canada, the phrase " 'Why has our white sister visited the wigwams of her red brethren?' was the salutation with which they broke silence—a question rather difficult to answer."[48] This relatively rare native voice acts as a necessary reminder that too seldom do British women acknowledge that their acts of scrutiny and judgment are not one-sided, and they are often startled or repulsed if their counterparts in the cultural contact zone between natives and Anglos behave in anything other than a deferential manner. The journalist and poet Emily Pfeiffer wrote with particular directness when, in 1885, she ascribed this lack of interest in the point of view of racial Others to the arrogance of white people: "Arrogance which makes communication impossible."[49] Moreover, there seems to have been relatively little awareness shown in Britain of the forms of resistance that were developing to positions predicated on the inevitability of extermination or the desirability of white-dominated assimilation. Reports of Paiute Sarah Winnemucca Hopkins's speeches, for example, reached a limited, and probably sympathetic, audience in the columns of the *English Woman's Journal* but did not make the *Times*. In general, native voices are for ventriloquizing, not for listening to. Few literary commentators seem aware of their own positioning; relating narratives designed to play on the reader's sympathy, they fail to put themselves in the role of observed as well as of observer, thus forestalling the development of what Julie Ellison has identified as the conventions of "liberal guilt," characterized by the "visualized or performed economy of inequality," in which the subject, the object, and the moral importance of their relation all come under awkward scrutiny.[50]

Far from it; often, the readiness of female travelers to purchase examples of "Indian curios" parallels the act of commodifying the picturesque vanishing Indian in poetry and prose. Visiting a Huron hamlet near Quebec in 1854, Amelia Murray records meeting an elderly Indian woman in terms that include a telling modifier: "She has decidedly the features of a squaw, but she is extremely intelligent, and speaks good Canadian French. . . . We bought little boxes, baskets, and pincushions, all made out of birch bark by Mrs. Paul and her husband; some of them very prettily embroidered."[51] Indeed, the increasing visibility of the Indian to the tourist and traveler within the United States or Canada's eastern seaboard—or, rather, the visibility of the dispossessed, semiurbanized Indian, whose economy and way of life has been completely disrupted—serves to dispel an earlier idealization and is a significant factor working against the sentimental portrayal of Native Americans. Touring an Indian village in Nova Scotia in the mid-1850s, Isabella Bird recalls how "we were going into one wigwam when a surly old man opposed our entrance, holding out a calabash, vociferous voices from the interior calling out, 'Ninepence, ninepence!' The memory of *Uncas* and *Magua* rose before me, and I sighed over the degeneracy of the race";[52] the failure of live Indians to match up to the expectations that James Fenimore Cooper had created remained a continual motif until the end of the century. But for those who did not believe that the "degeneracy" they saw was simply a matter of racial theory being proved correct in practice—evidence of a race ill adapted to modern life sliding toward extinction—the depressing conditions in which too many Indians were encountered provided further evidence of their victimhood and of a serious failure of responsibility toward them. This lesson, too, had repercussions that potentially stretched beyond the United States.

The implied connection between American conduct toward Native Americans and British imperial policies emerged with growing clarity during the later decades of the century, even if it was a latent presence long before then—as is evident even in the zoological displacement of a tiger into Cook's "Song of the Red Indian," as "exotic" stereotypes coalesce. George Eliot's broadening perspective on the Indian provides a telling paradigm of these shifting attitudes. In the early 1850s, she was stirred by the idea of the "great Western Continent, with its infant cities, its huge uncleared forests, and its unamalgamated races"; such a setting offered hopefulness for her—wistful hope—that this provided the ground on which the "higher moral tendencies of human nature" might yet develop.[53] Writing to Harriet Beecher Stowe in 1872, she owned that she "always had delight in descriptions of American forests since the early days when I read 'Atala,'" Chateaubriand's 1801 romance about French colonizers and the Indians they encountered in the Louisiana Territory at the end of the eighteenth century. This book was enormously influential in producing an idealized image of the Indian within France—even though, as Eliot understatedly put it, it was "half-unveracious."[54] By the 1870s, she had become decidedly more measured in her enthusiasm, however. When Rex, in *Daniel Deronda*, dramatically announces—after Gwendolen Harleth has rejected him—"that he should like to go off to 'the colonies' to-morrow," Eliot is satirizing—not without sympathy and affection—his earnest youthful idealism about the possibility of being able to start over in one's life in a blank space: Rex is much less playfully imaginative with the idea than was Shirley Keeldar.[55] His extravagant response is situated, moreover, in a novel marked by its critique of narrow-minded and uninformed Englishness, signaling Eliot's increasing frustration with her country's attitudes and its ignorance of what lies outside its national boundaries—a state of mind that she complained of, indeed, in her correspondence with Stowe. In "The Modern Hep! Hep! Hep!"— one of the essays in her next (and final) book, *The Impressions of Theophrastus Such* (1879)—Eliot explicitly links the treatment of Native Americans and more recent British colonizing activities when she makes a bitter connection between the relative powerlessness of the "Red Indians" and the "Hindoos," with both races being unwilling, or unable, to reproach the British for their policies of invasion. Nor, as Eliot sees it, were these races sufficiently informed of British history to be able to condemn her country for the violence in its past and its own earlier pagan practices, which in fact show that it was once as "savage" as the peoples over which it now claimed supremacy: "The Red Indians, not liking us when we settled among them, might have been willing to fling such facts in our faces, but they were too ignorant, and besides, their opinions did not signify, because we were able, if we liked, to exterminate them. . . . We do not call ourselves a dispersed and a punished people: we are a colonizing people, and it is we who have punished others."[56]

Eliot's voice is, of course, a heavily ironic one, but it represents a significant shift in the treatment of Native Americans in British women's literary writing. The discourse of mourning has been replaced by a tone of rage. Eliot's words need also to be placed in the fuller context of *Theophrastus Such*'s political commentary, especially the interest the text shows in nationalist movements. "That any people, at once distinct and coherent enough to form a State, should be held in subjection by an alien antipathetic government has been becoming more and more a ground of sympathetic indignation," she writes, with the Italian situation in mind.[57] But her attack on the policies of "an alien antipathetic government" proves, in relation to the treatment of Native Americans, an increasingly infrequent one in the latter years of the century. In part this is because, as we shall see, women's incorporation of the Indian into imaginative writing was often tied in with their participation in a new genre, that of the Western adventure story, with its tendency to divide Indians into "good" and "bad"—the same dynamics that were used to categorize indigenous peoples in stories located within Britain's own empire. So the heavily loaded criticism found in "Red or White?", a poem published by the journalist and poet Emily Pfeiffer in her 1889 *Flowers of the Night*, is, however powerful, a distinct rarity. It opens with the following:

> In a western city new-born from a withering fire,
> Fresh as a phoenix that rises renewed from the pyre,
>   I, musing aloft, far removed from the noise of the street,
> Looked down from my window and saw where the palaces spread
> In stony files o'er the wigwams of red men dead,—
>   Ground into dust in the march of the white men's feet.

Most likely, Pfeiffer had Chicago in mind, rebuilt following the great fire of 1871 and occupying the former territory of the Potawatomi (whose name, with neat irony, may be translated as "People of the Place of the Fire," or "Keepers of the Fire"). Pfeiffer goes on:

> Then I mixed with the crowd and beheld how the white men strive,
> Jostle and fret as the bees ere they swarm from the hive,—
>   Marked how with weapons newfangled the fight goes on,—
> And asked: "What good or to soul or to body's health

Has come of the change?" And the answer was: "Golden wealth,—
Golden each step we have made o'er the red man gone."[58]

The poem continues with a vicious attack on the motives that lay behind
the displacement of Native Americans. In part, the poem was stimulated
by Pfeiffer's own travels in the United States—written up and published
in 1885 as *Flying Leaves from East and West*—but the date of its appearance is particularly significant in its British context, for two years
earlier, Buffalo Bill's Wild West Show had played in London, prior to
going on tour in the provinces. It quickly became a must of the fashionable season, its participants and their vanishing lifestyle instantly being
commodified for a huge audience. We have already seen how the desire
to draw a positive connection between Indian sensibilities and what constitutes desirable forms of masculinity permeated several areas of early
and mid-Victorian representation. But the rhetoric that surrounded the
Wild West Show was differently oriented, working relentlessly to link
together the manliness of westward settlers, American armed forces, and
those who supported and executed British imperialist ideals. Pfeiffer's
poem, rather, offers a critique not just of the "affirmation of a white racial identity" that Cody's show put at the heart of American-ness,[59] but
of the possessive greed that lies at the heart of colonialism, whether
American or British. Linked to territorial ambitions and racial arrogance, such greed is universally unacceptable, whether the blame is to be
laid at the hands of the Americans or, potentially, be turned toward a
reading of British imperialism.

Moreover, such colonization is, ultimately, unhealthy. Pfeiffer's poem
contrasts settler and Indian from the point of view of their ethics and
their bodies. The Indian's word was to be trusted: in his premodern lifestyle (as the poet characterizes it), he not only maintained the bonds of
family with each "brotherly 'brave,'" he "simply plighted the word he
as simply kept." His buffalo-hunting existence might be characterized as
that of the "dull savage," but Pfeiffer quickly turns the tables, describing
he "who fashioned and threw the spear,/Deft-handed, swift-footed,
lynx-eyed, keen of scent, fine of ear." She makes it very clear that even
though he has in theory been supplanted by the "white man as red men
supplanted the beast," this is not some kind of evolutionary triumph.
Rather, to ally oneself with urban, modern life is to become unhealthy
and out of touch with the natural rhythms of one's own body. The poem
concludes with a question: "Will the red man or white, with his biliary
troubles to cheat,/With his advertised nostrums, his blundering fingers
and feet,/His sensory slowness, strained nerves, and his hurried heart-
beat,/Arise the more lean when they both shall have finished life's
feast?"[60] There can be no doubt of Pfeiffer's answer. Unlike many women

writers earlier in the century, she avoids sentimentalizing the Indian or borrowing his imagined attributes to bolster the image, reputation, or potential of British masculinity, past or present. Anger, for her—as for Eliot—has taken the place of the gentler and more politically evasive categories of compassion and nostalgia.

CHAPTER FIVE

Is the Indian an American?

The Great Exhibition of the Works of Industry of All Nations was held in the specially built Crystal Palace in London's Hyde Park from 1 May to 15 October 1851. Organized by the British and with Prince Albert taking a central role, it was intended as a celebration of modern industrial technology and design, its international exhibits grouped according to their country of origin. Two sculptures were prominently on show in the American section. At its entrance, visitors encountered Hiram Powers's *The Greek Slave* (1844), which depicted a naked woman, her wrists bound with the chains that tethered her to a draped post. Ostensibly a rendition of a captured Greek woman being sold at a Turkish slave market, it commanded attention both on aesthetic grounds—as an interpretation of classical beauty, which hence signaled America's artistic competency when working in the grand European tradition—and because of the strongly contemporary resonances of its subject matter.[1] Doubtless, too, it attracted the gaze of many visitors because of the novelty of seeing female nudity displayed on a mechanically revolving plinth.

The second notable work was Peter Stephenson's *The Wounded American Indian* (1848–50). The figure's muscled body is slumped over in pain, his head bowed over the wound from which he tries to extract an arrow; his collapsing form was commonly seen as symbolizing the Indian in terminal decline. The comments that initially appeared in the *Illustrated London News*, and that were subsequently recycled in various publications, offered a clear guide as to how to interpret this archetype.

> The figure is represented wounded and fallen, thereby typifying the race. While in the act of stringing his bow, he has received the wound; the moment the fatal arrow is felt he relinquishes the effort and hurriedly pulls it from the wound. In the moment that succeeds, he realises his danger, and his left hand drops powerless, partially clinging to the fatal arrow, while a faintness creeps over him. The right arm instinctively supports the body, and prevents its falling. Beneath the right hand is his own arrow, in his ears are an eagle's claw and a small shell. Sufficient ornaments and implements only have been introduced to give character to the subject. It is the first statue ever executed in American marble. It stands to the north-east of Power's Greek Slave.

Figure 9. Hiram Powers, *The Greek Slave*, 1844.

Figure 10. Peter Stephenson, *The Wounded American Indian*, 1848–50.

Is it not suggestive that the Americans, proverbially a 'cute people, should have so publicly drawn attention to slavery and the extinction of the aborigines of the far west?[2]

One might, indeed, ask. *Punch* was quick to exploit this suggestiveness, asking why there was no "Virginian slave in living ebony" to match the "Greek Captive in dead stone."[3] This inquiry was followed up a month later by John Tenniel's cartoon showing an African American woman, whose headdress and loose cloth draped around her waist serve to highlight the exposure of her naked breasts; unlike in Powers's work, the nakedness here cannot be seen as classical homage. The chains that bind her at the wrists are thick and heavy; the pillar is draped not in tasseled cloth, like Powers's, but in the Stars and Stripes; the plinth on which she stands is decorated with more chains and a motif of crossed whips, and the motto—deliberately ironic—"E pluribus unum"—is incised around its base.

Elizabeth Barrett Browning, who knew Powers in Florence, had already published a sonnet developing the antislavery theme suggested by the statue in her 1850 volume of poems. Opening with the lines "They say ideal beauty cannot enter/The house of anguish. On the threshold stands/An alien image with enshackled hands/Called the Greek Slave," the poem invites the statue to appeal "against man's wrong," to "strike

Figure 11. "E Pluribus Unum" *Punch*. June 1851.

and shame the strong,/By thunders of white silence, overthrown": a neat piece of doubleness that tropes both on the eloquence of the ironically ivory-hued marble and on the need to stir Caucasians into vocal protest against "man's crimes."[4] Rather than dwell on the impetus that the American section provided for the discussion of slavery per se—which, as Jeffrey Auerbach has noted, was "one of the foils, or counter-examples, used by Britons most frequently to assert their love of freedom and liberty" when they came to establishing their sense of nationhood against that of other countries—I want to explore the resonances of displaying a sculpture of a dying Indian in such a prominent way, and to consider the suggestions this sculpture threw out, in the context of the Great Exhibition, about the relationship between Native Americans, national identity, indigenous peoples, and what it meant to put the modernity of the United States on display in 1851.[5] How far, in other words, might a Native American be said to be an "American" at this historical moment? As we shall see, a very similar question was to be posed in relation to the development of a national literature just a few years later, in 1855, when Henry Wadsworth Longfellow's *Hiawatha* was published in Britain.

NATIVE AMERICANS AND THE GREAT EXHIBITION

As the *Illustrated London News* had been quick to point out, the American section of the Great Exhibition was a space that resonated with ironies. In any exhibition purporting to show the peoples or produce of a region or country, the area allocated to a display is complicated by its representational significance, since it both is and is not the territory of the land whose exhibits are ranged upon it. When such areas coexist in a bigger arena—such as the Great Exhibition—they provide a ready illustration of Foucault's concept of the heterotopia, a place "capable of juxtaposing in a single real space . . . several sites that are in themselves incompatible," most frequently in symbolic form.[6] This symbolic potential was seized upon by journalists keen to employ metaphors of cartography as devices around which to organize their accounts of the Crystal Palace. The surreal global rearrangement of countries could be invoked to promote that sentiment of "the coming Fraternity of Nations" which was ritualistically articulated in official speeches and accounts.[7] Or, more nationalistically, the proximate positioning of typical products allowed for the spread of the British Empire to be noted and celebrated, as by the *Morning Chronicle*: "The rude tents of Africa, the gorgeous pavilions of India, were alike open to the view; and the American bear skin, by its juxtaposition with that of the Bengal tiger—or the

Figure 12. The Great Exhibition of 1851: the United States section.

Canadian sledge in close contiguity with the New Zealand canoe—indicated more expressively than words can describe the vast extent of the British empire."[8]

The symbolic resonances of the floor space the U.S. section occupied were particularly strong and were played upon in a large number of press accounts. In what ways did the square footage given up to the country stand for its vast landmass, and in what ways might its apparent emptiness be made to resonate? The reportage was marked by an almost universal expression of disappointment, frequently voiced alongside a gleeful sense that the United States had not lived up to its boastfulness in advance of its display. It had asked for more space than had initially been allocated to it, something that the *Morning Chronicle* translated into a territorial ambition that had been acted out in miniature on the eighteen acres of exhibition space. "They wanted such a stretch of domain to themselves—they showed such symptoms of a desire to annex a slice of Russia, and to send a marauding expedition into the Zollverein—they got up, in short, . . . such a row about boundary lines, that all the world expected a most prodigious and 'tarnation display."[9] Such a display never materialized, however, and there is a palpable sense of relief that the United States had not yet manifested, in commercial terms, what the *Times* termed its "prospective greatness."[10] That newspaper, among others, was thus free to praise the energy that had gone into the production of such utilitarian objects as agricultural implements, buggies and sulkies, revolvers, false teeth, and wigs: items in which the United States could be seen to follow in Britain's footsteps in an unpretentious, unornamented fashion—Uncle Sam as subordinate family member.

But what struck commentators most of all was the emptiness of the American section. "She has here, as at home, large space unoccupied," commented the *Athenaeum*. "In the Crystal Palace, as elsewhere, the American must have plenty of elbow-room. The unsettled pieces of his country are suggested in the more than half empty areas of which he disposes.—The Belgian and Dutchmen can hardly stir in their well-stored compartments:—the American has wildernesses between his scattered stalls."[11] "The American department is the prairie ground of the Exhibition," wrote the *Times*, "and our cousins, smart as they are, have failed to fill it."[12] The *Morning Chronicle* similarly exploited the metaphorical possibilities of landscape and national icon: "The States find that they are not able to fill anything like the space over which that ugly flat eagle stretches its pasteboard wings, and that the virgin forest of their own uncleared territory is well represented in the bare expanses of flooring, dotted here and there with a stray piano or a stray sleigh, like frontier settlements scattered in the prairie."[13] However much Americans might mount a rational defense of the paucity of the display—information about the character and extent of the exhibition had been imperfectly circulated back home; Congress had appointed no funds to help exhibitors; the very size of the country meant that internal transportation was both expensive and inconvenient—it remained true that the floorage where they might have shown themselves to their best advantage stayed, in the term used by the *Morning Post*, "barren."[14]

One particular irony in all of this is that connotations of one kind of expansiveness cannot replace those of another. Probably the prime feature of the United States, upon which visitors invariably commented, was its vastness—vastness to the point of unrepresentability in the Europeanized language of the touristic sublime. One of the recurrent themes of emigration literature was the availability of territory for settling and cultivation. Nearly two decades after the Great Exhibition, "Americus," writing in the manual issued by the American Emigration Agency, *Where to Emigrate and Why,* could still claim that "the public domain of the United States is almost boundless. Its unsold acres, exclusive of Alaska, number nearly fifteen hundred millions, as yet covered only with the primeval forest or the wild and wanton vegetation of the prairies, 'wherewith the mower filleth not his hand, nor he that bindeth sheaves his bosom.' "[15] But this sense of space both as innately grand in its own right and as signaling economic promise and, by implication, the resulting territorial expansion—the potential expansion of a nation in terms of both land and economy—simply did not translate into the presentism of an exhibition. The "greatness" of the Americans, the *Times* opined, "lies in their expansive energies, and in the scale upon which they do everything," but the writer, observing that the display space failed to convey this, hypothesized that it would require the importation of a Mississippi steamer to make the point.[16] Rather than emptiness signifying possibility in its own right, this characteristic had to be identified by commentators as residing within raw materials or in the machinery with which to work them: in mineral nuggets or "ploughs, harrows, drills, waggons, sacks of corn, ears of maize, and barrels of salt meat." Such items made for unexciting display, yet when manufacturers attempted ornamentation, they tended to be accused of vulgarity, of loudness, and of producing "perfect triumphs of bad taste."[17]

When it came to the development of a national aesthetics, the *Standard* took comfort from *The Wounded American Indian*, which went far to prove, it claimed, "that America will not long remain behind hand in those aesthetic efforts which betray more than anything else the influence of education, the progress of taste, and the refinements that flow from the intercourse with Europe."[18] Like Powers's statue, which strongly suggested the Venus de Medici to many contemporary commentators, Stephenson's work was seen to provide a clear example of that republican art which looked to classical ideals, rather than to a British heritage, for its aesthetic validation.

Yet the fact that it was reminiscent, as journalists noted, of the *Dying Gladiator* in the Capitoline collection meant that some peculiarly complex questions were raised about the aptness of a statue of a Native American as an emblem not only of American art but also of America. This returns one to the issues that I raised in the opening chapter: whether the figure of an Indian represented an Other, *against* which narratives of American-ness were to be constructed, or whether, in fact, it carried the symbolic weight of being the country's original, and hence most authentic, inhabitant. This was the spirit in which William Gilmore Simms, just two years earlier, had been advocating the development of a national literature based on Indian themes, with indigenous people to serve, he said, in place of Europe's Gauls and Goths. As it happened, the classical statue of the Dying Gladiator did, in fact, represent a dying Gaul, since it was a copy of a Greek statue of a vanquished Galatian.[19] More than that, not only had the sculpted figure been appropriated, within Romantic literature, as a type of "dying *Hero*" (by Felicia Hemans),[20] but Byron had turned him into a political icon, seeing him as an exploited personage, a

Figure 13. The Dying Gaul. Capitoline Museum, Rome. Photograph by Jean-Christophe Benoist.

member of a powerless minority suffering at the hands of a relentless, merciless imperial power, providing an occasion to call for revenge in the name of justice. The poet squeezed poignancy out of the conceit that the dying Gaul's final thoughts were with his children—his "young barbarians"—playing in his "rude hut" by the Danube, while he has been "butchered to make a Roman holiday." "Shall he expire," Byron's poem concludes by asking, "and unavenged—Arise! Ye Goths, and glut your ire!"[21] What is especially significant is that both Stephenson's statue and its source are depictions of *dying* men; if this is heroism, it is unquestionably heroism in defeat.[22]

Thus *The Wounded American Indian* was a paradoxical presence at the Crystal Palace. It represented a pioneering national aesthetic, an example of the artistic enterprise that might be used to counter the common assertion that American creativity was limited to utilitarian objects. Yet Stephenson's choice of subject was also an appropriation, dependent upon those people whose dispossession—either territorial or cultural—was a precondition for settling that apparently promising empty prairie.[23] Moreover, when taken in the context both of the American section and of the exhibition as a whole, it helped to emphasize the connection of the persecution of Indians and other forms of exploitation of those who were commonly assumed to belong to inferior races. This connection was brought out explicitly in an engraving reproduced in the *Illustrated London News* on October 25, at the close of the exhibition. Entitled *The Great Exhibition—Official Award of the Prizes*, this work is deeply ambiguous. It shows a Caucasian figure in helmet and breastplate, yet waving an olive branch and towering over an African who is naked to the waist, as in many abolitionist representations of the slave; a turbaned Oriental man; and a Native American holding both tomahawk and rifle and nestling his head against the flank of a benign yet superior lion. The engraving is open to both triumphalist and satiric readings.

But most exhibition visitors, one suspects, did not think very deeply about the relationship between Native Americans and the realities of racial politics in the United States, nor in colonies more generally. Rather, the Indian stood primarily for a generalized type of exoticism: violent and unpredictable if provoked, but otherwise dignified, albeit emotionally remote. The intrinsic strangeness with which the Indian was invested is demonstrated by a contemporary one-act theater production, *Apartments, "Visitors to the Exhibition May Be Accommodated" etc. A Piece of Extravagance to "Suit the Times,"* staged in May 1851 at the Princess's Theatre, London. To quote from the *Times*'s mockingly xenophobic review,

> The notion, caught up with such avidity by our caricaturists, that one effect of the "Great Exhibition" would be the frequent assemblage of a great number of heterogeneous foreigners beneath the roof of a single lodging-house, has been embodied in a dramatic form by the younger Mr. Borough. A commercial traveller's wife, during the absence of her husband, has let her house to all sorts of outlandish occupants, including a Yankee, a Red Indian, a Frenchman, and a Highlander, who are stowed away in the most uninviting parts of the premises, such as the chimney, the dog-kennel, and so forth.[24]

If Stephenson's *Wounded Indian* worked to consolidate the idea that Native Americans were soon to face oblivion, the sense that Indians were more conspicuous by their absence in this surrogate national space than by their presence was, moreover, reinforced by the fact that hardly anything of Indian manufacture could be found within the United States department—a suggestion that their crafts not only had no place in the modern world but bore no organic connection with it. A Mr. Davis of Pittsburgh showed some "Indian ornaments"; Mr. Searle of Boston displayed a Sioux saddle and hunter's belt; there was an Indian cap and a bookmark; and that was all. This was in notable contrast to the Canadian section (inevitably praised by the British press), where costumes and carved and beaded items were to be seen. Severed from any ceremonial context, some of the latter were in effect little more than goods produced for the tourist market. But the relative proliferation of Indian artifacts in this section, together with a range of raw materials, allowed for a much more coherent narrative to be extracted from those "different North American provinces over which waves the Union Jack" than from the spaces of Britain's former colony.[25] In part, it encouraged journalistic travelogues that attempted to map onto the objects a voyage from the eastern to the western seaboard: a route of colonization that mirrored, in reverse, the Victorian version of the progress of civilization. Thus one could move from agricultural produce, through blankets and warm clothes, solid wooden furniture, and elegant sleighs, until "a step or two further and you suddenly leave all trace of civilization and plunge into the back woods. The evidences of the wilderness surround you—birch canoes, snow shoes, the wampum belt, the tomahawk, and the mocassin of the Indian hang in trophies from the specimens of the trunks of vast trees."[26] Encounters and engagement with First Nations culture, in other words, were conceived of as being very much a part of a pioneering, adventurous British presence within Canada, even if native culture—the display suggested—must ultimately be supplanted. Nonetheless, rather than offering a chronicle of confrontation, the cooperation of native and settler is stressed, a cooperation brought about by shared trade interests, a mutual need to survive in inhospitable climates, and, indeed, shared opposition toward those who had been responsible for the severance of Britain's former colony from the parent nation. Thus visitors could see "the pretty models of an Indian family" from New Brunswick, "the kindness of whose character is attested by having protected two maiden ladies, whose father emigrated from the United States after the American war, and settled among the tribe some 70 years ago. The remnants of the Indians and the remains of the Royalists must have had many subjects of sympathy, and many feelings in common, to have maintained so long a career of mutual respect."[27] Once again, this commentary stresses—whatever the reality—the humane treatment of native peoples by the British in Canada, in contrast to the policies that were carried out south of the border.

Exhibits from other parts of the Americas—sparse as they were, due to the political instability of Central and South America at the time—also allowed the grand narrative that underpinned the whole exhibition to be told: one of the advancement of industry, and the cumulative ameliorative effect of labor. The *Illustrated London News* exhorted its readers to pay "careful and special attention to these Aboriginal products. They illustrate the primitive elements out of which the most advanced nations have elaborated the gorgeous and graceful, the eminently useful, and almost intellectual things, of which this whole assemblage mainly consists. The most polished nations may in them trace their own perfection backwards to its source." Indeed, this teleological triumphalism is advanced as a consolation for "the melancholy feeling too prevalent amongst us, that numerous portions of our race are doomed by Providence to perish at the approach of our more instructed brethren."[28] While the almost total absence of such artifacts in the U.S. section might promote an ethos of modernity, this simultaneously disallowed any argument that progress had been built on deep history, on accumulation and advance, and it refused to give any weight to the copresence of Indian cultures alongside the products of the new nation.

One further irony of the exhibition remains to be explored. The imaginary spaces on the map of the United States might be said to constitute what Paul Carter, in *The Road to Botany Bay*, has termed "imperial space . . . with its ideal, neutral observer and its unified, placeless Euclidian passivity, [which] was a means of foundation, a metaphorical way of transforming the present into a future enclosure, a visible stage, an orderly cause-and-effect pageant."[29] If the kinder commentators on this section of the exhibition suggested a parallel between vacant floor space and the possibilities that lay before the ever-expanding growth of American agriculture and industry, George Catlin saw a more immediate possibility for filling up another corner of the American section. Although the tribal members who had formed part of his show had returned to the United States in 1848, Catlin's diminished exhibit of artifacts and paintings was on display in Waterloo Place concurrently with the Great Exhibition. The prospect of the crowds of people who were visiting London offered a chance for him to continue both with his personal agenda of attempting to obtain a purchaser for his Indian collection and with his broader ethnological project of familiarizing European publics with the characteristics of these supposedly vanishing peoples.[30] As a result of his intervention, the *terra nulla* of the East Aisle of the Great Exhibition became a site for the display of models of two native figures. It thus acted as a further reminder that "imperial space" is rarely as vacant as the imperialist presents it as being.

The two figures Catlin showed at the Crystal Palace were an Iowa Medicine Man, his leggings fringed with scalp locks, and a Mandan woman. There is a melancholy aptness in the choice of a Mandan, for since Catlin had visited and painted the tribe in 1832, it had suffered a catastrophic outbreak of smallpox in 1837–38, which left only about 130 out of 1,600 alive;[31] "people," Catlin had written, "whose fate, like that of all their race is sealed; whose doom is fixed to live just long enough to be imperfectly known, and then to fall before the fell disease or sword of civilizing devastation."[32] The ultimate irony, whether intended or not, lay in the positioning of these two costumed effigies, for they stood directly underneath the draped Stars and Stripes. They were, therefore, images simultaneously of native identity and of the conquered; this, however unintentionally, speaks eloquently to the fact that colonial space is, invariably, contested space. Like the poignant figure of *The Wounded Indian*, they acted as a prescient reminder of internal displacement and dispossession within the United States: the violence on which the production of national identity depended. They both stood for Americanness and were the archetypes against which the dominant American self-imaging—of a country that was modern, technologically and industrially inventive—could be readily seen as being built.

HIAWATHA IN ENGLAND

These paradoxical questions—whether Indians belonged to the past or to the present, whether they were integral or excluded when it came to a national self-conception—were articulated in an even more sustained fashion a few years later, when Longfellow's *Song of Hiawatha* appeared. Responding to this long verse narrative, British reviewers were as concerned as their American counterparts with the issue of what constituted a distinct national literature, in terms both of subject matter and of style. Should such a literature be identified through its celebration of particular scenery or its response to certain human qualities and emotions? Did *Hiawatha* fit the bill? "Here then, at last, is a genuine American poem, by a native of America; a poem redolent of pine-forests and the smoke of wigwams," wrote John Stanyan Bigg in the *London Quarterly Review*.[33] Could a poem focusing, however sympathetically, on America's indigenous inhabitants indeed be said to be "a genuine American poem," or could such a description be used only satirically—as closer inspection proves, in fact, to be the case with Bigg's piece?

The British critical reception of *Hiawatha*, and the British critique of its relationship to the idea of a national poetic identity, looks in two directions. Reviews of Longfellow's work almost invariably engaged, if only in passing, with the contemporary conditions of Native Americans and thus they must be read alongside the broader traditions of social and cultural commentary that took American policy toward the Indian as an important signifier of aspects of the national character of the United States. Yet one must also remember that the subject matter of the poem was not startlingly novel, for, as we have seen, British readers of poetry would have been familiar with a number of melancholic poetic treatments foregrounding the dying, disappearing Indian. A number of these treatments, moreover, encouraged their consumers to consider their responses not just toward the dispossessed but also toward those who did the dispossessing.

Longfellow's journal indicates that he cared deeply about his British reception and waited eagerly for reviews of *Hiawatha*. This concern demonstrates the pull that transatlantic culture held for him. As the poet himself recorded, the majority of early British notices—the ones in the weeklies—were favorable, with the exception of the *Illustrated London News*, which termed *Hiawatha* "a great mistake, but the mistake, nevertheless, of a man of genius."[34] The quarterlies, while hardly antagonistic, were somewhat more measured in their assessments. Throughout almost all the responses, however, run the questions of what subject matter might be most fit for an epic of America and of the kind of history that the Americans should look to commemorate. The *Athenaeum* came out strongly in favor of Longfellow's choice of subject matter. At last, its critic claimed, here was a writer who recognized that many of the mythical and pictorial elements that had customarily been sought out in Europe were available on his own doorstep.

> Who has touched the sad and tender chords of Indian story? Who has seized the poetic features of the Red Man? Surely here are fine materials for the true poet! Neither is that tale of the White Man in America devoid of romantic interest. How full of movement, how stern and dramatic, how infinitely vast, and rapid, and complex, is that story—from Columbus to Raleigh, from Pizarro to Penn, from Las Casas to Oglethorpe! How much of passion, of intellect, of fancy, weaves itself into that bright and clouded web! How intensely poetical, too, are all the episodes and changes of that story—from the sailing of the three poor caravals from Palos down to the Declaration of Independence! Nay, it is, in our opinion, one of the most romantic tales on record. How full of movement, how stern and dramatic, how infinitely vast, and rapid, and complex, is that Neglect of such a theme by American poets, in favour of legends of European goblins, European cities and European literary fashions, has always appeared to us a serious impeachment of the national genius.[35]

This enthusiasm for the potential scope of the all-American epic is, from an English point of view, somewhat uncharacteristic in that it gives full weight to the history of the Americas as a whole and to the place of Spanish as well as British participants in the conquest of the native peoples—peoples who somehow are also to be celebrated, as though the magnificence of their preconquest existence adds luster to those responsible for their subsequent subjection. In such a context, "seizing" the poetic features of the "Red Man" appears, albeit unintentionally, like a further act of capture and appropriation, placing the poet alongside more militaristic company. *The Dublin University Magazine* offered a different, topographically grounded approach when it came to supporting Longfellow's subject choice. It typified America's East Coast as continually engaged in material and intellectual rivalry with the rest of the industrialized world (an image of the land very much in accord with its self-presentation at the Crystal Palace) and its writers—Irving, Emerson, and Hawthorne are singled out—as being driven by similar competitive rivalry. But "in its forests, the Anglo-American is another man. He has shaken off the trammels, with the costume, of social life. He has set his face, and his soul, Westward." Straining the metaphor dreadfully, the writer continues to praise Cooper for having "cleared a literature from the forest. With an arm inured to manly toil, hath he smitten into the tangled luxuriance of a primaeval race." The poet William Cullen Bryant also has tracked the "footsteps of nature," and now Longfellow has pushed "the explorations of his countrymen both into nature and into legendary lore—into the wildernesses of space and tradition—to a limit before unreached."[36]

Yet for *The Saturday Review*, the subject of the Indian, and the Indian as the subject of literature, was already passé. In part, in this, the periodical showed itself to be more American than British in its cultural emphasis; as Berkhofer puts it; "By the 1850s the Indian in general and the Noble Savage in particular began to bore the sophisticated reading public."[37] It was not, though, to the number of works with relatively high literary pretensions that had indeed anticipated Longfellow's choice of subject to which the critic referred—poems like James Wallis Eastburn's *Yamoyden*, William Hosmer's *Yonnondio*, or Elmer H. Smith's *Ma-Ka-Tai-Me-She-Kia-Kiak; or, Black Hawk, and Scenes in the West*,[38] but to works of popular culture that were already very familiar to a British (and of course American) readership. "Have we not had enough of these Red Indians," wrote the critic, "—nay, rather too much of them—since the days when Fenimore Cooper, with his pleasant dream of *The Last of the Mohicans*, deluded our young fancies into believing that the conquering white race had destroyed a transatlantic Arcadia, in which the quiet enjoyment of Theocritus's shepherds was combined with the valour of Homer's heroes?" Rather than engaging in such mythology, one should face both historical and contemporary *reality*. This might lead one to the pages of William Strachey's *Travaile in Virginia* (a new edition of this 1612 edition had appeared in 1849) or Edwin James's *Account of an Expedition from Pittsburgh to the Rocky Mountains* (1823), "not to speak," this commentator continued, in unspecific, ominous terms, "of recent facts (told us by unprejudiced eye-witnesses), too disgusting and horrible to relate." Nor did *The Saturday Review* wish to uphold a sentimental position; rather, it was this writer's view that races do not perish without a cause—that these "red-men had really been destroying themselves . . . long before the appearance of the white race, by cruelty and revenge, dirt and idleness, shameless and nameless profligacy."[39] Even the more charitable reviewer in *The Christian Remembrancer*, although feeling obliged to express the viewpoint that "so wonderful a thing as savage life ought to have its epic," recoiled from the idea of a literature dealing with the necessary specifics; "there is between cultivated and savage life a natural repugnance and alienation. Try as we will, reason as we may, the ideal of savages soon wearies and disgusts us."[40] The dismissive, derogatory, and fastidiously self-congratulating opinions expressed here offer a context in which the shift toward an angrier approach on the part of some imaginative writers can be placed.

Nonetheless, such a display of lack of sympathy is relatively rare. Rather than contest an Indian claim to heroism or nostalgia, most British reviewers who were chary of the Indian's position as the subject of this poem queried whether he could really be said to be "American" at all. Bigg, in the *London Quarterly* piece, lamented that the topic was so "aboriginal" that "the present inhabitants" of the United States "will fail to recognise in it any traces of their own habitudes of thought and feeling." Either he is assuming no Native Americans can read English, or he is presuming that they already count as extinct. Whereas the efforts of their Puritan forefathers, or of such backwoodsmen as Boon, Harrod, and Smith, might be fit topics for poetry,

> he who demands of American poetry that it be not merely the child of the forest and the prairie, the mountain and the river, but that it echo also the war-cry of the extinct race by whom the country was anciently populated, is about as consistent as he would be who should ask of an English poem, that it be constructed in imitation of the Anglo-Saxon poem of "Beowulf," or the ode on the "Victory of Athelstan."[41]

The anonymity of the review, however, conceals a level of irony. In 1848 Bigg had published *The Sea-King*, a metrical romance in six cantos with very detailed historical and illustrative notes, showing how the poem grew out of his study of Sharon Turner's *History of the Anglo Saxons*. His motivation could be termed Blairian or Herderian, one that associated national characteristics with a country's primitive poetry and that saw grounds for investigating and celebrating the work of earlier peoples based on the assumption that each country's culture and civilization develop according to an organic model, from childhood to maturity.[42]

As Helen Carr points out in her excellent chapter on *Hiawatha* in *Inventing the American Primitive*, such a viewpoint underpinned Walter Channing's well-known "Essay on American Language and Literature," published in *The North American Review* in 1815. This claimed that the United States lacks a literature "because it possesses the same language with a nation totally unlike it in almost every relation," apart from the "oral literature of its aborigines," which is "as bold as" the Indian's "own unshackled conceptions, and as rapid as his step."[43] The Indian formed an obvious choice of subject matter for American writers attempting to establish an American literature, but, as many commentators have noted, the enthusiasm was relatively short-lived. As we saw in relation to sculpture, some writers, such as Walter Gilmore Simms, Cornelius Matthews, and Mrs. M. M. Webster, were still maintaining, until well into the 1840s, that indigenous inhabitants should be at the center of a national aesthetic. But in general, westward expansion was starting to diminish public sympathy for Native Americans within their own country. The cultural and political turn in the United States (especially in the East) toward using the idea of the vanishing American as a stimulus for preservation and assimilation bolstered by arguments taken from evolutionary science and traditional theology, was a few years off.[44] In this context, Longfellow can be seen as a somewhat belated writer in his choice of hero—belated, that is, in terms of the consistently elegiac tone with which he ends up investing him. His belatedness is brought home when one puts him alongside the directly contemporary, historically preemptive, and very different case of Walt Whitman, whose *Leaves of Grass* was also published in 1855; this poem may be said to mark a new phase in the appropriation of the Indian by Anglo writers, an attempt (despite Whitman's continued ambivalence about actual Native Americans) to integrate their presence into the imagined, multiethnic nation— "the tribes of red aborigines," Whitman wrote in his preface, being part of the country's human and geographic "diversity." "I except not one . . . red white or black, all are deific."[45] In seeing the Indian as a vital resource, Whitman, to quote Michael Castro, anticipates modernist poets, regarding the native as "in touch with the spirit of the American continent and offering, for an emerging American consciousness and identity, 'new forms' of language and life-style. In writing of the Indian, he adopts imagery not of distance and decline, but of merger and renewal."[46] For Castro, too, Whitman's native acts as an ideal of physical and mental manliness and of a vibrant presentism—even though, one might point out, his is also a tourist Indian, his "squaw wrapt in her yellow-hemm'd cloth . . . offering moccasins and bead-bags for sale."[47]

In the case of Longfellow's far more archaized version of a hero, the question of a poetic return to some form of native authenticity is further complicated by the factor of style. In adopting the infamously insistent meter of the old Finnish epic the *Kalevala*, Longfellow could hardly be said to be going to the native languages of his own country in order to inject new life through an indigenously inspired form of stylistic innovation, even if—as Channing would have approved—he was cutting loose from the literary traditions of America's mother country. Yet his metrical novelty did not seem to trouble British commentators, at least insofar as it carried with it certain nationalistic associations. William Howitt, in a letter to the *Athenaeum* that formed a contribution to that journal's protracted epistolary debate about the origins of the poem's meter, even went so far as to claim that the Finnish component gave the poem an extra importance for British readers, given the ongoing events of the Crimean War: "Next year we shall probably inflict more severe injuries on the coast towns of Finland, for its unfortunate subjection to Russia, and perhaps destroy the very cradle of the renaissance of its literature. Under these circumstances, anything which may create in us a more lively interest in this little known, but highly endowed people, is desirable, and not the least merit of Longfellow's fine poem may turn out to be this."[48]

Nonetheless, the intellectually numbing nature of Hiawatha's repetitive meter was notorious from the poem's publication onward. It was frequently aligned with a developmental model that denigrated the native. The *Spectator* was typical in seeing the "monotonous chant" as being impeccably fitted "to the limited range of knowledge, the simple life and manners, the hopes and fears of the people, and their 'untutored mind' in reference to the origin of things."[49] "A cultivated measure," remarked the critic of *The Christian Remembrancer*, "with its artful cadences and recurring rhymes, its intricacies and linked harmonies, was too far removed from the subject to hope for success." For this critic, the poem is monotonous because it faithfully represents the conditions of Indian life; it repeats itself "because this is the inevitable action of the mind debarred from new impressions." Despite acknowledging that Longfellow is using an old Finnish form, this information is instantly ignored with the claim that the author has been completely successful in "adopting the tom-tom beat of the Indian drum for his lyre."[50] "Unhappily for the poet," wrote Margaret Oliphant in *Blackwood's*, the poem is written in "the very measure to attract the parodist. *Punch* has opened the assault."[51]

Punch's lines, or some of them, have frequently been quoted in discussions of the poem, but not contextualized, since they have habitually been regarded as a self-evident example of the satirical magazine's spiky pen, with the transnational implications of the parody going uncommented upon.

Should you ask me, What's its nature?
Ask me, What's the kind of poem?
Ask me in respectful language,
Touching your respectful beaver,
Kicking back your manly hind-leg,
Like to one who sees his betters;
I should answer, I should tell you,
'Tis a poem in this metre,
And embalming the traditions,
Fables, rites, and superstitions,
Legends, charms, and ceremonials
Of the various tribes of Indians,
From the land of the Ojibways,
From the land of the Dacotahs,
From the mountains, moors, and fenlands,
Where the heron, the Shuh-shuh-gar,
Finds its sugar in the rushes:
From the fast-decaying nations,
Which our gentle Uncle SAMUEL
Is improving, very smartly,
From the face of all creation,
Off the face of all creation.[52]

It is precisely when read in the light of American policies toward the Indians that *Hiawatha* has the potential to be read—particularly from a British perspective—as a somewhat different sort of American poem from that aimed at by Longfellow. As we have seen, British commentary on the U.S. government's treatment of Indians went well beyond newspaper reportage and discussion in the serious journals of what Francis Head, writing in the *Quarterly*, had called the "desolating march" of white people "over the territory of the Indians."[53] It was found in some of the best-known, most widely circulating travel writings of the first half of the century, writings that helped to set out an idea of contemporary America for those who had never visited the country and who were unlikely to do so. It could be met with, for example, in Laurence Oliphant's *Minnesota and the Far West* (1855, and reviewed in the same number of the *Spectator* as was *Hiawatha*). "It is useless," wrote Oliphant, "for the American Government to expect that their efforts to improve the moral and intellectual condition of the red men can ever be attended with success while they persevere in that system of deportation which must tend much more than anything else not only to retard their civilisation, but ultimately to exterminate these original possessors of the soil."[54] Isabella Bird voiced a similar sentiment a year later in *The*

Englishwoman in America. Again in a vein quite different from those reviewers who praised Longfellow for pushing back the boundaries of American literature as if he were embodying the pioneering spirit of the frontiersman, she remarked: "It is impossible to give an idea of the 'western man' to any one who has not seen one at least as a specimen. They are the men before whom the Indians melt away as grass before the scythe. They shoot them down on the smallest provocation, and speak of 'head of Indian,' as we do in England of 'head of game.'"[55]

However scathing their political indictments, it was hard for all of these midcentury commentators on the condition of the Indian to keep the performance of nostalgia out of their writings, and this was as true for reviewers of Longfellow's poem as it was for travel writers. Despite the potential for a politicized reading that *Hiawatha* brings with it, the doom of the "hapless races"—as more than one reviewer of the poem termed them—was customarily taken for granted. Undoubtedly, the combination of the unfamiliar and exotic—to an English audience—with the sustained atmosphere of nostalgia was a powerful factor in establishing *Hiawatha*'s transatlantic popularity.[56]

There were a number of easily identifiable reasons why Longfellow's poetry, taken as a whole, was greeted with enthusiasm by a broad cross section of British readers. Many of these were so readily spotted, indeed, that they were mocked. "Excelsior" was effortlessly jibed at by British commentators because it pressed easy buttons labeled "determination," "perseverance," and "progress." The reception of *Hiawatha* built on, and helped to consolidate, the preexisting, growing, and widespread enthusiasm for Longfellow within England. In 1859, albeit in a somewhat less than adulatory vein, Theophilus Davis remarked in the *National Review* that one meets with Longfellow's work throughout the country

> every where and in every form,—in complete editions on the counters of the regular booksellers, in stacks of little shilling volumes on railway bookstalls, and in gorgeously-bound and profusely-illustrated volumes on drawing-room tables. He is unquestionably the most popular poet of the day. Country newspapers habitually adorn their columns with his minor pieces; young ladies sing his pathetic poems at the piano; and lecturers at mechanics' institutions invariably quote his moral and didactic verses.

Such popularity, Davis snidely suggests, is a result of Longfellow's capacity to write so as to appeal to the sympathies and comprehension of almost any reader; his poems "express, always neatly, sometimes gracefully, and now and then beautifully, what nine-tenths of their readers think and feel on the subject, or rather what they know they ought to think and feel."[57] Piling on the low-key sarcasm, Davis maintains that

Longfellow is at his best when writing about forests, where his own limited range of experience and sympathy will be least noted.

Hiawatha's blatant emotional demands on its readership spoke directly to the mid-Victorian taste for nostalgia: a taste that the "dying Indian" had already played its part in forming and sustaining. Nostalgia is a literary mode that readily triggers popular response, and as Svetlana Boym has usefully written, it "inevitably reappears as a defense mechanism in a time of accelerated rhythms of life and historical upheavals . . . [it] is rebellion against the modern idea of time, the time of history and progress."[58] Longfellow's alteration of some of his source material worked toward increasing its already-elegiac connotations; his inclusion of the death of Minnehaha, the emphasis he placed on the sad outcome of the famine, the fact that he fails to grant Hiawatha any children and hence denies him, and his line, a future, all contribute to the poem's downbeat affect. The easy emotional responses that this poem sets out to stimulate found resonances in a British readership well prepared to celebrate its capacity for compassion at the loss both of a specific people and of an unrecapturable version of preurban society. On 12 April 1856 Hawthorne wrote to the poet from Liverpool in appropriately horticultural metaphors: "Your fame is in its fullest blow; the flower cannot open wider. If there is any bliss at all in literary reputation, you ought to feel it at this moment."[59]

The absence of a transatlantic copyright agreement makes sales figures for *Hiawatha* difficult to compute, but the British Library's catalogue indicate that three separate editions were brought out in 1855, published by D. Bogue, T. Nelson and Sons, and George Routledge and Company. (dated 1856, but reviewed in November 1855). At least eleven other editions appeared before the end of the century. Francis Newman, brother of the cardinal, published a translation into Latin in 1862, albeit more inspired by the poem's plot than by its vocabulary, and feeling at liberty to abridge and to engage in "arbitrary alteration, especially where the native legends which he has followed appeared to me too puerile, tedious or obscure."[60] As *Punch*'s spirited response manifested, Longfellow's relentless hexameters readily inspired parodies. These included an 111-page imitation chronicling London street life, "A Drop O'Wather" (1856),[61] by the Shakespearean actor and critic Mary Cowden Clarke, and Lewis Carroll's "Hiawatha's Photographing," which uses the meter to mock the cultural and social pretensions of the British middle classes and, to quote the photographer Brassaï's essay "Carroll the Photographer," "the vanity and fatuousness of people demanding the most flattering portraits."[62] Indeed, Longfellow's appeal to the unthinking middle-class audience of the day was what above all characterized the poet to his English obituarists.[63] At the time of his death, the *Spectator* even managed simultaneously to praise *Hiawatha*, condescend both toward native people and toward the poem's unsophisticated audience, and damn Longfellow by claiming that this was his most successful poem because the writer's innate simplicity, his "childlike and yet not unstately verse," found its most apt subject when writing about "the childlike races."[64]

What is more, *Hiawatha* inspired musical spin-offs, ranging from the Hiawatha Polka of 1856 to Robert Stoepel's *Hiawatha: A Romantic Symphony*, an ambitious (and critically well received) work performed at Covent Garden in 1861 and combining "narration, solo arias, descriptive choruses, and programmatic orchestral interludes."[65] Most notably, at the end of the century, the black English composer Samuel Coleridge-Taylor wrote a choral trilogy, *Scenes from "The Song of Hiawatha."* (*Hiawatha's Wedding Feast*, 1898; *The Death of Minnehaha*, 1899; and *Hiawatha's Departure*, 1900). This was the most popular English oratorio between 1898 and 1912 and was revived in spectacular fashion by Thomas Fairbairn, with grandiose scenery and a chorus of some five hundred "braves and squaws" in 1924—a production that, feeding off the enthusiasm for cinema Westerns, was revived annually until the later 1940s.[66] The oratorio provides a powerful example of late-nineteenth-century circum-Atlantic cultural traffic. Coleridge-Taylor's compositions were popular in the United States as well as in Britain, and the composer was lauded there as an example of black achievement. Particularly after he read W.E.B. Du Bois' *Souls of Black Folk* in 1904, he worked to incorporate slave songs, African dance melodies, and other black folk music into his work (he included the melody "Nobody Knows the Trouble I See" into a separate work, the *Overture to the Song of Hiawatha*). It is, however, unclear to what extent a political alertness underlay his treatment of Longfellow. The British composer Sir Hubert Parry claimed that Coleridge-Taylor "said that he was mainly attracted to Longfellow's poem by the funny names in it. At any rate it was simple, unanalytic, straightforward pleasure in the simple story which appealed to him,"[67] Michael Pisani, however, has recently offered a more nuanced and speculative reading, one that notes the composer's incorporation of Indian musical phrasing into parts of his work and, building on the fact that Coleridge-Taylor suffered from some racial exclusion within his own country, suggests that

> in his embrace of Longfellow's poem, he may have been aiming to widen his country's sense of cultural identity. Perhaps his magnum opus, exotic trappings nothwithstanding, was intended to be understood as a beachhead in the battle for mutual tolerance between peoples of diverse cultural and racial origins, all the more potent for being

performed in the near-sacred national venue of [the] Royal Albert Hall.[68]

Writing his *Lives of the Famous Poets* in 1878, William Michael Rossetti included Longfellow as his only example of a living poet, and his only American one. He ascribes his considerable popularity to the fact that he was finely attuned to "the spirit of the age" and was adept at turning this to his account. "The question whether the popularity will be prolonged into enduring fame," however, "is much the same as the question in what degree the spirit of our own age will be operative in time to come."[69] Such uncertainty about Longfellow's overall durability is not, though, extended to *Hiawatha*. Rossetti regards the poem as particularly valuable for the part it has played in preserving "the native American legends and aboriginal tone of thought"; in this role, "I can hardly imagine it superseded, nor, until superseded, overlooked." This, he says, "leads us to consider for a moment whether Longfellow has impressed himself upon the time, or qualified for posterity, as the American poet *par excellence*. I do not think he has. *Hiawatha* will live as the poem of the American native tribes, not as the poem of America." His choice of the "real American poet" is Walt Whitman, "a man enormously greater than Longfellow or any other of his poetic compatriots" (390–91).

While *Hiawatha* clearly lacks the grandiose rhetorical and geographic sweep of Whitman, its implications for transatlantic cultural history were broader than Rossetti chose to suggest. Its grounds for being regarded as a significant "American" poem pivot around the very ambiguity of the identification of its protagonist in national terms: as a native inhabitant of America or as a figure against whom America's policies could be tested and found wanting. The very fact that the image of the Indian was not invested with the same iconic significances in Britain as it was in the United States allowed for the distancing perspective demanded by this latter interpretation. Read alongside other mid-nineteenth-century poetic appropriations of the figure of the Indian, *Hiawatha*'s strengths as a national poem ultimately lie, from a British point of view, not so much in its status as a record of cultural origins, a nostalgic relic of a passing race, as in the questions it raises about the directions in which mid-Victorian America was moving. In this, the figure of the native played a very similar part in relation to nationhood, as did the presence of Peter Stephenson's *Wounded Indian* in the ambiguously open spaces of the American section of the Crystal Palace.

ᐁ

Pisani concludes the section of *Imagining Native America* that deals with the musical representations of native America in the nineteenth century by reminding us of the rise of ethnographic disciplines toward the end of this period—a rise that, ironically, was made easier by the increasing confinement of Indians on reservations. If the musical work of Coleridge-Taylor and others incorporated some of the new ethnomusicology, thereby ensuring cross-cultural hybridity in these representations, it was nonetheless created at some distance from actual Indian people. The same could of course be said about Stephenson's sculpture—let alone the British reception of Longfellow's poem. And yet, in the first decade of the twentieth century, this distance was collapsed by a dramatic staging of *Hiawatha* that ran in London for six months. L. O. Armstrong, a Canadian entrepreneur, first put on his outdoor version of Longfellow's text in 1901 near the Garden River reserve in Ontario. It was translated into Ojibwa and used native actors. In 1903 the production traveled to Chicago, New York, Philadelphia, Pittsburgh, and Detroit, and in 1905 to London, where it was staged at Earl's Court. Alan Trachtenberg has brought out well the ironies inherent in Armstrong's *Hiawatha* pageants. As he shows, the press presented them as the occasion for a "Canadian-English artistic entrepreneur to 'restore' their forgotten culture to the Ojibways, including a chance for Christian Indians to perform rites of their ancient religion that Longfellow had sympathetically preserved," a chance that included the opportunity for the Ojibwa to perform their cultural loss "in someone else's version for the pleasure of white audiences and perhaps their own fun: Sacrifice was sublimated as entertainment."[70] These performers were native people who were a living denial of the imminent oblivion inherent in Longfellow's interpretation of the cost of American national expansion. Even if their roles were scripted, the pageant offered them a chance to keep alive their language and some aspects of their ceremonial dances and music—and to earn money simultaneously (although, one might note, they were not entirely successful at this; the London performers ran out of funds and were left temporarily stranded).[71]

London audiences had a chance to take on board a further set of ironies. When British spectators witnessed this double authenticity (Indians performing traditional Indianness, yet taking part in contemporary commercial culture), they watched men and women who were, as First Nations people coming from Ontario, members of the British Empire as well as of their own tribes. Their presence, therefore, had the capacity to act as a powerful reminder that even if the Indian of Longfellow's poem might be seen as an American, distancing oneself from the past and future of native peoples on the American continent was not, after all, a privilege of Britishness.

CHAPTER SIX

Savagery and Nationalism: Native Americans and Popular Fiction

In her autobiography, *The One I Knew the Best of All*, the children's novelist Frances Hodgson Burnett recalled how, as a girl, she used to play at being an Indian. The sitting room table, with its large hanging-down cloth,

> became a wigwam. The Doll was a squaw and the Small Person a chief. They smoked the calumet and ate maize, and told each other stories of the war-trail and the happy hunting-grounds. They wore moccasins, and feathers, and wampum, and brought up papooses, and were very happy. Their natures were mild. They never scalped anyone, though the tomahawk was as much a domestic utensil as the fire-irons might have been if they had had an Indian flavour. That it was dark under the enshrouding table-cloth made the wigwam all the more realistic. A wigwam with bay windows and a chandelier would not have been according to Mayne Reid and Fenimore Cooper.[1]

Burnett's play world, with all its clichés of generic Indian ethnicity, was typical of the imaginative space inhabited by very many British children from the 1830s onward. James Fenimore Cooper's novels established the terms in which Indians were popularly conceived across the Atlantic (as well, of course, in the minds of very many American readers), and this applied not just to suggestible young readers but to adult travelers as well. We have already witnessed Isabella Bird's disappointment that the Indians in Nova Scotia were nothing like Uncas and Magua, and she was far from alone in basing unrealizable expectations upon his fictions. The future author of boys' adventure stories John C. Hutcheson, writing in *Belgravia* in 1872, describes how Cooper's characters helped to preformulate the expectations he held of America: "Whether it was through childish reminiscences of the Pathfinder, Last of the Mohicans, Chingachgook, the Great Big Serpent, or the ill-fated deerslayer Natty Bumppo, who fared so badly in his love-affairs, I know not; but I always had the most wonderful ideas of the great West, and was in every way prepared to look at the country 'of the setting sun' and its people through rose-coloured spectacles."[2] His disappointment came not so much through any encounter with live Indians as with the realization that the spirit of contemporary America had little or nothing to do with the virtues with which Cooper invested the country's original inhabitants. Like so many English travelers, he swiftly moved into a lament for a total "absence of public, commercial, and private morality among its citizens, combined with a spirit of narrow-mindedness which is but all too apparent in every class of the community" (42). When Burnett described how her family emigrated in 1865 from the Lancashire mill town of Cheetham Hill, near Manchester, to Tennessee, she too complained that although the occasional Indian could be seen in their new locality,

> they were neither bloodthirsty or majestic. They did not build wigwams in the forests, or wear moccasins and wampum; they did not say "The words of the Pale Face make warm the heart of the White Eagle."
>
> "They gener'ly come a-beggin' somepn good to eat," one of the white house-owners said to her. "Vittles, or a chew er terbacker or a dram er whiskey is what *they're* arter. An he'll lie *an'* steal, a Injun will, as long as he's an Injun. I hain't no use for a Injun."
>
> This was not like Fenimore Cooper, but she persuaded herself that the people she questioned had not chanced to meet the right kind of Aborigine. She preferred Fenimore Cooper's, even when he wore his war-paint and was scalping the Pale Face—or rather pursuing him with that intent without attaining his object. (233)

It is now widely recognized that Cooper's portrayal of Indians was a composite one. As Robert F. Berkhofer explains, "like so many authors of his time, Cooper knew little or nothing of Native Americans directly, and so his works reveal the typical confusion of one tribe with another in customs, names, and languages. . . . Following the judgments of his chief source, the Moravian missionary John Heckewelder, Cooper's good Indians resemble Christian Delawares and his bad Indians behave like Heckewelder's descriptions of their enemies, the Iroquois."[3] But nineteenth-century British commentators, as well as crediting the novelist for predisposing readers in sentimental terms "to feel an interest in that extraordinary race of men,"[4] also perceived him as writing with accurate knowledge and understanding—so much so that the writer of Cooper's obituary in the *Athenaeum* felt able to make the grandiose claim that "hereafter he will be referred to by ethnological and antiquarian writers as historical authority on the character and condition of the Lost Tribes of America."[5] Particularly in the early 1830s, he was ushered into a representative role and lauded as " 'the great American Novelist' . . . the Sir Walter of the New World—one who was to do for his country what Scott had done for his"; a literary adventurer and pioneer; one who "stood, like another Columbus, on the ground he had discovered, and perceived that it was untrodden," who saw fertile territory ready for exploitation.[6] To be sure, there were dissenting voices. A critic in *The Dublin Review* in 1839—probably Catherine E. Bagshawe—complained at some length that "he has left wholly untouched the monster sin of the Americans—their conduct towards the people of colour—the red man and the black,"[7] and hypothesized that his reluctance to speak out against slavery, or against "the wars of extermination with the plundered and maddened Indians," must be the result either of humanitarian indifference or of moral cowardice; either way, she vehemently condemned the "degree of turpitude and disgrace deliberately and wantonly incurred by Mr. Cooper" (528–29).

This writer's attack, however merited, did not represent a majority opinion, and her labeling of Cooper as a "native American" on several occasions (490, 509)—albeit certainly not in a tone that suggests that she intended it as a compliment—points to the reason: his position within the developing literary history of the new country demanded that he be taken as in some way representative of his nation. Even if some commentators came to think that the comparison with Scott did not carry much weight and that Cooper, despite his vigorous style and the claims to novelty in his subject matter, had been propelled into fame only by a dearth of good American writers,[8] others were still, at the end of the century, building on the parallels between the two men. "What Scott did in WAVERLEY, ROB ROY, and THE LEGEND OF MONTROSE for a race of men scarcely known to the English public of ninety years ago," wrote T. E. Kebbel in 1899, "this Fenimore Cooper did for the Delawares, Mohicans, and Iroquois, of whom only very vague ideas existed on this side of the Atlantic."[9] Kebbel, moreover, touched on some of the reasons why Cooper should have enjoyed such enduring popularity. By calling attention to the repetitious structures of his plots, the eternal present in which his vivid scenery is encountered, how his characterization rested on stock types rather than sharp individualization, he demonstrated both the ways in which Cooper's five Indian novels offered a distinct yet predictable space into which readers could retreat and onto which, even more important, they could project elements from their own imagination, including their own desires to occupy a range of roles.

Cooper's "stirring novel[s] of adventure among Red Indians, which in the 'forties and 'fifties divided every school playground into Mohicans and Delawares, Pawnees and Iroquois,"[10] were widely circulated and frequently reprinted in Victorian England, and their influence lasted well into the twentieth century.[11] Cooper's "good Indians"—Chingachgook and Magua—endured in Britain as compelling stereotypes of courage, resourcefulness, and general manliness. Their methods passed into generations of scouting practice. For example, Robert Baden-Powell, in *Scouting for Boys* (1908), emphasized the importance of practicing one's powers of observation. "There is an interesting story by Fenimore Cooper," he writes, "called 'The Pathfinder' in which the action of a Red Indian scout is well described. He had 'eyes in the back of his head,' and after passing some bushes he caught sight of a withered leaf or two among the fresh ones which made him suspect that somebody might have put the leaves there to make a better hiding place, and so he discovered some hidden fugitives."[12] How successive generations of readers visualized Indians may be gauged from the changes in the dominant visual stereotypes that appear in the illustrations to these volumes. In 1838 an unnamed illustrator for *The Novelist*, which serialized Cooper's novel, presented scantily clad Indians with the characteristic shaved head and erect pony-tailed crest of the Woodland Mohican. Yet by the time that A. F. Lydon came to illustrate the novel in 1875, when Groombridge and Sons published it, Cooper's heroine Cora had changed from a figure from a keepsake annual into a Pre-Raphaelite medieval maiden, and the Indians who surround her sport more feathers than hair (and appear to possess a markedly more degenerate physiognomy). By 1900, when the prolific illustrator of adventure stories Henry Matthew Brock had his chance at depicting the dramatic incidents in the novel, Cora's assailants appear in the fully feathered headgear associated with Plains tribes such as the Sioux: a telling indication of how these latter Indians came to provide the iconic image (reinforced by Buffalo Bill's Wild West) of Native Americans. These illustrations, in their turn, demonstrate the two endlessly recurrent stereotypes of generic "Indianness" that were already in existence but that were further eased into popular circulation through the pages of Cooper. As Jane Tompkins explains, in the context of the development of American national identity,

> Cooper's good Indians often embody "lost" virtues associated with the heroes of epic, romance, and the Old Testament, while the tribal life they lead incorporates values associated with pre-Revolutionary stability and cohesiveness. Their radically and ethnically homogenous societies, hierarchical, governed by ancient customs and traditions, dignified, rooted in and respectful of the past, stand for a (quasi-feudal) way of life, imagined to be ordered and secure, that Americans believed they had lost when they overthrew the British crown. It is the use of Indians to represent qualities that white America lacked that motivates the nostalgia for Indianness pervading these fictions, even as they affirm the impossibility of union with the "dusky" race and acquiesce in its extermination.[13]

The Death of Cora.

Figure 14. Anonymous artist, "The Death of Cora," illustration to *The Last of the Mohicans;* in *The Novelist* (1838).

Figure 15. A. F. Lydon, "Cora and the Indians," illustration to *The Last of the Mohicans* (London, Groombridge & Sons, 1875).

Le Subtil seized the nerveless arm of the unresisting Delaware.

Figure 16. Henry Matthew Brock, "The Death of Cora," illustration to *The Last of the Mohicans* (London, Macmillan, 1900).

Their antithesis, of course, is violent, savage, and mercilessly cruel, with—as Kebbel put it—"all the ruthless ferocity and vindictive passions of the true savage."[14]

Yet the question of what constituted a "true savage" was a vexed one throughout the remainder of the nineteenth century. George Stocking explains how, in the 1850s, a growing amount of empirical evidence allowed scholars to ponder both this issue and the significance of the category of "savage" for understanding the development of human races as a whole, a preoccupation that stood at the core of early anthropological institutionalization.[15] The diverse types of American Indian culture—the similarities and differences between tribes on the North American continent, and the parallels and distinctions that may be drawn not just between them but between their appearance and cultures and those of other indigenous peoples—necessarily played a central role in the development of this discipline in Britain, North America, and continental Europe. Outside anthropological and ethnological circles, the term was bandied very loosely, and as Gillian Beer notes, "For nineteenth-century readers the scope of a term like 'savage' was larger than it can now be for us: it includes distance and superiority but need not imply repudiation."[16]

Very frequently, Indians were made to stand for a generic type of "savage," detached from any specific cultural or national frame of reference. As the eleventh (1910–11) edition of the *Encyclopedia Britannica* notes, "Indian," by the end of the century, had come to signify anything that could be thought of as somehow wild, strange, or non-European—Indian corn, Indian file, Indian summer. In particular, it was invoked when an allusion to cruelty or bloodthirstiness was called for. Thus Caroline Norton, a determined campaigner in efforts to redress the injustices suffered by married women, in *A Plain Letter to the Lord Chancellor on the Infant Custody Bill* (1839), cites Washington Irving's anecdote of the Indian "who struck down his favourite wife, killing her at a single blow, and then sate in stupid despair by the corpse for three days," and the chief who dashed his own child to the earth as the result of a slight offense, where it lay senseless and bleeding, and then forces the reader to challenge his or her own value systems. "We read these and other wild stories," she writes, "and exclaim 'Such are the acts of the *savage!*' But I fear, if all were told, we might find savages more cruel in our own civilized country."[17] The Indian, in other words, could be a stereotypical figure with which to articulate the idea of savagery, yet "savages," exhibiting humanity at its worst, may be encountered in a society such as England's that takes pride in being "civilized." This represents, of course, a considerable shift in the associations of the "savage" from those borne by the word in the eighteenth century and which, with the resurgence of a cultural valuation of primitivism, it was to start to bear by the end of the century. But that time had not yet arrived, and, writing in 1885, the linguist and anthropologist Max Müller was confidently able to give a succinct history of the word's shift in meaning.

> There was a time when the savage was held up to the civilized man as the inhabitant of a lost paradise—a being of innocence, simplicity, purity, and nobility. Rousseau ascribed to his son of nature all the perfection which he looked for in vain in Paris and London. At present, when so many philosophers are on the look-out for the missing link between man and beast, the savage, even if he has established his right to the name of man, cannot be painted black enough. He must be at least a man who maltreats his women, murders his children, kills and eats his fellow creatures, and commits crimes from which even animals would shrink.[18]

DICKENS AND THE NATIVE AMERICAN

This double-edged definition of the savage was one with which Dickens ironically played when he entitled his notorious 1853 piece in *Household Words* "The Noble Savage." Dickens's attitude toward Indians is far less stable than this offensive essay would suggest. In part, this inconsistency is characteristic of his journalistic practice. His opinions about these figures sway around according to what appear to be far more deep-rooted commitments to the underlying ends served by his references to the Indian. To some extent, this mutability is made possible because, as we have seen, the figure of the Indian was not incorporated into a national imaginary, nor did it, in Susan Scheckel's words, "haunt the national conscience and . . . pose troubling challenges to national character and legitimacy,"[19] as it did in the United States. Dickens nonetheless repeatedly adopted it for his own nationalistic ends. Whether he depicted Indians in a positive or a negative light depended, above all, on the part he wished them to play in relation to his moral critique of English society. As Amanda Anderson has written, "Dickens's nationalism is largely a frustrated ideal, not bald chauvinism,"[20] and it is therefore fitting that his expression of it should be built on antitheses rather than example. It was a nationalism built on not so much any ideal of statehood as one of responsible community, a nationalism posited on looking inward, not out—except for purposes of comparison. His antitypes can be located in the treatment that Indians received, or in elements that were projected onto the Indians themselves; in other words, they were antitypes of both collective and individual behavior. In both cases,

Dickens is a perfect exemplum of the maxim that "nationalism defined itself against 'others.' "[21]

Dickens's first notions of Native Americans came from his visit to Catlin's show—before live Indians joined it—and from Catlin's writings. He claimed, "I am greatly taken with him, and strongly interested in his descriptions,"[22] and his remarks about the Indians he encountered during his 1842 American trip were clearly inflected through the American's standpoint.[23] Sunset over the prairies, he wrote to his friend and future biographer John Forster, "looked like that ruddy sketch of Catlin's."[24] Finding the scenery monotonous, with endlessly repeating forest and swamps, he wrote to the painter Daniel Maclise: "I dress up imaginary tribes of Indians, as we rattle on, and scatter them among the trees as they used to be—sleeping in their blankets, cleaning their arms, nursing brown children, and so forth. But saving an occasional log hut, with children at the door, or a slave house, or a white man with an axe and a great dog, long miles and miles are wholly destitute of life, or change of any kind."[25] The depopulation of land through the removal of its original inhabitants was placed in its fuller political context when Dickens saw the treaties made with the "poor Indians" that were kept in the capital in Harrisburg. Eighteenth-century representatives of the Delaware, Iroquois, Susquehanna, and other Indian lands had signed these treaties, often with drawings representing their names. Dickens wrote to Forster about the way in which these marks moved him and, in *American Notes*, expanded the point to draw the Native Americans close to a vanishing English rural, rooted tradition, simultaneously idealizing and infantilizing the primitive.

> I could not but think—as I looked at these feeble and tremulous productions of hands which could draw the longest arrow to the head in a stout elk-horn bow, or split a bead or feather with a rifle-ball—of Crabbe's musings over the Parish Register, and the irregular scratches made with a pen, by men who would plough a lengthy furrow straight from end to end. Nor could I help bestowing many sorrowful thoughts upon the simple warriors whose hands and hearts were set there, in all truth and honesty; and who only learned in course of time from white men how to break their faith, and quibble out of forms and bonds. I wondered, too, how many times the credulous Big Turtle, or trusting Little Hatchet, had put his mark to treaties which were falsely read to him; and had signed away, he knew not what, until it went and cast him loose upon the new possessors of the land, a savage indeed.[26]

A month afterward, he saw the process of land dispossession at first-hand. At Upper Sandusky, a village inhabited by the Wyandot Indians, Dickens's visit coincided with the presence of the American government's representative, Colonel John Johnston, "who had just concluded a treaty with these people by which they bound themselves, in consideration of a certain annual sum, to remove next year to some land provided for them, west of the Mississippi, and a little way beyond St Louis." Johnston gave Dickens what he terms "a moving account of their strong attachment to the familiar scenes of their infancy, and in particular to the burial-places of their kindred; and of their great reluctance to leave them. He had witnessed many such removals, and always with pain, though he knew that they departed for their own good." Dickens added that this tribe had discussed the question of whether they should go or stay a couple of days previously. When the result was known, "the minority (a large one) cheerfully yielded to the rest, and withdrew all kind of opposition" (216–17). One wonders what kind of choice the Wyandot really felt they had; Johnston notes in his memoirs that "the night they agreed to give it up, many of the chiefs shed tears."[27] The sense of regret at dispossession that Dickens had voiced a few chapters earlier, writing of "one's feelings of compassion for the extinct tribes who lived so pleasantly" on the banks of the Allegheny (178), seems muted both by his personal contact with Johnston and the reasoning that he advanced, and also, doubtless, by the fact that the Wyandot he met were somewhat short on appeal to the picturesque imagination. "They are a fine people, but degraded and broken down. If you could see any of their men and women on a race-course in England, you would not know them from gipsies,"[28] he wrote to Forster, keeping the comparison in *American Notes* and adding the consumption of alcohol as a further reason for their decline; state prohibition of liquor on Indian lands did not, he observed, prevent them from buying it from peddlers.

The comparison with Gypsies was not a novel one. It had been made back in the eighteenth century by Frances Brooke, when Arabella Fermor, corresponding from Canada, asked her friend Lucy whether she did not think that "my good sisters the squaws seem to live something the kind of life of our gipsies? The idea struck me as they were dancing. I assure you, there is a good deal of resemblance in their persons: I have seen a fine old seasoned female gypsey, of as dark a complexion as a savage: they are all equally marked as children of the sun."[29]

Walter Scott, in *Guy Mannering* (1815), wrote of the Gypsies of Scotland that they had not been greatly altered by the passage of time, and that they remained "the Pariahs of Scotland, living like Wild Indians among European settlers, and, like them, judged of rather by their own customs, habits, and opinions, than as if they had been members of the civilized part of the community."[30] The comparison between Gypsies and Native Americans was frequently made by travel writers as well, and it formed a point of reference for transatlantic travelers in both directions. Marianne North described the seasonal migrations of the Huron: "They were spread about, some hunting, and some doing small pedlaring at watering-places in the way our gipsies do at home;"[31] while Lydia Sigourney commented on the English Gypsies that she encountered in the Lake District: "Pilfering and palmistry are said to be indigenous among them; yet, like our aboriginal Americans, they have some strong traits of character, susceptibilities both of revenge and gratitude."[32] The terms in which Gypsies were described shifted during the century, however. Rather than being seen as alien figures, they were increasingly invoked to suggest an alternative, attractive, and escapist mode of existence that was somehow in tune with nature, opposed to what Matthew Arnold, in "The Scholar-Gipsy" (1853) famously termed "this strange disease of modern life,/With its sick hurry, its divided aims,/Its heads o'ertax'd, its palsied hearts."[33] This usage readily spilled over into the comparisons that were made between them and Native Americans. So when in 1894, Lindesay Brine, the former vice admiral of the British navy, published *Travels amongst American Indians* and described his 1869 visit to a Sioux encampment in Minnesota, his perspective was strongly inflected by an attitude toward Gypsy life that Deborah Nord has located, in her turn, among the members of the British fin-de-siècle Gypsy Lore Society. This attitude was positioned "between scholarship and mystification, between a serious, empirical attempt to uncover the nature of Gypsy culture and language and an insistence, born of the lorists' own need to find remnants of a golden age, that the chimera of the wholly authentic Gypsy"—or in this case, Indian—was real.[34]

Good fires were burning brightly in the centre of the wigwams, the kettles were hung over them, the water was boiling, and the interiors were cheerful scenes of enjoyment. The life within and without, was similar to what may be seen in an English gipsy encampment in the New Forest in Hampshire. There was something singularly attractive in the habits of life amongst these wandering nomads, and the warmth and comfort inside the tents, was in pleasing contrast to the cold and wintry aspect without. This simple and natural state of existence, has unquestionably a great charm for those whose natures are essentially Bohemian.[35]

Dickens's comparison of Indians and Gypsies is much less of an exercise in personal projection than that which Brine was wistfully to put across. In recognizing the degeneration that the consumption of alcohol and other factors had brought about, he was supported by many contemporary and subsequent travelers, who rarely encountered indigenous peoples who did not live on the edge of white settlements, and who were hence particularly vulnerable to the availability of cheap liquor. They habitually noted, too, the dislocation caused by the disappearance of customary patterns of Indian life: a combination of factors that rendered them—in William Kingston's terms—"miserable, melancholy specimens of humanity, brought thus low by a pseudo civilisation."[36] Again and again, we hear commentators lamenting, like Frederick Marryat, "how the proud Indian warrior, the most eloquent of his race, the last chief of the six nations, would demean himself by begging for a sixpence to buy more rum."[37] Major Sir Rose Lambart Price notes, still less sympathetically, that "any one desirous of seeing the 'noble savage' can get plenty of him all over Utah . . . as the Mormons encourage and feed them for purposes of their own, there are usually plenty idling the time away, with dirty blankets, painted faces, and half drunk."[38] Not only is a drunk Indian a sign of a propensity toward degeneration—something that may, in turn, be seen to signal the potential, inevitable downward course of the Indian race as a whole—but the effects of alcohol are often interpreted as magnifying the Indian's presumed natural traits: "The Indian when intoxicated is ready for any outrageous act of violence or cruelty; vinosity brings out the destructiveness and the utter barbarity of his character; it makes him thirst tiger-like for blood."[39]

Dickens's encounter shows him to have been well aware of the immediate social problems many Native Americans faced as their societies came into contact with a white settler society that was moving with unprecedented speed. Not only his alertness to the rapidity of change, but his unmistakable frisson of shock that native peoples could and did easily adopt the practices of Anglos come across in his typographically registered surprise when, on board a river steamer, he encounters Pitchlynn, "a chief of the Choctaw tribe of Indians who *sent in his card* to me" (184). Peter Pitchlynn (Hat-choo-tuck-nee, or Snapping Turtle), wearing European dress, converses readily about Walter Scott's poetry, praises Catlin's gallery, for which his own portrait has been painted, and explains to Dickens that he is returning home after some seventeen months, which he has largely spent in Washington attending the negotiations between his tribe and the government.[40] He is pessimistic about the outcome of these and thinks Congress lacks dignity—a sentiment that was very likely to appeal to Dickens, given how disillusioned he was becoming with American institutions. Nor did Pitchlynn hold a much stronger opinion of Dickens's own country. When Dickens promises that Pitchlynn will be well treated if he visits England, as he longs to do, the Choctaw "was evidently pleased by this assurance, though he rejoined with a good-humored smile and an arch shake of his head, that the English used to be very fond of the Red Men when they wanted their help, but had not cared much for them, since" (186). Pitchlynn seems to alternate between the two current prophesies for the Native American.

Figure 17. Charles Fenderich, *Peter Perkins Pitchlynn*. Lithograph, 1842.

On one hand, he fears that Indians will take the extinction route, "the gradual fading away of his own people," but he also speculates about the frequently aired alternative—one of incorporation—saying "several times that unless they tried to assimilate themselves to their conquerors, they must be swept away before the strides of civilised society" (185). This Choctaw chief's presence is valuable in *American Notes*, since it gives an unsentimentalized portrayal of a Native American actively involved—as far as he was able—in shaping the future, for himself, his tribe, and natives more generally, and not remaining as a picturesque or degenerate relict. Dickens's final verdict on him is that he was "as stately and complete a gentleman of Nature's making, as ever I beheld" (211). Despite the obvious contradictions contained within this statement—"naturalness" is a very slanted claim to make on behalf of someone who has been deliberately engaged in constructing an outward appearance and demeanor that would quite ensure he would be treated with respect by members of the dominant society—Dickens's portrayal of Pitchlynn constitutes a counterblast from a popular author to the idea of the Indian as no more than a picturesque anachronism.[41]

The figure of the Native American makes one more appearance in *American Notes*, at the end of the powerful chapter on slavery. Here the broader context of Dickens's sympathetic treatment of native peoples in this work becomes even more apparent. He claims it would be hypocritical to denounce tribal savagery—which lay behind the popular image of the bloodthirsty scalping Indian—and yet "smile upon the cruelties of Christian men." Indeed, cruelty against the country's indigenous population is, he writes, inseparable from the inhumanity of slavery. Dickens asks whether we should

> exult above the scattered memory of that stately race, and triumph in the white enjoyment of their broad possessions? Rather, for me, restore the forest and the Indian village; in lieu of stars and stripes, let some poor feather flutter in the breeze; replace the streets and squares by wigwams; and though the death-song of a hundred haughty warriors fill the air, it will be music to the shriek of one unhappy slave. (265)

The Native American, in short, here has been co-opted into the service of Dickens's more general diatribe against the dehumanizing tendencies inherent in American institutions and into his attack on slavery in particular. The greed of white settlers has become conflated with Dickens's dislike of the superficial materialism that he finds in the United States, and the dispossession of Indian lands forms part of the "'smart' dealing" (267) against which he protests in his conclusion. In the line he takes, Dickens, however unwittingly, is consolidating a lasting theme that has already been voiced in an important contemporaneous article written by Francis Head, the controversial lieutenant governor of Upper Canada between 1836 and 1838, and published in the *Quarterly Review* in 1840. Head bluntly pronounces that the American government lacks a sense of responsibility, even human compassion, in its treatment of the "red man" and claims that it is guilty of "flagrant immorality."[42] More than this, Head, in the course of complaining how indigenous inhabitants "have gradually been superseded by the usurpers of their soil, until thousands of miles have been so completely dispeopled," protests against another form of expropriation: "By an act of barbarism unexampled in history, their title of '*Americans*' has even been usurped by the progeny of Europe," something compounded by the fact that they continue to be called "'*Indians*,' although the designation is as preposterous as if we were to persist in nick-naming them '*Persians*' or '*Chinese*.'"[43] However, despite the fact that Head uses an inclusive "we" when critiquing this inaccurate nomenclature, he does not lump the British together with the Americans in his condemnation. Rather, he takes as his starting point an assertion of what he designates as a fundamental attribute of Britishness: a concern with the underdog. For him, "there exists no trait more characteristic of that innate generosity which has always distinguished the British nation, than the support which an individual, in proportion as he is weak, friendless, and indeed notwithstanding his faults, has invariably received from it whenever he has been seen, under any circumstances, ruined and overwhelmed in a collision with a superior strength."[44] This was to remain a dominant line in British and Anglo-Canadian rhetoric throughout the nineteenth century, presented as a strong contrast with Americans when it came to attitudes toward racial "inferiors" and put forward as a badge of presumed national superiority.

Dickens's aim was not, though, specifically to point up Britain's preferable moral standpoint toward the disempowered but to express dismay at the "foul growth" of America, which he saw as having been nourished by—among other things—its noxious press. This was one of the chief agencies through which, he lamented, "year by year, the memory of the Great Fathers of the Revolution must be outraged more and more, in the bad life of their degenerate Child" (287).[45] Rather than Dickens employing the familiar trope of the Noble Savage as child, the infantilized party in this relationship is modern America, the unruly offspring of the mother country.

And yet, just over a decade after he published *American Notes*, Dickens wrote quite differently. In "The Noble Savage," his *Household Words* article of 11 June 1853, he looked back with scorn at Catlin's show. He flattered this particular American as an individual, as "an energetic, earnest man who had lived among more tribes of Indians than I need reckon up here," but reviled his live exhibits:

> With his party of Indians squatting and spitting on the table before him, or dancing their miserable jigs after their own dreary manner, he called, in all good faith, upon his civilised audience to take notice of their symmetry and grace, their perfect limbs, and the exquisite expression of their pantomime; and his civilised audience, in all good faith, complied and admired. Whereas, as mere animals, they were wretched creatures, very low in the scale and very poorly formed.[46]

He wrote of the natives in the same breath as the "Zulu Kafirs"— eleven men, one woman, and a child who were currently exhibiting at St. George's Gallery at Hyde Park Corner. In other words, he herded together not only all Native Americans but all "savagery," invoking Georges-Louis Leclerc, Comte de Buffon in support of his view that the "howling, whistling, clucking, stamping, jumping, tearing savage" was "a something highly desirable to be civilised off the face of the earth" (560). No longer is savagery a consequence of dispossession, of being uprooted from one's native soil. The Noble Savage myth was now, for Dickens, a con, a piece of false idealism, invested in by people whose senses, if only they would apply them, must surely give the lie to the image. Unsurprisingly, in the light of this, little redeems the figure within Dickens's fiction of this period. When he needed the obverse of civilization, the Native American came to mind. Here he was doing no more than reflect the fact that outside the serious press, the impact made by Catlin's show in particular and by the idea of the Native American in general was not, in many instances, seen in any direct relation to the historical trajectory of aboriginal populations. Rather, as he confirmed, the homogenized Indian increasingly functioned as a byword for strangeness and otherness in Victorian England, frequently with the added connotations of violence and uncouthness. Mid- and late-Victorian fiction is studded with references that casually recycle familiar, degrading typologies. In Ellen Wood's *East Lynne*, an unpopular parliamentary candidate is ducked in a pond, and the local youth, "in wild delight, joined hands around the pool, and danced the demon's dance, like so many red Indians."[47] In the New Woman writer George Egerton's short story "Virgin Soil" (1894), a tale attacking the preternatural naïveté with which respectable young women were expected to enter into marriage, the unhappily married girl complains, "My dear mother, the ceremony had no meaning for me, I simply did not know what I was signing my name to, or what I was vowing to do. I might as well have signed my name to a document drawn up in Choctaw."[48] It comes as a welcome surprise when the pattern is turned against the accuser; Elizabeth Robins, in her suffrage novel of 1907, *The Convert*, in which Dick Farnborough, a supercilious young man, belittles a suffragette speaking at a meeting—" 'She was yelling like a Red Indian, and the policeman carried her out scratching and spitting,' "[49]—places him definitely in the wrong. All of these examples form part of the popular imaginary concerning the Native American and, like more sympathetic expressions, depend for their impact upon what readers already think about natives, history, authenticity, and the wilderness.

One diluted response to the apprehension of otherness is, of course, ridicule, and this option is taken up by Dickens in *Bleak House* (1852), when he tries to raise a laugh by inventing the apparently absurd name of the Tockahoopo Indians—the tribe on whom the overzealously philanthropic Mrs. Pardiggle insists that her eldest son bestow five and threepence of his pocket money. " 'At the mention of the Tockahoopo Indians, I could really have supposed Egbert to be one of the most baleful members of that tribe, he gave me such a savage frown,' " remarks Esther.[50] Dickens's sense of the pressing need of England's social problems had apparently made him less than sympathetic toward the needs of those overseas, something that Richard Altick has plausibly linked, in relation to the Noble Savage article of the following year, to the fact that the reception of Harriet Beecher Stowe's *Uncle Tom's Cabin* overshadowed that of *Bleak House*, and that her visit to England coincided with the "Zulu Kafir" show.[51] This, Altick asserts, aroused Dickens's competitive instincts, despite his earlier firm support for the antislavery cause. Certainly, he was not ready, in *Bleak House*, to co-opt the plight of indigenous peoples so that they could be used to parallel his concerns with contemporary English society, as Charles Kingsley had done when, in chapter 4 of *Alton Locke* (1850), he attempted to shock the reader into considering the harsh otherness of working-class life. Kingsley has the Chartist Crossthwaite explain to Alton how tough life is for working men, either making survivors of them or forcing them under.

> "When we do come out of the furnace, [we] come out, not tinsel and papier maché, like those fops of red-tape statesmen, but steel and granite, Alton, my boy—that has been seven times tried in the fire: and woe to the papier maché gentleman that runs against us! But," he went on sadly, "for one who comes safe through the furnace, there are a hundred who crack in the burning. You are a young bear, my boy, with all your sorrows before you; and you'll find that a working man's training is like the Red Indian children's. The few who are strong enough to stand it grow up warriors; but all those who are not fire-and-water-proof by nature—just die, Alton, my lad, and the tribe thinks itself well rid of them."[52]

In contrast to the line that he had taken in *American Notes*, Dickens no longer seemed prepared to treat the Native American with even Kingsley's seriousness. When the boys return to Mr. Creakle's school in *David Copperfield* (1849–50) and see the placard that proclaims David to be a biter, "some of them," remarks the narrator, "certainly did dance about me like wild Indians."[53] In *Little Dorrit* (1857), Arthur Clennam visits Frederick Dorrit, who lodges upstairs in Mr. Cripples's small private school. The boys stare at this respectable-looking visitor in silence until he "was at a safe distance; when they burst into pebbles and yells, and likewise into reviling dances, and in all respects buried the pipe of peace with so many savage ceremonies, that if Mr. Cripples had been the chief of the Cripplewayboo tribe with his war-paint on, they could scarcely have done greater justice to their education."[54]

Dickens's response to the Native American does not end with these fictional examples; an increasingly xenophobic trajectory, against which his concern with contemporary England could be positioned, would be simply enough traced if it did. His treatment was, in fact, highly inconsistent. In an *All the Year Round* piece of 1863, subsequently reprinted in *The Uncommercial Traveller*, he considered what he called the "medicine men of civilisation" and examined the strange costumes and rites found at home and abroad, wondering, in strained mock seriousness, whether

> the Medicine Man of the North American Indians [is] never to be got rid of, out of the North American country? . . . I always find it extremely difficult, and I often find it simply impossible, to keep him out of my Wigwam. For his legal "Medicine", he sticks upon his head the hair of quadrupeds, and plasters the same with fat, and dirty white powder, and talks a gibberish quite unknown to the men and squaws of his tribe. For his religious "Medicine" he puts on puffy white sleeves, little black aprons, large black waistcoats of a peculiar cut,[55]

and so on. The presentation of a Medicine Man to a principal chief provided the none-too-subtle parallel to a drawing room at Saint James's Palace, and the article moved toward its main aim, an attack on the wordy futility and absurd pomp of the House of Commons. "A council of six hundred savage gentlemen entirely independent of tailors," commented the Uncommercial Traveller, "sitting on their hams in a ring, smoking, and occasionally grunting, seem to me . . . somehow to do what they come together for; whereas that is not at all the general experience of a council of six hundred civilised gentlemen very dependent on tailors and sitting on mechanical contrivances" (288).

Once again, it is instructive to compare Francis Head and his determination to draw parallels between Indians and members of British society. For, as we shall see at greater length in the next chapter, a form of comparative ethnology was a very handy rhetorical tool through which British writers either tried to gain sympathy for their subjects as individuals or, as in Dickens's case, attempted to show that forms of social ritual, however different in their details, in fact constitute a common thread that links human being across very different cultures.[56] Head does this throughout his article. Can one, he asks, really call the Red Man barbarous when one considers the practices that Europeans adopt in battle, running their opponents through with bayonets, smashing them with round shot and grapeshot, riding over their dying bodies with cavalry? Scalping, he informs his readers, is "not perpetrated by the Indians as a punishment, but on the principle on which our hunters proudly carry home with them, as a trophy, 'the brush' of the fox they have run to death."[57] Catlin, in his *Letters and Notes*, was also to write that before we condemn the practices of Indian tribes too readily, we should yet pause and enquire whether in the enlightened world we are not guilty of equal cruelties—whether in the ravages and carnage of war, and treatment of prisoners, we practise any virtue superior to this; and whether the annals of history which are familiar to all, do not furnish abundant proof of equal cruelty to prisoners of war, as well as in many instances, to the members of our own respective communities."⁵⁸ Head, like a number of other Victorian commentators, draws parallels between certain religious beliefs and Christianity. But what is startlingly fresh about his attempt to instill the importance of cultural relativism in his readers is his determined paralleling of Native American and domestic British scenarios, such as the husband who comes home too tired for conversation and the wife who, having fetched his moccasins, tries to find out what kind of day he has had at work and at his club by means of familiar little signals.

The fact that Dickens moves, without apparent discomfort, from a sympathetic view of native dispossession based on firsthand observation to a satiric sneering at racial otherness, to a labored but not uncharitable form of comparative ethnology—in which British institutions come off worse, if anything, than Indian cultures—is symptomatic of the fact that different narratives concerning Native Americans ran in tandem with one another in Victorian Britain, pulling in various and coexistent directions. Dickens's writing typifies the way in which Native Americans mattered less in their own right than because they readily provided rhetorical tropes, something that subordinated them as racial subjects. Whether they are treated offensively or with a measure of sympathy, their position emerges as of far less importance than the damage caused by injustice, cruelty, and ineptness at home.

INDIANS AND ADVENTURE FICTION

Tracing the impact that James Fenimore Cooper made in Britain involves, as we have seen, acknowledging the importance of American literature when it came to establishing cultural stereotypes of the Indian, stereotypes that were reinforced, at the end of the century, first by Buffalo Bill's Wild West and then by the import of films from the United States which drew on many of the same motifs. Alongside Cooper, Frances Hodgson Burnett mentioned the impact of Mayne Reid on her childhood imagination, and she was not alone in this. Like the earlier writer, Reid's influence was an enduring one, particularly when it came to conjuring up landscapes of the prairies, the Rockies, the Southwest, and the Florida swamps.⁵⁹ Reid was the best known of all the British fiction writers who dramatized life in the American West; his influence, like that of Cooper, stretched well beyond the English-speaking world.⁶⁰

Reid's Indians shared many of the same polarized characteristics as those of Cooper and his American successors.⁶¹ Either they were violent, bloodthirsty, and a threat to white women and men, or they were presented as loyal, courteous allies and guides, indispensable to those attempting to cross or settle unfamiliar and hostile territory. Moreover, unlike many British authors, Reid engaged with the central role that the Indian played in the national mythmaking that took place around acts of settlement, in what Arnold Krupat synoptically termed America's "narrative of the inexorable advance of civilization toward the fulfilment of its manifest destiny, the extension of the frontier ever westward, ever forward, to establish a continental arch from sea to shining sea."[62]

Although undoubtedly, and urgently, motivated by economic pressures to serve up sensationalist incidents, Reid's agenda was a complex one. His transatlantic background positioned him to be able to write with firsthand knowledge of native peoples, and also to situate and interpret their concerns within a broader picture of American racial politics, especially as they were being lived on its southern borders. He had considerable experience of the United States.[63] Born in 1818, Reid traveled to New Orleans in late 1839, where he was employed by a large commission house and had charge of slaves. He left after he refused to whip them, and his experiences there generated his hatred of the practice of slavery. His career for the next decade was a varied one; he seems to have made a brief attempt at running a school, was involved in two trading expeditions involving Indians on the Red River, organized game-hunting expeditions, was active in the Philadelphia literary scene, fought with the First New York Volunteer Regiment, and, after being wounded badly in the thigh at the Battle of Chapultepec, returned to England in 1849. He completed what was to be his first successful novel, *The Rifle Rangers*, and continued to write prolifically, aiming books at both juvenile and adult markets. Indeed, he was so productive, and increasingly formulaic, that his titles, at least, could easily be parodied. In the satiric magazine *Judy*, in 1867, one learns that "Capt. Rayne Meade also authored the Prairie Pumpkin, The Indian Thief, 'Possum Chief, Kitchen Rangers, Mouse Trappers, The War Whoop of the Ojabberways, Humbug of the Rocky Mts., Mosquito Hunters, Flea Hunters, Holman Hunters, etc."[64] Increasingly, Reid came to write as much for an American market as for a British one. His early fiction, like *The Scalp Hunters; or, Romantic Adventures in Northern Mexico* (1851) and the vehemently anti-Catholic *The White Chief: A Legend of Northern New Mexico* (1855), is accompanied by full, informative footnotes, but he adopted an increasingly racy, populist style, with many paragraphs no more than a sentence long. When, in 1867, he returned to the United States for three years, he launched a short-lived magazine entitled *Onward: A Magazine for the Young Manhood of America*. His articles were composed in much the same manner, whether they were praising George Catlin—"a name too little known and too slightly treated," according to Reid—attacking slavery, or emphasizing the importance of democracy.[65] For at the same time that he deployed his punchy rhetorical technique to enhance the dramatic impact of his fast-moving plots, he used it, both outside and within his fiction, to press home his radical political ideals.

Despite his radicalism—a subject to which I shall return shortly—and his expressed belief in racial equality, Reid failed to avoid some prevalent clichés. Firsthand knowledge and ethnographic reading collide with the expectations of the markets for which he is writing. His stereotyping is as conspicuous in relation to his white characters as it is to his Indians. In Reid's novels, one can easily locate the four interweaving myths that Leslie Fiedler identified as creating the image of the Far West: "The Myth of Love in the Woods"; "The Myth of the White Woman with a Tomahawk"; "The Myth of the Good Companion in the Wilderness"; and "The Myth of the Runaway Male."[66] *The Headless Horseman* (1865) condenses many of these aspects. The reclusive Maurice Gerard—Maurice the Mustanger—disabuses the idealistic Louise Poindexter of her desire " 'to see the noble savage on his native prairie,' " pointing out that the average Comanche, " 'the noble savage' you speak of, is not always so sober upon the prairies, and perhaps not so very gallant as you've been led to believe' ";[67] the romance between the two, forged in their mutual love of the wildness and solitude on the prairies, is ultimately validated when it transpires that Maurice is son and heir to an Irish aristocratic family.

But despite this put-down of the noble savage stereotype, the virtues of many of Reid's native characters are often brought to the fore, and in a much more nuanced way than one finds in many adventure writers. The English Family Robinson (in the eponymous novel of 1852)—initially victims of an emigration scam that seems to have been lifted straight out of *Martin Chuzzlewit*—are apprehensive of Indians when they settle in what seems to be New Mexico, but they soon learn to rely on these "children of nature" for the environmental knowledge that is necessary to their survival.[68] Reid's early novel *The Scalp Hunters* certainly contains plenty of "savage" Navajo, capable of mutilations and other forms of violence as well as kidnappings, but his portrayal of the Navajo medicine man gives insight into what it might mean to act from the guiding principles of one's own culture. Moreover, his invention of El Sol, in the same novel, provides a striking example of a quite different type of Indian, one who has internalized Western education and values, complete with Oxford education, a background of travel, and a sound knowledge of both government and the natural sciences. Improbable as El Sol is, this is exaggeration for effect on Reid's part, bringing home, albeit in a very stylized manner, the potential for intellectual and social assimilation that he sees as providing the Indians' best hope. *The Scalp*

Hunters is significant, too, in its setting. Like Reid's earliest work, as he eased himself into writing fiction—"Sketches by a Skirmisher" (1847), *War Life; or, The Adventures of a Light Infantry Officer*(1849), and *The Rifle Rangers; or, Adventures of an Officer in Southern Mexico* (1850)— it drew from his experiences in Mexico as well as New Mexico, this time as a trader in the early 1840s, rather than from his army service. Reid continued to situate dramatic plots in the Mexican-American border area throughout his writing career, partly because its settings provided the potential for highly evocative depictions of beauty and wildness, but also because it aided his sustained belief in the "manifest destiny" of the United States. In this context, Mexicans are presented as corrupt, evil, and dissolute, their Catholicism attacked by Reid, to quote Steele, "for its alliance with constituted authority against the forces of freedom and democracy."[69]

In other words, Reid's adoption of the volatile political situation of the borderlands had much in common with the popular fiction Shelley Streeby discussed in *American Sensations* (2002). It constituted his acknowledgment that 1848 represented "a 'watershed year' in the history of U.S. empire, a year when the boost to U.S. power in the world system provided by the U.S.-Mexican War, combined with the distracting social upheavals in Europe, made the United States a major player in the battles for influence in and control of the Americas," something that, in its turn, "must also be placed within a longer history of U.S. empire-building at the expense of North American Indians."[70] In many ways, Reid was an enthusiastic supporter of what he presented as the progressive forces of American expansionism, seeing in them a drive energetically propelled by ideals of democracy that, at least in principle, offered both opportunities and ideals of social equality not to be found in mid-Victorian England. Writing, as he was, from outside the United States, he frequently displayed a sophisticated and on occasion very critical understanding of the relationship between the U.S. government and its forces and native peoples, an understanding far more critical than the popular fiction writers whom Streeby discusses.

Reid's Indians occupy a complex position in his racy adventure novels. On occasion, they fullfill the role of the savage other, yet members of certain tribes also appear as oppressed: not necessarily by the American government (although Reid has some harsh things to say about their policies), but by the Mexicans. They are positioned to realize that—as the narrative voice states in *The White Chief: A Legend of Northern Mexico* (1855)—"their deliverers from the yoke of Spanish tyranny would yet come from the East—from beyond the Great Plains."[71] Although in this guise they act as supporters of American westward expansion, the way in which Reid presents their tribal boundaries, which fail to correspond to other national borderlines, reveals a conceptualization of native Indian cultures as potentially trans-American.

Reid continued to work over his Indian themes during his whole career, maintaining the duality of savagery (Comanche, Arapaho) and virtue (for example, the Ute), often combined with the tragedies attendant on dispossession and injustice (especially the Seminole). In *The White Squaw* (published in America in 1868 and in England in 1871), the "signally beautiful" Alice Rody, a type of Caucasian beauty with golden hair, "a forehead of snowy whiteness, and a neck and shoulders admirably rounded,"[72] falls in love with Wacora, a Seminole chief, after he rescues her twice, first from the cellar in which she is hiding after a hostile Indian attack, and then from a swollen stream. Gloomily, the smitten Wacora thinks that she could surely consider him only a "vain savage" (148), a misapprehension that is turned first into an opportunity for educating Alice (and the reader) on the historical wrongs of European behavior toward Indians, and then—after Alice declares her feelings for him—into an expression of his sense of racial inferiority. Wacora explains how futile he had believed his love to be; how he had thought that " 'I, an Indian savage, was not accounted worthy to indulge in thoughts of love that had sprung up within my heart, like a pure flower, only to be blighted by the prejudices of race; that all my adoration for the fair and excellent, must be kept down by the accident of birth; and that while nurturing a holy passion, I must crush it out and stifle it for ever' " (153). Yet Alice not only marries Wacora but shares in his tribe's displacement by the government, the striking biracial couple attracting attention as they are moved westward. Although Reid is rarely this enthusiastic about the social potential of miscegenation, their alliance enlists the ideals of chivalry, as exemplified in the Seminole's behavior, in order to point out a way through which Indians might move forward.

Even more striking about *The White Squaw* than this racial optimism is Reid's strong awareness of the force exerted on individuals by their internalized racial prejudice and the way in which he uses this awareness to link the position of the Native American to that of the African American. Even if Crookleg, the African American in *The White Squaw*, is presented through a number of derogatory racist clichés—he has an "apish" skull; his eyes are "rolling and sparkling in a field of white"; he refers to himself as "dis chile" (24–26)—he is given space in which to explain the fact that his own bitterness and antagonism toward white people is a result of the treatment that he and his mother have received and to explain—to one of the white villains of the novel—that "if I war a black man I war still a human bein', although you and de likes of you didn't think so" (104). Reid's antislavery position is voiced more strongly in *The Quadroon* (1856), which Dion Boucicault substantially plagiarized for his highly successful play *The Octoroon* (1859), and in *The Maroon* (1862).[73] But his attack on the practice does not only provide an occasion for British readers to feel superior toward the Americans—the response that, in many respects, Dickens provoked from the audience of *American Notes*. Rather, Reid increasingly lambastes his domestic consumers for their passivity around this issue.[74] In *The Headless Horseman* (set in 1850 but published after the Civil War), for example, he asks whether it was a change for the better when, on the Poindexter estate, the "red children of Azteca and Anahuac" were replaced by "the black sons and daughters of Ethiopia."

> There was a time when the people of England would have answered— no; with a unanimity and emphasis calculated to drown all disbelief in their sincerity.
>
> Alas, for human weakness and hypocrisy! Our long cherished sympathy with the slave proves to have been only a tissue of sheer dissembling. Led by an oligarchy—not the true aristocracy of our country: for these are too noble to have yielded to such deep designing—but an oligarchy composed of conspiring plebs, who have smuggled themselves into the first places of power in all the four estates—guided by these prurient conspirators against the people's rights—England has proved untrue to her creed so loudly proclaimed—truculent to the trust reposed in her by the universal acclaim of the nations.[75]

Reid is certainly no consistent promoter of what Eric Lott has termed "the mythology of plantation paternalism."[76]

Without doubt, as Joan Steele has observed, Reid's treatment of Indians largely works as a reinforcement of Roy Harvey Pearce's thesis that where Indians are depicted in literature, "the interest is not in the Indian as Indian, but in the Indian as vehicle for understanding the white man, in the savage defined in terms of the ideas and needs of civilized life."[77] Inarguably, too, as she also points out, he frequently objectifies the male Indian by eroticizing him. Moreover, at the same time that Reid believes in Indian survival— "I do not believe that any race possessing the organization of manhood so perfect as they, can be 'shuffled' from the earth's surface so easily"[78]—he is, by and large, a committed assimilationist, his plots advocating this not just through cultural change but through intermarriage. Yet Reid, in addition to fueling the demand for incident, drama, and strong heroic models—and these include an exceptionally large number of courageous, independent-minded, and proactive women—ensures that his fictions, even at their most populist, provoke their readers into thinking about the moral implications of dispossession and of racism, lessons that he considers Britain would do well to absorb and apply. He makes this point forcefully in *No Quarter!* (1888; serialized in the *Boys' Illustrated Newspaper* in 1881–82), where he writes that it is difficult to think of any war in which Britain has been engaged since the seventeenth century that has not been "undertaken for the propping up of vile despotisms, or for selfish purposes, equally vile, to the very latest of them—Zululand and Afghanistan, *videlicet*."[79]

In Reid's somewhat rambling address to the American Thanksgiving dinner of 1863, held, in the middle of the Civil War, at St. James's Hall, London, he speculates why "England, so long wedded to a detestation of slavery," should in any way support the South.[80] For him, the answer lies in a deeply ingrained response to political terminology, since "the English child is generally trained to detest the word 'Republic,' from the time he is able to lisp it. He is taught hostility toward it, he is taught to hate it, he is taught to hate it in his church and his school, he finds it in his Common Prayer, and meets with it in his primer and spelling book. . . . How then can you expect most Englishmen to do otherwise than hate the Republic?"[81] Both in this speech and in his two seventeenth-century historical novels, *White Gauntlet* (1864) and *No Quarter!* Reid makes no secret of his enthusiasm for republicanism, whether of the past or of the present. He firmly links it to American as well as British history; Henry Holtspur, the Parliamentarian hero of *The White Gauntlet*, has passed some of his life "under the shadows of primeval American forests—on the war-path of the hostile Mohawk,"[82] and returns to England with an Indian servant, Oriole, who makes excellent tactical use of his superior tracking powers. At the Restoration, Reid portrays the spirit of republicanism, "together with many of its staunchest supporters," as taking flight to America, "there to breathe freely, live a new life, call into existence and nourish a new nation," which, in turn, would come to "control the action of every other, in the civilized world."[83]

Reid does not go so far as the Corn Law poet Ebenezer Elliott had done in the 1830s when, in tracing the export of republicanism to the United States in the seventeenth century, and in making its rhetoric enter the speech of those involved in King Philip's War, he presented the parliamentary rebels as finding support, and some common cause, among Indians.[84] But Elliott did not reach a broad audience, and his somewhat archaic poetic style, though clearly supporting the abstract cause of "freedom" with as much passion as did Reid, is far from easy to follow. Reid, by contrast, was employing and exploiting a popular genre for both commercial and ideological ends. To be sure, his enthusiasm for the message of manifest destiny is a reflection both of his own support for the ethos of American idealism and of his eye on the American market. Unlike many writers of popular fiction, he was writing from a basis of firsthand experience and knew that the neat binaries that characterize this genre do not readily map onto social realities. Much more than this, he was writing from Britain, away from the countries that provided the social and political arena for almost all of his fiction. Not only did this afford the perspective from which he, like Dickens, could see the mismatch between the inspirational language of the Declaration of Independence and its working out in practice, particularly in relation to peoples of color, but it also enabled him to voice political and racial axioms in a way that was deliberately applicable to societies other than the United States. For Reid, Indians certainly provided dramatic subject matter for his American fictions. Additionally, their presence, like that of his African American characters, enabled the articulation of principles that, in his mind, had transnational relevance. The political reach of Reid's Indians stretched far beyond the conventional arena of the popular Western.

INDIANS, SAVAGES, AND IMPERIAL FICTION

Reid continued to be widely read into the twentieth century. His portrayal of life in the West not only entertained a wide audience but proved inspirational to emigrants. Yet the transatlantic politics he saw as latent within adventure fiction were not developed by other popular writers. Rather, with the surge of nationalism in England during the last quarter of a century that looked outward to the growth and consolidation of a cultural, as well as a militaristic and economic, imperialism, this genre was easily co-opted to such aspirations. It also tended to present the empire in such a way as—to quote Patrick Duane—"to inspire confidence and devotion among the vast adolescent reading public."[85] Whether published straight out in volume form or after it had appeared in periodicals such as *Chambers Magazine*, *Cassell's Illustrated Magazine*, and the *Boy's Own Paper*, much of this fiction fell under the general category of "adventure writing for boys"; even though it was read by both sexes, and by a range of ages, such labeling established its niche in the market. Nonetheless, and partly as a result of the recognition that girls frequently enjoyed their brothers' books more than those which were specifically targeted at them, and partly in accord with the greater emphasis in girls' fiction on active, enterprising, and outdoors types, young women were also placed in hair-raising situations in Indian country.[86] Although Bessie Marchant's fiction—almost always located, as Sally Mitchell has put it, "in the wilds of empire or in exciting foreign places where laws of modesty and decorum do not obtain"[87]—is for the most part set too late for Indian encounters to provide major dramatic incidents, the threat of Indian violence is periodically introduced in a way that echoes the theme of Burnett and others: that reading had the capacity to provoke unrealistic expectations. In *Sisters of Silver Creek* (1908), for example, Mrs. Elstow says that she has never known a case of the Indians "breaking out" of the nearby reservations, " 'but you have only got to read stories with Red Indians in them to know very well what may happen one day when you least expect it.' "[88]

The settings for all these adventure fictions offered the potential for dramatic incident following hard on dramatic incident; as William H. G. Kingston phrased it in the first paragraph of his *Adventures of Dick Onslow among the Red Indians* (1873), "In few countries can more exciting adventures be met with than in Mexico, and the southern and Western portions of North America; in consequence of the constantly disturbed state of the country, the savage disposition of the Red Indians, and the numbers of wild animals, buffaloes, bears, wolves, panthers, jaguars, not to speak of alligators, rattlesnakes, and a few other creatures of like gentle nature."[89] The authors sometimes sought the chance to educate the reader, to some extent, about unfamiliar places, enabling such works to make the implicit claim that they carried superior literary status compared with the Western adventures that were published "penny dreadfuls," the British equivalent of dime fiction. Above all, they provided plenty of opportunities for the hero to display that admixture of qualities thought admirable in the young male of the time: heroism, loyalty, coolheadedness, resourcefulness, and protective behavior toward women. These qualities were ritualistically trotted out as prerequisites—or more like wish lists for character attributes that were unlikely to be satisfactorily fulfilled—for young men, whether they were to remain within the British Isles or to administer the empire and Britain's colonial outposts. Ernest R. Suffling is quite explicit on the matter when he states, in his preface to *The Fur-Traders of the West; or, Adventures among the Redskins* (1896), that his fiction is designed to show that while "courage and energy are traits to be admired, [it] also goes far to prove that truth, sincerity, and magnanimity should also form integral parts in the composition of the character of the boys of Great Britain."[90]

Almost all the best-known writers in this genre attempted at least one novel in which Native Americans figure to some extent. R. M. Ballantyne, who had gone out to Canada to serve as a clerk with the Hudson's Bay Company in 1841, introduced a number of novels that contain Indian characters, most notably *The Young Fur Traders* (1856), *The Pioneers: A Tale of the Western Wilderness* (1872), and *The Prairie Chief*, which featured a white trapper and a converted Indian with enlightened views:

One of the peculiarities of Whitewing was that he did not treat women as mere slaves or inferior creatures. His own mother, a wrinkled, brown old thing resembling a piece of singed shoe-leather, he loved with a tenderness not usual in North American Indians, some tribes of whom have a tendency to forsake their aged ones, and leave them to perish rather than be burdened with them. Whitewing also thought that his betrothed was fit to hold intellectual converse with him, in which idea he was not far wrong."[91]

Throughout, his plots celebrate Christian manliness, whether in a settler or a convert. But he could be unsympathetic to cultural collisions. In his novel of the California gold rush, *The Golden Dream* (1861), for example, there is a cameo encounter with a Digger Indian which is used to illustrate the absurdity of native peoples who attempt to assimilate by donning European clothes, but with no sense of how they should be worn: "Glitter and gay colour were the chief elements of attraction. . . . Sometimes a naked savage might be seen going about with a second-hand dress-coat put on the wrong way, and buttoned up the back."[92]

G. A. Henty's *Redskin and Cow-boy* (1891)—one of a handful of novels that he set in the western Plains and the Rockies—offers a lively celebration of cowboys as the essence of homosocial decency: frank, good-tempered, looking out for one another, keeping the "Injuns" in check, and adhering to a strict code of conduct that differentiates them from the Red Man. Unlike them, they would not shoot "at squaws or kids," even in revenge.[93] And W.H.G. Kingston's *Dick Onslow* was enormously popular. The future Methodist minister William Lax, growing up just outside Wigan, claims that his eyes were opened

> for the first time to a domain far beyond my native hearth. He introduced me to the Rocky Mountains, and to the wild life of the vast hinterland of the Dominion of Canada. I was entranced. I no longer lived in Hindley. In imagination I turned native and lived among red men and hunters, tomahawks and scalps. I transformed my beloved Bordsane Wood into a bit of the rolling prairie, and watched the characters of the book living, trapping, fighting, scalping.[94]

As this catalogue of actions suggests, Lax was unlikely to develop any nuanced understanding of Indians from Kingston's work; his hero ricochets from encounters with ferocious "Indian warriors, with plumes of feathers, uplifted hatchets, and red paint," attacking an emigrant wagon train (13), to rattlesnakes, a huge grinning black bear that has to be shot, a "red-skin warrior" who appears at his tent doorway grasping a tomahawk in his right hand, "which quivered in his eagerness to take possession of our scalps" (31), and nights disturbed by howling and presumably hungry wolves—and that's just within the first forty pages. The remorseless violence of the Indians, on occasion fueled by their

Figure 18. Anonymous artist. "Ned Linton and Tom Collins Meet with a Native." Illustration to R. M. Ballantyne, The Golden Dream; or, Adventures in the far West. J. F. Shaw & Co., London, 1861.

consumption of brandy, poses a torment to Dick's conscience, since he feels that his Christian repulsion toward any kind of retaliatory action is continually tested. His reasoning about the natives' behavior—is it a manifestation of human brutality at its worst, or is it in some way redeemable?—at first looks like an occasion for some general meditation on the nature of the savage, which starts off with a pessimistic view, but then changes into a celebration of the power of Christianity. One strongly suspects that the excitement of a quick-moving adventure story like *Dick Onslow* is, at least in part, the bait used to hook in the reader to the text's evangelical message.

> Talk of the virtues of the savage—I do not believe in them. He may have some good qualities, but he is generally the cruel remorseless monster sin has made him. Civilization has its vices,—I know that full well,—and bad enough they are, but they are mild compared to those of the true unadulterated savage, who prides himself on his art in making his victims writhe under his tortures, and kills merely that he may boast of the number of those he has slaughtered, and may exhibit their scalps as trophies of his victories. It is a convincing proof to me that the same spirit of evil, influenced by the most intense hatred to the human race, is going continually about to incite men to crime. The Dyak of Borneo, the Fijian of the Pacific, and the red savage of North America, are much alike; and identically the same change is wrought in all when the light of truth is brought among them, and the Christian's faith sheds its softening influence over their hearts. (52–53)

Kingston's churlishness toward the "savage," however, was not universal. Ballantyne, for one, is insistent about the point that indigenous peoples are not congenitally brutish but need good exposure to Christianity to become "civilized," for at base, as he puts it when describing the Inuit in the preface to *Red Rooney* (1886), they experience "joys, sorrows, hopes, fears, perplexities, and aspirations after the good, true, and beautiful,—very much like ourselves."[95]

Recognizing human equality in all its positive aspects was, however, only a step away from the growing perception, at the very end of the century, that there might be something like the "savage" innate within all of us. This is the "dim suspicion" of "remote kinship" that so troubles Marlow in *Heart of Darkness*,[96] and it is the sentiment that underlies Andrew Lang's dedication to Rider Haggard in *In the Wrong Paradise and Other Stories* (1886). Reading Haggard, he declares, is to "make one a boy again," as when one "hunted long ago with Chingachgook and Uncas." For "we are all savages under our white skins. . . . We are hunters again, trappers, adventurers bold, while we study you, and the blithe barbarian wakens even in the weary person of letters."[97]

A pioneering anthropologist, Lang was to put forward a far more reasoned version of "savagery" in his major work, *Myth, Ritual, and Religion*, which appeared the following year, defining the savage as one who was nomadic, not settled; a hunter-gatherer, not an agriculturalist; an animist, a believer in metamorphosis and in ancestral ghosts and spirits; one who is a totemist and credits natural objects with sacred properties. What links savages globally, according to Lang, is what also links them to members of more "developed" societies: the foundational role that they accord mythmaking.

Clearly, Lang was not immune to employing "savagery" in its more populist sense as well. The attitude toward Indians that he simultaneously put forward to Haggard and to his broader readership played into a new mythologizing of the Indian that started to take place at the end of the century, one that went beyond seeing the savage simply as uncouth. Not coincidentally, of course, this occurred at precisely the same moment that Indians, whether in the United States or in Canada, ceased to pose a significant military threat.[98] It was not yet quite that pull toward the idealized idea of the primitive that was eagerly taken up, on both sides of the Atlantic, by modernist writers in the early decades of the twentieth century—an ideal based, as Marianna Torgovnick writes, on a denial of the complexity of primitive societies, a nostalgia for some presumed lost simplicity in the past, and on an adoption of such cultures as a site on which to project feelings about both the present and the future.[99] Rather, in the late-Victorian period, the idea of the Indian was incorporated into fiction that looked to borrow from his supposed bravery and resourcefulness, appropriating, rather than expelling, the characteristics of otherness. Ironically, however, these traits were pressed into the service of a different enabling mythology: one of bold masculinity and a different mode of communal, national identity. They were called upon to inspire precisely those forces that sought to suppress, or at least hold in check, the distinctiveness and autonomy of native peoples themselves.

CHAPTER SEVEN

Indians and the Politics of Gender

"When quite a small boy," wrote J. S. Campion in the late 1870s,

> I was for a short period much in company with Mr. George Catlin, the American traveller, then on a short visit to my father. I listened with delighted attention to his anecdotes of Western life, and spent hours poring over his folio of drawings; amongst these, certain sketches of buffalo hunts (the finished paintings from which, by the way, now hang in the Ethnological Room at the Luxembourg) most strongly impressed my imagination. It seemed to the ardent young mind of a born sportsman, that to become a buffalo hunter was a wild and glorious, if most unattainable ambition. Catlin and buffaloes were, however, soon supplanted in my childhood's reveries by other youthful vagaries, and for many years I thought neither of him or them.

Yet in the early 1860s, the opportunity arose for Campion to go hunting on the Great Plains, an expedition that allowed him to "become familiar with savages and savage wiles, with Nimrod's modern representative, perhaps direct descendant—the Red Indian. He has taught me due respect for his grand old prototype, 'the mighty hunter.'"[1]

Campion was one of a number of British sportsmen who visited North America and recorded their experiences (as well as participating in the decimation of the buffalo), especially during the 1860s and 1870s. They were among the many travelers—some of them employed by American companies, some of them tourists—who witnessed the rapid transformation of the West in the midcentury, a phenomenon about which they wrote in terms blending fascination at the metamorphosis of the social landscape with the inevitable, requisite requiem for what was passing. William Abraham Bell, photographer and medical attendant to General William J. Palmer's survey party for the Kansas Pacific Railway Company in 1867, recorded how they

> left Fort Harker on the morning of the 11th, and, three miles beyond, passed through Ellesworth, a wonderful place, having seven or eight "stores," two hotels, fifty houses of other kinds, occupied by nearly a thousand persons, and yet just one month old. Six weeks ago the wild buffalo was roaming over its site, and the Indians scalped a foolish soldier whom they caught sleeping where the new school-house now

stands. The day of the buffalo and Indian have passed for ever; never again will the one graze, or the other utter a war whoop on this spot.[2]

Bell's text stands for a moment of transition when it came to writing about encounters with Indians during the nineteenth century. While he employs the trope of disappearance, he is also instrumental in circulating ideas about continuing "savagery." He represents native peoples in the language of adventure fiction ("the sneaking Apache or the treacherous Comanche") (1:28), and he goes to some pains to illustrate the cruelty of which they were capable, even as he understands the circumstances that lead them to attack whites. For him, this violence is not imagined, nor a matter of report, but observed at firsthand. He recounts the conflict he saw at Fort Wallace: "I have seen in days gone by sights horrible and gory—death in all its forms of agony and distortion—but never did I feel the sickening sensation, the giddy, fainting feeling that came over me when I saw our dead, dying and wounded after this Indian fight" (1:61). The bugler was stripped naked, five arrows were driven through him and his skull was smashed. "Another soldier was shot with four bullets and three arrows, his scalp was torn off, and his brains knocked out" (1:62). He was especially horrified by the manner in which one soldier had been killed. The Englishman Sergeant Wylyams, who had been helping him develop his photographs just the previous day, was left naked on blood-stained ground, his body mutilated, cut, and slit to show the signatures of the different tribes that had been involved in his killing: "The muscles of the right arm, hacked to the bone, speak of the Cheyennes, or 'Cut arms;' the nose slit denotes the 'Smeller tribe,' or Arapahoes; and the nose cut bears witness that the Sioux were also present. There were, therefore, amongst the warriors Cheyennes, Arapahoes, and Sioux" (1:63).[3] As well as employing his ethnologist's eye, Bell turned his lens onto Wylyams's corpse and sent a copy of the resulting photograph to Washington, from whence it became a widely diffused image in the government's propaganda war against the Indians.

In both of these cases, Campion and Bell may be seen as bolstering their masculine identities through the ways in which they relate to the figure of the Indian. Bell not only gains authenticity as a participant-observer, witness to outrages that epitomize his readers' worst fears about Indians, but shows himself to have a strong stomach and plenty of presence of mind while under stress. Campion positions himself—even as he also acknowledges the atrocities that he sees Indians to have committed at firsthand—as one who partakes in the positive side of their hunting culture, and in this he is not alone. Visiting sportsmen relied on the skills of native scouts and companions, on the fact that they, to quote

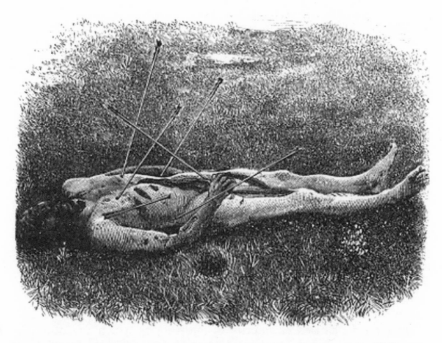

Figure 19. Sergeant Wylyams's body. Engraving after photograph by William Abraham Bell, reproduced in Bell, *New Tracks in North America: A Journal of Travel and Adventure whilst Engaged in the Survey for a Southern Railroad to the Pacific Ocean during 1867–8* (London: Chapman and Hall, 1869).

Francis Francis's *Saddle and Mocassin* (1887), "are wise as serpents, prudent as elephants, well armed, and intimately acquainted with every cañon, cave, and water-hole in the country," an accolade instantly undermined by the verb Francis appends in "in the country that they infest," as though they were kin with rattlesnakes.[4] Arthur Pendarves Vivian sets up his metropolitan, fashionable self in mildly ridiculous contrast with the native who is attuned to nature, as he commends the skills of the Micmac John Williams. He can trace their prey from rearranged forest debris and nibbled saplings, and blends silently with his surroundings: "With what a marvellous quiet stealth did those mocassins glide through the timber, not breaking the smallest twig; whilst I, trying to follow most carefully in my London-made shooting-boots, broke so many dead and rotten twigs, and made so much noise, that I felt truly ashamed of myself, before I encountered John's half-astonished, half-reproachful looks at my misbehaviour."[5] Away from centers of white settlement, whether frontier towns or army outposts, these visiting game hunters are in a position to observe Indian culture as it adapted to the opening up of the West, something that often involved presenting themselves as daringly bold.[6] Parker Gillmore, for example, sets out to repudiate the view that " 'Indians are poison,' " which he sees as "very indicative of the feelings with which the red-man is regarded by our trans-Atlantic cousins," since he has grounds for entertaining a more favorable opinion of them: "When the hunting-ground of a tribe lies so far to the north as to be out of the track of the white man, the adventurer may safely trust himself among them, for they are brave, honest, and proud."[7] Not only is there the implication that these qualities may somehow rub off through association, but these visitors also employ a different kind of privilege: that of the outsider who is able to give an authoritative overview. Thus Vivian, for example, writes of the "dishonesty," the "slackness and corruption" that mark the administration of the Indian agents; condemns the policies that ensure the mismanagement of undersized reservations; and even acknowledges his implicit role in ecological destruction when he records the "sickening data" about how many bison have been killed in "wasteful and sinful slaughter" by white men "armed with repeating rifles and six-shooters, and possessed with a wanton spirit of destruction."[8]

These works carried an imprint of authenticity which adventure fiction could not possess. Surveying the field in 1916, F. A. Kirkpatrick remarked that travel writing had probably been more widely read in Great Britain than any other genre apart from novels. Books of travel, and books inspired by travel, he claimed, "have provided the substance of a thousand books for boys; and thus, both directly and indirectly, have guided and fired the inclinations of many generations of boys. And every reader, whether boy or man, finds in his favourite books of travel some image of himself and some hint towards moulding himself."[9] This cultural self-affirmation was frequently built, moreover, on the assumption that life in wild, "uncivilized" surroundings somehow put one in touch with one's "natural" being. This, at any rate, was the spin put on such experiences by Mary Kingsley when editing her father's *Notes on Sport and Travel*. George Kingsley visited the United States and Canada several times between 1870 and 1875 (in turn, he had been strongly influenced by reading of Lewis and Clark's expeditions). His letters home chillingly describe the attitudes of the two trackers who accompanied him and Lord Dunraven on their hunting expeditions, who manifestly understood the grievances of the Indians, yet described their shootings of them as coolly as if they "were describing a shot at a rabbit, and would have heard the death shrieks of squaw and warrior with equanimity, if not with pleasurable excitement." They have, he writes, "the same feeling for Indians that the true sportsman has for game, 'they love them, and they slay them.' "[10] One of these trackers, incidentally, was Buffalo

Bill. Nor were these callous attitudes the sole property of American scouts. Major Sir Rose Lambart Price recalled hunting near Wyoming in 1874, armed with Springfield and Express rifles, a thousand rounds of ammunition, and several varieties of shotgun: "Thus equipped we were fully prepared for grizzly bear or Indians, the only two dangerous animals we were likely to come across."[11]

Kingsley's daughter, however, makes it quite clear that her father's sympathies did not lie with the attitudes of his companions, nor with the majority of white people who are desirous of wiping out the "poor brutes," although he did not believe that the world can "afford to give up enormous tracts of valuable land in order to enable a few bands of wandering savages to live in idleness."[12] Yet Mary Kingsley projects onto him an identification with a more mythical mode of Indian life than he seems to have encountered at firsthand. Despite her own adventurousness as an explorer and ethnologist (and her remarks surely owe a good deal to her reading in this latter field), Mary Kingsley had notoriously little sympathy with the growing feminist consciousness, and when she looked back to the effects of her father's absences from home, she indicated a latent fellow feeling with the phenomenon of the Indian who went out hunting while leaving his wife behind to perform domestic tasks. For her, such conduct exemplified her father's closeness to "natural," as opposed to socialized, behavior:

> I confess in old days I used to contemplate with a feeling of irritation the way in which my father used to reconcile it and explain it to himself, that because he had a wife and family it was his dire and awful duty to go and hunt grizzly bears in a Red-Indian-infested district, and the like. I fancy now that I was wrong to have felt any irritation with him. It is undoubtedly true that he could have made more money had he settled down to an English practice as a physician; also undoubtedly true that he thoroughly enjoyed grizzly bear hunting and "loved the bright eyes of danger"; still, there was in him enough of the natural man to give him the instinctive feeling that the duty of a father of a family was to go out hunting and fighting while his wife kept the home.[13]

Mary Kingsley's determination to collapse racial and cultural distinctions into a common humanity was, as we saw in the last chapter, a relatively frequent ethnographic maneuver when it came to trying to encourage an understanding of native cultures based upon principles of relativity. This "romance of translation"—to borrow Eric Cheyfitz's phrase—is nonetheless a technique that relies upon the reader's having a strong preexistent sense of racial hierarchy, which forms the context in which "the other is translated into the terms of the self in order to be alienated from those terms."[14] It was particularly revelatory when it employed a form of presumptive cross-cultural bonding among men. Çharles Murray, writing of life among the Pawnee, describes how at about the age of twenty, they are allowed to hunt and seek other opportunities for distinction, something he compares to an Oxford graduate's first appearances in London after taking his degree (1:261). The *Westminster Review*'s critic of Hubert Bancroft's *Native Races of the Pacific States of North America* (1876) takes up a similar line of argument when he considers the rationale that underpins tribal initiatory practices. Young men are toughened up by nettle beating and other trials:

> To have your friends kindly irritating venomous ants to sting you is not nice; yet, as this is attended, not by the ignominy of punishment, but by a sense of manliness already achieved, and coming glory, it may perhaps be more pleasant than painful, just as the bruises and blisters of cricket and boating are welcome trophies to the Englishman of eighteen.[15]

This is part of the strategy whereby he seeks to challenge the tendency to describe those from races "uncultured and unprogressive" by emphasizing difference (or as Berkhofer influentially put it, "since Whites primarily understood the Indian as an antithesis to themselves, then civilization and Indianness as they defined them would be forever opposites").[16] The reviewer acknowledges that native peoples may have very different standards of cleanliness, taste in food, body painting, piercing, and tattooing from those with which the reader is familiar, but asks that these be seen as the product of "climate, necessity, long usage, and dominant fashion," just as a "savage" might be bewildered by such oddities as boots that "pinch and crush and aggravate our feet, or the short dresses of the ballet, or the tight-lacing of fair ladies" (421, 423).

At the end of the century, T. E. Kebbel, offering a retrospective of Cooper's career, returned once again to the topic of the social role of torture, explaining that the "ability to bear it was with the American savage what veracity in a man and virtue in a woman are among ourselves."[17] Kebbel's apparent assumption that failing to endure torture without giving voice to one's agony was equivalent, in its capacity to produce shame, to failing to resist impulses toward falsehood (in a man) and extramarital sexual activity (in a woman) is notable in that he brings women (albeit white women) into the comparative equation. As Patricia C. Albers and William R. James have remarked, "During the past century, the most familiar image of the American Indian has been masculine. As stereotypically portrayed, the Indian is a tipi-dwelling, buffalo-hunting, equestrian warrior replete with warbonnet and fringed buckskin clothes."[18]

Although their formulation owes a good deal to the packaging of the Indian by the Wild West Shows and the movie industry, the tendency to regard the male Indian as exemplary of the race was almost ubiquitous among nineteenth-century British travelers. Their assessment of Indian women, as they encountered them in real life, was rarely tinged with the sentiment and pathos that, as we have seen, marked women's portrayal in romantic-inflected poetic works. Rather, in both the United States and Canada, those travelers, both male and female, who comment on the women they encounter very frequently do so in highly derogatory terms. Again and again we read: "Of the men among the Indians some were fine-looking fellows enough, but the women were, without exception, intolerably ugly,"[19] that the "squaws . . . were far more hideous than the men."[20] Nor did women appear to judge by different standards—that is, supposing even that they acknowledged they were looking at people of the same species and gender at all. There is an especially depressing and revelatory moment in Isabella Bird's *A Lady's Life in the Rocky Mountains* (1879) when, visiting Denver in 1873, she pronounces the crowds in the street "almost solely masculine," adding, "I only saw five women the whole day"; later, in the very same paragraph, she writes that she saw "hundreds of Indians on their small ponies, the men wearing buckskin suits sewn with beads . . . and squaws much bundled up, riding astride with furs over their saddles" (139–40).

Tested against contemporary British standards of feminine beauty, Indian women were almost invariably found wanting. John Donkin, an Englishman who served with the Canadian North-West Mounted Police between 1884 and 1888, was more explicit than most about precisely what type of Indian woman a white visitor was most likely to encounter in the streets of frontier towns. On arriving at Regina, his impression of the prairie as "flat and cheerless like a ghostly sea" was not improved by the sight of

> a Cree squaw, with painted vermilion cheeks, gaudy blanket drawn over her unkempt head, and bedraggled crimson leggings, [who] was standing at the corner of the Pacific Hotel, looking utterly forlorn, though dull apathy was written on her sullen countenance. Her tepee was visible across the railway track. These dusky beauties are periodically ordered back to their reserves; only to reappear again as soon as they fancy the official storm has blown over. It is one of the evils which follow civilization.[21]

This allusion to prostitution brings another angle to the denigration of native women: a distancing takes place that not only is a part of racial superiority, but is an affirmation of English masculine propriety, suggesting that those men who articulate their repulsion to Indian women are above, or immune to, the sexual temptations presented by frontier life. On other occasions, the register used to describe native women shifts from an uneasy curiosity with the explicitly sexualized to a yet more distancing type of literary set piece, in which the writer's cultural as well as racial credentials are placed on display. Bell visited the hacienda of a Mr. Maxwell, a large ranch holder near Raton, in northeastern New Mexico—a man who appears to have had an easy and relaxed relationship with the families of those Mohuhache, Ute, and Jacarilla Apache who worked for him. After noting the "motley group of squaws, papooses, and warriors" who clustered around Maxwell on the doorstep to his house, Bell passed around to the back, where he

> discovered the old hags of this party hard at work cutting up two sheep, which had been given to them as a present; and I can assure my readers that no manager of Drury Lane ever produced three more hideous or unearthly witches than were these half-naked, withered old creatures, their faces striped with red and white paint, their matted grey hair hanging from their huge heads over their sunken shoulders, their pendent shrivelled breasts, and their scraggy arms; while their eyes brightened and their huge mouths grinned with excitement as they plunged their claws among the entrails of the sheep, and scrambled for the tit-bits.[22]

This pejorative treatment was not universal, all the same. John Francis Campbell noted with decided approval the "graceful figures" of the women who plied their "embroidered nick-nacks" to tourists taking steamers across the Saint Lawrence and readily aestheticized them: "When night comes they make their camp amongst the boxes, roll their heads and drape their figures in some picturesque gear, and lay them down to sleep on the boards in graceful postures worthy of sculptors' models. There is no unseemly sprawling—there they rest with the native grace of a healthy young savage, still as veiled figures on a bronze tomb."[23]

At the same time that native women were being rated according to the degree to which they measured up to (or fell short of) conventional standards of Anglo-American female attractiveness, the label of effeminacy—readily attached either because the man was perceived to be lazy, leaving the women to do too much visible work, or because he seemed overfond of bodily decoration—was a recurrent means of denigrating the male Indian. British travelers and commentators seemed unable to think around the conventions of the binary divisions of gender, unaware of the fact that in societies where beliefs about gender roles were constructionist, "cross-gender and mixed-gender symbols, ritual experiences, work, and sexuality are a part of many people's lives," to quote Will Roscoe.[24] Roscoe's pioneering work on the role of the berdache, and the complex play of gender identities at play in daily and ceremonial life in many tribes, shows that it would have been almost impossible for travelers not to have encountered cross-gendered shamans or warrior women who defied the stereotype of the submissive squaw, but they rarely figure at all prominently in any British accounts. Anna Jameson's record of a woman who fought in the 1813 war is a rarity.[25] Yet despite the conventional association with bellicosity, a certain suspicion of Indians' unmanliness filtered right through to the popular press. In 1903, for example, the *Bristol Press* complained that the men in Buffalo Bill's Wild West Show were extremely fussy about the designs they painted on their bodies: "Such vanity is almost feminine. Certainly the love of feathers shown by these tribesmen is unmasculine."[26] However, Luther Standing Bear, who visited England with the Wild West in 1902–3, allows one to see how British conventional distinctions between "masculine" and "feminine" in terms of appearance did not necessarily translate into other cultures. When the Indians returned to Chicago after their trip, Standing Bear took all the men up to Marshall Field and Company's store, where they wished to buy fur overcoats, and while shopping in the city, "Some of the boys even indulged in some 'make-up,' such as they had seen white girls using, and it was not long before they could decorate their lips, cheeks, eyebrows, etc., as expertly as any white girl."[27]

"Lois the Witch" and Outsider Women

When it came to commenting on gender in relation to Native Americans, the usual strategy, whether consciously invoked or silently underpinning the representations, was to read Indian society in relation to the customary standards of white British or on occasion Anglo-American, culture. There is little to surprise here. Such assumptions of cultural and racial normativity have been extensively commented upon in discussions of ethnography, travel writing, and representation. As well as revelatory of dominant social attitudes, and illustrative of how shared assumptions can be used to consolidate bonds between authors and readers at both national and transnational levels, such writing illustrates the enabling role of the socially familiar when it comes to making vivid something strange. Similar rhetorical strategies are found, after all, in reverse. Maungwudaus wrote of the English social customs he encountered when visiting London in 1843:

When the tea got ready, the ladies were brought to the table like sick women; it took us about two hours in eating. The ladies were very

talkative while eating; like ravens when feasting on venison. . . .
They are very handsome; their waists, hands and feet are very small;
their necks are rather longer than those of our women. They carry
their heads on one side of the shoulder; they hold the knife and fork
with the two forefingers and the thumb of each hand; the two last
ones are of no use to them, only sticking out like our fish-spears,
while eating.[28]

Nor is it surprising that those who lived among Indians for a while had
their stereotypes disrupted. Nowhere is this more evident than among
women—settlers and missionaries in particular—who found common
practical and emotional ground in food preparation, medicine, ailments,
and child rearing. In the 1830s Susanna Moodie's "heart followed" a
woman who vainly brought her consumptive child for help; she recounts
a number of little anecdotes of mutual support, driven by a domestically
derived interpretation of history that led her to claim that the "real character of a people can be more truly gathered from such seemingly trifling
incidents than from any ideas we may form of them from the great facts
in their history."[29] Anna Jameson, who traveled to Canada in 1837–38,
wrote of how hard it was to get a proper sense of the Indian character
because "the very different aspect under which it has been represented
by various travellers as well as writers of fiction, adds to the difficulty of
forming a correct estimate of the people, and more particularly of the
true position of their women" (1:26–27), and in the third volume of
Winter Studies and Summer Rambles in Canada (1838), she sets out to
redress this. The Indian agent and proto-anthropologist Henry Schoolcraft, with whom she stayed at Sault Sainte Marie, wrote rather sulkily
of Jameson that she "appeared to regard our vast woods, and wilds,
and lakes, as a magnificent panorama, a painting in oil."[30] In fact
Jameson was notable for the care with which she recorded Ojibwa language and tales (much of her information came from Schoolcraft's half-
native wife, Jane) and for the attention that she paid to the status of
women within their society. Concerned as she was to gather as truthful
and sympathetic a view as possible of native people, she turned her observations into an occasion to comment on British and European gender
politics—in other words, to position First Nations women not only in
relation to their specific domestic and tribal lives, but also in the context of more broadly applicable, abstract principles of justice and
equality.[31]

So Jameson finds plenty to praise when it comes to describing Ojibwa
domestic life: the gentle ways of bringing up children, the common sense
of the women who take knives and other weapons away from their menfolk when they get drunk; their delicacy and modesty; and the fact that

they possess considerable property rights. But more than this, she puts into perspective the criticism that the men do nothing but hunt all day while the women stay at home and toil; this complaint, she writes, is predicated on a notion of hunting that equates it with riding to hounds in Leicestershire, "or at most a deer-stalking excursion to the High-lands—a holiday affair;—while the women, poor souls! must sit at home and sew, and spin; and cook victuals." Rather, for the Indian, hunting is dangerous and uncertain labor (3:301). What matters above all to her is that the women in Ojibwa society are not, as she sees it, in any *false* po-sition with relation to the state of society and the means of subsistence. The life of a First Nations woman may be a hard one, Jameson observes, but at least it is conducted in a symbiotic relationship with the need to provide for her own subsistence and for that of the society around her; she is not rendered a toy, a victim, or "idle and useless by the privilege of sex" (3:312).

Looking around her for atypical as well as typical examples of Ojibwa womanhood, Jameson recounts the case of one woman she learned about who had remained unmarried by choice. As the result of a dream she had when still young, the woman not only regarded the sun as her manitou, or tutelary spirit, but "considered herself especially dedicated, or in fact married, to the luminary." She used a rifle, hunted, and in her lodge had set up an image of the sun: "The husband's place, the best mat, and a portion of food were always appropriated to this image" (3: 71). As Jameson remarks, this woman would probably have been burned at the stake, "corporeally or metaphorically" (3:72), had she lived in European society. Advanced as a further example of native tolerance, as compared with bigoted British thinking, Jameson, once again, is engaged in comparativist, transnational thinking.

Witchcraft is central to Elizabeth Gaskell's novella "Lois the Witch," a tale that dramatizes issues of power and agency, seeing their parallel and intersecting trajectories in relation to variables of both race and gender. Set in Puritan New England in 1691, and firmly grounded in the historical materials that Gaskell took from the Reverend Charles W. Up-ham's *Lectures on Witchcraft*, published in Boston in 1831, it was serial-ized in Dickens's new weekly magazine *All the Year Round*, in October 1859. From the moment that she arrives from England, Lois hears of the dangers of the new colony, where the new settlers are continually, as Widow Smith tells the young girl, " 'on the look-out for the wild Indians, who are for ever stirring about in the woods, stealthy brutes as they are!' " Rehearsing what have become, by the late 1850s, very familiar stereotypes of popular culture, the older woman tells how she goes on dreaming, " 'now near twenty years after Lothrop's business, of painted Indians, with their shaven scalps and their war-streaks, lurking behind the trees, and coming nearer and nearer with their noiseless steps.'"[32] Others in the community present the Indians as, by turn, wily creatures capable of the most cunning disguises as they plan their attacks; as devils—"the evil creatures of whom we read in Holy Scripture"; and as political enemies, not only "in league with those abominable Papists, the French people in Canada," but in their pay (114). Although Captain Holderness, an old sailor, gives just a hint that Indian attacks on the English might have been prompted by the fact that they were inadequately compensated for the loss of their lands, he is soon speaking of them in the same breath as the pirates who infest the seashore and as witches.

Witches, as the title of Gaskell's tale suggests, are key to this story about the operations of prejudice. Lois goes on to express a certain sympathy for them, and how they (whom, from her experience, she sees as elderly women living on their own with cats) get persecuted because of people's tendency toward suggestibility and associationism, rather than as a result of any hard evidence for any damage they might caused. Almost immediately, she heads off to live with her uncle Ralph in Salem, a location that, to any historically alert reader, would probably have carried ominous associations as the infamous site of witch trials. One of the servants in her uncle's household is an elderly Indian woman called Nattee, a name that despite the negative visualization of her appearance as "of a greenish-brown colour, shrivelled up and bent with apparent age" (119), links her positively (and cross-racially) with Cooper's archetypal pioneer and backwoodsman Natty Bumppo. Nattee becomes Lois's conduit for native knowledge as she sits by the fireside at night, telling stories of human sacrifice made by her people out of appeasement, stories that, Gaskell indicates, are told partly out of a desire to wreak emotional revenge through the compelling power of strong narratives. The old Indian "took a strange, unconscious pleasure in her power over her hearers—young girls of the oppressing race, which had brought her down into a state little differing from slavery, and reduced her people to outcasts on the hunting-grounds which had belonged to her fathers" (127). Certainly, she reduces Lois to a state of acute apprehension when Lois goes out at night to fetch her aunt's cattle home. She fears, for example, that she will fall foul of one of the spells, left lying around like traps by wizards, that had the power to change people's natures on the spot, or that she will encounter the (curiously phallic) double-headed snake who lurks in bushes ready to surprise passing white maidens so that "loathe the Indian race as they would, off they must go into the forest to seek out some Indian man, and must beg to be taken into his wigwam, adjuring faith and race for ever" (127). Gaskell is swift to point out that we would be wrong to regard these stories as merely the products of another race, or to attribute credulity only to gullible "young imaginative girls. . . . We can afford to smile at them now," she writes, "but our English ancestors entertained superstitions of much the same character at the same period, and with less excuse, as the circumstances surrounding them were better known, and consequently more explicable by common sense than the real mysteries of the deep, untrodden forests of New England" (127). She is explicitly seeking to diminish the differences between Indian and English, and simultaneously shows that such things as the belief in a devil-like figure of evil, and other forms of irrational emotions that stir up feelings of fear, not only cross cultures but lie at the root of social persecution.

Gaskell certainly does not give an idealized portrayal of Nattee. Her description of the woman chanting "over some simmering pipkin, from which the smell was, to say the least, unearthly," is uncomfortably reminiscent of Bell's Macbethian witches (141). Praying together with the household, "the poor creature" is said, somewhat derogatorily, to have "muttered the few words she knew of the Lord's Prayer; gibberish though the disjointed nouns and verbs might be" (143). She is, for much of the story, an estrangement device, made to play her role in rendering Lois powerless and misunderstood in her new country, as the girl unwittingly becomes trapped in a train of romantic misinterpretations involving her cousins, young people who, the story increasingly reveals, are nothing if not somewhat mentally unbalanced. Manasseh wishes—despite receiving no encouragement—to marry Lois. His sister Faith is in love with the minister, Mr. Nolan—but he, too, is far more interested in Lois (again, this interest is unreciprocated). All this takes place against a background of the fear of spiritual possession—and of evilly prompted strange manifestations—that was slowly gripping Salem and that resulted in the hanging of the first "witch," Hota, the Indian servant of Pastor Tappau—in large part due to the testimony of Tappau's young daughter, Hester. Lois's third cousin, Prudence, is clearly fascinated, if not just plain jealous, of the amount of attention that a girl her own age has received and the amount of agency that she appears to have possessed. As Faith becomes increasingly, and unjustifiably, jealous of Lois and Mr. Nolan's friendship, Prudence seizes her chance to grab the same kind of prominence as Hester. She falls down in a faked fit at the meeting house and names Lois as the person who bewitched her. Shortly afterward, Grace, Lois's aunt—who has become increasingly angry with her niece for not wanting to marry Manasseh—further accuses her of having driven her son crazy (she willfully ignores the fact that he was decidedly strange even before his cousin arrived on the scene). Lois is thrown into jail, condemned to hang, and the day before her execution, another "witch" is thrown into her cell:

> And lo! it was Nattee—dirty, filthy indeed, mud-pelted, stone-bruised, beaten, and all astray in her wits with the treatment she had received from the mob outside. Lois held her in her arms, and softly wiped the old brown wrinkled face with her apron, crying over it, as she had hardly yet cried over her own sorrows. For hours she tended the old Indian woman—tended her bodily woes. . . .
>
> . . . In the deep dead midnight, the gaoler outside the door heard Lois telling, as if to a young child, the marvellous and sorrowful story of one who died on the cross for us and for our sakes. As long as she spoke, the Indian woman's terror seemed lulled; but the instant she paused, for weariness, Nattee cried out afresh, as if some wild beast were following her close through the dense forests in which she had dwelt in her youth. And then Lois went on, saying all the blessed words she could remember, and comforting the helpless Indian woman with the sense of the presence of a Heavenly Friend. And in comforting her, Lois was comforted; in strengthening her, Lois was strengthened. (189)

Both women are hung. Gaskell concludes her story by opening this localized moment in New England history to a wider historical perspective, describing how the people of Salem became aware of their delusions and subsequently made declarations of regret.

At the most obvious level, this tale may be read as an affirmation of Gaskell's Unitarian beliefs: her reliance on a form of practical, straightforward, generous, and inclusive Christian faith. Moreover, in the way in which Lois reaches out to Nattee, and in the manner in which Nattee apparently takes comfort and sustenance from the Christian message, Gaskell may be placed alongside those who were actively promoting the role that Christianity could play in "improving" the lot of the Indian and, in helping them assimilate into Euro-American society, in ensuring the continuation of their race. Gaskell had long been a friend and correspondent of William and Mary Howitt. Her first published fiction appeared in *Howitt's Journal* in 1847–48 under the pen name Cotton Mather Mills (somewhat ironically, the name of an influential Puritan minister who was a friend of three of the five judges in the Salem witch trials), and there is a strong similarity between the ethos of the conclusion of "Lois the Witch" and that of Mary Howitt's *Popular History of the United States of America*, which appeared in the same year. Here, the part played by women, both as agents of education and as apt learners, is strongly brought out. "As regards the Indian," Howitt writes, "missionary labour is increasing among his people, and where they are capable of receiving the instruction and civilisation of the whites, it is given. In 1850 there were 570 missionaries, more than half of whom were women, labouring earnestly in the wilderness, together with 2,000 preachers and helpers among the natives themselves."[33] An asterisk references "Miss Bremer's *Homes of the New World*"—which Mary Howitt had translated—as this text's source.

But more is at stake than Gaskell's support for the Christianization of the Indian. It is clear that Lois and Nattee bond in the end not just because both take sustenance from the message of redemption through sacrifice, but because both have been set up as "witches," as outsiders. As Jenny Uglow has observed, this is a story "in which communal hysteria is suggestively fused with private sexual persecution and jealousy." Lois is caught up in a domestic plot driven by male desire and by female jealousy (and by their desire to have some kind of power). Uglow picks up, moreover, on the allusion to Coleridge's "Rime of the Ancient Mariner" when Gaskell tells how Pastor Nolan, affected by Lois's innocence, " 'blessed her unawares.' " For those who recall how the Ancient Mariner was, in fact, blessing the "slimy things" that "crawl with legs upon the slimy sea" at this point, the reference is, she claims, "curiously disturbing," suggesting that "although Lois is innocent, there is some 'wild' element in women that both attracts and frightens men, some force that links them with the dangerous depths, with the untamed and the primitive—with the Indians and the forest."[34] Yet to read Gaskell's text in this way is perhaps to put too anachronistic, even too negative, a spin on her treatment of Lois, making her sound like a prototype of the New Woman writer George Egerton's identification of the "eternal wildness, the untamed primitive savage temperament that lurks in the mildest, best woman."[35] It is, moreover, to fall in with rhetorical patterns that depend on an identification of the Indian as Other. However, both Gaskell's Christian message and her less obvious but nonetheless quite identifiable feminist one stress the parallels between the English girl and the native woman. Both of them are victims of prejudice—prejudice in which, moreover, Gaskell implicates readers by getting them to collude in her own racialized portrayal of Nattee before we are led to see her as being as much a subject to injustice as is Lois. For as Uglow also points out, both suffer as a result of "public ignorance" and of people's "fear of the unknown" (475). As a single woman who fails to fall in with the plans of her relatives, Lois represents some undefinable form of threat, a threat that should be seen in the light of the animated discussions around women's autonomy, education, and employment which were taking place in Britain in the late 1850s.[36] Gaskell's fiction seeks to neutralize this threat by showing the human tragedy that can ensue when prejudice against the unknown overwhelms both compassion and reason.

POCAHONTAS AND THE NEW WOMAN

In *Bentley's Miscellany* for 1848, T. A. Warburton published an article entitled "Pocahontas, the Indian heroine." He opens in full elegiac mode, claiming that the "aboriginal children of the lake and wood" are now gone forever from the shores of the Atlantic, with only a "few miserable remnants" left wandering in the remotest forests (a state of affairs that is blamed on the contemporary "Yankee" who now "treads the hunting-grounds where the honest, faithful Indian roamed of yore, and the breeze that fanned his free bosom is heavy and polluted with the breath of slavery"). Consigning these native peoples to near extinction perhaps freed him up to mythologize their virtues, for unlike the travelers cited earlier in this chapter, he praises the bold, heroic, constant warrior and "the affectionate nature of the Indian woman—her persuasive gentleness of mien—her winning delicacy—her beauty of face—her symmetry of form—her bewitching and almost universal sweetness of voice" (41–42). This is all by way of a prelude to telling the story of Pocahontas pleading to her father to save John Smith, and the subsequent history of Jamestown; and the impression that this gentle, affectionate, beautiful, dignified, and intelligent woman made on John Rolfe. Although Warburton admits that it would have made a better story if Pocahontas had ended up with Smith, not Rolfe, he nonetheless celebrates the fact that "her life had found its appointed shelter in the affections of an English husband," and in the brief amount of life left to her, she had no forebodings that her own departure from her native land was some kind of prefiguration of the fate awaiting her people.

By the mid-nineteenth century, the name of Pocahontas was, in England, shorthand for an idealized version of Indian womanhood. Sarah Hale writes in *Lessons from Women's Lives* (1867) that it was by her that "the races were united; thus proving the unity of the human family through the spiritual nature of woman; ever, in its highest development, seeking the good and at enmity with the evil: the preserver, the inspirer, the exemplar of the noblest virtues of humanity."[37] Mrs. Octavius Freire Owen quotes these words of Hale as part of her own encomium to this representative of that "unmixed excellence [that] has always sacrificed self to the call of duty, at the shrine of public good."[38] When George Warrington, in Thackeray's *Virginians*, sets to writing a play with an American theme, ambitious to make a name for himself on the London scene, he hits on the legend of Pocahontas.

> An Indian king; a loving princess, and her attendant, in love with the British captain's servant; a traitor in the English fort; a brave Indian warrior, himself entertaining an unhappy passion for Pocahontas; a

medicine-man and priest of the Indians . . . , capable of every treason, stratagem, and crime, and bent upon the torture and death of the English prisoner—these, with the accidents of the wilderness, the war-dances and cries (which Gumbo [his African American servant] had learned to mimic very accurately from the red people at home), and the arrival of the English fleet, with allusions to the late glorious victories in Canada, and the determination of Britons ever to rule and conquer in America, some of us not unnaturally thought might contribute to the success of our tragedy. (715)

But the production is not a success; the audience hisses, whistles, and heckles. Most likely—although the narrator leaves us to infer it—this is due in large part to George's lack of skill as writer and director. He refuses to recognize that there might have been something absurd in the staging—" 'Miss Pritchard as Pocahontas, I dressed too as a red Indian, having seen enough of *that* costume in my own experience at home. Will it be believed the house tittered when she first appeared?' " (716). His old friend Parson Sampson surmises that the verisimilitude might just have been too much for the spectators—" 'would you have had Caractacus painted blue like an ancient Briton, or Bouduca?' " (718)—and George is in part willing to go along with this speculation; moreover, he starts to consider the implications of the fact that some of the sentiments he had put into the mouths of "some of the Indian characters (who were made to declaim against ambition, the British desire of rule, and so forth) were pronounced dangerous and unconstitutional, so that the little hope of royal favor, which I might have had, was quite taken away from me" (725). George's blindness when it comes to the transatlantic dynamics of Anglo-American relations in the 1760s is, at one level, just another way of showing the naiveté that accompanies his enthusiastic nature. Serialized in England in 1857–59, with a plot heavily dependent on twin brothers and containing the sympathetic (if slightly burlesqued) figure of Gumbo, Thackeray's novel inescapably invited its readers to draw comparisons and contrasts between the fraternal nations, Britain and America, and their linked but separate histories.[39]

As a number of scholars have recently shown, the narrative of Pocahontas has provided "literary and visual artists with a flexible discourse that came to be used to address a number of racial, political, and gender-related issues"[40]—something that has held true in Britain as well as in the United States. Back in 1859, Mary Howitt deftly highlighted how her young death at Gravesend served this process by removing her from being a witness to historical process while enabling her to endure as a potent symbol: "She fell a victim to the English climate, saved, as by the hand of mercy, from beholding the extermination of the tribes whence she sprung; leaving a spotless name, and surviving in memory under the form of perpetual youth."[41] Within America, the predominant image of this Powhatan young woman shifted during the nineteenth century from a model for an assimilated, miscegenated Anglo-Indian racial future, something predicated on her role as John Rolfe's wife and the mother of their son, Thomas, to one of protector, the savior of John Smith, who had emerged as a stereotype for the American hero. "By the early nineteenth century," Robert Tilton writes,

> Pocahontas had become an American historical personage, one who was in the ambiguous position of being both "other"—in that she was by birth a "savage"—and also (at least in spirit) an American—for her display of compassion that saved John Smith and with him the Jamestown colony. Indeed, to this day that act ties her to most Anglo-Americans far more strongly than her later adoption of the religion and culture of the English. (54)

Pocahontas's most interesting British reincarnation can be found at the end of the century, in a novel set in contemporary England: Gilbert Parker's *Translation of a Savage* (1894), which was a best seller. Parker noted in 1913 that "the book has so many friends—this has been sufficiently established by the very large sale it has had in cheap editions,"[42] and the same year it was made into a film for the Edison Film Company by Walter Edwin. Born and educated in Canada, Parker moved to London in 1890, where he lived until his death in 1932. A popular novelist on both sides of the Atlantic—he published around thirty works of fiction—he sat in Parliament for Gravesend (ironically enough, the location of Pocahontas's death and burial) from 1900 to 1918, where, an ardent Federal Imperialist, he was looked upon as a spokesman for the colonies.[43] The ostensible "savage" of Parker's title is Lali, the daughter of Eye-of-the-Moon, a First Nations chief from Fort Charles. She is married to a young British trader, Frank Armour. The chivalric overtones of Armour's name are surely ironic: his motivation was not love but revenge—revenge on his English fiancée, who had jilted him, coupled with a desire to shock his bourgeois family. He writes, tauntingly, to them giving the news that he has "married into the aristocracy, the oldest aristocracy of America" (18), and that his new bride is on her way to joining them. But from the start, Frank is placed clearly in the wrong, and Lali, his new bride, is idealized. We obtain a very favorable description of her as seen through the eyes of a sympathetic older woman on board ship. Racial markers are suppressed. Her skin color is passed over when the shipboard widow notes her "modest bust and shapely feet and ankles," her "large, meditative, and intelligent" eyes, her excellent hands, "perfectly made, slim yet plump, the fingers tapering, the wrist supple"; she was "superbly fresh in appearance though her hair still bore very slight traces of the grease which even the most aristocratic Indians use" (27–28). Notably, on board ship, many positive tales rapidly circulate about her—that she saved Armour's life from tribal warfare or from dying in the woods; in other words, she is easily written into preexistent narrative forms. Yet, for that matter, she can easily be slotted into the vocabulary of racial prejudice. When the letter arrives from Frank telling his family precisely whom they may expect, his brother, Richard, breaks the news that he's now married to a "wild Indian." " 'Indian? Indian? Good God, a red nigger!' cried General Armour harshly, starting to his feet" (34). Richard and Frank's sister, Marion, is just as outspoken, designating Lali as " 'a common squaw, with greasy hair, and blankets, and big mouth, and black teeth, who eats with her fingers and grunts!' " (34–35). However, the Armour parents, used to doing their duty, go to meet her at Liverpool and take her into their home, and it slowly dawns on them that she has feelings too, that she is embarrassed when people stare at her as though she is a sideshow (hardly surprising, since the headlines in the evening papers show that the press have gotten hold of her story). Understandably, they are at something of a loss, nonetheless, to know quite how "to turn the North American Indian into a European" (57). Richard—consistently the most sensitive English person in the novel—points out that almost certainly, as the daughter of a chief, she would have been used to respect in her own country, and he suggests that they would all come off better "if we treat her as a chieftainess, or princess, or whatever she is, and not simply as a dusky person" (60). All the same, Marion expresses some skepticism that it might be possible to present her "in a drawing room, 'and pose her, and make her a prize,—a Pocahontas, wasn't it?' " (61).

As Lali adapts to English society, the narrative unfolds to ensure that she has the opportunity to manifest many of the most positive sides of her Indianness—or, one might say, to ensure that she displays a range of positive stereotypes. Her love of nature, as well as her womanly compassion, is instantly demonstrated when she arrives at the Armours' house, since she exclaims with delight at the parklands that surround it and bursts into tears at the sight of a deer. She makes one spectacular assertion of her "wild" Indianness and independence—after she had been made to feel especially Other by being stared at in the drawing room—when she dashes to the stables and rider off on a spirited horse. Her ensuing fall, and the blow she receives to the shoulder, usher in a transition: "With that strange ride had gone the last strong flicker of the desire for savage life in her" (90). Moreover, she gains a new form of enlightenment regarding "the position she held towards her husband: that he had never loved her; that she was only an instrument for unworthy retaliation" (90).

Her circumstances change in a further way: she is pregnant (here, of course, one might note that had Parker not wished to pursue the theme of miscegenation as a totally viable way forward, or had he wished to show Lali as selfish in her equestrian pursuits, like Rosamond in *Middlemarch*, this riding fall could have resulted in an opportune miscarriage). The birth, indeed, unites the best of English and Indian not so much in the person of the (conveniently fair-haired) child, as in the First Nations woman herself: "Coincident with her motherhood there came to Lali a new purpose. She had not lived with the Armours without absorbing some of their fine social sense and dignity. This, added to the native instinct of pride in her, gave her a new ambition" (91). As Lali starts to move in London social circles, so other "native" instincts become apparent. She employs "the latent subtlety of her race" when she encounters her husband's former girlfriend—even though "her fingers ached to grasp this beautiful, exasperating woman by the throat. But after an effort at calmness she remained still and silent, looking at her visitor with a scornful dignity" (112)—the same clichés in posture and expression, in other words, that countless travelers had recorded.

Parker is careful not to present Lali's sense of her own assimilation into English society as entirely smooth. She remains acutely self-conscious that she is the object of curiosity on the double grounds of ethnicity and gender, and as someone who has dramatically crossed cultures, Parker imagines her "dual or multiple personality" as—in Gloria Anzaldúa's description of one who comes from the borderlands—"plagued by psychic restlessness," in a state of perpetual transition, unsure about which cultural collectivity she should listen to.[45] But she refuses to remain a passive outsider in her new life. Rather, she learns to capitalize on her position, not for personal ends but on behalf of her race. When the London press—the *Morning Post*, the *World*—shows an interest in her, "she did not hesitate to speak of herself as an Indian, her country as a good country, and her people as a noble if dispossessed race; all the more so if she thought reference to her nationality and past was being rather conspicuously avoided" (119). She acknowledges her sense of isolation—not just from her people, especially her father, but from her own language, as she says; "one can only speak from the depths of one's heart in one's native tongue" (97–98). As the novel's title indicates, the question of translation is central to it, and it is applicable in ways that reach well beyond the most obvious meaning, the "civilization" of a native woman, "though in part a savage,—now transformed into a gentle, noble creature of delight and goodness" (151). Parker plays with the fact that cultural, as well as verbal, translation may and may not be possible. He goes so far as to intimate a racial essentialism here, one that may well signal his adherence to a developmental theory of how different ethnicities relate to formulating and transmitting their perceptions. While he speaks with some awe of "that one great element in Lali's character—that thing which is the birthright of all who own the North for a mother, the awe of imagination, the awe and the pain, which in its finest expression comes near, very near, to the supernatural," he goes on to explain that "Lali's mind was all pictures; she never thought of things in words, she saw them; and everything in her life arrayed itself in a scene before her, made vivid by her sensitive soul" (230). This sensitivity, however, manifests itself as a kind of awareness of cosmic unity. In a passage that incorporates some Cree in the original, Lali acknowledges that the natural world, as demonstrated both in the curve of the dark night sky and in the presence of her own child, provides a continuity that links peoples and countries, however much social forms may differ. She looks out of her window, and sees the heavens,

> all stars, and restful deep blue. That—that was the same. How she knew it! Orion and Ashtaroth, and Mars and the Pleiades, and the long trail of the Milky Way. As a little child hanging in the trees, or sprawled beside a tepee, she had made friends with them all, even as she learned and loved all the signs of the earth beneath—the twist of a blade of grass, the portent in the cry of a river-hen, the colour of a star, the smell of a wind. She had known Nature then, now she knew men. And knowing them, and having suffered, and sick at heart as she was, standing by this window in the dead of night, the cry that shook her softly was not of her new life, but of the old, primitive, childlike.
> *Pasagathe, omarki kethose kolokani, vorgantha pestorondikat Oni.*
> *"A spear hath pierced me, and the smart of the nettle is in my wound. Maker of the soft night, bind my wounds with sleep, lest I cry out and be a coward and unworthy."*
> Again and again, unconsciously, the words passed from her lips—
> *Vorganthe, pestorondikat Oni.*
> At last she let down the blind, came to the bed, and once more gathered her child in her arms with an infinite hunger. This love was hers—rich, untrammelled, and so sacred. No matter what came, and she did not know what would come, she had the child. There was a kind of ecstasy in it, and she lay and trembled with the feeling, but at last fell into a troubled sleep. (164–65)

Neither this intense maternal bonding, however, nor the assurance of the overarching night sky can entirely make up to Lali for that which she has lost and for which no equivalence can be found. This is brought home during an episode in which Marion—by this stage, entirely happy with her sister-in-law—begs Lali to sing "The Chase of the Yellow Swan" in the Armours' London drawing room on the occasion of Frank's eventual return. (Parker's early career in Canada and Australia as a public reader must have given him insights into the power of performances.) This ballad had, like Lali herself, gone through a metamorphosis. Lali first sang it for Marion back in her early days at Greyhope "with the few notes of an Indian chant" (177), and it had subsequently, with the help of the musicians who had taught her European styles of music and singing, been translated and set to music—without, however, losing the flavor of the original entirely: "The song had the wild swing of savage life, the deep sweetness of a monotone, but it had also the finè intelligence, the subtle allusiveness of romance" (181). Understandably, Lali was apprehensive about singing it before someone who might completely fail to understand her attitude toward her past: she looked at it

> from the infinite distance of affectionate pity, knowledge, and indescribable change, and yet loved the inspiring atmosphere and mystery of that lonely North, which once in the veins never leaves it—never. Would *he* understand that she was feeling, not the common detail of the lodge and the camp-fire and the Company's post, but the deep spirit of Nature, filtering through her senses in a thousand ways—the wild ducks' flight, the sweet smell of the balsam, the exquisite gallop of the deer, the powder of the frost, the sun and snow and blue plains of water, the thrilling eternity of plain and the splendid steps of the hills, which led away by stair and entresol to the Kimash Hills, the Hills of the Mighty Men? (178)

Yet she was determined in part to perform the ballad so that Frank could understand, simultaneously, quite how far she had come, and that she could nonetheless sing of her past with pride and without blushing. Moreover, the song carried an allegorical message, one that is not particularly easy for either Frank or the reader of the novel to interpret (and that hence enhances Lali's own claims to a thoughtful and subtle cultural inheritance): it seemingly suggests that a wife's homage can coexist with a refusal to abnegate herself and accept a subordinate position, and that autonomy will win out over self-sacrifice. It is a message that moves Frank, who tells his wife that he will do any kind of penitence if he can only wipe out the damage he has caused. She, however, softens only slowly, and partially, toward him.

In part, the role of this modern-day Pocahontas is to rescue the central male protagonist not from hostile Indians but from himself. The enemy, in Parker's novel, is a composite of emotional selfishness, crude racism, and a sense of masculine entitlement exerted with no cognizance of a woman's self-respect or individuality. Even before he returns to England, Frank comes to feel ashamed of his actions, despite expressing his repulsion that he was "yoked for ever to—a savage!" (120). His initial promptings to lead a better life come from Lali's father, who impresses him with his dignity, solemnity, and moral resolution as he points out how Frank has been responsible for his own awareness of emotional severance. His feelings about the loss of his daughter act as a synecdoche of how First Nations people perceive themselves to be robbed of their identity by white settlers in far more general terms. " 'You,' " Eye-of-the-Moon says, " 'are of the great race that conquers us. You come and take our land and our game, and we at last have to beg of you for food and shelter. Then you take our daughters, and we know not where they go. They are gone like the down from the thistle. We see them not, but you remain' " (125). In a moment of improbable coincidence, at that very moment a trader enters, bearing a very old newspaper containing an account of Lali's riding accident, Frank rushes to do his duty: " 'It isn't wise for a white man and an Indian to marry, but when they are married—well, they must live as man and white should live . . . I am going to my wife— your daughter' " (129). And yet, even as he is on the verge of meeting Lali again, he fails to see her as anything other than a generic Indian, re-membering her looks as "showing her common prairie origin" (132). It is made quite obvious that the superiority rests with her, with her strong "desire to triumph over her husband grandly, as a woman righteously might . . . she was keen to prove her worth as a wife against her husband's unworthiness" (131). At no moment is this clearer than when she takes him to meet his son, and he asks her why she has kept him in ignorance of little Richard's birth, only to be told, " 'You married me—wickedly, and used me wickedly afterwards' " (142). Her teaching takes place not through out-and-out vengeance toward the self-centered young man who married her, and who was callously prepared to exploit her emo-tionally, but through a carefully calibrated moral economy.

One of the things that make *The Translation of a Savage* so interesting is that it is a generic hybrid. Given its publication date of 1894, it may profitably be read alongside examples of New Woman fiction. The figure of Lali seems in part to be borrowed from her spirited, articulate, sensi-tive, and artistic fictional peers. She is, without a doubt, presented as far superior, in moral character, to her husband. What is more, this novel refuses any happy ending according to the conventional terms of ro-mance plotting. Lali resists the temptation offered by Frank's kind, thoughtful, and sexually attractive brother, Richard (and he, for his part, restrains himself from giving way to the temptation that she presents to him). But neither does she give in to Frank sexually on his return; rather, she shrinks at the thought of doing her "wifely duty" to him (161), and it is left ambiguous, at the close, why they never have any more children. Yet in some ways, this is a socially conservative novel, which depends on the stability of the ideal of the traditional family to make its points about belonging and acceptance. For the true conclusion comes with Lali's assimilation into the order of her new family. Although this absorption takes place on English soil, not on the ground of new settlement, it has a good deal in common with what Amy Kaplan has described as the movement toward "manifest domesticity" apparent in relation to both Indians and African Americans in mid-nineteenth-century American fiction. As Kaplan writes, "The empire of the mother thus embodies the anarchy at the heart of the American empire; the two empires follow a double compulsion to conquer and domesticate—to control and incorporate—the foreign within the borders of the home and the nation."[46] The dynamics of embodiment are arguably even stronger in Parker's work, since the father—a man with a military past, at that—is so inseparably a part of the final family tableau. Lali receives, at the last, a letter "in the Indian language" from her own father, telling her, in terms both descriptive and prophetic, that "thou hast become great with a great race, and that is well. Our race is not great, and shall not be, until the hour when the Mighty Men of the Kimash Hills arise from their sleep and possess the land again" (232–33). It is enclosed in a letter from the factor at Fort Charles. General Armour gently tells Lali that her father dictated this on the day of the Feast of the Yellow Swan and that he then, that night, set out on a long journey.

> "My daughter," he said, "you have another father."
> With a low cry, like that of a fawn struck in the throat, she slid forward on her knees beside him, and buried her face on his arm. She understood. Her father was dead. Mrs Armour came forward, and kneeling also, drew the dark head to her bosom. (237)

Like the "Song of the Yellow Swan," it is impossible to read *The Translation of a Savage* in anything other than allegorical terms: Lali is the individual First Nations woman and stands—as did Pocahontas in her subsequent cultural incarnations—as a synecdoche for her race. Moreover, she is explicitly created to illustrate the fact that "translation" into a "civilized" state is by no means a process that is inevitably drawn out over generations. Parker describes how he believed his novel illustrated "the transformation, or rather the evolution, of a primitive character into a character with an intelligence of perception and a sympathy which is generally supposed to be the outcome of long processes of civilisation and culture."[47] Thus Lali offers an optimistic model for her race's easy assimilation, one that is rendered natural through Parker's deployment of the cultural politics of gender and the way in which she embodies a "womanly" tendency toward dependency. Yet when one considers *The Translation of a Savage* in the light not only of late-nineteenth-century sexual politics, but also of the ways in which they were affecting popular fiction, one sees that even in this relatively conservative novel, Lali is allowed some autonomous power. Although she is apparently lovingly absorbed into her new family, something brought home by this final tableau, the metaphor of the wounded deer suggests that this taming and domestication may well be at a painful cost to native identity and allegiances. If integration through marriage, and through a blending of cultures, offers for Parker the most optimistic way of looking at the future of First Nations people, he also knows that this process cannot be equated with the manufactured happiness of the ending to a fictional romance.

What is more, conservative though Parker's domestic and transnational politics are in many ways, this novel, like "Lois the Witch," inculcates and demands respect toward other beings, whatever their race or gender. Writing in the tradition of authors who have used Indian characters in tandem with their concern for the socially inferior or disadvantaged position of British women, Parker, in his novel, dramatizes a model for the future that works both in terms of the domestic drama of his own plot and as an allegory for white-native relations more generally. This model is predicated on ideals involving integration and mutual understanding: one that may not be easy, or complete, in its achievement, but that is essential to strive for. Moreover—and this makes the novel stand out from those theories, in both Canada and the United States, that depend upon a simplistic vision of assimilation—*The Translation of a Savage* gently hypothesizes that interracial communication and comprehension need not involve the loss or total sublimation of either individual or tribal identity. Furthermore, it moves far beyond the conventional ideas of what an Indian woman might bring to an interracial marriage—striking looks and submissiveness. It suggests that by her actions, her courage, and her strength of character, Lali has the capacity to act as an example to the person who set out to try to exploit her.

This represents a significant shift in the gendering of the literary Indian. In the earlier decades of the century, the ideal of the heroic Indian warrior was invoked as a model for British manhood: stoical, courteous (if reticent), and with extraordinary powers of endurance. And then, increasingly—and on both sides of the Atlantic—Indians were seen as an Other against which masculinity could be tested and proved, thus rendering them, symbolically speaking, feminine. Their culturally subordinate position nonetheless meant that they, and the sentiments raised by their historic persecution, could be appropriated in the interests of contemporary women. By the end of the century, informed to a mild extent by current feminist thinking, Parker's Lali is used to turn the tables: her strengths and virtues will reform and translate British manhood from its selfish preoccupations and expose the crudity of the unthinking racism that exists within British imperialism.

CHAPTER EIGHT

Indians and Missionaries

In 1838 the Quaker William Howitt launched a blistering attack on the results of missionary activity. The object of his volume *Colonization and Christianity*, he announced, was

> to lay open to the public the most extensive and extraordinary system of crime which the world ever witnessed. . . . We talk of the heathen, the savage, and the cruel, and the wily tribes, that fill the rest of the earth; but how is it that these tribes know *us*? Chiefly by the very features that we attribute extensively to them. They know us chiefly by our crimes and our cruelty. It is we who are, and must appear to them the savages. What, indeed, are civilization and Christianity? The refinement and ennoblement of our nature! The habitual feeling and the habitual practice of an enlightened justice, of delicacy and decorum, of generosity and affection to our fellow men. There is not one of these qualities that we have not violated for ever, and on almost all occasions, towards every single tribe with which we have come in contact. We have professed, indeed, to teach Christianity to them; but we had it not to teach, and we have carried them instead, all the curses and horrors of a demon race.[1]

Howitt spends five hundred excoriating pages detailing the atrocities of Spanish Roman Catholics in the Americas, in Cuba, in Jamaica, and in other Caribbean islands, of the Portuguese in India and Brazil, and the Dutch in India. The French in Canada, he writes, "treated the Indians just as creatures that might be spared or destroyed,—driven out or not, as it best suited themselves" (314). Nor should the British think themselves "free from the guilt of colonial blood and oppression" (18). For a start, the "scene of exaction, rapacity, and plunder which India became in our hands, and that upon the whole body of the population, forms one of the most disgraceful portions of human history" (252). When it came to America, the behavior of Protestants is to be regarded as particularly disgraceful, since, although "pretending to abandon the corruptions and cruelties of the papists, they did not abandon their wretched pretenses for seizing upon the possessions of the weak and the unsuspecting" (331). Howitt sets up a Utopian vision in place of the atrocities that he delineates, demanding that those individuals or nations who consider themselves Christian interrogate the true meaning of the word. "Imagine," he urges, that the original European settlers "came amongst the simple people of the New World, clothed in all the dignity of Christian wisdom, the purity of Christian sentiment, and the sacred beauty of Christian benevolence; and what a contrast to the crimes and the horrors with which they devastated and depopulated that hapless continent!" (15).

Howitt's vehement protestations against policies that had been executed in the name of Christianity emphasized the religious hypocrisy that could be used to bolster both colonial expansionism and national and racial proclamations of superiority. While he may have been far from expressing a majority opinion, his volume acts as a powerful reminder of the fact that Victorians were not oblivious to such hypocrisy: we have already seen Eliza Cook using very similar language. Moreover, when it came to Native Americans, the British were strongly implicated in the symbiotic connection between religion and colonization. Within British Canada, as within the United States, missions designed to convert native people to Christianity and to what was, for many, its synonymous byproduct, "civilization," proliferated.

Because of the degree to which Howitt draws Britain's own activities into his critique, his attack is not synonymous with the way in which Dickens, among others, distanced his country from the United States and the hypocrisy inherent in that country's lip service to the ideals of democracy. It should, rather, be seen in the context of other contemporary manifestations of concern about the relationship between colonization and humanitarianism, many of them nonconformist in origin.[2] Just the year before Howitt published his critique, for example, the *Report from the Select Committee on Aborigines (British Settlements)* of 1837 invoked divine authority in proclaiming:

> He who has made Great Britain what she is, will inquire at our hands how we have employed the influence He has lent to us in our dealings with the untutored and defenceless savage; whether it has been engaged in seizing their lands, warring upon their people, and transplanting unknown disease, and deeper degradation, . . . or whether we have, *as far as we have been able*, informed their ignorance, and invited and *afforded them the opportunity of becoming partakers* of that civilization, that innocent commerce, that knowledge and the faith with which it has pleased a gracious Providence to bless our own country.[3]

But assessing the ideological and political implications of the work done by British missionaries does not prove as clear-cut as Howitt would have his readers believe, even if it is tempting to set him up as offering a paradigm of radical thought on the matter. Missionary culture has, of course, tended to divide commentators. A significant number of histories of missionary activity have been written from an openly Christian position and hence offer a sympathetic narrative of progressive enlightenment, yet these have been offset by an energetic tendency in much of twentieth-century literature and cultural criticism to adopt a very similar tone to Howitt's, offering scathing indictments and satiric mockery of missionary work. Robert F. Berkhofer, for example, in *Salvation and the Savage* (1965), takes a very uncompromising line in his examination of Protestant mission work in the United States between 1787 and 1862, showing how such activity proceeded hand in glove with the military, governmental, and educational effort to bring about the principles of manifest destiny. "Not only were the goals of mission societies prescribed by the sponsoring civilization," he writes, "but even the method used to achieve these aims developed in line with a preconceived image of the Indian rather than through field experience . . . no custom was too picayune for censure and change, and no demand too sweeping and drastic in the missionaries' attempts to revamp aboriginal life in conformity with American ideals."[4]

More recent studies, however, have started to bring out the complexities involved in assessing the damage, the value, and the transformative agency of missionary work. The role of the missionary in cultural mediation has come under increasingly nuanced scrutiny in the wake of Johannes Fabian's demand that not only "the crooks and brutal exploiters, but the honest and intelligent agents of colonization need to be accounted for."[5] More pertinently for my argument here, Anna Johnston has drawn our attention to the fact that "missionary texts are crucial to understanding cross-cultural encounters under the aegis of empire because they illuminate the formation of a mode of *mutual imbrication* between white imperial subjects, white colonial subjects, and non-white colonial subjects."[6] As she demonstrates in her study of such writings, concentrating on those produced by emissaries of the London Missionary Society who were active in India, Polynesia, and Australia, they constitute an important part of the "imperial archive," not least, she argues, because of their insistent focus on questions of gender, sexual practices, and domesticity. The anthropological detail that missionaries furnished about Native Americans dealt with many other areas besides—hunting practices; modes of traveling, tracking, and trading; rituals, feasts, and dances; natural remedies; the construction and decoration of tepees and houses; spiritual beliefs; language; and forms of social organization. It is, of course, significant that the vast majority of British accounts emanated from Canada, and therefore they not only were the product of different conceptions about the relationship of Indian to national identity from those held within the United States, but also frequently emerged from notably harsh physical circumstances where cooperation was a necessary fact of life. Undoubtedly, the books and articles written for a British audience by missionaries, the lectures they gave on their trips home, their meetings with those who had "collected money and had made garments to cover the poor redman";[7] the lantern shows that, together with bazaars and meetings helped fund-raising; the accounts written up by travelers whose visits included extended exposure to mission work;[8] the letters and reports that appeared in church and diocesan publications: all furnished a major source of information about native peoples—information that, if often biased so as to show the spiritual and social benefits of Christian belief, was rarely overdramatized. The crucial feature of these publications was the fact that they were often the product of sustained, firsthand knowledge and active friendships, often combined with fluency in indigenous languages. It was, in other words, from missionaries that Victorians were most likely to gain detailed, not especially romanticized, and often highly sympathetic portrayals of native life. These accounts tempered the sensationalism of adventure fiction and the Wild West Shows, even if, at the same time, they must be seen in a symbiotic relationship to these forms, since the image of the unpredictable, aggressive, hostile Indian of popular culture tacitly served (and on occasion could be manipulated) to suggest both the bravery of missionaries and the necessity of their work. Stock images of Indians could be used to lure young readers into tales with a strong message of the importance of Christian teaching and religious colonization. To give just one example: *On the Indian Trail*, by the prolific writer Egerton Ryerson Young, has a cover that promises adventure, bearing, as well as the adventuresome title, the image of an Indian with a rifle, pulling a sled. There is no visible clue (other than the name of the publisher, the Religious Tract Society) that this is a didactic text until one opens the cover and encounters the subtitle *And Other Stories of Missionary Work among the Cree and Saulteaux Indians*, with a portrait of Young, complete with clerical collar, on the facing page.

Memoirs, reports, and letters by those working in Canada completely belie, for the most part, Berkhofer's generalization about missionaries' being unable, or unwilling, to engage with, and to have their own attitudes modified by, their experience in the field. Many, indeed, write about having their preconceptions completely shifted as a result of actual contact with Indians. Often, they were working with natives whose societies were already undergoing—and in many cases had been undergoing for several centuries—considerable transformation as a result of contact, whether existing trading patterns were disrupted, tribal identities and boundaries shifted, or they were forced to negotiate the effects of disease, alcohol, or the more diffuse impact of people dependent on

Figure 20. Cover illustration to Egerton Ryerson Young's *On the Indian Trail, and Other Stories of Missionary Work among the Cree and Salteaux Indians* (London: Religious Tract Society, 1897).

different technologies as well as social assumptions. Significant prior contact, indeed, often made missionary activity particularly challenging. "It has been said even by white travellers," wrote Edward Wilson in 1886, "that they have found the pagan Indians of the North more honest and trustworthy than those in a semi-civilized and nominally Christian state. The Indian when he mixes with the Whites soon learns their bad habits, but is more slow to learn what is holy and good."[9] However much one might deplore the ways in which Christianity had undoubtedly been used to divide Indian against Indian—or, as Howitt put it, to encourage them "to betray and exterminate one another, and not only one another, but to betray and exterminate, if possible, their white rivals" (317)—and however much it was employed as an agency of assimilation into a society dominated by white values, these facts must be weighed against the more positive role many missionaries played in sustaining communities, in tempering and mediating cultural collisions, and in spreading understanding of native customs, beliefs, and ways of life— even as these were undergoing change. In particular, those missionaries who worked for the Church Missionary Society (CMS) during the secretaryship of the Reverend Henry Venn were encouraged to practice a form of adaptive, practical Christianity by integrating their Christian mission with local economic and political issues.

In this context, it is important to note that many nonconformist missionaries and their wives often came from nonprivileged backgrounds. George Stocking has suggested that the fact that missionaries were frequently "self-educated men of artisan origins" could mean that when they were

> confronted with peoples whose cultural values seemed at polar variance, they assumed that because they themselves had risen from ignorance and low estate by their own exertions and by embracing vital Christianity, the natives to whom they offered education and the word of God would do likewise. When these expectations were frustrated, they were quite capable of portraying fallen savage man in rather bleak terms, whether to vindicate their own disappointed efforts or to exhort those at home to greater ones.[10]

Yet one can argue for a very different interpretation of the attitudes that some of the missionaries manifested. Rather than seeking to impose some middle-class lifestyle, they had an understanding of close-knit communities in which mutual help and a careful husbanding of material assets were crucial, and in which education was important for giving people the tools with which to read the Bible, write business letters (including petitions),[11] and keep accounts. Many had themselves left school in their early teens and then been educated by the CMS, and so they did not have the theological—or social—training that a university education would have bestowed on them.[12] This lack of a sense of social and material entitlement may well have enabled a number of missionaries to identify more easily with the priorities of their flocks, which led, especially toward the end of the century, to their engagement in land-rights issues, to the angry dismay of settlers and traders (and on occasion the more senior members of their churches) who wished to locate missionary enterprise somewhat differently within a broader and transnational economic and social context.

The most notable case in point here was that of John Maclean, who gained a particularly detailed and subtle knowledge of the Indians of the Canadian Northwest (especially the Blood Indians, a tribe of the Blackfeet) after being sent by the Methodists to work among them in 1880. He published a number of highly informed and informative anthropological studies, including *The Indians of Canada* (1889) and *Canadian Savage Folk* (1896); he started from the premise that he wanted his readers to "have their ideas changed as mine have been, by coming into closer contact with our dusky brethren, through their languages, literature, native religion, folk-lore, and later Christian life." Although Maclean was, ultimately and somewhat reluctantly, an assimilationist, he believed that the absorption of the Indian into white society was merely a replication of history; after all, "the modern Englishman is a descendant of the Anglo-Saxon, Dane and Norman, and the American is a cosmopolitan, indeed."[13] As this comment suggests, he favored a comparativist approach. Although he understood that true cultural understanding entaired acknowledging and respecting difference—"We are all of us savages in the estimation of somebody," he pointed out—he felt that the way ahead was to note points of similarity and not dwell on differences (308). Nonetheless, he was determined to see cultural change from an Indian as well as a British perspective. In his preface to *Canadian Savage Folk*, he wrote how it had been "our" tendency to look "at the red man from our own point of view. . . . Put yourself in his place and the verdict will be different" (no page number). He wrote about how the Indians he knew were puzzled by the construction and function of Western clothes and by the absurdity of village balls ("They could understand men dancing alone and appreciate it, but to see men and women together was a subject for fools"), and understandably they were lacking in comprehension when it came to the efforts being made to educate their children. They wanted to be paid for this, he reported, "as they felt that some unknown advantage was sought by the white people" through their teaching. "Having an educational system of their own, they thought that they should receive something for allowing the white man's culture to displace their own" (308).

Maclean's ethnic interests were not popular with his Methodist superiors. As Grant writes: "The adoption of European patterns was believed to be the Indians' only hope for the future, [so] interest in their traditions was suspect."[14] Nonetheless, Maclean's writings provide eloquent testimony of how prolonged engagement with First Nations people led not just to an understanding of their lives but to a desire to disseminate this knowledge in a way that would lead to a greater comprehension of the beauty and sophistication of Indian cultures among those who knew them only through stereotypes.

To engage with the relationship between native peoples and missionary activity in Canada, as elsewhere, is to pose questions about the intersection of material circumstances with spirituality, and to ask what connections there may be between changed conditions of living and changed modes of belief when it comes to understanding what constitutes "modernity." This is true whether one examines the role of white missionaries and the values, practices, and habits of speech and thought that they brought from Western cultures or the role of native converts who became missionaries in their own right. Many of the white missionaries believed they were importing spiritual and material benefits that would allow their native flocks to engage more effectively with an increasingly technological, less localized, and less subsistence-based world. Native commentators who left accounts likewise often position themselves, however awkwardly, as mediators between old and new lifestyles and discourses. Although they often situate themselves quite confidently as supporters of progress, setting the supposedly ahistorical and primitive against the teleological imperatives that informed late-nineteenth-century social systems, this confidence often breaks down when it comes to the question of belief. Not only do they—both native and white—often seek to establish a common ground between native and Christian spirituality, but they have, perhaps inevitably, a blind spot when it comes to asking whether the substitution, or overlaying, of one belief system with another does, in fact, constitute a form of modernity. Moreover, the work of British missionaries was frequently compromised by the nostalgia that they projected onto traditional lifestyles, the respect that they afforded them and their accompanying customs and belief systems, or, on occasion, their own guilt at having been swept up enthusiastically into a ceremony.

Missionary Activities

Missionary accounts could work to disturb stereotypical versions of the Indian—especially those based on romanticized idealization—or "childish sentimentality," as John Maclean termed it (307). They could also give the lie to those who projected themselves into an idealized role in relation to these picturesque, potentially grateful heathens, the kind of role in which Egerton Ryerson Young was more than happy to cast himself and which he presented as vanishing along with the tribes whom he had served. "Romantic missionary work among the red Indians will soon be a thing of the past," he wrote in 1897. "Civilisation is reaching this people, and the iron horse rushes and shrieks where the Indian trail was once the only pathway. The picturesque garb is fast disappearing, and store clothes, often too soon transformed into rags anything but picturesque, have robbed the Indian of the interest that once clung to him."[15]

It was easy for novelists to mock missionary work predicated on starry-eyed attitudes, whether or not they ultimately supported the missionary enterprise. Charlotte Yonge, for example, despite the fact that she dedicated the profits from her fiction to religious causes, offers a thoroughly pessimistic view of missionary activity among North American Indians in her novel *Hopes and Fears* (1860). She suggests that conventional rhetorical constructions of the native have generated a sentimental idealism, which has very little to do with the squalid reality of the encounters that a missionary would experience; these ideas echoing those put forward by Susanna Moodie in her popular memoir/travelogue *Roughing It in the Bush* (1852), where she claims that the Indians are "a people whose beauty, talents, and good qualities have been somewhat overrated, and invested with a poetical interest which they scarcely deserve."[16] Yonge's novel opens with Honora Charlecote contemplating the impending missionary career of a certain Owen Sandbrook, so impressed by her vision of his potential in this role that she falls in love with the image she constructs of his success and therefore rejects the very favorable proposal of her cousin. Owen's career will, in Honora's view, be one of noble, inspiring self-sacrifice, set up in a telltale string of clichés that seem to have been lifted from lyric poetry.

> The nephew and heir of the great Firm voluntarily surrendering consideration, ease, riches, unbounded luxury for the sake of the heathen—choosing a wigwam instead of a West End palace; parched maize rather than the banquet; the backwoods instead of the luxurious park; the Red Indian rather than the club and the theatre; to be a despised minister rather than a magnate of this great city; nay, or to take his place among the influential men of the land. What has this worn, weary old civilization to offer like the joy of sitting beneath one of the glorious aspiring pines of America, gazing out on the blue waters of her limpid inland seas, in her fresh pure air, with the simple children of the forest round him, their princely forms in attitudes of

attention, their dark soft liquid eyes fixed upon him, as he tells them "Your Great Spirit, him whom ye ignorantly worship, Him declare I unto you," and then, some glorious old chief bows his stately head, and throws aside his marks of superstition.[17]

After he arrives in Canada, at first the authorities think it best for him to work with colonists. But

> by dint of strong complaints and entreaties, after he had quarrelled with most of his flock, he accomplished an exchange into a district where red men formed the chief of his charge; and Honora was happy, and watched for histories of noble braves, gallant hunters, and meek-eyed squaws.
>
> Slowly, slowly she gathered that the picturesque deerskins had become dirty blankets, and that the diseased, filthy, sophisticated savages were among the worst of the pitiable specimens of the effect of contact with the most evil side of civilization. To them, as Owen wrote, a missionary was only a white man who gave no brandy, and the rest of his parishioners were their obdurate, greedy, trading tempters! It had been a shame to send him to such a hopeless set, when there were others on whom his toils would not be thrown away. However, he should do his best. (1:21)

This best, it transpires, soon gives way to more worldly concerns, as he returns to Toronto, becomes a very popular preacher, marries a captain's daughter with whom he has two children, returns to England, and, after his wife dies, leaves them with Honoria while he travels on the Continent for his health. Honoria refuses his eventual proposal, recognizing that "her girlhood suffered from a great though high-minded mistake" (2:412). Although missionary work among First Nations people does not form a major theme in the book, its early presence is extremely important in establishing the novel's main moral: that religion is not all about romance and sentimentality and that fanciful idealism offers very imperfect guidelines by which to live.

Owen should have done his preparation more thoroughly. Accounts written by missionaries in British Canada were readily accessible in Victorian Britain. They could be accessed in volume-length publications, in newsletters and reports, and through the numerous lectures and presentations, sometimes accompanied with magic lantern slides, that missionaries delivered on their trips back home.[18] For the most part, these missionaries were members of the Anglican Church Missionary Society (CMS, founded in 1799) or the Wesleyan Methodist Missionary Society (WMMS, founded in 1813), and their writings tended to focus on the Great Lakes region, the Red River, and the Pacific Northwest. My task here is not to chronicle the jockeying for position between Anglicans, Methodists, and Roman Catholics (and, to a much lesser extent, Presbyterians and the Salvation Army). Nor is it to discuss the fluctuations within these missions—their internal politics; the commitment that could be generated by one pastor or priest and that evaporated when he moved on to another location; the accommodations that were reached with traders who interacted with Indians, especially the officials and employees of the Hudson's Bay Company; and the differing degrees of enthusiasm, toleration, indifference, or resistance that could be shown individual Indians or particular groups.[19] Rather, I ask *why* a domestic public back in Britain should be interested in learning about missionary activity in these colonial locations, what it meant for them to support such work, what kind of emotional investments they made in the idea of converting native people, and what this had to do with perceptions of colonial activity.[20]

Congregations, committees, and private individuals liked to sense that they were getting a return on their investment, whether the form that this investment took was funds, clothing, or prayers. This makes it hard to read both published accounts and the evidence of reports with confidence; upbeat narratives of conversion and cleanliness often—although by no means always—simplify the pragmatics and hardships of missionary fieldwork. At the same time, the rhetoric of those who penned these accounts may well have been an exercise in convincing themselves of their own worth and success; their optimism and narratives of difficulties overcome are frequently tempered by the realities of missionary life that turn up in correspondence. Letters back to England express frustration at the inability to supply even the natives' most basic wants. "Dear me," wrote the bishop of Algoma in August 1889, "how I wished for about twenty bales of good, serviceable clothing to give out. How some of these wretched, half-clothed creatures live out the winter I know not."[21] Emily Headland, in her biography of John Horden for the Church Missionary Society Workers series, describes how at the beginning of his forty-two years' work in the Northwest, the "terrible depravity of the Indians greatly distressed him. . . . Food was frequently scarce, and the bow-string was the easiest way to dispose of old people. It was equally terrible to discover that parents, tempted by famine, sometimes devoured their own offspring."[22] Isolation, intense cold, and mosquitoes characterized his life among the Cree Indians at Moose Fort, where the only relief was the *annual* ship, which brought them flour, tea, sugar, and a year's worth of letters and newspapers.

Questions of empirical reliability are an issue in published texts when it comes not so much to the material details of everyday native life but the internal responses of indigenous peoples to matters of conversion and acculturation. But these works are unquestionably valuable as expressions of projected desire on the part of their authors and readerships. When read today, some of the most striking moments come when symbols of colonial rule are invoked in the same breath as spirituality. Bishop Ridley of Caledonia, who had worked at Metlakatla, a coastal village in northern British Columbia, succinctly enunciated the underlying principle at stake: "Religion and loyalty are aspects of the same spirit; one as it relates to heaven, the other to earth."[23] So when Edward Sullivan, bishop of Algoma, who was attending the Lambeth Conference in 1888, reported that the Indians at Negwenenang, on Lake Neepigon, would like a Union Jack, partly to show their fidelity to the Great Mother and to fly on Sunday as a call to worship instead of a bell,[24] he was articulating a fusion of secular and spiritual allegiance. Even if the queen herself was not invoked, missionaries liked to remind their readership that native peoples were learning both to worship and to celebrate holy festivals, in ways that could be understood as both quintessentially English and demonstrating the adaptive capabilities of First Nations people— singing familiar hymns or decorating a tree with candles and small handicrafts for a children's Christmas party.[25] Little anecdotes were used to bring home the effectiveness of mission work. In one published fusion of public and private testimony, a sermon delivered by the commissary to the bishop of Columbia, Victoria, in St. Stephen's, Westminster, was printed together with a letter from the bishop to the well-known philanthropist Angela Burdett Coutts, reporting:

> The Indians are very quick and intelligent. A little girl, nine years old, in about an hour and a half, *learnt*, so as to *repeat*, to *point to*, and to *write* the English vowels. A diagram was placed upon the board, of small words and representations: one was PIG—pig. [The bishop here inserted a sketch of a pig.] The Indian was told to copy the letters of the second word as that for *writing*. Almost immediately he returned his slate, with both words well copied, and a capital drawing of a pig!—better than mine. We are going to have a grand clothing-day of the poor little girls, who now are in tatters and dirt.[26]

Probably the most widely available accounts of missionary work in Upper Canada that circulated in Britain were those by the prolific writer Egerton Ryerson Young, by birth a Canadian. His books were energetically distributed through the Religious Tract Society, and, judging by the frequency and tone with which they were promoted in advertisements, they were popular choices for Sunday School prizes and holiday gifts. Young is nothing if not self-congratulatory, both about the work he and his wife performed and about the vast superiority of the devout white Christian over the Indian. If on the one hand he acknowledges that native people have the skill in woodcraft, in trail finding, and in hunting that he lacks, he wastes little time in subordinating them to the aesthetics of the scenery: these "quiet, picturesquely garbed men in their statuesque attitudes added much to the attractiveness of the surroundings."[27] Presumptuously, he presents their lives as "lonely and monotonous" (69), relieved only by the periodic appearance of a missionary. Familiarizing Indians with the Bible was central to missionary work, and he claims the book was being carried everywhere, once it was known and loved. Studied on long hunting trips, "its startling incidents and stories [became] more prized than the legends and myths that have come down to them from their forefathers, and have been repeated over and over in their hearing by the old story-tellers of the tribe" (89). Yet even Young's enthusiasm for Westernization is tempered by the fact that he accepts that indigenous peoples are most likely to respond to the message of the Scriptures when these are set before them in their own languages. He shows the Indians as fascinated by learning the Cree syllabary—which he draws on a rock with burned sticks—and as overwhelmed with delight and amazement when they realize that they can puzzle out the letters in the Bible for themselves. On the other hand, he has them learn hymns, and—he explains—"Indians in their wild state have no music worth preserving, and so in all of our missions, our hymns and songs are translated, and the tunes of civilisation are used" (204–5).

Yet Young's mission, as he presents it, went far beyond teaching the meaning of the Scriptures; rather, it was a full-blown attempt at acculturation, which centered on domesticity as its chief agent, explicitly in addressing women. As Anna Johnston notes in a more global context, "missionaries educated potential converts in ways that sought to reproduce, at the colonial periphery, middle-class British social structures and values,"[28] and this is borne home when Young tells how he and his wife taught the Indian women how to keep a clean house—once they moved into houses after living in wigwams—and how to sew, patch, and darn Western-style clothes, with the result that the women "endeavoured to let their husbands and children see, that no longer did they wish to live in the careless way of the old pagan life, but, as now they had become Christians in their profession, so in their homes, they would have the neatness, and cleanliness, that should belong to those who are thus called" (61). Indeed, he seems particularly proud that Christianity has effected what he sees as a real change in the attitude of Indian men toward women, lifting them "from a condition of inferiority and degradation," into one where they are "honored and respected" (189). He gives, moreover, a practical emphasis to his endeavors, which is propelled by the impact of white settlement. Young notes how the fish stock, their traditional food source, is swiftly diminishing as a result of the rapid increase of the white population in the northwestern states and Manitoba,

GOD ON THE ROCK.

Figure 21. Illustration in Egerton Ryerson Young's *On the Indian Trail, and Other Stories of Missionary Work among the Cree and Salteaux Indians* (London: Religious Tract Society, 1897).

and how it is therefore the imperative duty of the missionaries not just to Christianize these people, "but to do all they can, in harmony with the government officials, to encourage them to raise cattle, to cultivate what land is available, and to raise those hardy crops which will come to maturity in such a cold northern region" (203). In other words, the reader is invited to make various forms of investment in the narratives of achievement that he tells. These include identifying with the figure of the missionary, who brings spiritual enlightenment; with his wife, who joins with him in demonstrating the material, physical, and familial benefits of an orderly, Westernized domestic life; and sharing in a sense of moral entitlement at the effects of white settlement when these have been properly assessed and, where necessary, counterbalanced.

Although the portrayals of before-and-after conversions here and elsewhere can come across in a two-dimensional way, they were extremely valuable in that they offered a model of change and development that frequently acted as a check and counterbalance to the "scientific" arguments promoting the existence of racial hierarchies or the inevitability of certain ethnic groups' decline and fading away. Some writers, such as

Young, do not seem to have worked very hard to suppress a condescending tone, and yet working against this was a sense of human equality under God, which was a mainstay of missionary discourse and was fostered by comparative approaches toward religion. Missionaries and others were quick to find grounds on which Christianity and Indian spiritual systems could be compared—drawing parallels between the Great Spirit and the Christian God, between heaven and the Happy Lands to be found in the West or in the Milky Way—mapping a good-evil dichotomy onto the Iroquois cosmic twins Hawenneyu and Hanegoategeh, who stood for pleasure and harm respectively, and pouncing enthusiastically on apparently similar myths of the Creation or of the Great Flood. This theological parallelism was extended to linguistics by Joseph Howse, who worked for twenty years with the Hudson's Bay Company and produced the first grammar of the Cree language in 1844, maintaining that the complex nature of its inflections gave the lie forever to the fact that this was the medium of an "untutored SAVAGE." Rather, he could not but "recognize in such a System, a regular organization of vocal utterance, affording to my own mind a circumstantially conclusive proof, that the whole is the emanation of ONE, and that a DIVINE mind."[29] Other writers were less concerned with locating specific theological parallels than with detecting broad moral characteristics of Christianity. Even Moodie wrote of the Ojibwa that "their honesty and love of truth are the finest traits in characters otherwise dark and unlovely. But these are two God-like attributes, and from them spring all that is generous and ennobling about them" (279). The Congregationalist minister Edwin Paxton Hood found such encouraging attributes as a desire to share one's possessions liberally and to express "conjugal, paternal, and filial affection" already inherent within native cultures.[30] He cited Johann Georg Kohl's *Kitchi Gami: Wanderings round Lake Superior* (1860)—a book that was reviewed with considerable enthusiasm by G. H. Lewes and by Eliza Lynn Linton, among others—in support of his point that some Christian teachings might even be easier for Indians to accept than for Westerners.

> That Divine injunction, "take no thought of the morrow," does not seem so strange to them as to us; a Protestant missionary told Mr. Kohl how, on the borders of Lake Superior, he had noticed this in an old Indian woman whom he had baptized; he found the poor old squaw eating her last meal of maize porridge, she had a little handful left, and she threw it into the pot for the missionary—"Art thou not alarmed," said he, with some surprise, "at thy solitude and thy empty larder?" "No," said the old woman, "I always pray well and easily." "But surely thou art alarmed for to-morrow's meal?" he said. "By no

means," said she, "God always sends me something at the right moment, even if I do not know precisely whence it will come." True, this was a converted Indian woman, but there is still plenty of evidence that this kind of dependence upon the Great Spirit, the Great Father, is the property especially of many of the tribes. (268)

It is very easy to see how, in a different context, this anecdote could be produced as a classic example of Indian "improvidence." But Hood demonstrates how, as Andrew Porter has put it, the search "for aspects of indigenous belief offering openings for the Christian message could be transformed into knowledgeable, sympathetic approaches to indigenous culture."[31] Indeed, so keen could missionaries be to find similarities in practices of prayer or prophecy that they could be decidedly oblivious of the fact that there were profound differences of belief as well, especially given that Indian conceptions of time—and hence of the very ends that religious belief served—were cyclical, rather than based on a linear notion of fulfillment for both the individual and society.[32] It is, indeed, in these different understandings of time that we may find one of the most clear-cut differences between traditional First Nations views of the world and the ethos of modernity. And the other notable chasm exists, indeed, in relation to individualism itself. If Christianity places an emphasis on individual salvation, and the internalization of conscience, native belief systems are predicated differently. Maclean makes the point that the Indians "could not understand the individuality of the white men, each laboring for himself, and apparently not caring for his brother-man, as they were firm believers in the brotherhood of the red men, and sought to put into practice the teachings of the wise men of the lodges."[33] Maclean, however, was, as we have seen, unusual in the emphasis that he put on the necessity of seeing the world from an Indian perspective as well as an Anglo one. Yet this was precisely what First Nations people had to do all the time, and nowhere was this more apparent than on their transatlantic visits.

Indian Missionaries in Britain

Missionary traffic was not just one-way. Significantly, a number of Indian converts visited Britain in a missionary capacity. Their accounts are valuable for a number of reasons. First, they offer clear evidence of how, even among those who were strongly Christianized, Indian beliefs, traditions, and linguistic patterns of translating both the transcendental and the everyday continued to coexist and blend with new influences, whether spiritual, material, or cultural. Second, the traveling converts offer a detailed picture of the networks that sustained connections between religion and humanitarian-based international political movements, including abolitionism. And then, like other visitors, they provide their impressions of how a modernizing, urban world seems from their perspective and what it offers by way of example or warning for the societies of which they consider themselves members. Yet unlike Catlin's Indians, or those who traveled with the Wild West, they were not primarily spectacles, performing Indianness in opposition to modernity—although, and sometimes uncomfortably, they often found it hard to escape from being regarded as objects of curiosity, even as they record being able to interact and converse with a wide range of British people.

Two men stand out for the accounts that they left of their visits to England: the Reverend Peter Jones and the more problematic, controversial figure of George Copway. Jones (half Mississauga, half Welsh, and brought up in traditional Indian ways) nominally became a Christian in 1820, when he was eighteen—motivated in considerable part, he recalled, by the fact that he might thereby "be entitled to all the privileges of the white inhabitants."[34] His true sense of a personal need for salvation and his turn toward a Christian life came, however, in 1823, at a Methodist camp meeting held at Ancaster (now incorporated into the city of Hamilton, in south-central Ontario). The following year, he opened a small day school and started to preach, and in April 1825 he began to keep his journal, noting in it that "the history of my life may now be considered that of an Indian Missionary" (16). At first, he largely traveled and preached among the Ojibwa and the Muncey, around Rice Lake and Lake Simcoe (and was highly critical of "their pagan customs and manners" [30]); then in 1829, he toured in the northeastern United States to raise funds for missionary work and to see his translation of hymns and the Scriptures printed. So when George Ryerson approached him in early 1831 to see whether he would be prepared to accompany him to Britain under the auspices of the Committee on Religious Liberty, to deliver petitions to the Colonial Office in relation to native land rights and to preach and raise money for Methodist missionary work, he was already something of a seasoned traveler, whose assessment, on landing, of Liverpool's buildings as "elegant" (296), for example, had some comparative basis within modern urban life.

Jones's account of his trips to England—he returned in 1837–38 and 1844–46—provide a highly detailed picture of the people and organizations he met. For example, in the early weeks of his first visit, he attended the Wesleyan Methodist Missionary Anniversary Meeting, the Anniversary of the Church Missionary Society, the British and Foreign Bible Society Anniversary, the Annual Breakfast of the Preachers' Children, and the Anniversary of the London Missionary Society. During the course of a stay of several weeks in Bristol, a city known for its noncon-formist-led opposition to slavery,[35] he preached at two Wesleyan chapels, St. Philip's and Ebenezer, and visited Kingswood School in celebration of John Wesley's birthday, where he dressed himself in Indian costume and spoke to the boys about the conversion of Indians in Upper Canada. Re-ligious activities, however, were inseparable, here as elsewhere, from the fact that he was a social curiosity. He sat for his portrait and visited the elderly Hannah More. She asked him about his

> country, nation, religion, and wished particularly to know whether we embraced the Protestant religion; and on informing her that we had, she said, "I am happy to hear that, for if you had become Roman Catholics I should not have thought anything of you." After telling Mrs. Moore of the wonderful change effected by the Gospel amongst the Indians of Canada, she seemed highly delighted, and said to her companions, "Come, let us go over to Canada and live among the In-dians and instruct them." She spoke this in a humorous way to sig-nify how willing she should be to go and do good amongst the poor Indians. (306)

She then gave Jones a copy of her book *The Spirit of Prayer* and £5 for the missions in Canada. Jones evidently and understandably found his role as a fashionable icon somewhat wearisome, remarking on July 1 that he was "engaged in writing in Albums and in scraps for the good ladies of Bristol, who give me no peace till they have a sample of my scraw" (311). He returned to London so that he and Ryerson could meet with a committee of the New England Company and give a report on the conditions of Indians back home and to "suggest a few plans of the Com-pany's operations in civilizing the Indians" (312); back again in Bristol, the visitors paid a call on George Pocock, "who showed us his inventions of the new air gloves, and the mode of travelling by kites" (315).[36]

To read Jones's journal is to see the muddying of the boundaries be-tween religion, politics, and—if one happened to be both an object of curiosity *as* an Indian and to feel curious about the country one was vis-iting—entertainment. The journal gives an excellent sense of the scope of his official duties: preaching; speaking both about the "superstitions" (321) of the Indians and what the Gospel has done for them; asking not just for funds but, in Sheffield, for local wares, such as joiners' tools and cutlery; writing to the committees of the Sunday School Union and the Sunday School Society for books for Indian Sunday schools; and receiv-ing the news that he would be paid by the British and Foreign Bible So-ciety for translating portions of the New Testament into Ojibwa. All in all, on his first visit, Jones addressed congregations in public a hundred times (it is unclear whether he means meetings by this, as opposed to church services), and preached sixty two sermons. He garnered £1,032.06 in donations (£300 from the Wesleyan Missionary Society, £174 1s 6d from Quakers, and £557 19s from benevolent persons in general) and, what seems of almost equal importance to him, the prayers of thousands of Christians.[37] In addition to the Sheffield metalwork, he took back with him work bags, pincushions, needle cases, needles, scissors, thread, bodkins, thimbles, and articles of clothing destined for the mission stations. Jones also carried away books that had been presented to him personally, and a box containing three hundred engravings of the portrait that had been painted of him. Fund-raisers chose to symbolize the technological progress of their own country through the very vehicles used to convey funds up to the platform. At a missionary meeting at St. Ives, in Cornwall, for example, a "missionary ship was presented on the platform during the meeting, containing a cargo of copper, silver, and gold, to the amount of more than £27. A steam-engine was also set in motion to bring up the precious metals of copper, silver, and gold from the bowels of the earth, and safely landed on the platform £20" (397–98).

But the value of Jones's journal goes even further than enabling us to see the extent and details of his British mission and the degree to which British people could feel that they had made a material, as well as spiritual, investment in his cause. Some of the contacts he made, or who sought him out, deepen our knowledge of Indians in England or those British people who had substantial knowledge of native culture. In February 1832 Jones visited Oxford in the company of Joseph Howse, "the Cree white Indian," and spent a few hours "giving him specimens of the Chippeway language for his Cree grammar" (339). Six years later he dined with Sir Augustus D'Este, a cousin of Queen Victoria's, who not only expressed considerable interest in Indian rights but had a full-length portrait of Mahkoons, an Indian who had toured England with a small dance troupe in 1834.[38] Five days later, Jones was visiting an Indian in Clerkenwell Prison, who claimed to have been drawn into a fight in self-defense. In a more peaceful context, when he had an audience with William IV and Queen Adelaide at Windsor Castle on 5 April 1832, he encountered a Micmac chief and his son from Nova Scotia—Roman Catholics, a point of contrast to which the king drew very marked attention—who were in England to purchase farming implements.[39] Jones was particularly struck by the openness of the royal couple and by the fact that "they seemed not at all to be proud"—something that provoked the patriotic effusion "Long may they live to be a blessing to their nation and people! May God direct them in the good and right path of righteousness! God bless the King and Queen!" (344).[40] This was not the only time he expressed great admiration and veneration for British institutions.

When he visited Westminster Abbey, he remarked not only on the statues, monuments, and tombs it contained but on the chairs used during the coronation ceremony: "I took the liberty to squat myself down upon them as we passed by, so that I can now say that I, a poor Indian from the woods of Canada, sat in the king's and queen's great crowning chairs" (338).

Jones clearly enjoyed traveling in Britain and (in 1838) to Ireland. He records with enthusiasm his visit to both the zoo and the diorama in Regent's Park and the Italian scenes that passed before his eyes on that occasion, as well as the panoramas of New Zealand and Quebec which he saw in Edinburgh. He was even more rhapsodic about the scenery along the Clyde and the fruit orchards in Worcestershire, asking ruefully, "When will my poor native land assume such a garden of paradise? Not in my day" (399). Yet Jones was not an unqualified Anglophile. Even if, in his *Life*, he does not express the critical angle on poverty and urban conditions with the frequency of Catlin's Indians in the 1840s, he was quick to draw a contrast between the two societies when it seemed apt. He was shocked by the revelations concerning those who robbed graves and sold bodies for dissection and remarked, "None of the American Indians, I am sure, would be guilty of such atrocious barbarity" (324). Jones was less cautious, however, when writing for a Canadian audience or when speaking to a congregation likely to be sympathetic to a critical perspective. In published letters to the editor of the *Christian Guardian*, the organ of the Methodist Episcopal Church of Upper Canada, he satirized those wealthy English Methodists "who live on roasted beef, plum-pudding, and turtle-soup [and] get very fat and round as a toad."[41] He noted how, in the streets, "you may see the poor man who knows not where he may get his next meal,"[42] and in his farewell sermon, he praised the beauty of the churches that he had seen and the sermons that he had heard but noted the contrast between these and the drunk, blasphemous men and women that he encountered outdoors.[43] Moreover, even though he seems to have been continually respectful in his dealings with authority, he did not pass up the opportunity to give the young Queen Victoria a lesson in the realities of the emotions involved in First Nations–English political issues. Meeting with her at Windsor in 1838, he presented a petition from the Credit River Indians respecting title deeds. Although he had just learned from Lord Glenelg, secretary of state for war and the colonies, that the governor had already been asked to grant this, he nonetheless gave it to her, thinking she would

> like to possess such a document as a curiosity, as the wampum attached to it had a meaning, and their totams [*sic*] marked opposite the names of the Indians who signed it. The Queen then said, "I thank you, sir, I am much obliged to you." I then proceeded to give her the

meaning of the wampum; and told her that the white wampum signified the loyal and good feeling which prevails amongst the Indians towards Her Majesty and Her Government; but that the black wampum
was designed to tell Her Majesty that their hearts were troubled on
account of their having no title-deeds for their lands; and that they
had sent their petition and wampum that Her Majesty might be
pleased to take out all the black wampum, so that the string might all
be white. (407–8)

Peter Jones presents his tone here as respectful and conciliatory; he was
to express himself far more vehemently in his *History of the Ojebway
Indians* (1861), where he bitterly exclaimed, "Oh, what an awful account at the day of judgment must the unprincipled white man give, who
has been an agent of Satan in the extermination of the original propri-
etors of the American soil!"[44]

Peter Jones's connections with England were necessarily consolidated
by the fact that on his first visit, he met his future wife, Eliza Field, a
young woman who had been strongly influenced by the social Christianity of Rowland Hill.[45] She prepared herself thoroughly for Canadian
mission work by learning practical cookery and needlework and by
reading *The Last of the Mohicans* and Basil Hall's *Travels in North
America*, which even mentioned her future husband's missionary work.
What she could not have prepared herself for—despite some initial opposition to her marriage from family members in England—was the racial abuse that, as we saw in chapter 3, was heaped on the occasion by
elements of the New York press, nor the fact that the union was widely
treated by Canadian journalists as an opportunity to talk about the
"amalgamation system," as the *British Colonial Argus* put it.[46] For
some, this was a scandalous disruption of the proper order of the uni-
verse (and the attitudes of many white settlers toward Eliza confirmed
this); for others it represented a possible future. What the debate passed
over, however, was not only the fact that Jones was the son of a mixed-
blood relationship, but that his own acculturation represented an amalgamation of traditional and Anglicized elements. This becomes clear
when we look not just at his writings but at the three likenesses that
were taken of him on his 1845 trip to Britain, by the Edinburgh photographers David Octavius Hill and Robert Adamson. In his costuming, he
appears both as an Indian, complete with leggings and pipe of peace
and seated on a low log in a simulated woodland setting, and as a more
conventionally dressed man of the cloth, in a formal Western coat,
poised—albeit slightly awkwardly—in a substantial leather armchair. A
third picture seems to bridge the contrasts: in Indian clothes, he sits
watchfully in the chair. In each, Jones's authority is unmistakable, but

Figure 22. David Octavius Hill and Robert Adamson, *Ka(h)kewaquonaby, a Canadian chief (Peter "Kahkewaquonaby" Jones)*. Calotype, 4 August 1845. © National Portrait Gallery, London.

Figure 23. David Octavius Hill and Robert Adamson, *Ka(h)kewaquonaby, a Canadian chief (Peter "Kahkewaquonaby" Jones)*. Calotype, 4 August 1845. © National Portrait Gallery, London.

Figure 24. David Octavius Hill and Robert Adamson, *The Waving Plume (Peter "Kahkewaquonaby" Jones)*. Calotype, 4 August 1845. © National Portrait Gallery, London.

the dress and props shift the potential source and scope of this authority in each case.

Unlike Peter Jones, George Copway was an independent lecturer rather than, strictly speaking, a missionary. Both as an individual and as an author, he proves a challenging figure to assess in a number of respects, as has been noted in several recent discussions of his work.[47] Copway, born in 1818, converted to Christianity in 1830, in large part as a result of Jones's influence. He became first an interpreter, then a lay preacher for the Wesleyans, moving between Canadian and American missions. He married the daughter of an immigrant Yorkshire farmer in 1840; "well versed in English literature and a proficient writer herself, it is more than likely that she played a key role in her husband's subsequent literary career," writes Bernd Peyer.[48] But he was expelled from the church in 1846 (supposedly for embezzlement), at which point he moved to the United States and worked the lecture circuit in the Northeast, proclaiming himself to be a (highly Christianized) tribal chief and publishing both an autobiography, *The Life History, and Travels of Kah-Ge-Ga-Gah-Bowh (George Copway)* (1847), and a history, *The Traditional History and Characteristic Sketches of the Ojibway Nation* (1850). In 1850 he was invited as a delegate to the third World Peace Conference, where he represented the "Christian Indians of America," and it is his account of this, and of his visit to Britain, that he published in 1851 as *Running Sketches of Men and Places, in England, France, Germany, Belgium, and Scotland*, which offers the most complex rendering of his engagement with modernity.

Running Sketches has been curiously ignored by those who have written on Copway.[49] It shares, nonetheless, some of the features of his two earlier volumes that serve to make Copway's such an unstable voice. It is composed in a collage of tones; apparently structured around journal entries, it also incorporates undigested chunks from guidebooks—among them, *Black's Railway Map*—extracts from newspapers (usually those which make very favorable mention of Copway), lists of his appointments, copies of letters that he sent back across the Atlantic, the texts of addresses that he delivered to audiences gathered by churches and by Mechanics' Institutes about the religious beliefs, poetry, eloquence, traditions, manners, and customs of the North American Indians, and passages—reminiscent of his earlier writings—of elevated, "literary" writing. Describing his *Life*, Cheryl Walker remarks, "Copway's own lack of psychological and cultural coherence is reflected in the text's confusing array of premises and styles."[50] Or, more generously, he comes across as a member of Homi Bhabha's category of the mimic, one of those parodists of history who, despite their intentions, "inscribe the colonial text erratically" in a narrative "that refuses to be representational," at least insofar as the aim of that representation is "to emerge as authentic, . . . through a process of writing and repetition."[51] But while this may be said of *Running Sketches* as well, the volume may be understood as an acknowledgment of the need for a fluidity of styles and registers when it comes to making some kind of sense and order of modern, urban existence. The points of comparison he makes in relation to his travels are both of the contemporary transatlantic moment and reflective of less urban vistas. Thus arriving in Liverpool, he notes that "the smoke of the town, or in fact of the whole country, is like the smoke of Pittsburg" (47); but when he notes how hotel servants prey on recently-arrived travelers, he calls them "constant plagues," asking for extra sums "like a regiment of starved turkeys clamoring for food" (50). People milling around a London rail station "swarm like bees" (89), but he claims that "there is a daguerreotype" of the sight of the red sun rising over the Atlantic in his memory (28).

Despite his acquaintance with America's eastern cities, London still came as a huge shock to Copway's sense of orientation. "My first day in the metropolis must be set down as a———" he wrote. "Yesterday I did nothing, with the exception of hunting after myself and feeling how strange it was to get lost. The longer I rode, hoping to get from one side of the city to the other, and to attain a position at a distance where I could look on, the more did it seem as if there was no other end to the city."[52] And he was certainly perturbed by the dirtiness of everything, noting that people and their linen readily became streaked with soot. Yet although he acknowledged a temporary sense of dislocation in the urban capital, Copway's reactions to England were almost entirely supportive of what he took to be modernity. He proclaimed ecstatically:

> The railroads of England, and the thousands of men who are employed in opening the gateways of light, are doing a great work. Steamboats, railroads, wires—all—all, are urging the "good time coming." The day-star is rising, and the glory it will shed down upon the earth will gladden the homes of poverty. Let it come where I live and stand over the place where the child of Humanity is born, that I may aid in the glad shout, "The world is free, and all nations are happy." (94)

He presented himself as fascinated by his observations of the country, whether these included the near-ubiquitous presence of policemen at street corners, steel production in Birmingham, which could be turned into instruments of agriculture or of war, or the bustle of the General Post Office: a bustle caused by the existence of a cheap postal service that, for this Ojibwa observer, brought all kinds of benefits with it. "This cheap postage," he wrote, is perhaps the greatest blessing the British Government has bestowed on its subjects. Whatever faults I may hereafter have occasion to find with the management of government affairs, let me here pay a just tribute to the men who have been instrumental in bringing about this great good. Such a boon should immortalize them; and doubtless it will. This is the great channel of the life-blood of English prosperity, which, flowing in rivulets over the country, will animate the fettered souls of the working classes. (93)

Overall, he came across not only as an admirer of Western modernity, but also as one who claimed authority for his ability to speak about the future of Indian lifestyles in part because of his mastery of its values and its discourses, and his ability to put both temporalities into relation with one another. By "values," I especially mean here an endorsement of industrial development, the consolidation of democracy and free speech, and a generalized affirmation of the ideal of progress; these he set against the fact that Indian people, mingling up "their early history in fictions and allegories, types and symbols" (134), frequently found it hard to distinguish between the symbolic and the historical. Despite his respect for his own culture, he chose—in a Liverpool lecture that directly preceded a concert by the Swedish soprano Jenny Lind—to explain its ways of thinking through similes drawn from the culture of his audience, tying the two worlds together when he described how "a beast, or a bird, a man, god, or devil, a stone, serpent, or a wizard, a wind, sound, or ray of light are so many causes of action vibrating along the mysterious chain connecting earth and skies as it were by telegraphic lines" (135). Yet throughout his travels, he was also, it would seem, thinking through the problem of reverse translation. How to describe the newly finished Houses of Parliament to people who had never seen Gothic architecture? "My friends must imagine they see a tremendous *gingerbread*, nearly a quarter of a mile long, 300 feet high, and 400 wide, and they will have a good conception of its size and looks" (112). Visiting the zoo, he paused momentarily in front of the eagle, thinking that this sad-looking bird would for once be seeing a sympathetic face, before puzzling on how he would describe the hippopotamus on his return—not like a beaver, nor a moose, nor a buffalo: "I have it—I shall tell my people that the hippopotamus looks something like a *fat, shaved Bear*" (124). One of the most disconcerting yet compelling features of *Running Sketches* is the fact that neither the position from which Copway wrote nor the audience whom he addressed seems at all stable.

Copway was well aware of his visibility both in literal terms, as a "copper-coloured" individual, and as a spokesperson for his people—as someone who could both capitalize on the associations of Indians with picturesque tradition and was, in his own person, an apparent example of what could be achieved through conversion and "civilization." He manifested no desire to blend unnoticed into British life, being highly alert to his representative role during his brief visit: "I will endeavor never to say nor do anything which will prejudice the mind of the British public against my people—In this land of refinement I will be an Indian—I will treat everybody in a manner that becomes a gentleman—I will patiently answer all questions that may be asked me—I will study to please the people, and lay my own feelings to one side" (55). To be sure, Copway's self-presentation was also an exercise in maintaining self-esteem. Although his appearance at the World Peace Congress was highly popular with some elements of the audience, this seems in large part to have been due to his novelty value, rather than the delivery of his speech. The *Times*, assuming its readers' familiarity with *Gertrude of Wyoming*, noted that this " 'stoic of the woods' luxuriating in the sound of his own voice, doubled the time" allocated to him;[53] Elihu Burritt, founder of the League of Universal Brotherhood and the man who had invited Copway, wrote in disappointed fashion in his journal that he had given "a long, windy, wordy speech, extremely ungrammatical and incoherent";[54] Copway himself indicated that witnessing the excellent speakers who preceded him—including Girardin and Cobden—had robbed him of his confidence. The most successful part of his performance seems to have been the presentation of a catlinite peace pipe to the president of the congress; what is certain is that he appeared incongruous from a number of viewpoints. Dressed in a plain black suit and a black hat, yet carrying a decorated staff and scepter and wearing his hair long, he was as much of a visual hybrid as Peter Jones was when sitting for his photographs.

Copway is fascinating as a figure of hybridity in his own right. His subsequent career showed him unable to settle: he wanted recognition from mainstream white society (whether in America, Canada, or Europe) and claimed to admire the outward manifestations of modernity, but he also expressed considerable anger at the dispossession of native people that he had witnessed. Although the details of his life are shadowy, he seems to have reverted at some stage to native beliefs and practices, working as a traditional healer, and then converted to Roman Catholicism on his deathbed. But we can also see him as exemplifying a particular moment in history, a type of what Marshall Berman, in *All That Is Solid Melts into Air*, calls the second phase of a modernity, one that he locates in the mid-nineteenth century. Copway is, as it were, a member of a public that

> shares the feeling of living in a revolutionary age, an age that generates explosive upheavals in every dimension of personal, social and political life. At the same time, the nineteenth-century modern public

can remember what it is to live, materially and spiritually, in worlds that are not modern at all. From this inner dichotomy, this sense of living in two worlds simultaneously, the ideas of modernization and modernism emerge and unfold.[55]

This inner dichotomy is manifested not just through his biography, but through the rhetoric of his writing.

Jones and Copway were by no means the only Christian converts to visit Victorian England. The Ojibwa Methodist John Sunday (Shawundais, or "Sultry Heat") traveled extensively in England in 1837 and was presented to Queen Victoria. Another Ojibwa, Peter Jacobs (Pahtaysagay, or "Come/Arrive Shining"), also a Methodist, went to England in 1842 and stayed with Robert Alder, the Wesleyan missionary secretary for North America; returning in 1851, he addressed the annual meeting of the society at Exeter Hall.[56] On his return, he performed the role of cultural informant and mediator, trying to impress on his hearers the advantages of becoming a Christian, and hence joining those who

> are rapidly advancing in civilization. I told them that I had been over the great waters to England, and had seen the *Great Female Chief* eight times during my last visit. They inquired how she looked, I told them that she was very handsome, that she lived in house or castles [*sic*] like mountains, was surrounded by many great men, soldiers, and great guns, so that none who intends evil to the great female Chief, can come near her. I told them also that England was a wonderful and a very rich country, everything wonderful was there to be found,— steamboats, and carriages, which go by steam, running very fast on iron roads, and the whole land is filled with people like the multitudes of mosquitoes in their own country.[57]

The Ojibwa Henry Pahtahquahong Chase visited Britain in 1876, 1881, and 1885 to raise funds for the Anglican church; on the third of these occasions, he was a guest of the Lord Mayor of London at the Banquet House.[58]

In 1872 Edward F. Wilson took the Ojibwa chief Buhkwujjenene with him to England on a fund-raising tour, where he spoke at meetings (through Wilson, since his own English was poor) and excited considerable interest. Again, his ethnicity was exploited sartorially in an effort to demonstrate the way in which an Indian could move between cultures: he spoke formally, asking for contributions to a "big teaching wigwam," wearing the respectable black coat of Anglo society, but then he changed into traditional costume in order to sing a war song. Like Jones, this mutability was recorded by a camera: "Several likenesses were taken— representing him as a Christian Chief in his ordinary dress; and as a

Figure 25. Chief Buhkwujjenene arriving in Liverpool. Illustration from
Edward F. Wilson's *Missionary Work among the Ojebway Indians* (London:
Society for Promoting Christian Knowledge, 1886).

Chief of former days in feathers and Indian costume."[59] He worked
hard, with two or three engagements a day and a meeting in the eve-
nings, met twice with the archbishop of Canterbury, and found himself
involved with such fund-raising events as speaking, in full native dress,
to a garden party in Mitcham, Surrey, and telling the assembled company the native story of the Flood that led to the creation of the world.

One learns little from Wilson about his responses—the transcription
of part of a public address uses predictable formal rhetoric—although
one certainly sees that without a framing context, an Ojibwa was completely unrecognizable on the streets of London as conforming to any
obvious stereotype: "Wherever he went, he wore his blanket coat, his
feather in his hat, his leggings and moccasins, and the skunk skin on his
arm. . . . Wide guesses were made at his nationality; one would take him
for a New Zealander, another for a native of Japan" (105–6).

Figure 26. Chief Buhkwujjenene speaking in London. Illustration from Edward F. Wilson's *Missionary Work among the Ojebway Indians* (London: Society for Promoting Christian Knowledge, 1886).

For Indians to feel that they had come into significant contact with modern Britishness, they did not, seemingly, have to cross the Atlantic. In 1872 Wilson translated and published the response of Little Pine, an Ojibwa chief and the brother of Buhkwujjenene, with whom he traveled to Toronto on a fund-raising mission. As

> [I]looked at the fine buildings, and stores full of wonderful and expensive things, the thought came into my breast: How rich and powerful is the English nation; why is it that their religion does not go on and increase faster? Surely they behave as though they were a poor people. When I entered the place where the "speaking paper" (newspaper) is made, I saw the great machines by which it is done, and the man who accompanied us pointed to a machine for folding up the papers and said: This is a new machine, it has not been long invented; and I thought then, "Ah, that is how it is with the English nation, every day they get more wise; every day they find out something new. The Great Spirit blesses them, and teaches them all these things because they are Christians, and follow the true religion. Would that my people were enlightened and blessed in the same way."[60]

Little Pine was swiftly somewhat disillusioned, however, by the fact that the money Wilson and he collected seemed insignificant by comparison with the opulence both of the city and of the "big . . . beautiful wigwam"—in other words, the church—in which he worshiped.

Figure 27. Chief Buhkwujjenene at a garden party in Mitcham, Surrey.
Illustration from Edward F. Wilson's *Missionary Work among the Ojebway
Indians* (London, Society for Promoting Christian Knowledge, 1886).

Little Pine's trip illustrates well a notable feature of native conversion.
While First Nations people could embrace their new religious beliefs
with considerable fervor, the very fact that not all white people shared
the same intense engagement with the Scriptures—nor, indeed, the same
concern with native peoples—as those who had originally inspired them
could readily lead to major disillusionment, both with Christianity and
with white society, quickly exposed as self-contradictory and hypocritical. As the contrasting cases of Jones and Copway suggest, while conversion, and the forms of assimilation—both cultural and textual—that
could come along with it, might give a sense of shape and purpose to an
individual's life, it could equally well be a factor in producing a state
of self-division. Yet it would be misleading to think that exposure to
two cultures led only to self-divisiveness among Indians. Wilson became
a translator between cultures in both a literal sense (he brought out

A Manual of the Ojebwayy Language in 1874) and a practical one—as a minister and a superintendent of mission schools, to be sure, but then as an amateur anthropologist and, increasingly, as a champion of native rights. His travels in the late 1880s in the American Southwest, together with his reading of Helen Hunt Jackson's *A Century of Dishonor* (1881), profoundly altered his views about social change among Indians. In articles that he went on to publish as editor of two magazines, *Our Forest Children* and *The Canadian Indian*, it becomes clear that he thought that white people had done more harm than good; that social change should be adaptive and voluntary rather than imposed; that it should look to blend with, and not replace, existing cultural practices; and that Indians were more than capable of running their own communities and autonomous institutions.[61]

White missionaries could be profoundly influenced by the people whom they set out to serve, and they could have their points of view significantly altered as a result; the case of Wilson is a clear testimony to this fact. There is, nonetheless, a difference between having the hegemonic attitudes of a dominant culture to which one belongs thrown into question and engaging with a culture that, despite the enlightened understanding of a minority of its members, continues, for the most part, to relate to one as an inferior being. Paulo Freire has written of how the internalization of colonialist attitudes leads to feelings of low-esteem and self-deprecation; Frantz Fanon famously explains how the oppressed learn to perceive the cause of their oppression in their own inferiority.[62] It is tempting, but too easy, to read the trajectory of Copway in these terms. What one can see happening in his case, and indeed in the case of all the men whose life histories are described here, is rather more complex in terms of their relationship to Western belief systems and white culture. David Scott's term "conscripts of modernity" is useful here. Following the lead of the anthropologist Stanley Diamond, and of Talal Asad's homage to his work, he suggests that "modernity was not a choice New World slaves could exercise but was itself one of the fundamental *conditions* of choice"; thus he proposes that Toussaint L'Ouverture, the revolutionary Haitian who fought against the British in the 1790s, and his colleagues "were conscripts—not volunteers—of modernity."[63]

It is certainly possible to see many Indian and some British missionaries alike as consciously and conscientiously attempting to bridge two worlds, to find space for the coexistence of different cultural formations and the rhetorical terms in which very distinct societies could be translated for each other: each world predicated, albeit in very different terms, on the necessity of mutuality and "brotherhood." But such an interpretation willfully overlooks the broader forces of contemporary economics and the racial hierarchies that were pressed to serve the political ends of those who, ultimately, wielded much more power than these missionaries. In Scott's terms, these are the conditions of tragedy, where we "see the ways in which acting in the world obliges us to expose ourselves to conditions and consequences not entirely of our own choosing," and where are raised "significant questions about the extent to which we are—entire and whole and perfect—the masters and mistresses of our ends" (159). In other words, both those who tried to show how First Nations people could change, adapt, and become a part of the modern world and those natives who expressed ecstatic support for modernity were, ultimately, interpreters of its outward manifestations alone. For what was ultimately at stake was a conflict based around incompatible versions of power and agency. Christian rhetoric, with its language of spiritual enlightenment and its predication of better times ahead as a heavenly reward for true belief and good conduct, offered a way of making sense of a changing world. This was especially true when its message was predicated around the concerns that animated individuals and their immediate communities—even when colonial rule was transformed into the familial language of a caring Great Mother working in consort with a loving God. But to expect that the secular forces of the modern world would be responsive to the same rhetoric was, to say the very least, an example of tragically misplaced optimism. This was, unsurprisingly, a lesson that many individuals were to learn at firsthand. Neither old nor new belief systems, in the end, could be relied upon to sustain either individual psyches or cultural formations in the face of unprecedented technological, social, and demographic change.

CHAPTER NINE

Buffalo Bill's Wild West and English Identity

Bram Stoker's short story "The Squaw" (1893) introduces the reader to an English couple taking their honeymoon in Germany. During their stay in Nuremberg, they join forces with a certain Elias P. Hutcheson. Through his very name, Stoker sets him up as an archetypal—indeed, near-caricatured—Westerner "hailing from Isthmian City, Bleeding Gulch, Maple Tree Country," Nebraska.[1] Leaning over the castle wall, he drops a moderate-size pebble. Hutcheson's intention is to startle a playful kitten, but in fact he knocks its brains out. The kitten's mother glares at the Nebraskan, turns her attention to her dying offspring, and then, realizing it is dead, she

> again threw her eyes up at us. I shall never forget the sight, for she looked the perfect incarnation of hate. Her green eyes blazed with lurid fire, and the white, sharp teeth seemed to almost shine through the blood which dabbled her mouth and whiskers. She gnashed her teeth, and her claws stood out stark and at full length on every paw. Then she made a wild rush up the wall as if to reach us, but when the momentum ended fell back, and further added to her horrible appearance for she fell on the kitten, and rose with her black fur smeared with its brains and blood. (88)

The violently vengeful cat rushes at Hutcheson, but the wall is too high for her to reach him. She is, he remarks, the "savagest beast I ever saw," with the exception of an Apache squaw he has known, who had had her "papoose" stolen by a "half-breed," and in turn managed to torture and kill him (88–89). The narrator's new wife speculates that the American may in turn be murdered by the cat; the cat hears him laugh at the suggestion, leaves off the frenzied assault, and returns to licking the body of her kitten:

> "See!" said I, "the effect of a really strong man. Even that animal in the midst of her fury recognises the voice of a master, and bows to him!"
> "Like a squaw!" was the only comment of Elias P. Hutcheson. (90)

A set of verbal parallels conflate the cat and the Apache woman in the reader's mind, before the tourists continue their excursion, visiting the

Torture Tower in the castle and examining swords, blocks where necks of victims had lain, chairs full of spikes, "racks, belts, boots, gloves, collars, all made for compressing at will; steel baskets in which the head could be slowly crushed into a pulp if necessary" (92). The American is fascinated by all this apparatus of torture; in a perverse way, the unabashed appetite for cruelty that it suggests makes contemporary America seem underdeveloped. " 'Pears to me,' " remarks Hutcheson, " 'that we're a long way behind the times on our side of the big drink. We uster think out on the plains that the Injun could give us points in tryin' to make a man oncomfortable; but I guess your old mediaeval law-and-order party could raise him every time' " (93–94). He insists on getting inside the infamous Iron Virgin, a roughly shaped figure of woman with a hinged section of her front configured so that a man can be placed within. Her innards are equipped with spikes—one set ready to pierce the eyes of the victim, and the lower ones his heart and entrails. Hutcheson wanted, it seems, to give himself a thrill by imagining what it might feel like to be on the point of violent death; he is, it is made clear, a man who has spent his adult life enjoying taking risks. At this point, the cat reappears and flings herself at the attendant holding the rope that had been keeping the Iron Virgin from crushing and piercing the American. This attendant, one of his eyes ripped through by a claw, lets go, dropping the torture machine down on Hutcheson's body. His skull is crushed, "and sitting on the head of the poor American was the cat, purring loudly as she licked the blood which trickled through the gashed socket of his eyes" (97). The narrator executes her.

Various contrary narratives come into play here. Certainly, the Native American woman, like the bereaved cat, is figured as physically cruel in her instincts of revenge. Yet this revenge is also presented as a completely understandable response, whether to thoughtless kitten murder or child murder. Hutcheson's own callousness is played up by the fact that his pocketbook is in fact covered in a piece of the mixed-race child stealer's skin. As his geographic address, and indeed his whole demeanor, suggests, not only does he stand for a crass vacationing American (this figure had become a fictional stereotype by the late nineteenth century), but his assumption of control and ownership is played up to the point of parody, in a way that serves to highlight a well-established British perception of the presumption of frontiersmen toward the indigenous peoples they found in their way. As Herbert Spencer wrote in the *Comparative Review* in 1883, "Especially out in the West, men's dealings do not yet betray too much of the 'sweetness and light' which we are told distinguish the cultured man from the barbarian."[2] Moreover, Stoker appears to make a deliberate comparative point through this story: is the cruelty of a persecuted Apache woman any greater—or even as great—as that of a supposedly civilized people who could create and use such instruments of torture as the Iron Virgin?

BRITISH RESPONSES TO THE WILD WEST

Stoker's story illustrates well something of the complexity of attitudes held toward both Native Americans and American nationhood in late-Victorian Britain: the period that, in the United States, was—in Jeffrey Steele's summary—an "era of warfare and legislation that effectively contained American Indian cultures on the margins of U.S. society."[3] Stoker himself had, as it happened, a direct connection with Buffalo Bill.[4] Stoker's great friend the actor Henry Irving had been among those who had strongly urged Cody to take the Wild West across the Atlantic. As we have seen, the direction in which American culture was moving could be employed, at the hands of British writers, as both a warning and a threat: a warning against the overdevelopment of democracy and the undesirable relaxation both of class hierarchies and of standards in behavior and decorum; a threat in that the overwhelming thrust of contemporary society was read as being commercially pushy, with, at times, the very real economic challenge that America posed being sublimated into a supercilious scorn of the vulgarity of commodification.

Yet this nation that both was and was not an Other could also be advanced as a model of progress, of modernity. On the occasion of the 1887 American Exhibition, at Earl's Court, the *Illustrated London News* proclaimed:

> "It would be unnatural to deny ourselves the indulgence of a just gratification in seeing what men of our own blood, men of our own mind and disposition, in all essential respects, though tempered and sharpened by some more stimulating conditions, with some wider opportunities for exertion, have achieved in raising a wonderful fabric of modern civilisation, and bringing it to the highest prosperity, across the whole breadth of the Western Continent, from the Atlantic to the Pacific Ocean."[5]

This anticipated the sentiments of Lord Ronald Gower, who, in the opening ceremony, voiced his hope that this exhibition might lead to "a new bond of amity between England and America; may it cement the friendship and good feeling between the two great Anglo-Saxon peoples; may it increase the unity between them, that unity of which Mr. Canning so eloquently wrote when he said that the two nations were 'United by a common language, a common spirit of commercial enterprise, and a common regard for all well-regulated liberty.'"[6] Less pompously, the

Times was to remark, on the day after the final London performance, that Cody "has done his part in bringing America and England nearer together. The nearer they are brought together, the less likely they are to quarrel."[7] Official tones were admonitory, as well as celebratory, however. There was a growing sense that the future of English-speaking peoples probably lay with the United States—certainly the increase in the population of this country suggested that this would soon be the case in purely numerical terms—and hence the onus fell on them to behave responsibly. As Gladstone put it when he visited the exhibition on April 29: "If they were about to become a people of such enormous power and resources, it would be incumbent upon them to set a correspondingly noble example; and if they attained that greatness without setting such an example, he was far from saying that in their case greatness and wisdom would prove to be synonymous."[8]

The message sent by the spatial organization of this American Exhibition was very unlike that of 1851. Instead of offering open ground that could be interpreted as signaling the vastness and promise of the as-yet-unsettled West, this was an urban United States. The floor was divided into four "avenues" (Washington, Cleveland, Lincoln, and Franklin); in further simulation of a city, the cross streets were numbered from 1 to 10; and the whole was illuminated by electricity. But it was not, on this occasion, the industrial exhibits in the main halls that drew the public's attention and curiosity—beyond the fact that the displays gave an unusual degree of prominence to porcelain teeth, extract of beef, and stuffed buffaloes—but the accompanying entertainment: Buffalo Bill's Wild West Show.[9] Public interest had been expertly stirred up by the modern techniques of Cody's publicist, Major John Burke, who planted newspaper stories, issued packs of information to the press, and ensured that large colored posters were plastered all over London.

> I may walk it, or 'bus it, or hansom it: still
> I am faced by the features of Buffalo Bill.
> Every hoarding is plastered, from East-end to West,
> With his hat, coat, and countenance, lovelocks and vest.
> Plunge in City or fly suburbwards—go where I will,
> Bill and Bill's "Billy-ruffians" appear on the bill.[10]

The first public performance was given to a packed house on May 9 (by special request, the Prince and Princess of Wales saw a "royal rehearsal version" on May 5). Two days later, the company played a truncated version in front of Queen Victoria, who, since the death of Prince Albert in 1861, had hardly been seen at a public entertainment, although her appearance at the Wild West was part of her slow process of emergence into public life prior to the celebrations marking her golden jubilee.

"The cow boys, are fine looking people, but the painted Indians, with their feathers, & wild dress (very little of it) were rather alarming looking, & they have cruel faces," commented the queen.[11] Press accounts of the occasion, although emphasizing its spectacular nature—thus adding to the blanket publicity that the Wild West was receiving—were decidedly critical of the queen's apparent elitism in claiming the privilege of a private performance. The *Referee* directly linked this to her political status, and this, albeit tacitly, made a comment about the similarity of external and internal territorial expansionism: "The Queen, with true imperial instinct, insisted on having the Wild West all to herself, undisturbed by the gaze of the common herd."[12]

Yet the British public was to have plenty of opportunities to visit the show. Between May and October, the show was put on in front of around 30,000 to 40,000 people a day (in all, 2.5 million tickets were sold in London) and then moved to Birmingham, Manchester, and—for one performance only—Hull. The Indians made numerous appearances in the arena: as part of the exhilarating grand entrance, together with the cowboys and Mexican vaqueros, which was immediately followed by a daily foot race—run for real—between a member from each of these groups; chasing the Pony Express; attacking an emigrant wagon train, pulled by oxen and mules, and terrorizing the women and children before Buffalo Bill led a rescue attack; and attacking the Deadwood stagecoach (with Cody, inevitably, coming to the rescue). As the program progressed, there was a bareback pony race between young Indians—with the audience being encouraged to choose a favorite and cheer for him—followed by a piece with some pretensions to ethnographic education, at least in its title, "Life Customs of the Indians." An Indian camp was set up in the arena, with the women doing the hard work while the men looked on, prior to performing a war dance, and demonstrating (to the repulsion, whether actual or feigned, of reporters) how to scalp a victim. One Indian threw glass balls in the air as an occasion for Cody to display his sharpshooting skills; the entrepreneur and a band of Indians enacted a buffalo hunt—though not to the death, since a point was being made, by alluding to the scarcity of buffalo, about the rarity value of all the performers. Finally, there was what was described in the program as an "attack on a settler's cabin, capture by the Indians and rescue by"—again, no surprise here—"Buffalo Bill and the Cowboys." The entire performance took place against a painted backdrop showing prairie, mountains, and trees; the arena's entrances were screened by live, imported native trees and shrubs.

While the show remained essentially the same in Birmingham (although Annie Oakley had departed for the United States), where competition with football matches was an important factor in the smaller

Figure 28. Buffalo Bill's Wild West Show: Native American group against painted backdrop, Earl's Court, 1892. Denver Public Library, Western History Collection, NS-376.

attendance figures, some significant changes were made by the time it opened in a huge new auditorium at a Manchester racecourse. These included the introduction of new spectacular effects—bears, elk, a tornado, a prairie fire—seven giant canvas panoramas, and seven new tableaux, representing "pages of passing history." One included Pocahontas saving the life of John Smith, and another the death of General Custer at the battle of Little Big Horn, concluding with Buffalo Bill, head bowed, hat in hand, standing over the body of his dead friend, a scene calculated to impress the audience with Cody's emotional investment in suppressing Indian violence. Nonetheless, the show as a whole, on this and subsequent tours, was full of the contradictions that the historian Louis W. Warren has articulated so well in his cultural biography of Cody; as he writes, the real question about the man is less one of how he "derived his sympathies for Indians than how he fashioned a persona of Buffalo Bill that could denounce Indian conquest at one moment and become its most visible advocate in the next. Of all Cody's characteristics, it is this profound ambivalence about Indians that seems most impenetrable."[13] It is, however, an ambivalence that played well to British audiences with very little national investment in the existence of actual Indians, but who were accustomed to witnessing different aspects of their image deployed to different pragmatic ends.

Nonetheless, these audiences were to some degree witnessing reenacted American history, and the show's publicity capitalized on this. Cody had served with the Fifth Cavalry in Wyoming and had taken part in its attempts to drive the Sioux onto reservations and to prevent them from joining up with the resistance movements led by Crazy Horse and Sitting Bull. He had carried the news of General George Armstrong Custer's death to the officers of the Fifth Cavalry after the Battle of Little Big Horn in 1876 and had personally killed, and scalped, an Indian warrior some ten days later. This "famous Single Combat with 'YELLOW HAND,' Chief of the Sioux," became an item on the 1891–92 tour and by spotlighting Cody's dramatic past helped to sell shilling copies of his first autobiography, *The Life of Buffalo Bill*.[14] Cody was, moreover, still engaged in activities against Indians on behalf of the U.S. government. At the time of the 1890 Ghost Dance movement, he was sent by Colonel Miles to locate Sitting Bull, a member of the company that had toured England, and arrest him.[15] Twenty-three prisoners of war from the Ghost Dance disturbances were released by the U.S. War Department to tour with Cody in Britain in 1891–92 (accompanied by nine "Indian policemen").[16] Cody readily incorporated his personal history into his self-promotion as a showman. Many of the members of his company had also participated in anti-Indian military activity. But what was taking place in the Wild West Show was, to quote Sarah Blackstone, the transformation of

> this authentic knowledge of actual events into a representation of generic Western incidents. Because of this transformation, audiences saw cowboys without cows, Indians without buffalo, battles where help always arrived in the nick of time, and guns that never killed anyone. The whole bloody and arduous task of taming an unsettled land was romanticized and glorified and the moral questions that that settlement entailed were glossed over and ignored.

Accuracy and myth were mingled, and the audience was left "with no way to distinguish truth from fiction."[17]

The ethos and implications of Buffalo Bill's Wild West Show have recently received a good deal of thoughtful academic attention, from Blackstone, Joy Kasson, Paul Reddin, Richard Slotkin, and others, with the emphasis falling on how the triumphalist myth of the West was consolidated, and exported, through these performances. Cody, for one, saw the idea of the West as inseparable from his version of American patriotism, which involved promoting the excellence of his country overseas.

"I am convinced," he wrote in *Story of the Wild West and Camp-Fire Chats* (1888), in which he reflected on the impact of his performances in Europe, "that our visit to England has set the population of the British Islands reading, thinking, and talking about their American kinsmen to an extent before unprecedented. They are beginning to know of this mighty nation beyond the Atlantic and consequently to esteem us better."[18] But understanding the ways in which Buffalo Bill's show was received in Britain, not just in 1887 but on its subsequent visits, involves exploring not only what British spectators might be encouraged to internalize about the American-ness from the shows themselves, but also what is revealed about perceptions of *British* national identity from their reception.

New features were added when the Wild West returned in 1891–92 and 1902–3. Henry Morton Stanley's troop of dancing Shuli warriors appeared with them in Scotland, as did some trained Burmese elephants. Argentinian gauchos and Russian Cossacks became part of the entertainment in London. Occasional events were staged that spoke directly to versions of national memory or identity: a benefit performance in Manchester for nineteen elderly veterans of the Charge of the Light Brigade at Balaclava featured a detachment of the Twelfth Lancers and their regimental band ("Unique Military Spectacle—Historic Heroes of the past—England's Defenders of the Present—Soldier Lads of the Future");[19] on another occasion, a bareback-mounted Native American rode in competition against an Englishman wearing full hunting regalia in a small-scale steeplechase. In January 1892 the Africans who had traveled back to England with H. M. Stanley were engaged to form part of the show in Glasgow, and press reports indicated that Indians and Africans communicated using sign language.[20] Still more international acts were added to the formal performances by the early twentieth century. But throughout, it was the "red man," the "children of the prairie," who invariably attracted the most attention. To a considerable extent, this interest grew, as one might have anticipated, out of the fact that Cody was manipulating stereotypes with which his British audiences were already familiar from literature. The *Morning Post*, on 5 May 1887, drew attention to the symbiotic commercial relationship between text and display when it noted that "the windows of London booksellers are already full of editions of Fennimore [*sic*] Cooper's novels 'The Path-finder,' 'The Deer Stalker,' 'The Last of the Mohicans,' 'Leather Stocking.'"[21] Cooper, inevitably, formed a constant point of reference for journalistic accounts of the Wild West, and to his name that of Mayne Reid was repeatedly added. "Haughty in mien, graceful in manner, picturesque in dress, the Red Indians of the Wild West Show and 'The Last of the Mohicans' are one and the same," proclaimed a representative from the *Globe* who went to greet them at Gravesend.[22] The *Sporting Life*'s correspondent, writing in a tone of embarrassed jocularity that typified a certain genre of writing about these visitors, went down to the Albert Docks to see the boat on which they arrived and, coming away, "raised my hand and discovered that (shades of Fenimore Cooper and Mayne Reid!) I had not been scalped."[23] "Readers of Fenimore Cooper and Mayne Reid," commented the *Liverpool Daily Post*, "cannot but help feeling interested in the fate of the red man." But, the writer continued, both "of these famous writers painted this race in somewhat glowing colours, and it is the purpose of 'Buffalo Bill' . . . to represent the Indian as he is."[24] For while fiction evidently played a central part in forming audience expectations, the particular appeal of Cody's show lay in the fact that—as was constantly reiterated—these were no artificial images, but real, live participants, ostensibly surpassing representational conventions. "We hear a great deal about realism on the stage," wrote a correspondent in the *London Evening News and Post* in 1892, "where a working model of a Westend drawing room is hailed as a triumph of art, but the Buffalo Bill Show is something more than realism—it is reality."[25]

The emphasis in Cody's extensive, and very efficiently distributed, publicity material fell on the fact that this was the authentic thing, not the product of romance. Yet precisely the ability to live up to the expectations created through literature paradoxically seemed to confirm this reality. These Indians, the *Manchester Guardian* was pleased to report, "are obviously the genuine thing. There is no adulteration of civilisation about them. Their dress and manners, their childishness, and their stateliness are charming proofs that they are exactly the people with whom 'Leather Stockings' had to do."[26] "The Indian," as in most commentary in the popular press, is, once again, homogenized, with little or no attention paid to tribal differences. Cody's shows, drawing largely on painted and feathered horsemen from the Lakota and Brulé Sioux, the Arapahoe, Cheyenne, Shoshone and Oglala, played, as has frequently been noted, a very significant role in consolidating the clichés that came to establish the Plains Indian as *the* Indian in countless twentieth-century movies. Moreover, the trademarks of the Wild West Indian, as reported in the British press—the scalping, the incessant and ferocious attacks on white settlers, the war whoops—provided the hallmarks that allowed the Indian to become the archetype for an exportable mode of savagery, with characteristics that could be adopted wholesale into descriptions of threatening native behavior elsewhere in Britain's colonies. Thus Simpson Newland, one of the Australian writers of the 1890s who set out to target the London market with adventure stories about the outback, clad the Aboriginal warriors of *Paving the Way* (1893) in a "glory of paint and feathers."[27] One further commonplace

Figure 29. Buffalo Bill's Wild West Show: Native American woman and child in camp at Earl's Court, 1892. Denver Public Library, Western History Collection, NS-422.

about the Native American that was endlessly repeated was the idea of the race in decline, on the verge of extinction: a cause for the celebration of the advance of "civilisation" for some and of cultivated melancholy for others, and easily appropriated to a commercial rhetoric as well—"see these specimens now, before they, and the way of life they represent, are gone forever." This also was transportable to a colonial context, so powerful was the tradition and apparently self-evident logic of the motif. Newland, again, writes of an Aboriginal leader: "Perhaps he saw dimly, as many of his people have clearly seen since and as the American Indian has had occasion to know, that the success of the white man entailed the ruin of the Aboriginal race. So he preferred to die defiant and free" (138).

When Buffalo Bill's show opened in Earl's Court, it and its attendant encampment became an instant feature of the social scene of the summer of 1887. Cody himself was rapidly lionized, as the volume of invitations he received during the London season attests. Early visitors to the show and its encampment included Ellen Terry, who was presented with an eagle feather by Red Shirt, and the Prince and Princess of Wales. The language in which this visit was reported suggests a certain unintentional

OVERHEARD AT EARL'S COURT.

Old Buffer. "Ugh! I'm tired to death of being Hunted! Blessed if I'll run away from those Blank Cartridges again!"

Broncho. "Yes, you bet! And I've made up my mind to quit Bucking. It's perfectly sickening having to do it from Year's end to Year's end!"

Figure 30. "Overheard at Earl's Court," *Punch*, 4 June 1892.

but telling parallelism between the different forms of indigenous species on display: "The Prince petted a half-breed Indian baby. . . . The corrall [*sic*], where the buffalo and other animals are confined, was then visited, and the ladies petted the gentle black-tailed deer."[28] The show retained something of its social cachet on its return visit to London, too, and again the company performed for Queen Victoria, this time at Windsor. *Punch* hinted at a certain weariness with the relentless publicizing of the Western theme and projected onto its animal participants a sense that its novelty had gone off the boil. But the majority of the cartoons that drew on the Wild West for their inspiration did no more than assume familiarity with the basic roles played by the show's performers.

The simpering pose Cody and Oscar Wilde shared in the 1892 *Evening News*'s cartoon "The *Wilde* West" suggests that the British were far from blind to a certain self-serving vanity in Cody's self-promotion. However, the existence of this cartoon also reminds one of another feature that Cody and Wilde shared: the way in which the impact of their carefully honed images was dependent on the disseminating powers of the mass media. What Shelton Waldrep has argued of Wilde applies equally to Cody: his "development of an identifiable public personality . . . was possible only as the technical means for the

Figure 31. "The *Wilde* West," *Evening News*, 19 May 1892.

reproduction of his type became available. . . [His] concept of his own creation as a type, in other words, could only have the influence it did through the various forms of rapid reproduction of the time such as photography, journalism, and publishing."[29] What was true for Wilde and Cody was undoubtedly true for the Indians themselves; the considerable amount of press commentary, posters, and publicity handouts that was generated by the tours, as well as the performances themselves, played a huge part in disseminating the popular image of Native Americans. As Warren rightly remarks, these Indians were, in themselves, "a commentary on mass production, on manufacturing, on mechanical reproduction of art at every level and of every kind." Although, as he argues, they thus "invited audiences to draw a line between real and fake, historical and representation," one could equally well claim that they rendered this line a very porous and confusing one. Nonetheless, as Warren maintains, they also "provided a thrilling display of courageous, authentic people who would not quail before a blizzard of representations that threatened to overwhelm them. . . . Much of the fun of the show was seeing the 'real' people and measuring how they stacked up against their own images."[30]

Yet this was not the only form of comparison that the presence of Buffalo Bill's performers provoked. Humorists, in particular, turned the topical theme of the Wild West into an opportunity to comment on a number of aspects of contemporary society, so that the subject matter became less of a theme in its own right—often completely detached from its transatlantic associations—than a vehicle for reflection on modern British life. As had been the case with the visit of Catlin's Indians, sexual politics were prominent in satiric responses. Cartoons from 1887, and from the next tour of the Wild West, suggested, once again, that fashionable women found the native performers particularly sexually attractive. This time, however, the joke was frequently against Englishwomen for their transparent interest in what was readily acknowledged as handsome manliness (reflected, too, in the grave, meditative profiles of the Indian subjects), the punch line usually relying on the presumed superior wisdom and sense of perspective of the native sex object. These works were still an expression of anxiety, at one level, about the volatility of female sexual desire, but this time it was presented as ridiculous, rather than as a threat. The appeal of the Indian is suggested by the caption to a cartoon in *Kensington Society* (see figure 32) and by the personages in *Fun*'s cartoon. Here, even more obviously, sexist humor is deployed in order to debunk an idealization of racial difference. It is suggested that the handsome native is just as sensitive to the embarrassingly predatory female as any right-thinking Englishman would be—with the advantage of being able to speak his mind. Moreover, if the critique of women's sexual appetite is much more muted than it was at the hands of satirists in the 1840s, the Native American is treated, both verbally and in visual representation, with a great deal more dignity—indeed, even superiority—in these examples. This is not to say that there were not some occasional grotesquely offensive racist responses. The *Illustrated Sporting and Dramatic News*'s correspondent sneered that he had ceased to wonder at the theory that Indians were descended from Israel's lost tribes, since the "Indian resembles nothing so much as a Jew whose nose has been in a prize fight."[31] And the native performer appears as the epitome of savagery in the cartoon that was published in *Ally Sloper* in 1892. But even here I should note that while the tomahawk-wielding, firewater-brandishing specimens in this image are the clear descendants of Dickens's "howling, whistling, clucking, stamping, jumping, tearing" "Noble Savage," the swaggering, red-nosed, cigar-smoking cowboy figure comes off almost as badly: this is in essence an anti-*American* cartoon.

Less easy than cartoons to assess, in terms of their register, are press comments that adopted a joky, half-embarrassed tone to deal with the transatlantic visitors. Some attempts at humor deliberately infantilize their subjects, as when the *Era*'s correspondent writes that "the drawings which adorn their dwellings, representing an elk with anatomical details, and another mysterious animal resembling a plum-pudding

Figure 32. "At the Wild West at Kensington," *Kensington Society*, 6 October 1892.

> FAIR DAUGHTER. "How I would like to marry a Sioux Indian."
> STERN MOTHER. "Gracious! Why?"
> FAIR DAUGHTER. "Think how delightfully he would throw up my complexion."

AT THE WILD WEST OF LONDON.
Possibly he knew it was Leap Year.
Gushing "Old-Young" Lady.—"OH, CICELY, DEAR, I MUST SHAKE HANDS WITH THIS NOBLE SAVAGE. WHAT A PITY HE CANNOT SPEAK OUR TONGUE."
Surly Bear (in good English).—"SURLY BEAR'S GOT ONE SQUAW ALREADY. ONE'S PLENTY." [*G. O.-Y. L. faints away.*

Figure 33. "At the Wild West of London," *Fun*, 23 May 1892.

> GUSHING "OLD-YOUNG" LADY—"Oh, Cicely, dear, I must shake hands
> with this noble savage. What a pity he cannot speak our tongue."
> SURLY BEAR (IN GOOD ENGLISH)—"Surly Bear's got one squaw
> already. One's plenty."
> [G. O.-Y.L. faints away.]

breathing forth flames, are also screamingly funny."[32] This blinkered defensiveness against unfamiliar forms of cultural representation is akin, in sentiment if not in register, to anxieties about human development and degeneration that the Native Americans could be made to serve in the more soberly phrased press. In such terms—curiously proleptic of Marlow's words in *Heart of Darkness* as he contemplates the natives dancing and howling on the bank of the Congo—a *Sunday Chronicle* reporter who visited the show when it was still playing on Staten Island considered that the fascination the Wild West Show offered "the imaginative mind" was in part

> due to the coming face to face with conditions that in some sense represent our own ancestral ones. These dusky Indians, with their un-

Figure 34. "Sloper's New Friends," *Ally Sloper*, 1892.

earthly streaks of colour on their faces, and their weird, monotonous, and hollow cries as they ride past, fine as many of the faces are, yet remind us of the earlier forms of savage man whence we have evolved, not by any manner of means always in the right direction.[33]

Cody himself, of course, did not miss out on opportunities to reinforce lessons about what he unequivocally took to be the "progress" of civilization, and he and the show's management were undoubtedly responsible in part for determining the emphasis on distinguishing between primitive and modern that characterized much of the press reportage. Such differentiation was intrinsic to the performative framing of his whole enterprise. To take just one instance: on 10 June 1887 Cody held a rib-roast breakfast. Inside the large dining tent, the Native Americans cooked the meat which was suspended on tripods over coals in a hole in the ground. Hominy, "Wild West pudding," popcorn, and peanuts were also served. While the guests, including visiting American politicians, ate with cutlery, the Indians squatted on the ground at one end of the table and ate with their fingers, enacting Cody's aim of showing quite how far "civilization" had come in respect to the development of table manners.

Other manifestations of journalistic jokiness explicitly played on well-established cultural norms, with attempts at denigration through absurdity. The points of reference were determinedly British, even if occasionally they drew on forms of domestic racial stereotyping: the *Field* claimed that the Indian dancing resembled a Highland reel, with whoops "suggestive chiefly of the whisky."[34] But more frequently, the ultimate target was the various forms that social and cultural modernity at home took, rather than anything to do with either America or the American Indian. According to the *Observer*'s reporter, Red Shirt's face, decorated in yellow paint, "might have been taken at first sight for an advertisement for Colman's mustard"—an instantly recognizable color, to be sure, but the metaphor serves to damn the Indian, just faintly, through association with mass marketing. In a jibe at Whistler's innovative painting, another member of the company was said to exhibit "a face which might be appropriately termed a nocturne in violet and gold, and would most certainly delight the president of the Society of British Artists."[35] The *London Gazette* dismissed the dancing as a "diabolical can-can" and, of the sounds that accompanied it, claimed that "the spectator who speaks of the crew as an Indian Salvation Army is unkind, but he raises a general laugh, for the comparison is accepted as happy."[36] In another musical comparison, the aesthetic avant-garde is ridiculed head-on and implicitly denigrated as primitive: in 1892 a correspondent in the *Sporting Life* wrote that the Indian music is "hard upon the nerves; there is nothing like it except Wagner."[37]

Further co-optation of Native Americans into a British context had more particularized social and political resonances, even if they did not always prove to be quite what they seemed at first sight. On 28 April 1887 William Gladstone visited the Indian camp. He was introduced to Ogilasa, "Red Shirt," as the "Great White Chief" (in fact, as a *Punch* cartoon marking the occasion makes clear, he was leader of the opposition, his party having lost the election the previous year—in multiple-punning terms, "Chief of the Opper Sishun Hinderuns").[38] "The member for Midlothian will doubtless have no difficulty in converting Ugli Sha to his views," commented the *Observer*, with a far from subtle twist of derogatory renaming. "The Red Indian is a confirmed home ruler already."[39] This turns out to have nothing to do with any concept of indigenous nationalism, but something to do with that commonly repeated sneer that the men stood around looking on while the women set up house in their tepees, and that this was some kind of marker of moral inferiority. However, other journalists engaged more directly with the party political capital that they could extract from Gladstone's visit to the Wild West. *Judy*'s comic strip made heavy weather of Gladstone "playing Indian": purchasing war paint and a Sioux wig and uttering—

inevitably—"Ugh, ugh." "We understand that the Great White Chief lives in the hopes of eventually taking the scalps of *all* the rival chiefs of the Commons and of Mr Swinburne," the caption to the final picture reads. "He has constructed a wigwam at his Hawarden home, at which Fenians and photographers are always welcome."[40] To portray Gladstone *as* an Indian, even a wannabe Indian, was, of course, to write him into a script of predestined defeat. The Irish question, Walt Whitman was to write three years later, could be understood as "our Indian question repeated."[41] Other, more pro-Liberal publications turned things round. The supporter of home rule was transformed into "Our Own 'Buffalo Bill'! On his Irish Mustang, Shamrock,"[42] while *Truth* tried to extract maximum value out of the juxtaposition of the Wild West and British politics, dressing up the Grand Old Man with headdress and tomahawk, yet also having him sing a ditty about the "Cattle Ranch" episode in the show:

> Now, this incident you've seen, and have watched with interest keen,
> > Is like the Irish question let me say,
> Since the hut for Ireland stands, while those savage Indian bands,
> > Are the Unionists who govern us to-day.
> Yes, young Balfour and his lot, try with bludgeon and buckshot,
> > And with fire and sword poor Irishmen to crush;
> But he will not have his way, for the Liberals of to-day,
> > Like the Cowboys, to the rescue boldly rush![43]

The response to Buffalo Bill's entourage, as we have seen, mapped onto sets of cultural expectations already formed by popular fiction—and for some older people, doubtless, by memories of George Catlin's tours. Moreover, the serious press continued to provide a steady stream of articles, which on occasion not only treated Native Americans with anthropological seriousness, distinguishing in minute detail between tribal practices, but also used the treatment that they had received in the United States as a means to attack, once again, the perceived inhumanitarian attitudes of that country by comparison with those standards that they wished to assert were upheld within the British Empire. What is more, the *Times*, in particular, carried regular reports on the continuing warfare between U.S. troops and Indians. Nonetheless, there was little direct reaction to American policies toward indigenous peoples in the press responses to the Wild West Shows (this may have something to do with the pervasive influence of the copious publicity issued by Major Burke, which, in making the task of many time-pressed journalists easier, had the effect of deflecting political reflection). The battles in which some of the participants, on both sides, had been actively and bloodily

THE GREAT WHITE CHIEF.

On the occasion of Mr. Gladstone's visit to the American Exhibition, Red Shirt, the Sioux Chief, was introduced to the ex-Premier, it being explained to him that the latter was the "Great White Chief" of this country.—*Vide Public Press.*

Figure 35. "The Great White Chief," *Judy*, 11 May, 1887.

involved were hardly contextualized except as exempla of the "conquest of the West."

Rather than looking in vain for repeated critical references to American policy toward Indians in the British press, it is far more telling to look at a further way in which Native American identities were used simultaneously to highlight aspects of Englishness and to defamiliarize it. Particularly before the opening of the first London show, the Indians were extensively reported on as they were taken around the city. This tourism was a part of Cody's means of stirring up public excitement about the forthcoming performances; it was certainly effective in setting up a deliberately provocative contrast between contemporary metropolitan society and the culture of the visitors, whether they were visiting Drury Lane, watching a performance of *Shadows of a Great City* in Manchester, or attending the Congregational Chapel in West Kensington, where they sang "Nearer My God to Thee" in Lakota—unremarked-upon evidence that missionary activity had not exactly left them unmarked by Anglo-American culture already.[44] On this and subsequent tours, reporters delighted to record them visiting sights in England and, indeed, other European countries. They were imaged riding on a Manchester corporation tram, attending an audience with the pope in Rome, riding in Venetian gondolas, and so on. This provided attention-grabbing material, playing upon expectations that the interaction of "primitive" and "civilized" would create a shock of incongruity.[45] This sightseeing could also be presented as a beneficial educational experience for the Indians, which added yet another component to the resulting publicity; it gave them, said Nate Salsbury, Cody's manager, in an interview, "a better idea of the white man's power, and of the ORGANISED FORCES OF CIVILISATION."[46] Yet, on other occasions, their presence could be commandeered in order to celebrate integral aspects of Englishness; bravery, one is led to infer, is what the warriors and the survivors of the Charge of the Light Brigade share—as well as the way both groups mutually reinforce a sense of each other's belatedness, their belonging to an era that is now past.

The Wild West Indians' Responses to Britain

What, however, may we learn of the responses of the Indians themselves to their experiences? Frustratingly, not as much as we would hope. Their reported reactions during the visits are not only brief but frequently very bland. This suggests a surface—and perhaps mediated—courtesy, with almost nothing of the edginess toward contemporary social conditions that came across in the comments that Catlin recorded some fifty years earlier. In 1887 the Sioux chief Red Shirt, for example, when asked his opinion of Goethe's *Faust*, in which he had seen Henry Irving star at the Lyceum, "opines, after a pause, that it was 'good,' and added, 'Big dream.'"[47] Visiting Westminster Abbey, the "Spirit Lodge" of Londoners, was for him an even more visionary experience:

> The words of the preacher I did not know but they sounded like the soft winds through a leafy forest and my eyelids were heavy. Then I heard soft music and sweet voices, and a great cloud came down towards me, and when it nearly reached me, it opened and I saw in a blaze of light the girls with wings and they beckoned me. And I was so certain that what I saw was true that I called out to my young men who were with

Figure 36. Members of Buffalo Bill's Wild West Show posing with survivors of the charge at Balaklava, Manchester, 1887. Denver Public Library, Western History Collection, NS-218.

me "Come and see what this is," and the young men replied, "You have been dreaming." But what I saw was true, for when I looked round the great lodge afterwards I saw on the walls the same girls with wings as I saw in my dreams. Our people will wonder at these things when we return to the Indian Reservation and tell them what we have seen.[48]

The interview with Red Shirt in which this lyrical passage occurs was relatively widely syndicated through the Central News Agency, but one is led to speculate on how much spin-doctoring lay behind the translation or even the opinions themselves. We learn—as though Red Shirt is repeating a lesson—that he believes "the United States Government is good. True it has taken away our land, and the white men have eaten up our deer and our buffalo, but the Government now give us food that we may not starve. They are educating our children, and teaching them to farm and to use farming implements. Our children will learn the white man's civilisation and to live like him."[49] Yet Red Shirt, when not mouthing material that had an unmistakable air of official propaganda, also came up with responses in different registers. On occasion, his words demonstrate the same capacity for cultural reappropriation that one saw in the earlier responses of Catlin's Indians and of Maungwudaus, offering up a double-headed use of metaphor, which is quaintly defamiliarizing to a native English speaker—that is, on this occasion, to the journalist and to newspaper readers—but which simultaneously can be seen as a translation into his own conceptual terms. Something of the grandeur of this language was spotted by at least one commentator, who wrote that "Red Shirt's impression of the white man's world reads like a fragment of the Odyssey. He sees 'great villages which have no end, where the pale faces swarm like insects in the summer sun.'"[50] Visiting the House of Commons, he apparently "does not think much of it" and then expands on his reasoning. "Laws are passed in his country, he says, a good deal more quickly than they are here."[51] His orthodoxy, moreover, does not entirely prevail when it comes to social manners. Meeting with Queen Victoria, he thanks her for her greetings. "After a pause he desired the interpreter to say that 'he had come a long way to see her Majesty, and was glad,' after which 'Red Shirt,' feeling the interview was over, strode abruptly away. His notions of Court etiquette are primitive, but for all that there was both dignity and respect in his manner."[52]

The best-known account by an Indian who traveled to England with Buffalo Bill is given by Black Elk, a Lakota Sioux holy man who, in 1886, had joined up with the Wild West in an attempt to help his people, both directly, through his earnings, and by returning to them with a broader perspective on white men's ways. "Now I know the white men's customs well," he wrote in Lakota from Manchester about two years after he left home. But his experience seemed to make him skeptical about cultural integration. "And many of the ways the white men follow are hard to endure," he continued. "And although the country is large it is always full of white men."[53] Much later, in 1931, he gave John Neihardt an account of his meeting with Queen Victoria and of her saying to him: "If I owned you Indians, you good-looking people, I would never take you around in a show like this. You have a Grandfather over there who takes care of you over there, but he shouldn't allow this, for he owns you, for the white people to take you around as beasts to show to the people" (249–50). There is no apparent recognition, though, of the appropriative colonial weight behind the idea of ownership, and Queen Victoria does seem to have convinced other Indians of her benevolent outlook, even if, in doing so, she was publicly putting forward the maternalist face of empire. The *Daily Mercury* reported that Red Shirt, speaking through an interpreter, "said that he and his young men had sat up all night talking about the 'Great White Mother.' [. . .] It pleased all their hearts that she came to them as a mother, and not with all her warriors around her. Her face was kind and pleased them, and every one of his young men resolved that she should be their great white mother."[54] Her private views, as expressed in her journal, however, suggest a far less empathic approach. "All the different people," she wrote, "wild, painted Red Indians from America, on their wild bare backed horses, of different tribes,—cow boys, Mexicans, &c., all came tearing round at full speed, shrieking and screaming, which had the weirdest effect."[55]

If the Show Indians were angry about their treatment—whether at the hands of Buffalo Bill or the American government back home—there is no prominent record of it. But as with Catlin's Indians, it is impossible to gauge what lies behind silence, reserve, and cautious, polite language: a reticence that at the time provided a blank space onto which journalists could write their own script. The *Leeds Daily News* was certainly alert to the political circumstances of some of the Indian performers who were appearing on the 1891–92 tour, but it managed to turn their presence and their appearance into an occasion that demonstrated how amenable these once-alarming people were to civilizing influences, as though all they needed was contact and kindness.

> A short conversation, through an interpreter, with one of Buffalo Bill's braves soon convinces one that in many cases, he is gifted with a thoughtful mind and an observant eye. Yesterday, Short Bull, leader of the ghost dancers and high priest of the "Messiah Craze" made a speech through the medium of an interpreter, which clearly showed that civilization had made him a philosopher. At one time he was a fanatic of the most dangerous type. It was curious to see him and his fellow braves bedecked in their gaudy garments of various colours and their faces besmirched with paints of every hue, listening with half closed eyes to all that was said. Not a word could they understand, but their wonderful power of interpreting a gesture or a facial movement, no doubt, gave them a clue to the conversation. With all their war paint they are very simple folk and their conversation consisted mostly of reminiscences of home, and simple but evidently heartfelt gratitude to Colonel Cody and his colleagues who had, as they naively put it, been so kind as to take them to different countries to see rare and wonderful things.[56]

George Crager, the interpreter for this tour, was not prepared to offer a translation when, on the last night of the tour, in Glasgow, Kicking Bear stayed behind in the arena to recount his heroic deeds in Lakota. Crager suspected an internal political agenda; many of the Sioux on this tour had, indeed, been hired from the Pine Ridge Reservation on Cody's promise to the commissioner that he would take with him Indians who were most likely to be troublesome when the spring arrived. Crager's sympathy toward native identities is seriously called into question, for that matter, by the fact that he sold fourteen Indian artifacts (and donated another fourteen), most notably a Ghost Dance shirt, to Glasgow's Kelvingrove Museum in December 1891.[57]

Occasional mentions were made in the British press that some of those taking part in the Wild West were, effectively, political prisoners. Usually this was a means of highlighting the sensationalism of the Lakotas' presence, although a journalist for the *Cardiff Evening Express* put a more empathic Celtic emphasis on the participation of Short Bull: "In the spectacle of this leader of a vanquished people exhibited to the gaze of the multitude in the arena we seem to find a modern parallel to that experience of Caractacus, who, exiled from his island home, was exposed to the gaze of the Roman populace."[58] For the most part, however, the British press generally shared the publicity that portrayed these participants as vanquished warriors; as Sam Maddra has put it, "Buffalo Bill's Wild West was engaged in the business of making a profit through entertainment, and it did not suit the show's needs to portray the Lakota Ghost Dancers as anything else but 'Hostiles.' "[59] Journalists do not seem to have asked probing questions around this issue. The sense of dislocation and alienation that many must have felt has to be inferred from circumstances: from Black Elk's relatively laconic account of being stranded in Manchester, traveling to Europe with another small Wild West Show, and there falling sick and being overwhelmed with homesickness; from the number of deaths, injuries, and illnesses that befell members of the company.

Perhaps the most vivid sense of estrangement from tribe and place comes, however, through imaginative fiction. James Welch's *Heartsong of Charging Elk* (2000), in which this contemporary Gros Ventre–Blackfeet novelist imagines himself back into a turn-of-the-century Show Indian, will be discussed in the concluding chapter. A much earlier short piece, Robert Cunninghame Graham's "Long Wolf," sought a very similar effect. In 1917 Graham wrote to Theodore Roosevelt, sending him a £20 check as his contribution toward a national memorial to Buffalo Bill. In the letter, he both praises Cody and places him somewhat ambiguously in a broad context of types of heroic, nationalist masculinity.

> Every American child should learn at school the history of the conquest of the West.
>
> The names of Kit Carson, of General Custer and of Colonel Cody should be as household words to them. These men as truly helped to form an empire as did the Spanish Conquistadores.

As we shall see in a moment, it is unclear quite how complimentary Graham intended this historical reference to be.

> Nor should Sitting Bull, the Short Wolf, Crazy Horses and Rain-in-the-Face be forgotten.

They too were Americans, and showed the same heroic qualities as did their conquerors. . . .

All of these men, and they were men of the clearest grit . . . were actors in a tremendous drama, set in such surroundings as the world never saw before, or will see again.[60]

As a result of the letter, Roosevelt's son Kermit invited Graham to compose a biography of Cody aimed at children, thinking that he was the writer best able to make him come to life on the page. The Englishman declined politely enough, claiming that "since his roaming in North America and participation in our frontier life had been largely confined to our South-West and to Mexico, he did not feel inclined to take up a work that would necessarily deal largely with the bleak frozen winters of the North-West, to which he was a stranger" (73–74). Instead, he sent a written sketch—one that, indeed, dwells on estrangement and opens with the idea of a hostile climate—of the neglected grave of Long Wolf in Brompton Cemetery, in London, who had died while on tour with the Wild West in 1892. "The English climate," he writes, has done its worst upon the headstone of this Sioux chief. "Smoke, rain, and then more smoke, and still more rain, the fetid breath of millions, the fumes of factories, the reek of petrol rising from little Stygian pools on the wood pavements, the frost, the sun, the decimating winds of spring, have honeycombed" it (74). Above all, Graham is moved by this man's isolation. Long Wolf is surrounded by English graves, representatives of every age and class, but united by their religion, their language, and their nation, and the Englishman meditates upon the difference of this scene, with its granite and marble tombstones, from the tepees by the riverside where the Sioux must have played as a boy to the trails that he must have ridden upon with war parties. His grave is rendered "more lonely than if it had been dug out on the prairies, by the crowd of monuments of alien folk who crowd about it." In being isolated from his native landscape, he is severed from his past. By implication, this has been the fate not just of this one dead Indian, although the degree of removal from the land of his birth has been acute; his own lost recollections of "the plains long ere the railroad crossed them and when the buffalo migrated annually, in countless thousands," are the precarious recollections of entire tribes once displaced from landscapes that themselves hold the prompts of the past. "What his adventures were, how many scalps he took, and what atrocities he saw committed, only he himself could tell and Indians keep no diaries except in memory" (79). Although the tale stays well clear of overt didacticism, it offers up the potential for a reading that is far from supportive of the "conquest of the West."[61]

NATIVE AMERICANS AND THE GLOBALIZATION OF
POPULAR CULTURE

By 1902–3 the elegiac tone in which Buffalo Bill's show was framed was more emphatic than ever. Coverage in the British press emphasized yet more strongly the notion that the public was being invited to a historical relict of a way of life that was rapidly passing, if it had not already disappeared: a microcosmic depiction of recent American history. "The native Indians are fast passing away, and the redskin warriors who terrorized the frontier of the Western United States will soon join the braves who have passed to the happy hunting-ground. The frontiersmen, scouts, and trappers have seen the day of their glory, and have won well-nigh imperishable fame in Indian warfare and in the progress of the nation."[62] Journalists repeatedly stressed that what was on offer was not only entertainment but education. They were following the lead of Major John Burke, Cody's colleague, who drew reporters' attention to the rapid transformation of the West—when Cody started out, beyond the Missouri was the Great American Desert, "peopled with wild animals and hostile savages. Now this section of the States is the granary of the world." More than this, he indicated that the show offered lessons that could be directly applicable to British colonies: "With Canada, South Africa, and Australia, what may not your people expect within the same time—thirty years—with more rapid methods, more confidence, from the experience of the courageous adventurers that have affected these magical conditions?"[63] The press was not passively content to let Americans pick up pioneering glory for themselves. The *Leicester Mercury* turned the fact that "the great Wild West has for hundreds of years past appealed strongly to the imagination of the British people" to long-lived national characteristics: it was the "love of freedom, the attraction of adventure, and the restlessness of spirit that animates the better part of the men of Great Britain that sent them across the seas to the great continent of America."[64] The *Cheltenham Mercury* extended the importance of transatlantic exports to horses, too, cataloguing the different breeds represented in the show and claiming that they were in themselves "an object lesson, telling what a factor England has been in the improvement of the general stock of all kinds so prolific in America."[65] It is tempting to speculate that this foregrounding of Englishness might both be related to a heightened consciousness of national identity during the period of the Boer War (something that Cody played upon by showing a Boers-versus-English scene set in the Transvaal) and operate as a response to the intensified Americanization of the show. In 1902–3, this included a reenactment of the Battle of San Juan Hill, between the Americans and the Spanish, thus playing up the claims of the United States as an imperialist power.

Two further tendencies stand out in the journalistic coverage of this third tour. The first is an increased acknowledgment that Cody's staging cannot, after all, entirely be said to be realistic. It was widely recognized that despite the authenticity of the participants, the performances were conspicuously enhanced by modern technology. Cody's company traveled with its own generator, and, as the *Daily Dispatch* noted, the effect of the "weirdly picturesque . . . war dances of the Indians . . . which are stated to be historically correct . . . was greatly heightened at the evening performance, when the flare of the arc lamps threw grotesque shadows behind the whirling, dancing figures."[66] More than this, the press started to reinstate what the Wild West Show silenced: the fact that many Native Americans now lived on reservations, and that reservation life brings other changes with it. In part, this fact was tied in with the claim—reflecting an ultimately unfulfilled American policy as well as prophecy that the American Indian "is now fast assimilating with the white man."[67] In the camp, it was noted that some of the younger natives could "speak English pretty fluently,"[68] even if in the arena Cody excised all signs of modernity, rather as Edward Curtis removed alarm clocks and automobiles from his photographs.[69] A dichotomy was being set up between the imaginary world of the Indian performances in the arena, where, in the phrase Philip Deloria uses about attitudes toward the modernizing Indian more generally, "Indian country was always to be seen as an anachronistic space,"[70] and the heterogenous world outside these enactments—including the changing cast of the Wild West itself.

The Native Americans who toured Britain with Cody in the early twentieth century were part of a globally inclusive show, which was moved around the country with military-style organization. "The interior of the dressing tent," reported the *Swindon Advertiser*'s correspondent,

> presented a curious spectacle indeed. Dusky Indians were stalking about in the most fantastical of garbs; negroes of the darkest hue and white gleaming teeth were at their toilette; in one corner was a swarthy nigger giving a Cuban a close crop; in another corner a Mexican was cutting a cowboy's hair . . . , in another part of the tent the Russian Cossacks were arranging their articles of clothing . . . in every part of this big tent was something taking place, and the more one saw the more he became interested, and thought what a really happy family these many coloured and strange tongued people were.[71]

The *Abergavenny Chronicle* became fancifully speculative when it wondered if the monks who inhabited the show's site of old ever dreamed "that one day the Red Indian, the Cossack, the Arab, and the men from

Uruguay would meet there in friendly conclave with the Briton, and sit down peaceably to dine with him."[72] What took place in the arena was, to quote Jonathan Martin, writing about Cody's show in the context of the politics of American identity, "an affirmation of a white racial identity, an identity that transferred the nexus of American-ness from class to race."[73] But this behind-the-scenes display of apparently comfortable cultural blending proved a more interesting and conceptually provocative sight than the orchestrated performances that were staged in the arenas. It both acknowledged the place of the Native American in a melting pot not so much of American national identity, but of globally distributed cultures in dialogue with one another, and offered, on British soil, a very visible model—however temporary—of peaceable racial coexistence and cooperation.

The fascination of Buffalo Bill's shows had worn off considerably for many commentators by the early twentieth century, even if this was not true for successive generations of spectators. The clichéd details of Indian life—the attacks, the war dances, the scalping—had become more familiar than ever.[74] Yet there remains one further appropriation of the figure of the Native American into popular culture at the turn of the century that suggests despite the well-worn nature of some aspects of these stereotypes—the war paint, the feathered headdresses, the grunting articulation—they could be turned to ends as slippery in their connotations as Bram Stoker's squaw.

J. M. Barrie's *Peter Pan* was first performed in 1904, a play with episodes based in part on Barrie's own reading of "penny dreadfuls."[75] Never-Never Land is a Ballantynian coral island, yet one furnished with basking mermaids; it is constantly threatened by pirates, but covered by a forest inhabited by "redskins." In other words, it represents as great a heterotopic fantasy as one could find backstage in 1902–3. Barrie's play, indeed, presents an extraordinarily crude compilation of stereotypes—so crude that one wonders at times if the stereotypes themselves are being burlesqued. Tiger Lily, "the belle of the Piccaninny tribe," enters. She puts her ear to the ground and beckons to Great Big Little Panther and the rest of the tribe:

> TIGER LILY.   Pirates! (*They do not draw their knives; the knives slip into their hands*) Have um scalps? What you say?
> PANTHER.   Scalp um, oho, velly quick.
> THE BRAVES.   (*in corroboration*). Ugh, ugh, wah.
> (*A fire is lit and they dance round and over it till they seem part of the leaping flames. Tiger Lily invokes Manitou; the pipe of peace is broken; and they crawl off like a long snake that has not fed for many moons.*)[76]

When Tiger Lily is kidnapped by the pirates, Peter rescues her; out of gratitude, the members of her tribe guard the Darling children for a while. Their role is simultaneously to be nurturing children of the forest and to be "picturesque." But they are not strong enough to withstand Hook and his crew, who become, in their turn, new versions of Western adventurers. They vanquish the Red Man, to be sure, and hence might be read as emissaries of progress by some, yet—like Elias P. Hutcheson— they are marked by a crude recourse to violence and are hardly to be ad- mired in themselves. Indians, in this play, seem to belong with childhood in a way that goes beyond the infantilizing maneuvers of those journal- ists who just wanted to designate Buffalo Bill's (and hence all) Indians as primitive and therefore faintly cute and amusing. They are part of a de- sire to hold time still, to remain young, against all logic and, indeed, against all probability.

Significantly, the reception of *Peter Pan* was quite different in England and in the United States. North American audiences saw a very particu- lar allegorical message in the inclusion of the Indians; indeed, the seri- ousness with which the play was analyzed greatly amused its author. To quote Andrew Birkin, Barrie's biographer: "The Never Land symbolized the New World. . . . Audiences suddenly became 'nursery-conscious, fairy- conscious, pirate-conscious' and, not least, 'Redskin-conscious', since Peter's intimacy with Tiger Lily and the Lost Boys' alliance with the Red Indians was seen to have a special and meaningful significance."[77] But in England, lacking the same vested interests in the drama that had played out on the Western frontier, *Peter Pan* was taken as a fantasy for both children and adults: pure escapism.

Richard Slotkin has noted how the Western movie, after the Second World War, was not only a highly popular genre, but had developed

> a visual language of great force, variety, resonance, economy, and the- matic reach that invited both cinematic virtuosity and critical intelli- gence. As a result, the genre was now developed intensively and with a high degree of consciousness by filmmakers who sought to use its vocabulary to allegorize a wide range of difficult or taboo subjects like race relations, sexuality, psychoanalysis, and Cold War politics.[78]

The reception accorded Barrie's psychologically strange play is but one of many instances that suggest this flexible co-option of the Native American happened much earlier in England than it did in the United States. A similar fluidity can be seen in the way in which Buffalo Bill was treated. For the English could, when it suited them, adopt him as one of their own—an exemplum of "manliness," an archetypal colonial figure. When his biography was published in London in 1901, it was, indeed, included in Methuen's "Colonial Library." The romance of his life was compared to a romance by Rider Haggard,[79] or the British public could be encouraged to admire Cody as a typical American—not just in the terms of his own self-promotion, as a fearless frontiersman, and hence the embodiment of progress, but as an occupational polymath, capable of taking on a number of careers and making a success of them. Only occasionally do we find notes of criticism: that he had played too personal a role in exterminating buffalo, that his aggressive advertising reeked of American over-commercialization.

Native Americans certainly could, in the popular mind, be linked to the inhabitants of the British Empire; the common factor here was a crude and ignorant racism, often reflecting a bastardized version of theories of evolutionary and degenerative development. But above all, by the turn of the century, the Native American was spectacle. And as spectacle, these peoples became a screen onto which various narratives of national identity were projected: versions of Englishness, versions of America. A literal screen, indeed; during Buffalo Bill's 1904 tour of Britain, the British Bioscope Company made over 300,000 "moving pictures," recording every moment of the show. Cody—and members of the press—saw the film in Manchester, shortly before his return to the United States. He took his own copy home with him; the ten reels depicting the performance were subsequently shown throughout Britain. Opening with William Sweeney and the Cowboy Band playing "The Star-Spangled Banner" and closing with "God Save the King," this movie's format suggests quite neatly how native peoples were enfolded, by Western popular culture, into national symbolic orders.

The symbolic order that counted, however, was a domestic one. Again and again, Buffalo Bill's Indians were invoked and deployed—ironically, as well as triumphantly—as a means of establishing a British sense of national identity and, above all, a distinguishable national culture. There were elements of both the jingoistic and the parochial about this, to be sure: a strategy of defense at a time when, unmistakably, America was becoming a notable challenge as a world power, whether in economic, militaristic, or ideological terms. Even if collaboration with this growing international force was increasingly perceived as advisable and pragmatic at a diplomatic and commercial level, and even if commentators within Britain were increasingly lamenting what they perceived as the "Americanization" of many aspects of life, popular culture offered an opportunity to appropriate a quintessential element in modern American mythmaking and turn it to local ends.

CHAPTER TEN

Indian Frontiers

Traveling in America in 1890, Rudyard Kipling recorded a number of his conversations. In Yellowstone Park, he chatted with the captain in charge of defending the Mammoth Hot Springs against such acts of violence as visitors' dropping soft soap into the water or chipping off bits of the geyser cones, and learned that this man "had read a good deal about [our] Indian border warfare and had been much struck with the likeness it bore to Red Indian warfare."[1] Another military man tells him: "I've been in Arizona. A trooper there who was in India told me that Arizona was like Afghanistan. There's nothing under Heaven there except horned toads and rattlesnakes—and Indians" (102). In a further discussion, with the lieutenant running the cavalry post at Yellowstone, Kipling found that this man

> had read everything that he could lay hands on about the Indian army, especially our cavalry arrangements, and was very full of a scheme for raising the riding Red Indians—it is not every noble savage that will make a trooper—into frontier levies—a sort of Khyber guard. "Only," as he said ruefully, "there is no frontier these days, and all our Indian wars are nearly over. Those beautiful beasts will die out, and nobody will ever know what splendid cavalry they can make." (105)

Later, crossing the Rockies by train, Kipling remarked, as many other travelers had done, on the miserable creatures that he saw—"Bundles of rags that were pointed out as Red Indians boarded the train from time to time"—but he also read what he witnessed as a form of proud, stoical independence. "Like the Punjabi, the Red Indian gets out by preference on the trackless plain and walks solidly to the horizon. He never says where he is going" (123). Although the response to this momentary vision is framed in terms that convey his learned respect for the difference of other cultures, Kipling's words also evoke, more conventionally, both the supposedly vanishing Indian of the closing frontier and the newly minted tourist Indian, displaying a picturesque primitivism that offers a safe yet indisputable counterpart to the forces of modernity. The aesthetic appeal, moreover, was, for Kipling, unrelated to the ethnicity of the objects of his gaze; on another occasion, he summarily dismissed Native Americans as "unlovely and only by accident picturesque" (74).

The ease with which the discourse of Kipling and his acquaintances could pass from one frontier to another—indeed, from the touristified American West to a wistfully glimpsed arena of danger and activity nine thousand miles away—is a reminder that despite the powerful and increasingly mythical resonances of the American Indian frontier at the end of the nineteenth century, the concept of the frontier was encountered in relation to a number of locations, including the contested fringes of the British Empire. Yet in late-nineteenth-century Britain, the term had rather different resonances from those that it bore within the United States, and it did not have an equivalent function in the establishment of a national mythography. To be sure, the romance of the American frontier played a significant role in adventure fiction—both homegrown and imported—and within travel writing, and the role of the frontiersman was co-opted into various versions of Anglo-Saxon manliness.[2] But at the same time, concerns about American coarseness, brutality, exploitation, and greed, as manifested in different aspects of frontier life, raised issues about the social directions that country was taking and about the dangers of atavism on the borders of "civilization." This anxiety held true for the edges of empire as well. Indeed, for the Victorians, the very term "Indian frontier" was highly ambiguous. Some works that incorporate the phrase—such as Henry Hartley Fowler's *The Indian Frontier Question* and General Sir John Adye's *Indian Frontier Policy: An Historical Sketch*—unsurprisingly deal with the troubled areas in the Himalayas and the Hindu-Kush, with anxieties about Russian invasion, and the terms on which relations with the local native tribes should be conducted; their year of publication is, after all, 1897, the date of the rising of the Pathan tribes on the Northwest Frontier and the resulting year-long campaign by British troops to regain the Khyber Pass. The contents of other texts are less immediately guessable. E. H. Aitken's *Tribes on My Frontier* turns out not to be concerned with human groupings at all but describes the rats, mosquitoes, lizards, ants, crows, bats, bees, wasps, butterflies, and bugs of "Dustypoor." F. B. Forester's *Beyond the Frontier*, however, is a novel, set some sixty years before its publication in 1914; it recounts the adventures of a young British man who goes to the United States to work as a government surveyor and has some hair-raising encounters with Indians. He concludes with a glance forward to a time "when the dominion of the white should spread and widen, cramping and dooming the tribes of the red,"[3] the narrator hearing "the spirit of the unconquered West . . . calling us, the pioneers of the civilization yet to come, out once more, back to the work awaiting us yonder in the wild, wide regions, the home of the red man and bison—the vast unsettled wilderness that lay as yet far Beyond the Frontier" (309). Although one might fairly expect Bessie Marchant's *Girl Captives: A Story of the*

Indian Frontier to be an adventure tale written in the tradition of captivity narratives, in fact, like *In the Toils of the Tribesmen*, also subtitled *A Story of the Indian Frontier*, it is set in northern India. And even if the first part of the title of Lascelles Wraxhall's fictional *The Backwoodsman; or, Life on the Indian Frontier* correctly points the reader to an America where shooting a Comanche is on a sporting a par with shooting a bear or buffalo, the presumably generic engravings of adventure that serve as illustrations do their best to confuse—they include elephants.

This confusion over the term "Indian" could be used to deliberate textual effect. In his account of traveling with native people in England, Catlin drew attention to their capacity to shock by telling how a hotel proprietor in Manchester was alarmed to see "Indians" who looked like this, and how a London landlady was incredulous that such "wild, black-looking savages" should come from the "Indies." He tells, with some ironic disparagement, of a London woman who gushed over him and protested her familiarity with his work: ' "I recollect the very day when you started for India—and I have followed you the whole way—I have your book—I bought several copies to give to my friends; I have read every word of it over and over again. . . . By the way, I don't suppose you were down much in the neighbourhood of Chusan (I've got a nephew there—a fine fellow—he's a surgeon. . .)." '[4] Chapter 15 of Edith Nesbit's 1899 novel for children, *The Story of the Treasure Seekers*, is entitled "Lo, the Poor Indian!" building on Alexander Pope's well-worn epithet, and in it the Bastable family learn that their mother's Indian uncle will be visiting. Overhearing their father in conversation with this gentleman, "about Native Races and Imperial something or another,"[5] they prepare a special dinner for him in the schoolroom. "We asked him about wigwams, and wampum, and mocassins, and beavers, but he did not seem to know, or else he was shy about talking of the wonders of his native land" (193). Inevitably, this white man not only hails from the India of the British Empire, but is rather well-to-do and showers them with gifts. Nesbit is—as throughout her book—making affectionate capital out of the well-meaning (if somewhat patronizing) intentions of the Bastables and their dangerous propensity to jump to conclusions without the knowledge available to the adults around them.[6] But this inference about an "Indian" would have been a natural one for children to draw in the 1890s, not least because of Buffalo Bill's British shows, which had resulted in a notable increase in fiction, picture books, and toys reinforcing the dominant late nineteenth-century American view of the Native American, of the conflicts that had taken place on the frontier, and the subsequent messages about the advance of "civilization"—for America, Britain, and the world—that might be derived from these wars.

With the closing of the *actual* frontier in the American West came the consolidation of its symbolic valences, both internally and externally constructed. The internally located frontier spirit was drawn along the familiar conceptual lines that take their bearings from Frederick Jackson Turner. He saw the movement from west to east as a "record of social evolution,"[7] with agrarian development followed by manufacture, all the while accompanied by "the extension of political organization, of religious and educational activity" (9–10). Turner characterized the frontier spirit as fostering a healthy combination of steadfast individualism and neighborliness in the face of adversity, whether that adversity comes in the shape of intractable landscape, harsh winters, or attacks from natives. Famously—notoriously—Turner's frontier was the border between "settlement" and "free land," "the outer edge of the wave—the meeting point between savagery and civilization" (3); in other words, he gave it both topographical and metaphorical currency. On the other hand, Theodore Roosevelt's extension of the frontier myth, especially in his speeches and writings about the Spanish-American War, looked outward rather than inward. It has been seen, by the doyen of frontier studies, Richard Slotkin, and by many others, as expressing the ethos that has lain behind the whole subsequent history of U.S. imperialism.[8] Roosevelt's frontier was more explicitly global in its potential, even as it drew on the same absolutist dichotomy, and was based on righteous violence—"peace by the sword"—rather than ideals of cooperation and democracy. As he saw it, "Whether the barbarian be the Red Indian on the frontier of the United States, the Afghan on the border of British India, or the Turkoman who confronts the Siberian Cossack, the result is the same . . . without force, fair dealing usually amounts to nothing."[9]

From the point of view of a significant number of Victorian British commentators, there would have been nothing new here, whether they reacted to Roosevelt's words with sympathy or with revulsion. As we have already seen, an examination of Americans' encounters with *their* native population had, for some decades, provided a ready ground for comparison with Britain's own policies. The Bastable response—the way in which the mention of an "Indian" instantly calls a vivid image to mind—serves as a reminder that in all kinds of contexts, the American Indian was what first came to mind when the term "Indian" was used. The American Indian, moreover, came to stand as the archetype according to which all kinds of native peoples were described and assessed. Nowhere can this be seen more than in early accounts of the British exploration of Australia, where Aboriginal shelters, or "humpies," were readily referred to as "wigwams"; where tribal cultures were misread and regarded as extraordinarily primitive because their structures did not correspond to North American ones, with clearly defined chiefs or leaders; where maps soon became scattered with names such as "Indian Head," "Indian Bay," "Indian Creek," "Indian Well," and "Indian Point" and where, in the wake of terrible massacres, the rhetorical form of "dying Indian" poems could readily be adopted for compassionate and critical ends. Eliza Hamilton Dunlop's "Aboriginal Mother," for example, written in the wake of the Myall Creek Massacre of 1838, is spoken by a woman fleeing with her baby in her arms, her other child beheaded at her feet, the menfolk slaughtered. Who, she asks, will teach the survivor she's carrying away the skills of his people? "The echoes of my homeless heart/Reply—the dead, the dead!"[10] Henry Kendall's "Aboriginal Death Song" (1862) and "The Last of His Tribe" (1864) romanticize the passing of the noble Australian native in ways that seem directly dependent on laments for the disappearing Indian, and another over-romanticizing poet, George Gordon McCrae, wrote an epic poem on an Aboriginal subject, "Mamba ('The Bright-Eyed'): An Aboriginal Reminiscence" (1867), which, as Janeen Webb and Andrew Enstice remark, "has many similarities to Longfellow's much better-known poem of native American life, 'Hiawatha.' "[11] The language of Kendall's "Death Song" betrays its heritage very obviously. "Hunter, and climber of trees/Now doth his tomahawk rust," he apostrophizes, as anachronistic in his delineation of native life as was Ettie A. Aycliffe, who in "Lubra" (1886), despite her desire to create an identifiable and sympathetic voice for the Aborigine, has him recollect: "Happy were we in the wild, and our wigwams builded at leisure."[12]

If the American Indian readily provided many stereotypes through which indigenous people could be approached and judged, so could the American frontier readily be seen as the archetypal frontier. It is easy to see why this should be the case. The frontiers of settlement were, after all, once Britain's own. Looking at policies toward native people in what had formerly been part of Britain's own empire offered opportunities for a range of reflections on the ways in which Britain was dealing with racial issues on her current frontiers. Comparisons of frontier policies could be turned into an opportunity for calling attention to the superior tactics of Britain's administrators and commanders within the current empire, and, as we have seen, deliberately flattering parallels with British expansionism were drawn by Cody's team in order to magnify the glories of the Anglo-Saxon spirit that had, they claimed, consolidated the American frontier. Yet the tables could be turned. For example, the administrator and diplomat Sir Lepel Henry Griffin, in *The Great Republic* (1884), maintained:

> In British India there are many aboriginal races, like Bhils and Gonds, who are of no account as a source of revenue or strength, yet the

Government takes fully as much care of their interests as if they were a rich and civilised community. In Canada, where the Indians are numerous, we have no record of constant Indian wars, and the white and coloured races live side by side orderly and peacefully. The difference is due to the care with which complaints are investigated and grievances redressed, while Indian affairs are conducted by officials who understand the business, instead of by the first adventurer who can bribe the wire-pullers of Washington to give him office.[13]

Griffin's emphasis falls not only on the presumed integrity of British officials, but also on the fact that he wishes to present them, and hence the type of rule they represent, as motivated by humanitarian rather than economic interests. Even though the United States is not openly mentioned here, its association with callous materialism was well enough established for it to provide an implicit point of contrast. The perceived difference in administrative competence and attitudes was even more explicitly brought out in an article published seven years later in *Macmillan's Magazine* by the prolific travel writer A. G. Bradley, who was to go on to write a book tellingly entitled *Britain across the Seas: America*. Here, he deplored the Indian agent as "the incarnation of everything that is scandalous in administration. . . . The contrast between the British Civil Servant in Bengal or Madras, and the American custodian of the native races in Arizona or Wyoming, who has individually more power for good or evil, is too great for definition in decent language."[14] Nonetheless, even when American policies toward natives were criticized, this was not invariably done from a presumed position of superiority. Indeed, the point was also made that the British should be cautious with how far they criticize U.S. policy when their own record did not always bear close inspection. Charles Dilke, among those who cautioned about drawing too neat an analogy between tribal peoples from different parts of the world, in *Greater Britain* proffered the warning that "it is not for us, who have the past of Tasmania and the present of Queensland to account for, to do more than record the fact that the Americans are not more successful with the red men of Kansas than we with the black men of Australia."[15]

Elsewhere, the very scale of the enterprise represented that the expansion of the British Empire, and the challenges that it faced, could be emphasized by a juxtaposition with the United States. Again, the Indian comes to function as the exemplar that supposedly proves the fact that "inferior" races, or those ill suited to adaptation, will decline and die out of their own accord. In this vein, the British-born H. M. Stanley, justifying the publication in 1895 of his letters relating to the Indian Campaigns of 1867, which form the first volume of *My Early Travels and Adventures in America and Asia*, argued, "The lessons derived from the near extinction of the Indian are very applicable to Africa. Savages have the minds of children and the passions of brutes."[16] But other strains of humanity, in fact, appeared to prove more resilient, failing to conform to the prevalent mythology of racial vanishing in which the Indian had played such a central role. Thus Anthony Trollope, in his 1877 book *South Africa*, remarked, "The North American Indian, the Australian Aboriginal, the Maori of New Zealand are either going or gone—and so in these lands there has come, or is coming, an end of trouble from that source." He then went on to speculate that the process may not, indeed, be a simple exercise in racial superiority, since "the difficulty as to the Savage has . . . not been solved in South Africa as in other countries in which our Colonies have settled themselves. The Kafir with his numerous varieties of race is still here, and is by no means inclined to go."[17] He noted, moreover, that the question is considerably complicated by issues of miscegenation. Also looking at South Africa, J. R. Seeley, in *The Expansion of England* (1883), was to remark on the problems of ruling when "the native tribes of South Africa, instead of disappearing and dwindling before the whites, greatly outnumber them, and show a power of combination and progress such as the Red Indian never showed."[18]

If the Indian frontier formed a continual point of return for many supporters of the imperialist enterprise, the language of the frontier was a global, interchangeable one. "He must blaze a nation's way with hatchet and with brand,/Till on his last won wilderness an empire's bulwarks stand," wrote Kipling in "The Voortrekker," and Turner quoted it in his "Pioneer Ideals and the State University" of 1910 (271), just as he cited Kipling's "Song of the English" in a piece written seven years earlier: "We were dreamers, dreaming greatly, in the man-stifled town;/We yearned beyond the sky-line where the strange roads go down" (262)— lines that, incidentally, form the epigraph to chapter 5 of Forester's *Beyond the Frontier*. Infamously, Turner's concept of the frontier is predicated upon a sharp distinction between the savage and the civilized. At the same time that American Indians were frequently being represented as the epitome of savagery, a number of British considered life on the American frontier from a more skeptical standpoint. Quite *who* could most emphatically be labeled "uncivilized" was a question repeatedly posed, not only within social and political commentary, and within some travel writing, but within popular fiction as well. This criticism of frontier behavior, as well as of government-sanctioned callousness, in part went back to that long-standing attack that understood and represented American policy toward the Indians as part of the same greedy and hypocritical mind-set that had supported slavery while giving lip service to democracy and opportunity. Such a condemnation of American internal imperialism was also very strongly linked to those growing anxieties within England about the vulnerability of its own economic and social frontiers to forms of American invasion. Louis Warren has written compellingly about how two different types of frontier transgressors have to be killed off by Bram Stoker in *Dracula*: the racially hybrid, sinister count hailing from "western civilization's first frontier with non-Christian peoples in Transylvania . . . his insatiable appetite for blood mimicking the bloodthirst and stagnation of the Balkan frontier,"[19] who threatens with one form of reverse colonization, and Quincey Morris. Morris bears an uncanny resemblance to Cody; as Warren writes, "by the time Stoker began to write *Dracula* in the 1890s, the ubiquity of Buffalo Bill's Wild West show would have made it practically impossible for Stoker to conjure up a western character without thinking of Buffalo Bill" (331). As such, he both represents a form of transatlantic Anglo-Saxon triumphalism ("If America can go on breeding men like that, she will be a power in the world indeed," says Dr. Seward of Morris)[20] and allows the expression of what Warren terms a fear of American "regenerative and military power" (331). This, moreover, is combined with anxiety about what life on the frontier can actually do to a man, since it can be a site of miscegenation (was Morris designed, as the manuscript suggests, to be just a bit more of a blood relative to Dracula than is eventually the case?) and of moral decay.

But to bring out popular unease about frontier morality, I want to dwell not on *Dracula* but on a less familiar work by one of Stoker's contemporaries, the Canadian-born Grant Allen. *The Devil's Die* (1888) is a novel that above all sets out to promote the idea that England is an extremely racially tolerant country, especially by contrast with America. It is also, for Allen, a country of possibility, whatever one's racial origins. The central figure in the story is a doctor from India, Mohammed Ali, who near the opening gratefully exclaims, "I'm glad I came to England. To stop in India is to starve one's own moral and mental nature. To come here is growth, development, emancipation, freedom!"[21] The novel offers a convoluted plot of affective relations, but the crucial section for my argument is the central one, where, following the dying wishes of his good friend Dr. Harry Chichele, Mohammed heads off to the United States to try to find Royle, the young artist who has been in love with the woman who is now Chichele's widow and whom that doctor wished her to marry after his own demise. From the day he sets foot in America, the Indian encounters considerable racial prejudice.

In any country of the old world, Mohammed Ali, well born, well bred, cultivated, refined, a gentleman by blood and race and education, would have been received as an equal with open arms in the society of all that was best and highest; in America alone, with all its noisy boasts, his black skin raised an insuperable barrier between himself and the lowest or vilest or most ignorant of white men. He had come to the land of the free to find himself for the first time in all his life subjected to the vile surviving prejudices of old world slavery; he longed to be back in the land which had conquered and enslaved him and his people, in order that he might feel himself once more a freeman. (208)

Things are even worse where Royle already is, out West, in a rough mining town, the epitome of what Richard Hofstadter describes as the "riotous land speculation, vigilantisim, the ruthless despoiling of the continent, the arrogance of American expansionism, the pathetic tale of the Indians, anti-Mexican and anti-Chinese nativism, the crudeness, even the near-savagery, to which men were reduced on some portions of the frontier."[22] This is not to say, however, that Allen advances a particularly enlightened view of Native Americans, but the native population is, despite the considerable condescension in the narrative voice, contrasted favorably with the white settlers. Royle "much preferred the unsophisticated red man of the wild west" to the frontiersmen he works among.

The simple children of nature stabbed and shot and got drunk without the faintest pretence that they were the pioneers of Aryan culture in the great west, or that they were planting the germs of American liberty on the rolling confines of the boundless prairies. Ivan rather liked his Indian guides, in fact. They were unpretentiously wicked. The innocent criminality of the born savage does not disgust one like the degenerate and decadent immorality of the outcast and off-scourings of European civilisation in its worst avatars. (209)

The landlord of the local saloon lumps African Americans and Indians together in his racist abuse, and then, after his arrival, has no hesitation in including Mohammed in this invective when he talks to Royle.

'Pears to me . . . that in Europe folks ain't got no proper pride in their position as white man. They ain't been brought into contact with inferior races, that's where it is. They don't recognize that a white man's got to shoot an Injun whenever the durned redskin misbehaves himself, or there wouldn't be no law and order anyway. Moral susation's necessary, for the inferior races; nigger and Injuns must do as they'er bid, or else you've got to chop 'em. Otherwise there ain't no maintainin' the Caucasian supremacy. There's a nigger come to town, too, by the way, since you were here last. . . . The toniest nigger I see, you bet. (210)

And so the rant continues. This offends Royle's very British sense of decency; he rescues "that tender, sensitive, chivalrous black man" (211) from taunts and jeers and finds that it is Mohammed, come to look for him. After they are both run out of town and suffer some more hair-raising moments, Mohammed is relieved to find himself on the (ironically named) boat home, where he can reflect:

Thank God, he was rid of America for ever!
Till that terrible journey, he had never known how great a privilege it was to be a British subject. As he paced the deck of the *City of Savannah*, however, ploughing her way across the sea to England, he felt at last like a free man; he recognized the truth that nowhere in the world is a person of his colour so raised above the reach of vulgar prejudice as within the four sea walls of Britain. (247)

Although the topic is nowhere specifically addressed by Allen, *The Devil's Die* prompts some useful reflections about the role of the frontier in the British popular imagination at the end of the 1880s. On the one hand it is a location that fascinates, carrying connotations of rugged individualism, danger, and opportunity—as well as hostile Indians. This is the appeal that, after all, led to Royle's being sent there by a publishing house to bring back some vivid, firsthand depictions. On the other hand it is a place that can be perceived as profoundly *un-British*—not so much because of its physical environment, but because or so Allen hopes—because of its *mind-set*. Britain's "four sea walls" function less as an impermeable barrier to those with non-European racial origins—or Mohammed himself would not be there—than as an ideological palisade, protecting free thought and speech, whereas—to quote Mohammed one last time—"in America, and even in the British colonies, individuality and liberty of opinion are wholly unknown" (247).

The idea of the frontier representing a clear line of demarcation, whether geographic or symbolic, has been repeatedly and deservedly called into question over the last thirty or so years. In the mid-nineteenth century, American legislation meant that it could, indeed, be regarded as a definitive dividing line. Setting out with a mule train for California in 1849, William Kelly writes of what lay just beyond Saint Louis: "The line of demarcation between the pale-face and the Indian—the extreme margin of civilization . . . the point at which the plough of the hardy settler was to stop—where the hunting-ground of the red-skin commenced, stretching away into illimitable space.[23] This line can be found on the map that accompanies Anthony Trollope's *North America*, with the names of states appearing on the eastern side and the names of tribes on the west. But by the late nineteenth century, the frontier seemed less securely fixed on the land's surface, unlike, say, Hadrian's solid broad wall curving over the northern landscape, envisaged by Kipling in *Puck of Pook's Hill* as the utmost outpost of civilization, separating Romans from ancient Britons.[24] Rather, it formed a symbolic divide, whether between savagery—however constituted—and civilization or between ancient and modern. It was, in Leslie A. Fiedler's words, a "mythological frontier which writers tend to identify with actual geographical frontiers, where men of a particular culture confront creatures of another, who challenge their definition of the human by living out possibilities which they themselves have rejected or not yet imagined."[25]

Yet even such an apparently gung-ho adventure story as Forester's *Beyond the Frontier* could contain within it the germs of recognition that there might well be perspectives other than those of Anglos looking west. Don, the hero, falls in love with Annie, a settler's daughter, who nurses him back to health after a rattlesnake bite. He asks her whether the life she leads on the western fringes of the plains is a safe one: he has heard a good deal about the hostility of the Indians from the scouts working with the government survey party.

> "The scouts?" she repeated bitterly. "Of course, the scouts would say that—they all hate the Reds, as they call them. I don't see the justice of it, myself," went on the fair speaker, warming to her subject, before I could get in a word, "nor do I wonder why there should be an eternal feud between Redskins and whites, when I consider how the former have been treated. Suppose the cases were reversed; suppose—if such a thing were possible—that the Indians should swoop down on the States, bringing herds of buffalo and wild horses into the country round Washington or Boston—how should we take it, then? That is the very thing, in their eyes, that we are doing now." (125)

Don's argument about the necessity for "progress and civilization" cuts little ice with her: she and her father have, up to now, lived in peaceful harmony with their Indian neighbors; moreover, she wants little truck with the material results of such abstract ideals. "'I love my beautiful woods and mountains far too well to want to see them spoiled by ugly black chimneys and railroads,'" she goes on, "'and I wish—I wish,' she declared half angrily, 'that the Government would not go sending its stupid surveys out West, if all they can do is spoil the lovely work of Nature, just to set up their ugly angle-posts and things'" (125). Needless to say, the plot works against such dangerous feminine sentimentalism, and shortly afterward, Don's encounter with the massacred bodies of his former colleagues proves Annie to have been naively misguided: "Ghastly traces they were, sights that—used as I have since become to frontier warfare, with all the nameless atrocities perpetrated by the savage, with the devil in him rampant—come back to thrill me even now with horror in my dreams" (142). Even Annie, as the situation becomes even tenser, gives way to Don, as though courtship has tamed her, admitting, "'I would rather have civilization, now'" (239).

But for a moment, there had been that recognition that things might look differently from the other side of the frontier, "facing east from Indian country," to borrow the title of Daniel Richter's recasting of early U.S. history from the native point of view. The Eurocentric version of both territorial and mythical frontier is, obviously enough, called into question if, say, one looks back to the Pottawattamie chief Simon Pokagon's 1893 "Red Man's Rebuke," a complaint printed on birch bark about the lack of representation of native views at the 1893 World's Fair: "The cyclone of civilization rolled westward; the forests of untold centuries were swept away; streams dried up; lakes fell back from their ancient bounds; and all our fathers once loved to gaze upon was destroyed, defaced, or marred, except the sun, moon, and starry skies above, which the Great Spirit in his wisdom hung beyond their reach."[26]

Yet not all Indian responses to the signs of advancing modernity emphasize the cruel violence of dispossession. We have already encountered a number of Indians who engaged with social situations and structures that we might term "modern," attempting both to understand them on their own terms and to evaluate how native cultures and peoples might have an active part to play in an evolving future. In other words, the frontier could not have seemed as definitively closed to native peoples as Turner or Roosevelt would have us think—with Indians firmly consigned to a primitive and ahistorical picturesqueness and accepting a state of subordination. Philip J. Deloria, in his excellent book on Indian modernities, *Indians in Unexpected Places*, asks, "Would Indian people have accepted such an assertion? . . . Even amid the onslaught of forced assimilation, allotment, linguistic genocide, and religious suppression," he maintains, one has a hard time "assuming the absolute end of religions, cultures, and social practices. Imagine," he invites, "an Indian Frederick Jackson Turner or Buffalo Bill Cody, a Native person offering Indian interpretations of the closing of the frontier, of violence and pacification, of modernity. I imagine such a person," Deloria continues, "not drawing the stark lines of epochs and eras, but rather recognizing that, while military conflict was no longer an option, the struggle between Native people and the United States had not concluded."[27] His primary concern is with those specific cultural sites where the struggle for representation among emergent forms of modernity could be found, and where Indians possessed, at least for a while, significant agency—among them the early days of the moving picture and athletics. He also emphasizes that despite the importance of the "cultural front," the Indian struggle was to continue primarily in legal and political channels.

The more that such intracultural engagement has been examined, the more shaky those binary connotations of that very linear term "frontier" have become, and so one witnesses calls for the term itself to be recuperated and transformed. Arnold Krupat, for one, wants to move beyond the Turnerean idea that it is "a series of those points apparently marking a clearly discernible line between 'us' and 'them.'" Rather, for the ethnocritic, he writes, "in a more relativist manner, the frontier is understood as simply that shifting space in which two *cultures* encounter one another. In James Clifton's recent formulation, 'a frontier is a social setting,' not a fixed or mappable, but, rather, 'a culturally defined place where peoples with differently culturally expressed identities meet and deal with each other.'"[28] Choctaw/Cherokee critic and novelist Louis Owens has reappropriated the frontier yet more radically, calling it "the zone of trickster, a shimmering, always changing zone of multifaceted contact within which every utterance is challenged and interrogated, all referents put into question."[29] And New Western historian Patricia Limerick, in her influential 1988 *The Legacy of Conquest*, began a campaign against the removal, in historical circles, of this dominant term. "Frontier," she wrote, "is an unsubtle concept in a subtle world."[30]

So, when is a frontier not a frontier? It begins to look rather like Richard White's "middle ground," his highly effective term describing the search for accommodation and common meaning between Indian and European in the Great Lakes region in the later seventeenth and eighteenth centuries, before this broke down and the Indians again came to be seen as aliens or exotics, and the whites as aggressors—mutual occupiers of "divided ground." The title of Alan Taylor's book, *The Divided Ground*, which examines the borderland between the British in Canada and Americans in the period after the Revolution, deliberately pays homage to White's work on an "earlier period of mutual accommodations where neither natives nor colonizers could dominate the other, but instead had to craft new customs and rhetoric to deal with each other as equals," for by the period about which he writes, natives had to cope on quite different terms "with an invasion of settlers, coming in greater and growing numbers to divide the land into farms, reservations, and nations."[31] Such an actual and figurative space resembles Mary Louise Pratt's familiar concept of the "contact zone," but "contact," nonetheless, sounds rather too brief, initiatory, or superficial for those intricate, engaged, and enduring patterns of social, imaginative, and intellectual transformations that take place as cultures meet. Perhaps better to go with Gloria Anzaldúa's *Borderlands/La Frontera*, a title that draws attention to the porosity of boundaries—in language, as well as on the ground, one reminding us that frontiers exist on the (slanted, forward-looking) vertical, as well as the horizontal axis, and that exploring the triangulation of Hispanic, Native, and Anglo life on the Mexican-U.S. border and the resulting *mestizaje* usefully restrains one from seeing frontiers in terms of cultural binaries. Nonetheless, the word "lands," like "ground," and "frontier," carries with it something very rooted and material: all are earthbound terms that like the more generalized and conceptual word "site" suggest a good deal about our desire to render our abstract ideas solid.

But the cultural politics of encounter are resistant to this in their very mobility, not least when the fluid medium of the "great water"—to use Black Elk's term—plays a part in the passage of both individuals and ideas.[32] The frontier might provide a powerful mythical location onto which white desires for opportunity, expansionism, and adventure could be projected (or where their avatars of boorish acquisitiveness and racism could also be found), even well after it ceased to exist in geopolitical fact. As William R. Handley has argued in his persuasive analysis of Turner's rhetoric, "the word frontier will continue to mean something as long as Americans want to give history a nationalist meaning."[33] However, its one-sided implications are laid bare when one sees how incongruous and inadequate it is as a term when the area of contact is not the product of western movement but of Indians traveling east.

Nahnebahwequay: A Credit Indian Woman Meets Queen Victoria

We have already considered the politics of cultural encounter on British soil in relation to those who toured with Catlin's and Cody's very differently conceived ethno-entertainments or those who traveled with a religious motivation or background. These were not, however, the only groups into which transatlantic Indians may be placed. Others who made the crossing include at least one sportsman, the Iroquois long-distance runner Louis Bennett (Deerfoot) in 1861–63, at the time when the Civil War had disrupted competitive sport in the United States;[34] First Nations people who came to petition the monarchy on land rights issues; and other speakers and performers, including, most notably, the Iroquois writer Pauline Johnson. The fact that a significant number of legal and cultural challenges to British policy took place on English, rather than Canadian, soil, by people who considered themselves British subjects, further complicates the idea of "frontier warfare."

The case of Catherine Sutton (Nahnebahwequay) illustrates these complexities well. Sutton—Nahnee, as she called herself—was a Credit Indian. Born Catherine Sunego in 1824, she was a close relative of Peter Jones.[35] She attended the mission school at Credit River until 1837, when she accompanied him and her aunt Eliza on a yearlong trip to Britain, coinciding with Queen Victoria's coronation, during which Jones presented a petition and wampum belt to the young queen in an effort to secure the lands of the Mississauga Band. In 1839 she married William Sutton, a Methodist convert, and they worked first at Credit Village, then on the Newash mission, before, in 1852, going to the Garden River Reserve, near Sault Sainte Marie, to supervise a model farm—renting out their own two-hundred-acre farm at Owen Sound. Judging by a poem she wrote or transcribed in her husband's ledger, Nahnee was no opponent of colonization; rather, she makes a disconcertingly enthusiastic endorsement of colonial strategies.

> From eastern land the white man came
> To seek a forest home
> Where the wild deer and the wilder Indian roam
> The law of truth was in his heart
> For God hath sent him here.[36]

But Nahnee's cross-cultural marriage meant that she suffered a particularly sneaky kind of dispossession. On the Suttons' return to Owen Sound, they found that her land, which had been deeded to her and her heirs in perpetuity by the Newash Ojibwa, no longer belonged to her, having been surrendered to the government in her absence by a few members of the local band. She tried to buy it back from the land agent but was told that she would not be issued a certificate of sale because she was an Indian; she then found that she was not eligible for the same annuity as the other Newash because she was married to a white man. She, together with her chief, David Sawyer (who had also lost his land while away doing mission work), and a schoolteacher, Abner Elliott, petitioned the legislature, to no effect; in her attempt to obtain justice, she was elected by the chiefs and people to try to gain an audience with Queen Victoria in order to plead her cause. She traveled first to New York, where her cause was taken up by Quakers; they helped her prepare the necessary materials and furnished her with letters of introduction. She then crossed the Atlantic to stay with Robert and Christine Alsop in Stoke Newington, London, who not only provided her with a home for nearly four months but also introduced her to members of the Aborigines' Protection Society.[37] A hyperbolic poem published in the *Friends Intelligencer* sent her on her way, speaking of the halo of faith that shines brightly around her head, of her own majesty that somehow is derived from her own—Indian—nation's wrongs and of the hopes that are held out by her friends.

> God bless thee, queen Victoria! may He thy spririt bless
> To understand the Indians wrongs, and knowing, to redr[ess]
> Thy sister, of the forest wild, makes her appeal to thee
> Oh, may'st thou as the name* she bears, thyself deserving

That future ages may record of England's matron Queen,
A true and upright woman's heart in all her acts was seen
The Noble, and the Peasant poor, the Indian in the woods,
United all in loving her, "Victoria the Good."

*Nah-Nee Bahwee-Qua, in the Indian Language, Signifies "An Upright Woman."

In fact, Queen Victoria's private attitude toward Native Americans does not seem to have differed significantly from that of the average, minimally informed middle-class Victorian, despite her meetings with First Nations subjects, and despite the fact that her advisers were usually well informed from firsthand Canadian experience. On hearing of Victoria's accession, Anna Jameson, who was traveling by boat down Lake Huron at the time, was filled with compassionate awe by the demands that the geographic scale of her possessions placed on the young ruler. She put great trust in what she saw as the innate properties of her womanhood, believing that if the young queen be "true-hearted, and straightforward," and her royal education had not proved to have "blunted in her the quick perceptions and pure kind instincts of the woman," the innate emotional propensities of her gender will mean that she will do far better for native peoples than "a whole cabinet of cut and dried officials." Nonetheless, Jameson wondered aloud whether Victoria knew, or cared about, this land, "young like herself," where "hearts are beating warm for her, and voices bless her—and hands are stretched out towards her, even from these wild lake shores!"[38]

But a much more muted, and decidedly condescending, sympathy comes out in Victoria's journal record of her meeting with the Credit woman on 19 June 1860—the same day that she also received two New Zealand chiefs from Auckland. "She is of the yellow colour of the American Indians," wrote Victoria in her diary, "with black hair, and was dressed in a strange European dress with a coloured shawl and straw hat with feathers." The entry continues: "She speaks English quite well and is come on behalf of her Tribe to petition against some grievance as regards their land. A worthy Quakeress, Mrs. Alsopp, with whom she is living, brought her. She seems gentle and simple."[39] Nahnee publicly professed to be impressed by the meeting, writing in a letter to relatives in Brantford, (it was immediately published in the *Brantford Courier*):

So you see I have seen the Queen. The Duke [of Newcastle] went before us, and he made two bows, and then I was left in the presence of the Queen; she came forward to meet me, and held out her hand for me to kiss, but I forgot to kiss it, and only shook hands with her. The Queen asked me many questions, and was very kind in her manners and very friendly to me. Then my Quaker friend spoke to the Duke,

Figure 37. Catherine Sutton (Nahnebahwequay), Grey County Museum, Owen Sound, Ontario.

and said, "I suppose the Queen knows for what purpose my friend has come?" The Duke said, "All my papers had been explained and laid before her Majesty, and I have her Majesty's commands to investigate the Indian affairs when I go to Canada with the Prince of Wales." Then the Queen bowed to me and said, "I am happy to promise you my aid and protection," and asked me my name. The Queen then looked at her husband, who stood at her left side, and smiled. She received me with so much kindness as to astonish me, when I saw her come smiling and so good to poor Indian [sic].[40]

These two women's comments offer a vivid encapsulation of a central aspect of frontier relations: they are invariably constituted as relations of inequality, whether this is a matter of military strength, legislative power, or, as here, more subtle patterns of hierarchized self-evaluation amounting to internalized colonization. Yet despite Nahnee's apparent deference, a closer examination of her visit and other fragments of her extant writing suggests that there might well have been a performative element to her rhetoric, with an eye to pleasing both her own supporters and those who might be in a position to aid Indians more generally. Not only does she seem to have been more forthright in her approach to the queen during her audience than her own account suggests ("I have been told that the Queen extended her hand for just a touch but our Indian friend took the Queen's hand and gave it a good hearty shake such as she had been accustomed to do with her Methodist friends in this neighbourhood," wrote a local resident back in Canada),[41] but she was also well aware of the strategic importance of self-presentation. Just before she sailed back across the Atlantic, Nahnee spoke at a public meeting organized by the Aborigines' Protection Society in Liverpool, where she explained why, against the initial wishes of her tribal council, she had worn European-style clothing and when "I have been asked by different people why didn't I fetch my Indian dress," "I tell them I had none; this was my dress; this was the way we dress. I tell them we are not pagan, that we try to be like white people—to be clean and decent, and to do what we can to be like the civilised people."[42] Moreover, in this address—delivered, according to the press report, "with a great composure," with her "strong emphasis" giving "additional point to the words"—she was very explicit not just about the ways in which Indians were increasingly being driven off their land—often after improving it for white settlers to take over—but also about the hypocritical double standards that prevailed when it came to landownership. To purchase land, which she has just learned from her husband now seemed possible,

Why, the Indian must be civilized; he must talk English, talk French, read and write, and be well qualified for everything before he can purchase land. Why, the poor Indians, none of them can go there. Poor things, how are they to get their education? And is that the way they do with your own people? Why, I can tell you something. I have seen some people in our own country that came from your country that could neither read nor write; and they came to buy Indian land. But the poor Indian must be so well qualified before he can have a house of his own![43]

Here and elsewhere in her speech, Nahnee ritualistically employs Pope's phrase "the poor Indian," using it almost like a refrain, a prompt to activate sympathy along established lines.

Despite the enthusiastic applause of the Liverpool audience and the help that she received from her London friends and supporters, with whom she stayed in contact, Nahnee had good reason to feel bitterness and disappointment about the fact that her trip to England did not result in the restoration of her land. The Duke of Newcastle, who had been deputed to look into the wrongs, spent a derisory five minutes listening to a deputation consisting of both white men and Indians, and indeed he seems to have suspected Nahnee herself of land speculation. His view that she was a white woman, since she had married a white man, was particularly galling to her sense of racial and cultural identity. "I should like to know," she riles against the Indian Department, "if you have a law in England, that would deprive a woman of Property left her, by her Fathers will or if you please inherited property—I ask have you a Law that would deprive that woman of her property because she got married to a Frenchman?"[44] Clearly, she was in ignorance of the terms in which married women could—or could not—hold property before the passing of the Married Women's Property Act in 1882; her assumptions, of course, unwittingly throw into relief the way in which women's property rights in England also went against fundamental justice.

Catherine Sutton died in 1865, having suffered from asthma for a couple of years: only after her death did her husband receive the deed to the land; neither Sawyer nor Elliott was successful. Nahnee's increasing anger at the racial prejudice Indians suffered was confirmed and fed by the experience of her visit and is articulated most forcefully in a letter that she wrote to British-born Charles Lindsey, editor of the *Toronto Leader*, who had penned a derogatory piece in which he referred to Indians as monkeys. They looked, she satirically replied, most unlike the animals that she'd seen in London's Zoological Gardens. Indians, she thought, "were always considered to be human beings, possessing living souls." While Lindsey seemed to resent reservations as a public nuisance, Nahnee spoke up for Indians' rights to good reservations and for proper compensation for confiscated land, concluding, pessimistically, by saying that "our present administration can extinguish the red mans title at pleasure, what hope is their [sic] for the remnant that are yet left to whom can they go for redress who will help them or are they entirely without helper."[45] All the evidence of Nahnee's activities and of her own writing suggests that she saw herself in several lights: both *as* a "poor Indian"—"poor" in the sense of being cheated of land rights and treated in a racially insulting manner—and more successfully "civilized" than many of those for whom she spoke. It is as though she was a new type of Indian, one who was pragmatically adapting her lifestyle, to be sure, but not at the expense of her Indianness—her unnegotiable ethnic identity. Nor—unlike Copway, say—does she come across as confused by the experience of double consciousness; confusion, if there was any at all, was quickly translated into anger, vocalized as a bitter lack of comprehension in those white people who refused to regard Indians as fellow, and equal, human beings.

Caughnawaga and the Nile Campaign

Louis Jackson, a very different type of transatlantic traveler, was the Caughnawaga captain of a contingent of fifty-six Caughnawaga, who at the express desire of General Lord Wolseley, formed part of a contingent of three hundred *voyageurs* who went to Egypt in 1884 to serve in the Nile campaign and to lend their skills of porterage and boatmanship to the successful navigation of that river. If the impression that they gave to some who saw them embark was straight out of adventure fiction— "Quel assemblage étrange! Pas d'uniformes—des habits de toutes couleurs—des figures hâlées, quelques-unes aux traces durs et féroces—ça et là les sinistres visages des Iroquois de Caughnawaga,"[46] remarked a French priest, Father Têtu, melodramatically—Jackson's account is that of an interested, engaged professional, and, what's more, one who confidently writes from his own Indian perspective. The circumstances of his trip to North Africa required that he be in the employment of the British government, not the Canadian (John A. Macdonald, the Canadian prime minister, insisted on this, to avoid any accusation that the Canadian government was directly supporting an imperialist adventure), but Jackson maintains as carefully calibrated an observational eye on the British forces as he does on the inhabitants of the land through which he travels. To some extent, he is, at least during the first part of the trip, a tourist (or a frustrated tourist: they were obliged to pass by Thebes and Luxor without a chance of visiting them, and when some of his men went off to look at the statues of Rameses and the temple of Abu-Simbel, he had to stay behind to receive stores and cholera belts). He is struck by the poverty and the flies on children's faces; by the ubiquitous use of mud for building; by the crocodiles sunning themselves on the banks; by Egyptians' custom of putting a small coin into the mouth of a person they are burying; and by a very different form of spectacle, the military funeral of a Gordon Highlander. He is a comparative traveler ("Another curiosity was the protective fencing for the road, made of cornstalks to keep back the sand, as we make board fences against the snow")[47] and a compassionate one. Jackson was concerned that when his men stopped, they must inevitably have done damage to the crops that were being grown on the very narrow strips on either side of the Nile, and hence to the lives of poor people living on subsistence farming. He is also strongly aware of his people's visibility—but not as members of a performing show or as curiosities for a passing white visitor. Rather, "the natives came rushing out of their huts with their children, goats and dogs and stood on the beach to see the North American Indian." He and his men are in a position of agency and mobility and are to be wondered at by those whose lives have exposed them to less of the world (26).

Jackson expresses great admiration for the British army—for the physique of the soldiers, for the discipline with which it was run, and for the way in which he and his men were treated and provided for. What dominates the conclusion to his account of the trip, however, is a sense of pride in his race, in a formulation that both singles out the Iroquois and sees them as part of a broader, heterogenous national grouping: "We sailed from Alexandria on February 6th, 1885, well pleased with what we had seen in the land of the Pharos [sic] and proud to have shown the world that the dwellers on the banks of the Nile, after navigating it for centuries, could still learn something of the craft from the Iroquois Indians of North America and the Canadian voyageurs of many races."[48] This account differs from all the other writings by Native Americans that I have considered, since Jackson's comments involve comparing one non-European group to another. What is significant about these brief descriptions of interracial contact is the terms of relative human equality on which they are set up, despite the Caughnawaga's indisputable sense that he is in a privileged position in relation to those whom he is observing.

Pauline Johnson in London

But inequality among races returns center stage when we examine the case of Pauline Johnson (1861–1913), poet, fiction writer, journalist, performer, half Mohawk and half English, who grew up on the Six Nations reserve in a household that brought her into contact with distinguished members and guests of the Canadian government. Living the life of a leisured young woman until her early twenties, she started to write seriously after her father's death in 1884, composing some works that dealt lyrically with the natural world and others that directly addressed First Nations topics—including a poem written to commemorate the re-interment of the Seneca orator Red Jacket in 1885, in which she states outright that "copper-tinted face and smoldering fire/Of wilder life, were left me by my sire/To be my proudest claim" (lines that formed the epigraph to *The White Wampum*)."[49] Some of her early occasional poems, nonetheless, offer unabashed support for various forms of colonial activity. "A Request" (1886), written for the Woman's Auxiliary of Missions to the Church of England in Canada, addresses an imaginary Indian mother, telling her that missionaries are not to be thought of in the same light as military forces. No longer can it be said of Britain that " 'she treats her Indian wards as foes.' No! These are different men,/Their strength is not in rank and file, no martial host they lead,/Their mission is the cross of Christ, their arms the Christian creed."[50] "For Queen and Country," composed for Queen Victoria's birthday in 1890, is even more fulsome in its praise of imperial rule: "To-day her reign seems to have been/A benediction of vast liberties."[51] During the 1880s, she published widely in periodicals, gaining increasing recognition within Canada, and the inclusion of two of her poems in William Douw Lighthall's anthology *Songs of the Great Dominion* led Theodore Watts-Dunton, in his *Athenaeum* review, eulogizing Johnson, "the cultivated daughter of an Indian chief," and to call her, "on account of her descent, the most interesting English poetess now living."[52] In 1892 she embarked on a career as a recitalist of her own work, and for the next fifteen years she toured Canada and parts of the United States and, in 1894 and 1906, visited and performed in England.

Pauline Johnson has attracted a good deal of intelligent critical commentary in recent years, most noticeably from Veronica Strong-Boag and Carole Gerson, whose *Paddling Her Own Canoe* does an excellent job of placing her in relation to her First Nations identity, her position within the developing Canadian political and cultural scene, and the position of women at the close of the nineteenth and opening of the twentieth centuries. As they put it, hers "was a complicated, contentious, and passionate personality whose life blurs the borders of what it means to be Native, a woman, and Canadian."[53] Onstage, Johnson did not so much blur these borders as flamboyantly call attention to them in order to make increasingly political, as well as theatrical, capital from assumptions surrounding her ethnicity. Her show divided into two halves; in the first she wore a version of native dress, and in the second she appeared in conventional elegant evening wear. Johnson's costume did not belong specifically to any tribal group but included an asymmetrical buckskin dress decorated

Figure 38. Pauline Johnson in her Indian stage costume, William Ready Division of Archives and Research Collections, McMaster University Library, Hamilton, Canada.

with various symbols of native culture, including fur pelts, Iroquois silver medallions, wampum belts, her father's hunting knife, and, in time, a necklace of bear claws—an ensemble apparently influenced in part by the dress worn by Minnehaha in illustrations to popular editions of *Hiawatha*.[54] Her publicity photographs also show her dual attires: in her Indian outfit, and then carefully, provocatively, demurely, and languorously posing for the camera in the standard attitudes of a stage celebrity, in full corseted evening dress. To a question about consistency, she reportedly responded, "Oh *consistency*! . . . How can one be consistent until the world ceases to change with the changing days?"[55]

Deliberately liminal, Johnson set out to deconstruct, as well as exploit, frontier binaries, and this was especially apparent on her two major trips to England. On an 1894 visit she chose to start foregrounding her Indian identity and lineage by taking the stage name of Tekahionwake—her paternal grandfather's name—which also appeared on the title page of her first book of poetry, *The White Wampum*, put out in 1895 by the adventurous London publisher John Lane at the Bodley Head. Yet whatever messages her sartorial flexibility and the parallel streams of her poetry's subject matter sent, offstage *and* on she took it upon herself to speak for an Indian, rather than an assimilationist, agenda. Johnson's shift to a poetry that was much more upfront in expressing anger against the injustices experienced by First Nations people dates from the year before her first British visit. If overall she was not anti-imperialist, in emphasizing the indivisibility of First Nations people from modern Canada, she repeatedly returned to the fact that the British owed their 1812 success against the Americans to Iroquois warriors, and that this put the British under a strong obligation toward them. On both sides of the Atlantic— and again in a triangulated Canadian-U.S.-British space—she emphasized the need for white people to recognize the rights, the feelings, and the needs of the land's original inhabitants and to stop denigrating them as savages, noble or otherwise—a theme that continued throughout her career. "These Indians *look* savage," a train conductor tells a white boy in "A Night with 'North Eagle'" (1908) "in their paint and feathers, but King Edward of England has no better subjects; and I guess it is all the same to His Majesty whether a good subject dresses in buckskin or broadcloth."[56]

Yet lying behind Johnson's appearances and her public statements is the nationalist position she expressed in an interview she gave to the *London Gazette* in 1894. Her adherence is neither to the British throne nor to Canada, and still less to the United States; she couches herself as a member of an imaginary, pan-Indian nation. In asking her readership to imagine this, she poses the question: what if power relations were otherwise, and a form of reverse colonization had taken place? Johnson

Figure 39. Pauline Johnson in evening gown, William Ready Division of Archives and Research Collections, McMaster University Library, Hamilton, Canada.

taps into contemporary anxieties about invasion that were circulating in the popular literature of the mid-1890s when she hypothesizes:

> Suppose we came over to England as a powerful people. Suppose you gave us welcome to English soil, worshipped us as gods, as we worshipped you white people when you first came to Canada; and suppose we encroached upon your homeland and drove you back and back, and then said, "Oh, well, we will present you with a few acres— a few acres of your own dear land." What would you think of it all? So we think. We are without a country. I cannot say America is my country. The whole continent belongs to us by right of lineage. We welcomed you as friends, we worshipped you, and you drove us up into a little corner.[57]

Strong-Boag and Gerson write about how the ambiguity of Johnson's person—and persona—highlights the "quandary of living in an imperial world that, willingly or not, was increasingly multicultural and multiracial. Perhaps," they speculate, "observers were puzzled not so much that she appeared to cross the racial line at will, moving from Native 'Other' to Imperial 'I' with the change of a dress, but that she made the return voyage. If she could pass as one of the dominant, what then drew her back to the margin?"[58] To be sure, one answer to this lies in the commercial appeal of the Indian—and, indeed, the shape-shifting Indian—as entertainment. Johnson's self-presentation differentiated her from the Indians of Wild West Shows in a way that went far beyond the contrast between mass spectacle and solo show, however; it made her stand out as someone with agency, not a member of a race for whom the script was already written. And underlying her stage performances, the interviews that she gave, and many prose pieces that she published is a canny understanding of how she could manipulate the outward signs of her ethnic identity (as Indian, but also as half white) in order to claim the authority to speak for those less able than herself—both linguistically and socially—to address those who occupied positions of relative power and privilege. In some of her poems that directly address Indian issues, Johnson appears to revisit familiar themes. In "Silhouette," for example (first published in 1894 and reprinted in her second volume, *Canadian Born* [1904]), she imagines a Sioux chief standing at the doorway of his solitary tepee like a shadow: "He looks towards the empty west, to see/The never-coming herd of buffalo." This is no nostalgic lament, but rather the evocation of a postapocalyptic scene of ravaged desolation. In his view are "only the bones that bleach upon the plains/only the fleshless skeletons that lie/In ghastly nakedness and silence, cry/Out mutely that naught else to him remains."[59] This slaughter of the buffalo created the hunger that drove Indians to crime. In "The Cattle Thief" (1894, and included in *The White Wampum*), Johnson takes up the meter of a popular ballad to tell how a gaunt, starved, hollow-eyed Cree is shot down by a yelling band of vengeful settlers. His furious daughter hurls herself on his body to prevent them from mutilating it and points out what drove him to steal nourishment: "'Look there, at that shrunken face,/Starved with a hollow hunger, we owe to you and your race,'" and these men, in the poem, are explicitly "English settlers," "their British blood aflame." The Indian woman continues to interrogate them: "What have you left to us of land, what have you left of game,/What have you brought but evil, and curses since you came?/How have you paid us for our game? How paid us for our land?/By a *book*, to save our souls from the sins *you* brought in your other hand.'" These lines represent an angry revision of her earlier, and more conciliatory, response toward mission work. She demands that the settlers take back their new religion and restore to the Indians what belongs to them, and the poem concludes on this sustained, determined note of grievance: "Give us back our land and our country, give us back our herds of game;/Give back the furs and the forests that were ours before you came;/Give us back the peace and the plenty. Then come with your new belief,/And blame, if you dare, the hunger that *drove* him to be a thief" (99).

In the poem with which she often began her recitals, "A Cry from an Indian Wife" (1885, reprinted in slightly revised form in *The White Wampum*), she also addresses the issue of rightful ownership head-on. Written at the time of the Riel Rebellion, it is spoken by an Indian wife to her warrior husband and derives its force from its willingness to shift its point of view. "Yet stay," the speaker exhorts at two points in the poem. The first time she cuts short her own train of thought comes after she has been egging him on to attack the British forces mercilessly. She redirects her sympathy, seeing things from another point of view, realizing that the foreign soldiers are political instruments, rather than agents in their own right, and urging him:

> Revolt not at the Union Jack,
> Nor raise Thy hand against this stripling pack
> Of white-faced warriors, marching West to quell
> Our fallen tribe that rises to rebel.
> They are all young and beautiful and good;
> Curse to the war that drinks their harmless blood.
> Curse to the fate that brought them from the East
> To be our chiefs—to make our nation least
> That breathes the air of this vast continent.
> Still their new rule and counsel is well meant.
> They but forget we Indians owned the land

From ocean until ocean; that they stand
Upon a soil that centuries agone
Was our sole kingdom and our right alone.
They never think how they would feel to-day,
If some great nation came from far away,
Wresting their country from their hapless braves,
Giving what they gave us—but wars and graves.

Had the monologue concluded there, the speaker would have performed an act of turning the tables not unlike the one Johnson did in her newspaper interview, asking her white audiences to imagine themselves in the position of the powerless, and this mode continues for a while as she encourages her hearers to think that she is not the only woman who is pale faced and anxious about the fate of a beloved husband or son: some woman's white face, she tells her husband, "quivers thus to think,/ *Your* tomahawk his life's best blood will drink." But then the poem shifts once more as the speaker determines that, after all, the white women toward whom she extends her imaginative sympathy are not going to be thinking of her. The lines "She never thinks of my wild aching breast,/ Nor prays for your dark face and eagle crest" function as a reminder of the conventional sentimentalism of white women's poetry about Indians: however benevolent in its intent, it was very rarely the product of thinking about the feelings of a racial Other in a specific and immediate political situation. "Go forth," the speaker therefore concludes, encouraging her man to "win the glories of the war." "Go forth, nor bend to greed of white men's hands,/ By right, by birth we Indians own these lands,/ Though starved, crushed, plundered, lies our nation low . . ./ Perhaps the white man's God has willed it so" (14–15). The final ellipses put particular stress on the word "Perhaps," and, in turn, the force of this— uncertain, sarcastic, or boldly challenging—depends very much on its mode of delivery.

Johnson was, without doubt, a practiced performer, her stance and diction deployed to create an impression and to convey political messages, and, as Strong-Boag and Gerson note, from 1892, her "literary work was almost always received and assessed in relation to her performance" (117). When Gilbert Parker, author of *The Translation of a Savage*—who was to go on to write the introduction to her book of short stories, *The Moccasin Maker* (1913)—met her in London, she struck him very much as though she were the reincarnation of Lali, the heroine of the novel he had just published: "The feeling of the wild looked out of her eyes, stirred in her gesture, moved in her footstep. I am glad to have known this rare creature who had the courage to be glad of her origin without defiance."[60] But her appearances in London (whether as a guest and performer in private drawing rooms on the first occasion or in more public venues on her return) are of less concern here than the way in which she took her point of view into the press, especially on her second visit.

In 1906 Pauline Johnson published a series of four articles in the *Daily Express*. Each of them critiqued British social rituals and institutions of government from behind the protective veil of a faux-innocent Indian voice, asserting the cultural equality, even superiority, of tribal cultures, modes of governance, and responsible education. Johnson had literary tradition behind her; she reverted to the model pioneered in much earlier English, European, and American writing, whereby a supposedly naive visitor is well equipped to see to the heart of current social ills.[61] The difference here, of course, is that Johnson's persona both is and is not that of an imaginary Indian. Unlike her predecessors, she had the authority to write of native life from her own experience and her own blood allegiance; what she chose to conceal was her cosmopolitanism. Thus the sound of Big Ben, for example, "thundered out from the white man's strange time-piece set in the carven square tower that rises majestic and inviolate as the tallest pine in the undiscovered wildernesses of the West"—a simile that in no way precludes the precision of her critique of British government.[62] Like other Indians, such as Arthur C. Parker and Charles A. Eastman, she acted Indian—to use Philip Deloria's phrase—by "mimicking white mimickings of Indianness."[63]

These articles drew particular resonance from the simultaneous presence in London of three chiefs—Joe Capilano (Squamish), Charlie Tsilpaymilt (Cowichans), and Basil (Bonaparte)—who had traveled from British Columbia to protest against hunting restrictions and against railroad surveys that were passing through their burial grounds. The chiefs served as a prescient reminder that Indian issues could not be safely contained by the condescending language employed in much of the press reporting on the visitors. The *Daily Express* characterized them as "pitifully, childishly impressed with the King's power and benevolence"[64] and as being unnerved by modern urban society: "By day the bustle and never-ending procession of men and women in the streets unnerves them, and at night the rattle of motor-cars brings on horrible nightmares."[65] Both their own eloquence and the powers of their interpreter are demeaned by the newspaper articles that represented the complaints of the "child of the Far West" in pidgin English: " 'White man say Indian no shoot deer or duck. Indian no fish. How then can Indian live? We come to tell the King.' "[66] This infantilization contrasted sharply with Johnson's writing. "A Pagan in St. Paul's Cathedral," which appeared on the page preceding these protests, was articulate in the contrasts that it drew between native and British belief systems and practices, refusing to grant

Figure 40. British Columbian chiefs in London, 1906. *From left to right*: Simon Pierre (interpreter), Chief Charlie Isilpaymilt, Joe Capilano, and Chief Basil Bonaparte. *Daily Express*, 3 August 1906.

supremacy to either, and at the same time suggesting that the former could and would not be subsumed by the latter. Much more pointedly, in the context of the chiefs' visit, "The Lodge of the Law-Makers: Contrasts between the Parliaments of the White Man and the Red" showed up the weaknesses of Britain and Canada's political system, which refused the rights of citizenship to native peoples, which was inherently unstable and mutable, and which failed to grant women the authority that they held in Iroquois society. Notably, at a time when the suffrage movement was gathering momentum, Johnson concluded with a challenging contrast: "I have not yet heard of fifty white women even among those of noble birth who may speak and be listened to in the lodge of the law-makers here."[67] Nonetheless, the *Express* rejected as unsuitable for publication a further piece in which Johnson used Iroquois life as the basis from which to critique gender issues (it appeared in the weekly magazine *Canada* later in the year). "In all the trails I have travelled," she had written, "to the whiteman's camping grounds I do not see that his women have the importance either in his Council or his Camp, that we have given to our womenkind these many centuries." In this article, too, Johnson wrote directly about the greed that she saw as characterizing white people: the "paleface," she alleged, "is never content unless he is risking his possessions to acquire those of another man."[68]

Johnson's first London visit alerted her—if she was not already aware—to the poverty and social conditions that could lie behind emigration, economic imperatives having created a class of what she termed, with a deliberate double edge, "city savages." Her primary concern, initially, was the impact that such undesirable emigrants could have on native life. Visiting Muskoka in the company of a missionary, she wrote, in 1896, that "your heathen in Africa . . . is nearer the light of civilization than those wretched Whitechapelites, that poison the airs of the great clean forest lands, and rot the morals of the simple but blameless Indian."[69] The language here is formulaic, however, distancing the London poor and also, in the last phrase, her own people. Yet on her return to England, she seems to have encountered urban deprivation far more directly. Records of private conversations indicate how shocked she was to be in a capital city where a woman could be attacked and murdered in the street in front of her, and where a clergyman who was lodging in the same house as she came to her late one night, shaken, having returned from a trip to baptize a dying child. She recounts his telling her what happened: "Men and women were lying in a drunken sleep all over the bare floor, but standing near the wall with a young child in his arms was a man who was sober; 'This child will be dead in an hour,' he said with stricken face, 'and it wasn't baptized; but it's only fair to tell you that the young woman lying drunk at my feet is its mother, and I am both its father and its grandfather.'" Rather like the Ojibwa Jim, sixty years earlier, Johnson finished her account by remarking: "With slums like this in the heart of London, they'll dare to send missionaries to our Indians in Canada."[70] Yet Johnson never put such direct, open criticism of British domestic policies into print. She expressed her critique of settler activities in poetry, to be sure, but even then there was an element of obliquity created by her favoring the medium of the dramatic monologue. Her British newspaper articles, as we have seen, sheltered the polemical thrust of her opinions by employing an exaggerated, mannered "Indian" voice. Johnson's access to the modern media came at a price. Unlike, say, the British Columbia chiefs, her education, her background, and her contacts ensured that she had access to publications and to a range of performance spaces. But dependence on writing and recitation for her livelihood meant, inevitably, that she had to shape the expression of her views with a broad public firmly in view. Bitterness, anger, and a powerful sense of the injustices native people experienced are definitely present, but channeled, continually, through irony, metaphor, and archaism. This, of course, makes Johnson's work aesthetically challenging, but its literary sophistication is at the expense of direct political impact.

꙰

In November 2003 President George W. Bush, staying at Buckingham Palace, was shown the program for Buffalo Bill's Wild West Show on the occasion of Queen Victoria's 1887 visit and her diary entry recording the day. One can see that advisers might have thought this would interest a president given to talking about "riding herd" over Middle Eastern governments and "smoking out" enemies in mountain passes; yet according to reporters, he looked bored. Perhaps his mind was on the speech he was to give that evening: " 'The Three Pillars of Peace and Security': The Whitehall Palace Address on Iraq Policy." Bush opened this by looking back to what America had gained from the British. "We're sometimes faulted for a naive faith that liberty can change the world," he said. "If that's an error it began with reading too much John Locke and Adam Smith." He proceeded—with an apparent will to flatter—to locate the origins of American moralizing zeal, religion, and puritanism in the United Kingdom, and then went on to say that "to this fine heritage, Americans have added a few traits of our own: the good influence of our immigrants, the spirit of the frontier."[71]

Nothing could function better as a reminder of the ways in which, as Slotkin has shown, the Rooseveltian language and imagined polarities of the frontier have remained firmly enshrined within rhetoric, as well as the foreign policies of the United States. Yet one should also recall that Slotkin himself issued an important caveat about the frontier's flexible location, proclaiming, indeed, that "the first Frontier was the transoceanic."[72] In its turn, this may encourage us to think of this "first Frontier" not in terms of two locations separated by a large body of water, but in terms of the very fluidity and changeability that this aqueous medium offers to our habit of making metaphors. Rather than dwelling on the materiality, territorial possession, and dominion that are evoked through the terminology of ground, zone, or even "frontier," this transoceanic space allows for the flow and intermingling of peoples, goods, ideas, and temporalities. This transatlantic flow disrupted those apparently neat binaries of "traditional" and "modern," "savage" and "civilized," on which nineteenth-century ideas of the frontier rested so heavily: ideas that were, indeed, directly challenged by the mobility, and visibility, of certain pioneering native individuals.

Indians, Modernity, and History

In 1908 a full-blooded Mohawk man dressed in tribal costume won third prize in a male beauty pageant held on Folkestone pier, coming in behind the captain of the town's lifeboat and a comedian who had been engaged for the summer season. John Ojijatekha Brant-Sero was born on the Six Nations reserve in 1867 and enjoyed a varied career—as a machine hand, a performer, and a lecturer.[1] First visiting England in 1891, he settled there permanently in 1900 until his death in 1914. His motives for participating in the beauty pageant are unclear; he may have hoped for the first prize, a Raleigh bicycle (instead he won a pair of field glasses); he may have been looking to draw attention to native peoples; or he may have enjoyed the camaraderie of such a contest—a chance to put his masculinity on display.[2] But Brant-Sero's career may be seen to stand for the complex, contradictory positions Native Americans held in England in the early twentieth century. On the one hand, he was an object of spectacle, willing to play up Indian stereotypes. "In full native dress, with feathery headgear, he might have stepped out from the pages of a book by Fenimore Cooper or Mayne Reid," commented the *Folkestone Express*. Yet he was also someone who sought to inform both the general public and specialist organizations (such as the British Association for the Advancement of Science) about Mohawk history and customs, and who spoke out, in Germany, against the way in which Indians were portrayed in that country's "penny dreadfuls."[3] He illustrated how the Native American could play a role in popular entertainment and also be both the subject and the agent of serious cultural inquiry.[4] Could he also act as if he were a full British subject? Seemingly not. Although Louis Jackson had served on the Nile, Brant-Sero was rejected when he went to the Cape colony and volunteered for a mounted rifle regiment, since he was not, he wrote in a protest letter to the *Times*, "a man of European descent." Instead, he found a position at the Queenstown remount depot, where his work "consisted in taking animals up to the front and bossing the Kaffirs."[5] Not British enough, perhaps, to serve in an active role, but certainly comfortable with falling into the dominant culture's casual language of racial hierarchization. Brant-Sero, in other words, was negotiating his position as a First Nations person who was making his way in a transnational, commodified modern world, negotiating with both its possibilities and its restrictions. Yet his British residency, and the adaptive roles that he played, highlighted his individualism at the same time that he played on his tribal roots: his engagement with modernity never fed back into the life of the Six Nations.

As we have seen, since colonization, an increasing number of Native Americans engaged, voluntarily or otherwise, with the phenomena of cultural and social modernity, but the impact of such features on native life during the nineteenth century involved unprecedented physical and psychic violence and ensured modification, resistance, compromise, and transformation on a large scale. These phenomena—whether one considers migration (forced or otherwise); changing forms of agriculture, of transportation, and of labor; the growth of urbanization, commercialization, and the mass media—all come under the heading of what Dilip Parameshwar Gaonkar has identified as "societal modernization." He goes on to explore the ways in which, in mid-nineteenth century Europe, "cultural modernity" developed against it.[6] This provides the context for the fact that by the early decades of the twentieth century a number of writers, both American and British, came to look at the Indian through a new type of idealized lens, seeing in him (almost invariably *him*) a symbol of defiance to mechanized, fragmented modernity. As such, the Indian partook in a broader cult of primitivism, with its adulation of the instinctual, the archaic, the communitarian, and the natural: the elements against which the rational, individualized, and industrialized modern world defined itself through suppression and exclusion.[7]

The responses of D. H. Lawrence, Aldous Huxley, the painter Dorothy Brett, and others to native culture were, with respect to cultural modernity, very similar to those of their East Coast literary and artistic peers. "Transatlantic in scope and sources," Jackson Lears writes,

> antimodernism drew on venerable traditions as well as contemporary cultural currents: republican moralism, which promoted suspicion of urban "luxury"; romantic literary convention, which elevated simple and childlike rusticity over the artificial amenities of civilization; a revolt against positivism, gathering strength toward the end of the century, which rejected all static intellectual and moral systems, often in the name of a vitalist cult of energy and process; and a parallel recovery of the primal, irrational forces in the human psyche, forces which had been obscured by the evasive banality of modern culture.[8]

At the cusp of the nineteenth century, when it became increasingly apparent in global terms that Britain had more to gain from treating the United States as an ally than as a rival, the need to assert national difference from the United States became much less compelling than it had been earlier in the century. By the same token, that which distinguished British and American attitudes toward Native Americans became far less clear-cut. The increasingly close literary parallelism of British and American modernists in relation to the Indian stands in a synecdochal relationship to the two countries' political positioning; little distinguishes them in their desire to adopt the Indian as an antimaterialist figure, in touch not just with the land but with deeper spiritual forces (in this regard, and particularly in the Southwest, we see high art occupying much the same ideological space as the tourist industry). Lawrence, most conspicuously, manifests this through his promotion of the Indian as emanating the intensity that, for him, should lie at the core of the human being: the "beautiful, barbaric tenderness of the blood."[9] Thus he writes with awe of visiting Taos Pueblo on a snowy morning, where one can feel "the old, old root of human consciousness still reaching down to depths we know nothing of."[10] Yet for all his portentousness, Lawrence also expresses unease at the degree to which he *was* inescapably an outsider, a participant in tourist experience. He knows all too well that he cannot avoid looking through predetermined cultural filters when he visits "New Mexico, the picturesque reservation and playground of the eastern states, very romantic, old Spanish, Red Indian, desert mesas, pueblos, cowboys, penitentes, all that film-stuff" (141).

"All that film-stuff": Lawrence's self-mocking dismissive term serves as a reminder of how popular culture emanating from America continued to shape British ideas about Indians. Prewar cinema, in Britain as in America, presented a far more varied set of impressions of Indians than did the later Westerns, with their reliance on stereotypes.[11] Cinema, as we have seen, helped to diffuse the impressions of Buffalo Bill's tour, and the impact of American imports was quickly felt. At least twenty-four films featuring Native American themes were described and discussed in 1909—to take an early year—in Britain's weekly film newspaper, the *Bioscope*. Emanating from a range of studios—including Pathé, Lux, Vitagraph, Lubin, Selig, Edison, and Essanay—some of these were adventure stories, including captures and violence by bloodthirsty warriors, or, alternatively, rescues by friendly Indians, while others included the historical documentary *Buying Manhattan*; the idealized tale of a romance between Indians, *The Mended Lute*; and a slapstick comedy (in which an Indian is sold to a cigar store owner as a living advertisement, but eventually gets his own back on his exploiter). Emphasis falls on the beauties of the settings, whether plains or mountains, and on verisimilitude, with Vitagraph's *Red Wing's Gratitude*, in which "the leading roles [were] sustained by real Indians," who were especially singled out.[12] Well aware of the impact of film, Lawrence pits the performers who dress up as Indians in *The Lost Girl* (1920, but set in 1913) against the new vogue for the cinema; they verge on the ludicrous, with their war paint and feathers and striped Navajo blankets. The crowd who watches them parade senses that they are something of an anachronism—dressing up, not providing the deceptive illusion of access to the real thing that the cinema can give, " 'where,' " as Miss Pinnegar puts it, " 'you see it all and take it all in at once, you *know* everything at a glance.' "[13]

Lawrence's three visits to Taos, and his friendship with Mabel Dodge Luhan, ensured he not just observed but talked and socialized with Native Americans at firsthand, gaining a less culturally packaged form of knowledge. He was well aware that geographic and cultural distance fostered idealism. "It is perhaps easier," he wrote in *Studies in Classic American Literature* (1923), "to love America passionately, when you look at it through the wrong end of the telescope, across all the Atlantic water."[14] Some passionate attachments on the part of British people to the idea of the Native American survived the Atlantic passage, most notably in the case of Grey Owl, the Hastings-born Archie Belaney, who, after emigrating to Canada in 1906, lived, wrote, broadcast, and appeared as a First Nations ranger, hunter, and fervent environmentalist until his death in 1938. Others were never put to the test, relying on the idea alone: the long-term spirit guide of the Wimbledon medium Estelle Roberts was Red Cloud. In this, she was following a path taken by mediums on both sides of the Atlantic, since the later nineteenth century of depending upon the heightened sense of the spiritual associated with native religions and practices.[15] Lawrence, however, was skeptical about the degree to which white and red could get along harmoniously in actual life without a damaging degree of compromise on either side. It seemed to him, he wrote, that "the white man and the red man cause a feeling of oppression, the one to the other, no matter what the good will." Nonetheless, the spirit—in Lawrence's particular sense of an essence that lies at the core of a person's inner life—can change. In his customary abstract, somewhat nebulous, but passionate terms, he suggests that the white man's spirit "can cease to be the opposite and the negative of the red man's spirit. It can open out a new great area of consciousness, in which there is room for the red spirit, too."[16] Yet the topographic metaphors of this last sentence betray Lawrence's assumptions. Despite his sympathetic use of irony in his travel writing, which works against the stereotypes of the degenerate and disappearing Indian, and which gently undermines the old ideal of the noble savage, and even despite the emphasis that he places on the magnificence of their muscular, golden bodies, Lawrence's Indians are still, nonetheless, subordinates. Moreover, they are objects without agency, except insofar as that agency is employed to reinforce an idea of their existence outside of Europeanized time.

For Lawrence—and for a number of other British and American writers, artists, and photographers—a considerable part of the Indians' appeal lay in the degree to which these people could be seen, and preserved (in writing, in paint, in actuality), as enduring examples of the "primitive," the antimodern, and the ahistorical. Nowhere was this more true than in the American Southwest, where Lawrence developed his notions, and where the work of artists and anthropologists coexisted with the efforts of promoters of the tourist trade. The world of the Indian appeared, or could be made to appear, in harmony with the earth and the seasons; one about which, too, as pioneering art instructor Dorothy Dunn put it in 1935, writing about Pueblo culture, it could be said that "for thousands of years," the people "have woven and modeled, carved and painted, sung songs and made dances, until art and their daily life have become one."[17] This version of native life, to the outsider, collapsed actuality and representation. As playwright and novelist J. B. Priestley, who traveled to Albuquerque by train in the mid-1930s, exclaimed: "New Mexico—what a film you could make out of it, not with handsome leading men and doll-faced actresses, but with the real people here, the wrinkled ranchers, the sombre Mexicans, the mysterious Indians, the desert and the rocks and the shafts of sunlight!"[18] The perspective of the cultural tourist, like that of any other kind of tourist, is one, of course, that denies the observed their own geographic, social, and cultural mobility. Like Harriet Martineau looking at the immobile, solitary Indian near Buffalo, it implicitly demands that they stay picturesque and static, without considering what the implications of stasis may be.

Contemporary Hopi/Miwok poet Wendy Rose writes:

FOR THE WHITE POETS WHO WOULD BE INDIAN
 just once
 just long enough
 to snap up the words
 fish-hooked
 from our tongues.
 You think of us now
 when you kneel
 on the earth,
 turn holy
 in a temporary tourism
 of our souls.
 With words
 you paint your faces,
 chew your doeskin,
 touch breast to tree

as if sharing a mother
were all it takes,
could bring
instant and primal
knowledge.
You think of us only
when your voice
wants for roots,
when you have sat back
on your heels
and become primitive.
You finish your poem,
and go back.[19]

The desire of Lawrence and his contemporaries to displace the Indian from the "modern" world, or to preserve native peoples in an imagined timelessness, was not, as I have indicated, a desire that native people necessarily shared. For those who have determinedly sought to preserve their separateness and to maintain traditions and lifestyles in as unchanging a way as possible, this has been an act of determined resistance: a radically different aim from that of existing as a defining Other of Eurocentric culture. But other native writers have sought to explore their people's relationship to white history and the interminglings, antagonisms, and unevenness of different cultures—not just in relation to the United States and Canada, but with an eye to the importance of the transnational as well. So I turn finally to a couple of novels that very explicitly explore Victorian transatlantic encounters from an Indian perspective: James Welch's *Heartsong of Charging Elk* (2000) and Leslie Marmon Silko's *Gardens in the Dunes* (1999).

Through the imaginary figure of Charging Elk, Gros Ventre/Blackfeet novelist Welch visualizes what it was like for an Indian to travel to Europe with Buffalo Bill in 1887. He draws on contemporary accounts: on Red Shirt's meeting with Queen Victoria and, more directly, on Black Elk's experiences after he and three other members of the Wild West show became lost in Manchester and missed connecting with the boat that would have carried them back to the United States. The Sioux then joined Mexican Joe's show, traveled around Europe, fell sick, lived with his girlfriend's family, saw his Pine Ridge home in a vision, was given up as dead, was reunited with Buffalo Bill, and eventually, in 1889, returned, to his mother's joy.[20] Black Elk makes a cameo appearance near the beginning of the narrative, long enough to articulate that he has "lived in the *wasichu* [or white man's] world for two years and I do not like what I see. Men do not listen to each other, they fight, their greed prevents them from being generous to the less fortunate, they do not seem to me to be wise enough to embrace each other as brothers." He might be echoing those observations made by Catlin's Indians in Britain in the 1840s, shocked by the poverty and lack of communal care. Welch's Black Elk continues: "I have learned much from this experience, much that will help me teach our people the right road when I get back to my country," sentiments that directly call on the reasons recorded by John G. Neihardt that Black Elk gave for traveling with the Wild West.[21]

Of particular interest are the ways in which Welch imagines the combination of curiosity, pride, and alienation that the Wild West Indians experienced in Europe; and his linguistic experimentation, showing—through the same type of careful, simple English that characterized the reported speech of those Indians interviewed when in Europe—that although Charging Elk was excited and intrigued by what he saw, he could read this society only through his own cultural terms. Moreover, the question of return—of what it might mean to reintegrate into Indian society after living in the late-nineteenth-century white man's world—becomes increasingly pertinent for Charging Elk as the novel progresses. When, finally, he has the chance to return to the Pine Ridge Agency—to his people, to his mother—he chooses to stay in France with his pregnant French wife: a particularly significant decision in the context of the emphasis Lakota culture, and narrative, places on ancestral ties and lineage. He is distressed by what he has learned from the new generation of Wild West Lakota—that the young people now have to go away to school to learn to be like white Americans and that they are forbidden to speak their language or to perform ceremonies. It is, it seems, less of a compromise to keep his Indian identity inviolate and private and to stay in France, heading into an unknown, partly assimilated, and hybrid transatlantic future.

The story the Laguna writer Leslie Marmon Silko, tells in *Gardens in the Dunes* is, by contrast, a more optimistic and even mildly utopian one. Also set in the late nineteenth century, it is the story of a young girl, Indigo, from a disappearing tribe of Colorado River Indians, who is taken up by a white American couple after she runs away from Indian boarding school. The woman, Hattie (loosely based, Silko has said, on a combination of Margaret Fuller and Alice James),[22] is a church historian; her husband, Edward, is a botanist who visits the Amazon jungle—something that allows Silko, in this ecologically aware novel, to demonstrate how even the most exuberant manifestations of natural life are becoming subject to the international commercial trade in botanical specimens. The threesome make a trip to England, where the site of the old slave market in Bristol offers a convenient excuse to comment not just on the triangulated Black Atlantic but on the selling of young Indian children to cattle ranchers and miners. The narrative shows various tensions between natives and whites in the Southwest, whether through the damming of a river to provide water for the expanding city of Los Angeles, forced migration by native peoples, or the Ghost Dance movement. At the same time, it seeks to underscore quite how much whites have to learn from indigenous peoples, not only within the United States but also worldwide. Silko shows how cultures, whether ancient British or desert Indian, may be linked through their mythologies, as demonstrated by various forms of attachment to stones, snakes, and plants. This is not to say that Indigo's responses would necessarily have been shared by nineteenth-century Indians. The missionary Peter Jones, visiting Cornwall in April 1838, records in his journal that on the way to Redruth, he "called to see the remains of a Druidical Temple, called *Carnbrea*, where human sacrifices used to be offered to their gods. We saw several of the rocks hollowed out into basins, where the poor creatures were slain, and these basins to all appearances caught the blood of the victims. Surely," Jones piously remarked, "God has done much for England."[23] But Silko's reading of comparative anthropology, whether the cultures under consideration have left their archaeological traces on the American continent, in England, or in Italy, is based on the imagery and mythology of nonpatriarchal societies: societies, at the very least, that were comfortable with overt images of fertility and with the easy crossing over of human and animal species. In an elaborate Tuscan garden full of black gladiolus and strange hybrid sculptures, Edward is relieved, he thinks, that Indigo had "missed the serpent figures. The child was from a culture of snake worshipers and there was no sense in confusing her with the impression the old Europeans were no better than red Indians or black Africans who prayed to snakes. Hattie agreed; they must help the child adjust to the world she was in now."[24] Yet not only had Indigo already seen enough of these ancient Italian sculptures to feel a comforting kinship with another culture, but the encounter stirs Hattie's own discomfort with her sterile and repressive marriage—which leads her not only to a recognition of her own sexual needs, but toward finding emotional and social support from women. She stays with Indigo, reunited with her sister and cultivating a flourishing vegetable and flower garden in the desert, but both parties know that the connections between Indian and white women, if deep in some ways, must be tenuous in others—something that is finally symbolized by the distance suggested through the transatlantic nature of Hattie and Indigo's final correspondence. Nonetheless, Silko's fundamental grounds of difference are posited not in racial divisions but in the divisions that exist between those who exploit and those who are exploited, whether the exploitation is of humanity or of the land. The fertile garden that provides the tentatively harmonious and hopeful setting of the book's conclusion is a manifestation of the fact that utility and beauty can coexist. It is a reminder that in such matters as irrigating a particular environment, effective "modern" technology may have been developed many centuries ago, and, above all, it is a proof that native peoples (and native women in particular) have the energy, adaptability, and endurance to enable them to learn from transnational experiences and contacts, and then come home to try to make their own futures.

Arjun Appadurai has written that "it is the imagination that will have to carry us beyond the imagined communities of the past."[25] In their fictional re-creation of new forms of living—in Europe, in the Southwest—both of these novels engage with the themes of transformation and adjustment. Both employ transatlantic crossings to explore the sense of dislocation that Native Americans inevitably felt when engaging with European modernity, as well as to dramatize the accommodations that they inevitably made. That the novels should be so different may in part be due to the very different histories of the tribes from which Welch and Silko come. Both, however, offer imaginative rejoinders to Seeley's 1883 version of history when he asserted, "The American race had no more power of resisting the European than the sheep had of resisting the wolf."[26] By writing this fiction today, both Silko and Welch reclaim and rewrite the possibilities inherent for native peoples in the late nineteenth century. In so doing, they demonstrate that despite the importance, then and now, of tradition as both concept and practice within Indian society, identity, and modes of thought, it stands not isolated from modernity, but rather in mediation and dialogue with it. They emphasize the importance of community, and the centrality of the concept of community to notions of identity, whether the identity at stake is individual or social. At a time when critical attention within American studies has increasingly turned toward imperialism and transnationalism, to explore the importance of the transatlantic Indian is to provide an important reminder that the internal colonial relations of the United States cannot be separated from these other trajectories.[27] Finally, this book brings to the fore the complex social, emotional, and cultural importance of transatlantic relations to Native American culture and, in turn, the ways in which native culture, both real and represented, throws light on the developments and attitudes that characterized British modernity—not just now, in an era of globalization, but in its roots within the Victorian and Edwardian past.

Notes

CHAPTER ONE. FIGURING AMERICA

1. For this tradition, see Honour, *The European Vision of America*.

2. For details of the Albert Memorial, see Bayley, *Albert Memorial*; Brooks, *Albert Memorial*; particularly Colin Cunningham, "Iconography and Victorian Values," 206–51; Dafforne, *Albert Memorial; and Handbook to the Prince Consort National Memorial*.

3. The conditions surrounding the near extermination of the buffalo have produced a considerable amount of recent controversy; my interpretation follows the pro-Indian school of ecological history. For a full discussion, see Geist, *Buffalo Nation*; Flores, *Natural West*; Krech, *Ecological Indian*.

4. Charles Dickens, "The American Panorama," *Examiner*, 16 December 1848, reprinted in *The Dent Uniform Edition of Dickens' Journalism*, vol. 2, *The Amusements of the People and Other Papers*, ed. Slater, 137. For more on the New York–born John Banvard, see Altick, *The Shows of London*, 204–6, and Collins, *Banvard's Folly*, 1–24.

5. Torgovnick, *Gone Primitive*, 3.

6. See Brantlinger, *Dark Vanishings*.

7. Dafforne, *Albert Memorial*, 51–52.

8. The works that have the most relevance to my own and that have had the greatest impact on my thinking include Berkhofer's *White Man's Indian*; Bordewich's *Killing the White Man's Indian*; Brown's *Bury My Heart at Wounded Knee*; Nabokov's *Native American Testimony*; and Pearce's *Savagism and Civilization*.

9. When I write of the United States without any qualifiers, I refer to the geographic and political area as presently constituted by this term, not the growing spaces thus designated during the nineteenth century.

10. Undated cutting from *Daily Mercury*, Buffalo Bill Collection, Denver Public Library.

11. The shift in relative economic stature that took place in the last decades of the nineteenth century may be gauged by the fact that in 1880, the United Kingdom produced 22.9 percent of the world's manufacturing output, and the United States 14.7 percent; by 1900, the figures had become 18.5 percent and 23.6 percent respectively. See Orde, *Eclipse of Great Britain*, 1.

12. See, for example, Robertson and Robertson, *Our American Tour*, 68. Not all British visitors and commentators condemned the administration of reservations and the work of government agents, however; examples of a contradictory viewpoint may be found in Gladstone, *Englishman in Kansas*, 194–96, and Price, *A Summer on the Rockies*, 25–38, 64–73.

13. Berlant, *Anatomy of National Fantasy*, 5.

14. Deloria, *Playing Indian*, 29–31. See also Olson, *Emblems of American Community*, 77–78; Fleming, "From Indian Princess to Greek Goddess," 39–46, and "Symbols of the United States: From Indian Queen to Uncle Sam," in *Frontiers of American Culture*, ed. Browne, Crowder, Lokke, and Stafford, 1–24.

15. Sollors, *Beyond Ethnicity*, 102–3.

16. Smith-Rosenberg, "Subject Female," 485.

17. See Deloria, *Playing Indian*; Susan Scheckel, *Insistence of the Indian*; Walker, *Indian Nation*. Helen Carr has also written usefully about the progressive nineteenth-century movement away from regarding the Indian as an image of "natural man," which the figure had held within the revolutionary rhetoric through which the United States initially distinguished itself; see *Inventing the American Primitive*, 11.

18. Norton, in *Reflections on Political Identity*, quoted by Scheckel, *Insistence of the Indian*, 9.

19. Walker, *Indian Nation*, 7.

20. Maddox, *Citizen Indians*, 5.

21. For the tendency to generalize from a specific tribe or tribe about "Indians" in general, see Stewart and Newman, "Historical Résumé"; McNickle, "American Indians." One cannot ignore the fact that many contemporary Indians refer to themselves (albeit with varying degrees, on occasion, of self-irony) as Indians, often cautious of the Anglo supremacy hiding behind those who are often keenest to employ the supposedly politically correct term "Native Americans." This, at any rate, seems to hold true within the United States; indigenous Canadians often seem more comfortable with the term "First Nations," and I have used this when fitting. Since there is no clearly appropriate way to describe the original inhabitants of the United States, I have deliberately used both "Indian" and "Native American" to designate them.

22. Thackeray, *Virginians*, 121.

23. Psomiades, "Heterosexual Exchange," 109.

24. Churchill, *Reminiscences*, 60.

25. Balsan, *Glitter and Gold*, 71.

26. James, *Portrait of a Lady*, 123.

27. See Dickason, *Canada's First Nations*; Daniel Francis, *Imaginary Indian*; J. R. Miller, *Skyscrapers Hide the Heavens*; Moyles and Owram, *Imperial Dreams*.

28. Oxley, "Indian in Canada," 194.

29. See Rich, *Hudson's Bay Company*, and Saum, *Fur Trader*.

30. In my account of Sitting Bull's stay in Canada, I have drawn particularly on Francis, *Imaginary Indian*, 69–72. See also MacEwen, *Sitting Bull*, and C. Frank Turner, *Across the Medicine Line*. Founded in 1873 and modeled on the Royal Irish Constabulary, the exploits of the Mounties provided the staple for much adventure fiction featuring bloodthirsty Indians—notably that written, in the late 1890s and the early decades of the twentieth century, by "Ralph Connor" (the Presbyterian clergyman the Reverend Charles Gordon). See Daniel Francis, *Imaginary Indian*, 72–82.

31. See Ged Martin, "Canada from 1815," in *Oxford History*, ed. Porter, 522–45, esp. 530–32, and Marsh, *Conscience of the Victorian State*, 173–213.

32. William Wilson, "England and British America," *Christian Guardian*, 23 May 1838, reprinted in *History of the Ojebway Indians*, by Peter Jones, 192–97. Wilson died shortly after leaving Upper Canada Academy, at Coburg, where he had been educated.

33. Sproat, *Scenes and Studies of Savage Life*, 4.

34. Trant, "Treatment of Canadian Indians," 508.

35. Wilkie Collins, *Hide and Seek,* 179.

36. The case of the Pueblo Indians of the southwestern United States created a blurring of the boundaries here, since they had been colonized by successive waves of the Spanish who traveled up from Mexico—from about 1540 to 1610, in the 1680s and 1690s, and from the 1770s through the 1790s—and, despite their periods of conflict, had adopted some of their customs and beliefs. The juxtaposition of Spanish and Indian cultures here certainly could be worked in the latter's favor. Alma Strettell commended the simplicity and affability of Pueblo Indians compared with their neighbors of Castilian or "better class" Mexican ancestry. "Indian Festival," 21.

37. Colley, *Britons*, 6.

38. Colley gives much more weight to America in her *Captives.*

39. See Gibson, *Black Legend.*

40. Roberto Fernández Retamar, "Against the Black Legend," in *Caliban and Other Essays*, 60.

41. See Aguirre, *Informal Empire,* and Forman, "When Britons Brave Brazil."

42. Seeley, *Expansion of England,* 14.

43. Mignolo, *Local Histories/Global Designs,* 133.

44. Saldívar, *Dialectics of Our America,* 9.

45. José Martí, "Our America" (1891), in *José Martí Reader,* ed. Shnookal and Muñiz, 112.

46. A different sort of pan-Indian movement had been established in the mid-eighteenth century with the aim of thwarting Anglo-American expansionism; for the consorted efforts of the Delaware, Shawnee, Cherokee, and Creek nations, see Dowd, *Spirited Resistance.*

47. See Fryd, *Art and Empire,* and Scheckel, *Insistence of the Indian,* ch. 6, "A Guide to Remembrance: The Capitol Tour and the Construction of a U.S. Citizenry," 127–151.

48. James, *American Scene,* 266–67.

49. Dickens, *American Notes,* 210–11.

50. James, *American Scene,* 267.

51. Roach, *Cities of the Dead,* 13.

52. Giles, *Virtual Americas,* 1.

53. Recently there has been a shift in this respect, however, in relation to the period preceding that covered by this book; see Bickham, *Savages within the Empire;* Fulford, *Romantic Indians;* and Pratt, *American Indians,* all of which appeared while I was in the closing stages of this book.

54. Gilroy, *Black Atlantic,* esp. 1–40.

Chapter Two. The Romantic Indian

1. For comparisons of Indians with people of antiquity, and the idea of relating ancient and modern paganism, especially in the writings of Bernard Le Bovier de Fontanelle and Joseph François Lafitau, see Manuel, *Eighteenth Century Confronts the Gods*, 42–43.

2. Quoted in Egerton, *Wright of Derby*, 130.

3. Hayley, *Essay on Epic Poetry*, 226–27.

4. This source was recognized by Honour, *European Vision of America*, cat. no.184.

5. For Adair, see the introduction to Samuel Cole Williams's *Adair's History*. His *History* is remarkable not just for the anthropological and sociological information that it gives concerning the southeastern tribes, but for the sustained argument that he puts forward for the Jewish origins of Indian peoples. Its material not only achieved circulation in its own right, but was one of the texts substantially plagiarized by Jonathan Carver in his *Travels through the Interior Parts of North America*. The idea that the Indians were descended from the Jews had been advanced since the early days of the continent's occupation.

6. Samuel Cole Williams, *Adair's History*, 195–96.

7. For a discussion of these paintings, see Tobin, *Picturing Imperial Power*, 81–109.

8. Richter, "Native Peoples," 348. See also Breen, "Empire of Goods"; Axtell, *Beyond 1492*, 25–51; and, for a mid-nineteenth-century corroboration, George Catlin, *Life amongst the Indians*, 35.

9. See Stevens, "Christian Origins."

10. Warton, "Dying Indian," 272. Warton's anger is directed against European greed: the Indian in "The Revenge of America" tears at his "feathery crown," breaks his arrows, and stamps on the ground in defiance of the "plunderers": "I see all Europe's children cursed / With lucre's universal thirst" (271).

11. Carver, *Travels through the Interior Parts of North America*, 338–40.

12. Fulford, "Romantic Indians," 208. Fulford's chapter titled "The Indian Song," pp. 140–55 of *Romantic Indians*, offers an excellent discussion of the genre. See further Farley, "Dying Indian," and Wind, " 'Adieu to All.' " The dying Indian is one of the topics treated in two works that have been indispensable to the writing of this chapter: Bissell's *American Indian* and Fairchild's *Noble Savage*.

13. Thomas Babington Macaulay, "Milton" (1825), in *Miscellaneous Works of Lord Macaulay* 11:11–12.

14. Gisborne, *Poems, Sacred and Moral*, xxx.

15. The genre of the "dying Indian" poem would undergo something of a mutation at the hands of a number of women poets in the 1820s and 1830s, and it was not exclusively associated with men before then; in her 1782 journal, Hester Thrale Piozzi recorded Anne Hunter's "North American Death Song, Written for, and Adapted to, an Original Indian Air" (reprinted in *Eighteenth-Century Women Poets: An Oxford Anthology*, ed. Roger Lonsdale [Oxford: Oxford University Press, 1989], 364.)

16. Robert Southey, "Song of the Chikkasah Widow" (1799), in *Complete Poetical Works*, 144.

17. Fisher, *Vehement Passions*, 57.

18. For Southey's literary connections at this time, see chapter 4, "Prospects, 1796–1799," in *Robert Southey*, by Storey, 84–121.

19. William Wordsworth, "Preface" (1802), in *Lyrical Ballads*, 63.

20. Fulford, *Romantic Indians*, 170.

21. Wordsworth, "Ruth" (1798), in *Lyrical Ballads*, 281.

22. See Carver, *Travels*, 187. In writing the poem, Southey drew on William Warrington, *The History of Wales* (London: J. Johnson, 1786), and John Williams, *Enquiry Concerning the Discovery of America by Prince Madog* (London: B. White, 1791).

23. The legend continues to intrigue some historians, of variegating historical reliability, and to inform popular fiction, such as Pat Winter's two-volume *Madoc Saga* (1990–91) and Anna Lee Waldo's yet more fanciful *Circle of Stars* (2001).

24. As well as Helen Maria Williams's vehemently anti-Spanish *Peru* of 1784, and such works as Thomas Morton's 1792 *Columbus; or, A World Discovered* and the 1797 Covent Garden pantomime *Harlequin and Quixotte*, which took Peruvian settings, 1799 saw the publication of seven English-language adaptations or translations of Kotzebue's *Die Spanier in Peru*, by Sheridan, Thomas Dutton, Anne Plumtre, Matthew Lewis, M. West, Richard Heron, and "a North Briton."

25. Storey, *Robert Southey*, 56. For the genesis of the poem, see also Bernhardt-Kabisch, *Robert Southey*, 109–27.

26. Once again, Erillyab is presented as an Indian widow:

> By the door,
> Bare of its bark, the head and branches shorn,
> Stood a young tree with many a weapon hung,
> Her husband's war-pole, and his monument.
> There had his quiver moulder'd, his stone-axe
> Had there grown green with moss, his bow-string there
> Sung as it cut the wind.
>
> (2:1121–27)

27. William Wordsworth to Sir George Beaumont, 29 July 1805, *The Letters of William and Dorothy Wordsworth*, arranged and edited by the late Ernest de Selincourt, 2nd ed., 8 vols. (Oxford: Clarendon Press, 1867–1993), 1:610.

28. Philip Freneau, "The Dying Indian" (1784), in *The Poems of Philip Freneau*, ed. Fred Lewis Pattee, 3 vols. (Princeton: Princeton University Library, 1903), 2:245.

29. Stafford, *Last of the Race*, 84.

30. Southey employed the figure of the "last of the race" more directly in *Thalaba* (1801) and *Roderick: The Last of the Goths* (1815).

31. Stafford, *Last of the Race*, 87.

32. Goldsmith's rather mixed view of the "savage" more generally may be gauged from his *History of the Earth and Animated Nature* (1774), 6 vols. (London: Richardson, 1822), 2:88.

33. John Leyden, "Scenes of Infancy: Descriptive of Teviotdale," in *Poetical Remains,* 396–99. Leyden's notes to his poem, published in the 1803 edition of "Scenes of Infancy," show that he used Adair's *History of the American Indians* as his source.

34. Kupperman, *Indians and English,* 29. She cites Nathanael Carpenter, *Geography Delineated forth in Two Bookes: Containing the sphœrical and topicall parts thereof,* 2 vols. in one (Oxford: John Lichfield and William Turner, 1625), 281–82.

35. The watercolor drawings of John White, in the British Museum, may be visited on-line, together with the corresponding engravings of Theodor De Bry, at www.virtualjamestown.org/images/white_debry_html/jamestown.html.

36. Blair, *Lectures on Rhetoric,* 177. See chapter 2 of Carr's *Inventing the American Primitive,* 53–100.

37. Shelley, *Frankenstein,* 116.

38. Heckewelder, *History, Manners, and Customs,* xl.

39. For the British reception of Bryant, see Nadal, "William Cullen Bryant," and Bradfield, "William Cullen Bryant," both of which celebrate him as a poet of place and of nature and suggest that he is more popular in America than in Britain precisely because of the particular landscapes about which he writes.

40. William Cullen Bryant, "The Indian at the Burial-Place of His Fathers," in *Poems of William Cullen Bryant,* 67–68. For Bryant's 1844 trip to Britain and some account of his meetings with British poets, see Charles H. Brown, *William Cullen Bryant,* 304–11. Bryant's 1816 poems utilizing Indian narratives had been stimulated by Walter Scott's poetry about Scottish Highlanders (Brown, 116).

41. Ellison, *Cato's Tears,* 7.

42. Ibid., 18.

43. Ibid., 123.

44. See, for example, Frank Sayers's "Dying African," which appeared in the *Gentleman's Magazine* in November 1791, and More's own "Slavery: A Poem," in *Works of Hannah More,* 28.

45. Thomas Day, dedication to *The Dying Negro,* viii–ix. For Day, see Gignilliat, *Author of Sandford and Merton.*

46. Arthur Barlow, writing in a tract intended to promote settlement in late-sixteenth-century Virginia, quoted by Krech, *Ecological Indian,* 18. Krech's book provides a sustained analysis of the long-cherished idea of the Native American living in peaceful harmony with nature, relating this to the environmental history of the United States.

47. Butler, *Journal,* 1:98.

48. I am much indebted to Deirdre David for the suggestion that Kemble, in her writing, may be seen as a rhetorical performer, just as she was accustomed to adopting roles when onstage.

49. Others, however, were generally distrustful of Europeans or wanted to keep trading connections active with whatever side. For the complexities of British-Indian relations during this period, see Robert S. Allen, *His Majesty's Indian Allies;* Calloway, *Crown and Calumet* and *American Revolution;* Richter, "Native Peoples of North America"; and Richard White, *Middle Ground.*

All of these historians emphasize that—in Richter's succinct formulation— "there would never be *one* British policy towards Native Americans, but rather a host of British people pursuing a variety of interests within parameters set by historical experience, Imperial structures, and finally, basic characteristics of Indian political culture" (349).

50. Thomas Scott, n.d., in Douglas, *Familiar Letters,* 2:345. In his turn, Norton translated Scott's *Lady of the Lake*—as well as the Scriptures—into Mohawk. See Calloway, *Crown and Calumet,* 114. For Brant's visits to London, see Thompson, *Joseph Brant,* 162–74, 379–91. Another contrast is made by the 1776 portrait by Benjamin West of Colonel Guy Johnson, Brant's friend and companion on his first visit to London and recently appointed superintendent of Indian affairs, who was painted with Indians—albeit somewhat shadowy ones— in the background.

51. Kupperman, *Indians and English,* 9.

52. Thackeray, *Virginians,* 104.

53. [Burke], "History of Europe," 111.

54. Quoted in S. T. Coleridge's *Lectures,* 56n.

55. For an interesting discussion of Lennox's transatlantic fictions and, in particular, of her treatment of the nationalistic implications that English manners and codes of politeness bear in *Euphemia,* see Bannet, "Theatre of Politeness." For *Euphemia* more particularly, see Howard, "Seeing Colonial America."

56. In this respect, *Euphemia* may profitably be compared to the memoirs of Anne MacVicar Grant, a Scotswoman whose father had been posted to Albany and who married into a prominent local Dutch family. See her *Memoirs.*

57. Lennox, *Euphemia* 3:124–25.

58. See Batten, *Pleasurable Instruction.*

59. Voltaire's "ingénue" is a young Frenchman brought up in America as an Indian, who arrives in France anxious to learn about the country. Ostensibly set in 1689, it is in fact an indictment of many contemporary aspects of the ancien régime.

60. [Young], *Adventures of Emmera* 2:185.

61. This inference is not just drawn from the novel's plot; in a draft of a letter to her own husband, Lennox referred to his "despotick will." See Isles, "Lennox Connection," 425.

62. [Blamire], *Poetical Works,* 22.

63. See Charlotte Smith, "The Captive Escaped in the Wilds of America" and "Supposed to Have Been Written in America," sonnets 56 and 61 of her *Elegiac Sonnets.* For captivity narratives, see Burnham, *Captivity and Sentiment;* Castiglia, *Bound and Determined;* Ebersole, *Captured by Texts;* and Namias, *White Captives.* Further notable treatments of Indian captivity can be found in Frances Brooke's *Emily Montagu* (1769) and Robert Bage's *Hermsprong; or, Man as He Is Not* (1796).

64. Thomas Day, *History of Sandford and Merton,* 425.

65. For the treatment of the Indian in eighteenth-century British philosophy— putting it, additionally, into a European context—see the very clear account given in Emerson's "American Indians."

66. The term "noble savage" has been extensively discussed, most recently by Ter Ellingson, in *Myth of the Noble Savage*.

67. See, for example, Edmund Burke's appropriation, in *Reflections on the Revolution in France*, of Native Americans as a type of "savages" to whom those responsible for the French Revolution should be equated. For a discussion of Burke and the concept of savagery, see Luke Gibbons, "'Subtilized into Savages.'"

68. Samuel Johnson, *Preface to Shakespeare* 7:88.

69. Oliver Goldsmith, "The Deserted Village," lines 47–48.

70. Wind, "'Adieu to All,'" 42.

71. [Irving], "Biographical Sketch," 247. For the critical response to "Gertrude," see Miller, *Thomas Campbell*, 62–67; see also Duffy, "Thomas Campbell."

72. [Scott], "Gertrude of Wyoming," 243.

73. Hazlitt, *Lectures on the English Poets and Spirit of the Age*, 150.

74. Thomas Campbell, "Letter to the Mohawk Chief," 97. Wild, *Travels through the States of North America*.

CHAPTER THREE. "BROUGHT TO THE ZENITH OF
CIVILIZATION": INDIANS IN ENGLAND IN THE 1840S

1. Catlin, *Life amongst the Indians*, 30.

2. The literature on Catlin is relatively extensive. In particular, I am indebted to Brian W. Dippie, *Catlin and His Contemporaries;* Gurney and Heyman, *George Catlin*—the catalogue of the magnificent exhibition, first shown at the Renwick Gallery, which displayed the complete collection of paintings that made up Catlin's "Indian Gallery"; Treuttner, *Natural Man Observed*; and Reddin, *Wild West Shows*, 1–52.

3. Catlin, *Catlin's Notes* 1:296.

4. "The Encampment," Handbills, Indian Gallery. George Catlin Papers, 1840–60, Smithsonian Institute, quoted in *Wild West Shows*, by Reddin, 41–42.

5. Cooper, *Last of the Mohicans*, 25.

6. Catlin, *Letters and Notes* 2:10.

7. See Fiona Stafford's excellent book *Last of the Race*.

8. Catlin, *Notes* 1:62. Catlin was not exactly disinterested in making this suggestion—to which he would return in subsequent years; he entertained the hope that the purchase of his own collection might form the foundation of such a museum.

9. Prichard, "On the Extinction of the Human Races," 166–70.

10. Brantlinger, *Dark Vanishings*, 2.

11. Catlin, *Notes* 1:99.

12. Charles Augustus Murray, *Travels in North America*. For Murray's life, see Maxwell, *The Honourable Sir Charles Murray*.

13. Catlin, *Notes* 1:78.

14. I use the First Nations name Ojibwa; in the United States this tribe is known as the Chippewa.

15. [Rankin], *Short History*, 6.

16. For a discussion of the Iowa visit, see Winona Stevenson, "Beggars, Chickabobbooags, and Prisons," 1–23.

17. I take this phrase from Lindfors, "Ethnological Show Business," 207.

18. W. Richard West, introduction to *George Catlin,* ed. Gurney and Heyman, 20–21.

19. See Foreman, *Indians Abroad.*

20. Hakluyt, *Divers Voyages,* 23.

21. Mossiker, *Pocahontas,* 209. There is a copious amount of literature concerning the Pocahontas story; see especially Tilton, *Pocahontas*; Faery, *Cartographies of Desire*; and, written from a nativist perspective, Paula Gunn Allen, *Pocahontas.*

22. "He stands six feet two, and, dressed in his splendid native costume, presents a most imposing and warlike appearance. The chief was introduced last week to his excellency the American minister, who received him with much kindness." *Manchester Guardian,* 18 November 1843, 5. Very few Sac Indians had survived the "Black Hawk" removal war of 1832–33, after which they had had to concede their last six million acres in Illinois for a tiny piece of land in central Iowa.

23. See Donald B. Smith, "Maungwudaus Goes Abroad."

24. Catlin, *Notes* 1:108.

25. Ibid. 1:120. The *Manchester Guardian* of 22 November 1843(4) notes that Cadotte, the interpreter, refused to allow a cast of his head to be made.

26. *Manchester Guardian,* 22 November 1843, 4. The trade in photographs was not just one-sided. Rankin notes that when the Ojibwa were staying in London, they became friendly with an elderly neighbor, a Mr. Saunders.

> On a late occasion, after a repast, the Old Chief was noticed to be in a close conversation with his followers, and at length made an harangue after his usual mode, and to this effect:—He had a favour to ask. His brother (Mr. Saunders) had shown great kindness to his people. They loved him, and when they were again in their own land it would be pleasant to see him still. They wished to have his face (meaning a portrait). They would be able to show to their tribe the man who had been a father to them! The old gentleman kindly complied with the request, and the Ojibbeways, at their own expense, purchased a Daguerreotype likeness, which will, doubtless, for many years hereafter, be handed down as a heirloom in the forests of the far West. (*Short History,* 19–20)

27. *Manchester Courier and Lancashire General Advertiser,* 18 November 1843, 6.

28. Ibid., 25 November 1843, 7.

29. Catlin, *Notes* 1:153–54.

30. Lindfors, "Ethnological Show Business," 210.

31. Slavery was indeed an issue in the Webster-Ashburton Treaty; the United States agreed to station ships off the African coast in an effort to detect Americans engaging in the slave trade, but Webster rejected a request to allow the boarding of American ships by the British navy.

32. For the development of racial theory as it bore on relations between the sexes, see in particular Young, *Colonial Desire*.

33. See *Gentleman's Magazine* 25 (1765), 95.

34. Quoted by Fairchild, *The Noble Savage*, 73.

35. See Felsenstein, *English Trader*.

36. Felicia Hemans, "The American Forest-Girl," in Hemans, *Felicia Hemans*, 389–91.

37. Thomas Gray, "Elegy Written in a Country Churchyard" (1751), line 93.

38. Sigourney, *Pocahontas, and Other Poems*, 23.

39. Colley, *Captives*, 228.

40. Jemison, *Life of Mrs. Mary Jemison*, 207.

41. Mary Howitt, "Elian Gray," in *Ballads and Other Poems*, lines 81, 194.

42. Kingston, *Western Wanderings* 2:188.

43. Hancock, *Emigrant's Five Years*, 240–41. Sarah Haynes died in March 1851; Alexander Cadotte (b. 28 March 1820) married Celenise Baril or Bay on 20 June 1853 and died on 30 January 1901. See the genealogical research on the Cadotte family at www3.sympatico.ca/sneakers/.

44. Catlin, *Notes* 1:110.

45. Malchow, *Gothic Images of Race*, 217.

46. Donald B. Smith, *Sacred Feathers*, 139.

47. *Commercial Advertiser*, 12 September 1833, quoted in *Sacred Feathers*, by Donald B. Smith, 141.

48. "The 'Strong Wind' in St. Martin's Church," *Punch*, 20 April 1844, 173.

49. "The London Lass and the Ojibbeway Indian," Bodleian Library: Harding B (13) 174, lines 15–17.

50. "The Ojibbeway Indians and Love," Bodleian Library: Harding B (13) 156, lines 34, 36; "The London Lass," lines 19–20.

51. Young, *Colonial Desire*, 181.

52. Maungwudaus, *An Account of the Chippewa Indians*, title page.

53. For the fullest and most useful discussion of the complex language and translation issues at stake here, see David Murray, *Forked Tongues*.

54. Briggs and Bauman, " 'The Foundation of All Future Researches.' "

55. Copway, *Traditional History and Characteristic Sketches*, 125.

56. For a discussion of the issue of authenticity, see especially Susan Bernadin, "Authenticity Game," as well as many of the other essays in *True West*, ed. Handley and Lewis, 155–75.

57. Catlin, *Notes* 1:121. The astonishment, incidentally, was two-sided: "In one large room, where 1,300 power looms were attended by six hundred and fifty girls, the girls were so astonished or affrighted at the appearance of the Indians, that they lost the broken threads for some minutes." *Manchester Courier and Lancashire General Advertiser*, 18 November 1843, 6.

58. It may be noted, however, that the Manchester press at this time does not write of current industrial disputes in terms that would corroborate Catlin's account.

59. Friedrich Engels, *Condition of the Working Class*, 84.

60. See Lyotard, *The Differend*. For an illuminating discussion of Native American silences, see Glenn, *Unspoken*, 107–49.

61. Catlin, *Notes* 1:129. Catlin notes that the Iowa had very similar attitudes toward the street sweepers, spending some time deliberating which tribe of Indians could possibly demean themselves so far as to sweep the street, before determining on the Ojibwa. Although Catlin enlightened them, Jim stuck to the derogatory appellation, can be seen in a later encounter, when he told Catlin that

> they had found another place where there were two more ojibbeway [Ojibwa] Indians (as he called them), Lascars, sweeping the streets; and it seems that after passing them they had ordered their bus to stop, and called them up and shook hands, and tried to talk with them. They could speak a few words in English, and so could *Jim*: he was enabled to ask them if they were Ojibbeways, and they to answer, "No, they were Mussulmen." "Where do you live?" "Bombay." "You sweep dirt in the road?" "Yes." "Dam fool!" *Jim* gathered a handful of pennies and gave them, and they drove off. (2:70)

The repetitions in Catlin's prose do, admittedly, afford material for some questions about evidence, accuracy, and memory.

62. George Catlin to his father, 3 March 1842, in *Letters of George Catlin,* ed. Roehm, 237.

63. Vizenor, "Edward Curtis," 181.

64. Donald B. Smith, "Maungwudaus," 6–11.

65. Frank Little, "Early Recollections of Indians about Gull Prairie," read before the Kalamazoo Pioneer Society, 15 August 1895, *Michigan Pioneer and Historical Collections* 27 (1896), 336.

66. In giving this account of the features of modernity, I am greatly indebted to the opening pages of Marshall Berman's *All That Is Solid,* 17–19.

67. Fabian, *Time and the Other,* 1983, 31.

68. For a sustained treatment of transformation in relation to postcolonial cultures, see Ashcroft, *Post-Colonial Transformation.* This is not to say, however, that I regard Native American or First Nations people, then or now, as unproblematically postcolonial, bearing in mind the complexities created by the relationship of reservations to state or province and to nation.

CHAPTER FOUR. SENTIMENT AND ANGER: BRITISH WOMEN
WRITERS AND NATIVE AMERICANS

1. Brontë, *Shirley,* 441.

2. To take a contemporary example: Robert Ballantyne wrote of his experiences among the Cree: "The Indian women are not so good-looking as the men. They have an awkward slouching gait, and a downcast look,—arising, probably, from the rude treatment they experience from their husbands; for the North American Indians, like all other savages, make complete drudges of their women, obliging them to do all the laborious and dirty work, while they reserve the pleasures of the chase for themselves." Ballantyne, *Hudson's Bay,* 45.

3. Felicia Hemans, for one, readily signals her indebtedness to various American sources. "Child of the Forests," published in the *New Monthly Magazine* in

1824, was later subtitled "Written After Reading the Memoirs of John Hunter", whose highly popular account of his upbringing in captivity at the hands of the Kansas and Osage had been published the previous year, and her "Indian Woman's Death-Song" (1828) includes a sentence from Cooper's *Prairie* among its epigraphs. See Hemans, *Felicia Hemans*, 371. John Hunter's popular volume was entitled *Memoirs of a Captivity among the Indians of North America, from Childhood to the Age of Nineteen* (Philadelphia, 1823). For the biography of Hunter, and a considered discussion of the impact of his work, see Drinnon, *White Savage.*

4. See Julie Ellison, "Race and Sensibility in the Early Republic: Ann Elizabeth Bleecker and Sarah Wentworth Morton," *American Literature* 65 (1993), 445–48.

5. Goslee, "Hemans's 'Red Indians,' " 237–61.

6. Fulford, *Romantic Indians*, 198–201.

7. Wolfson, *Borderlines*, 60.

8. Festa, *Sentimental Figures*, 2–3.

9. Sigmund Freud, "Mourning and Melancholia," in *The Penguin Freud Library*, ed. Albert Dickinson, vol. 11, *On Metapsychology* (Harmondsworth: Penguin, 1990), 252.

10. Midgley, *Women against Slavery*, 5. See also Bolt, *Anti-Slavery Movement and Reconstruction* and "Anti-Slavery Origins," 233–53; and Ferguson, *Subject to Others.*

11. Goslee has persuasively argued that Hemans may well have written about Indians in part because her family background and her father's business connections in Liverpool prevented her from treating the cause of African enslavement directly. "Hemans's 'Red Indians,' " 241. For Hemans and imperialism, see also Sweet, "History, Imperialism." For further relevant revisionist considerations of Hemans, poetry, and gender, see two articles by Susan Wolfson, " 'Domestic Affections' and 'the Spear of Minerva' " and "Gendering the Soul."

12. Armstrong, *How Novels Think*, 13.

13. Jacobus, *Tradition and Experiment*, 192.

14. Lootens, "Hemans and Her American Heirs," 244.

15. Eliza Cook, "The Song of the Red Man," in *Poetical Works of Eliza Cook*, 498–99.

16. In making this general argument, I have been influenced by the approach Tricia Lootens took in "Hemans and Home."

17. Morrison, *Playing in the Dark*, 51, 53.

18. Felicia Hemans, "The Indian with His Dead Child," *Songs of the Affections*, 51.

19. Felicia Hemans, "The Aged Indian," in *Translations from Camoens*, 71

20. Butler [Kemble], "The Red Indian," in *Poems*, 31.

21. Contrast the far less ideologically loaded formulation of Wordsworth: "My journey will be shortly run,/I shall not see another sun," in "The Complaint of a Forsaken Indian Woman," in *Lyrical Ballads*, 255.

22. Rosaldo, *Culture and Truth*, 69, 70, 86. The usefulness of Rosaldo's work to the discussion of Native American culture was brought home to me by Laura Romero's stimulating article "Vanishing Americans: Gender, Empire, and New

Historicism," *American Literature* 63 (1991), 385–404, although my use of his work is somewhat different from hers.

23. Tocqueville, *Democracy in America*, 328. See further Liebersohn, *Aristocratic Encounters*.

24. See especially Girouard, *The Return to Camelot*, and Kestner, *Masculinities in Victorian Painting*.

25. The counterview was also expressed, that the beauties of nature are wasted on the indigenous inhabitants: "The chance which opens to the meditative the almost untouched regions of nature, is a rare one; and they should not be left to the vanishing savage, the busy and the sordid." Martineau, *Society in America* 1:212–13.

26. Eliza Cook, *Jottings from My Journal*, 324–25.

27. Frances Trollope, *The Old World and the New* 2:126.

28. For Indian-white intermarriage, see Faragher, "Custom of the Country"; Swagerty, "Marriage and Settlement Patterns"; Van Kirk, *Many Tender Ties*; and for a more theoretical overview, Pascoe, "Race, Gender."

29. Moran, *Interracial Intimacy*, 54. See also Weierman, *One Nation, One Blood*.

30. Maddox, *Removals*, 39.

31. Ibid., quoting William Gilmore Simms, *Views and Reviews in American Literature: History and Fiction, First Series*, ed. C. Hugh Holman (Cambridge, MA: Harvard University Press, 1962), 112.

32. Frances Trollope, *Domestic Manners*, 178.

33. Ibid., 221–22. Her understanding of the plight of Native Americans may be juxtaposed with the attitudes of her initial traveling companion, Frances Wright, who did not share her sympathetic attitude, writing that "the savage, with all his virtues, and he has some virtues, is still a savage . . . holding a lower place in creation than men who, to the proud spirit of independence, unite the softer feelings that spring only within the pale of civilized life. The increase and spread of the white population at the expense of the red is, as it were, the triumph of peace over violence." She went on to speak, in blinkered ignorance, of the "wise and humane" treaties between the federal government and the Indians, which "have never been violated." Wright, *Views of Society*, 106, 108.

34. Frances Trollope, *Refugee in America*, 2:161.

35. Frances Trollope, *Whitlaw* 3:132.

36. Murray, *Letters from the United States* 1:185.

37. Ibid., *Letters*, 184–85.

38. Seemingly, *The Old World and the New* spawned at least one imitation later in the century that provoked similar questions in a yet more popular form. Robert Louis Stevenson noted that Ohio

> had early been a favourite home of my imagination; I have played at being in Ohio by the week, and enjoyed some capital sport there with a dummy gun, my person being still unbreeched. My preference was founded on a work that appeared in *Cassell's Family Paper*, and was read aloud to me by my nurse. It narrated the doings of one Custaloga, an Indian brave, who, in the last chapter, very obligingly washed the paint off his face and

became Sir Reginald Somebody-or-other; a trick I never forgave him. The idea of a man being an Indian brave, and then giving that up to be a baronet, was one which my mind rejected. It offended verisimilitude, like the pretended anxiety of Robinson Crusoe and others to escape from uninhabited islands. (Robert Louis Stevenson, *Travels and Essays,* 108)

39. Browder, *Slippery Characters,* 11.

40. H[owitt], *The Desolation of Eyam,* 243.

41. Eliza Cook, "Song of the Red Indian," in *Poetical Works,* 177.

42. See Jon W. Finson, "The Romantic Savage: American Indians in the Parlor," chapter 7 of *Voices That Are Gone,* 240–69, and Sanjek, *American Popular Music,* 60–67. The music to Russell's version of Cook's "Song" may be heard at http://www.pdmusic.org/russell.html. For Russell's interest in native music, including his research trip with Catlin (which served to disenchant him with the idea), see Pisani, *Imagining Native America in Music,* 110–12, and Russell, *Cheer! Boys, Cheer!* 159–73.

43. Eliza Cook, "Did God So Will It?" in *Poetical Works,* 336.

44. Eliza Cook, "Song of the Red Indian," in *Poetical Works,* 177.

45. Ibid., 178.

46. Howitt, *Popular History,* 2:404.

47. Martineau, *Retrospect of Western Travel* 2:89.

48. Isabella Lucy Bird, *Englishwoman in America,* 50.

49. Pfeiffer, *Flying Leaves,* 136.

50. Ellison, *Cato's Tears,* 181.

51. Amelia M. Murray, *Letters* 1:109. My formulations about commodification draw on some of the essays concerning the production and consumption of Native American artifacts for the tourist trade; see the chapter in Phillips and Steiner, *Unpacking Culture,* and especially Aldona Jonaitis's "Northwest Coast Totem Poles," 104–21.

52. Bird, *Englishwoman in America,* 48–49.

53. Eliot, *George Eliot Letters* 2:85.

54. Ibid. 5:279–80.

55. Eliot, *Daniel Deronda,* 77. To some extent the portrayal of Rex here must be read in the light of the fact that George Lewes's sons Bertie and Thornie went to seek their fortunes in South Africa: Mr. Gascoigne's reply to his son that he had no right to expatriate himself until he had tried to see what he could do with his education in England indicates that Eliot may well have regarded emigration as something of a last resort. For Eliot, race, and empire, see especially Henry, *George Eliot,* as well as McKay, *George Eliot.*

56. Eliot, *Impressions of Theophrastus Such,* 239.

57. Ibid., 259.

58. Emily Pfeiffer, "Red or White?" in *Flowers of the Night,* 18–19.

59. This is Jonathan Martin's formulation of the cultural work performed by William Cody's shows; see Martin, " 'The Grandest and Most Cosmopolitan Object Teacher,' " 107.

60. Pfeiffer, "Red or White?" 21.

CHAPTER FIVE. IS THE INDIAN AN AMERICAN?

1. Powers also produced two notable sculptures with Indian themes: *The Last of Her Tribe*, showing a young Indian woman in flight, and the resigned and melancholy *Indian Chief Contemplating the Progress of Civilization*. For an extended discussion of *The Greek Slave*, as related to the broader contexts of nineteenth-century American sculpture, see Kasson, *Marble Queens and Captives*, 46–72.

2. Exhibition supplement to the *Illustrated London News*, 3 May 1851, 432. The *ILN*'s comments on the exhibition were widely disseminated through subsequent volume publications, such as *The Illustrated Exhibitor*.

3. *Punch*, 24 May 1851, 209; 7 June 1851, 236.

4. Browning, "Hiram Powers' Greek Slave," in *Selected Poems*, 211. "Mr. Powers the sculptor is our chief friend & Favorite," wrote Elizabeth Barrett Browning to Mary Russell Mitford on 15 September 1847; "A most charming, simple, straightforward, genial American." She continued: "The sculptor has eyes like a wild Indian's, so black and full of light." *Letters of Elizabeth Barrett Browning* 3:222.

5. Auerbach, *The Great Exhibition of 1851*, 168.

6. Foucault, "Of Other Spaces," 25.

7. *Athenaeum*, 3 May 1851, 477.

8. *Morning Chronicle*, 8 May 1851, 3.

9. Ibid., 31 May 1851, 2.

10. *Times*, 15 May 1851, 5.

11. *Athenaeum*, 3 May 1851, 478.

12. *Times*, 15 May 1851, 5.

13. *Morning Chronicle*, 31 May 1851, 2.

14. *Morning Post*, 4 June 1851, 3. For a succinct explanation of the problems facing American exhibitors, see letter to The *Times*, 28 May 1851, 7.

15. "Americus," *Where to Emigrate and Why*.

16. Perhaps a better sense of the scale of the United States would have been conveyed by the "Moving Mirror of American Scenery," concurrently on show at the Baker Street Bazaar—a diorama "presenting views of the Mammoth Cave of Kentucky, a journey across the Western Prairies, the River and Falls of Niagara in winter and summer, and the natural Bridge of Virginia." *Spectator*, 17 May 1851, 476.

17. *Morning Chronicle*, 31 May 1851, 2.

18. *Standard*, 3 May 1851, 1.

19. The Dying Gladiator "is in fact a dying Galatian, and is a Roman copy of one of the statues from the monument set up in Pergamum by King Attalus I to commemorate his victory in about 230 B.C. over the Galatians, a Celtic people settled in Central Asia Minor." Betty Radice, *Who's Who in the Ancient World* (London: Penguin, 1984), 107.

20. Felicia Hemans, "The Statue of the Dying Gladiator," in *Felicia Hemans*, 3.

21. Lord Byron, "The Dying Gladiator," in *Childe Harold's Pilgrimage*, canto 4, stanzas 140–41.

22. One might note, however, that Indians could well be compared far more favorably with the statuesque. Observing the pilots of Canadian timber floats on the Saint Lawrence in late 1864, John Francis Campbell wrote that they might well be "some old Indian, wrapped in a buffalo robe, still as Nelson on his column in Trafalgar Square." [John Francis Campbell], *Short American Tramp,* 248.

23. It should also be noted that Indian bodies had already been compared to ancient Greek statues. Johann Winkelmann made the parallel in *Thoughts on the Imitation of Greek Art in Painting and Sculpture* (1755); five years later, visiting Rome in 1760, Benjamin West, on seeing the Apollo Belvedere, famously exclaimed, "How like a young Mohawk warrior!"

24. *Times,* 15 May 1851, 8.

25. *Morning Chronicle,* 16 May 1851, 6.

26. Ibid.

27. *Illustrated London News,* 24 May 1851, 459–60.

28. Ibid., 457.

29. Carter, *Road to Botany Bay,* 304.

30. Treuttner notes that at the time that Catlin exhibited these two figures, he was in a poor financial way, painting fifty five copies of paintings in his Indian collection at £2 each to repay a debt to Sir Thomas Phillips. Treuttner, *Natural Man Observed,* 53. Catlin's small show, incidentally, provided the opportunity for four Iroquois to show their beaded purses, caps, and shoes; they had turned up at the Crystal Palace not having understood that this was not a commercial fair. *Spectator,* 15 August 1851, 788.

31. There is a further irony, one involving the idea of reverse colonization. Catlin was obstinately fixated on the idea that the Mandan were descendants of the Welsh, of those who had come across with Prince Madoc.

32. Catlin, *Letters and Notes* 2:249.

33. [Bigg], "*The Song of Hiawatha,*" 333.

34. Unsigned review, "Poetical Works of Henry W. Longfellow," 630.

35. Athenaeum, "*Song of Hiawatha,*" 1295.

36. Unsigned review, "Longfellow's Song of Hiawatha," *Dublin University Magazine* 47 (1856), 90–91.

37. Berkhofer, *White Man's Indian,* 95.

38. See Schramm, "*Hiawatha* and Its Predecessors."

39. Unsigned review, "The Mystic," 34.

40. Unsigned review, "Poetry of the Past Year," 270.

41. [Bigg], "*Song of Hiawatha,*" 336.

42. Bigg cites Sœmund Sigfuscon's *Edda* on a number of occasions in his notes to *The Sea-King* (London: Whittaker, 1848): this connects with Longfellow's well-known description of *Hiawatha* in his notes to the poem as "This Indian Edda—if I may so call it." Henry Wadsworth Longfellow, *Poetical Works,* 575.

43. Quoted in Carr, *Inventing the American Primitive,* 108–9.

44. See Chapter 9 of Dippie, *Vanishing American,* 122–140.

45. Whitman, *Leaves of Grass,* 711, 126. Ed Folsom, in *Walt Whitman's Native Representations,* 55–98.

46. Castro, *Interpreting the Indian*, xvii–viii. For the British reception of Whitman, see Blodgett, *Walt Whitman in England*.

47. Whitman, *Leaves of Grass*, 42.

48. William Howitt, letter to the *Athenaeum*, 17 November 1855, 1337.

49. Unsigned review, "Longfellow's Song of Hiawatha," 1200.

50. Unsigned review, "Poetry of the Past Year," 270–72.

51. [Margaret Oliphant], "Modern Light Literature," 135.

52. Unsigned poem, "The Song of Hiawatha (*Author's Protective Edition*)."

53. [Head], "The Red Man," 408.

54. Laurence Oliphant, *Minnesota and the Far West*, 231. This book originally appeared in article form in *Blackwood's Magazine*, April–September 1855.

55. Isabella Lucy Bird, *Englishwoman in America*, 156–57.

56. The poem's incantatory style, and the resultant temptation that it offered to schoolteachers, was doubtless a further factor in its enduring popularity (in 1963, when I was an eight-year-old in London our teacher still had us learn chunks of the poem by heart) Eric Robinson, writing the first British study of Longfellow shortly after his death, notes:

> Memory carries the writer back to days when Longfellow's "Hiawatha" was eight years old, and in a class of four ill-spelling Scottish boys, there was a prodigy of childish learning. Although but seven years of age, he could repeat from beginning to end both Scott's "Lady of the Lake" and Longfellow's "Hiawatha," and many an afternoon did he keep his fellows spellbound with this song of the American forests. On these occasions they gathered under an old piano in a disused room, and the solemn-faced little oracle—now he is in the cavalry!—chanted forth Longfellow's trochaics unswervingly, while the audience remained suspended between curiosity to find him halt and awe and dimly-understood utterances that seemed like fairy tales out of the Bible. When they arrived at the passage where Kabibonokka, the North Wind, "to the lodge came wailing," one little lad put down the pedal of the ruined old square piano, while another would strike his head, like a drumstick, against its belly, and make it shudder and loudly sigh. This was Kabibonokka, the North Wind. Could the poet have seen that oft-gathered group of children, not one of whom—no, not the reciter himself—really understood a line of the poem that entranced them, how he would have enjoyed the picture!
>
> This slight reminiscence may serve in its way to exemplify the wonderful power that "Hiawatha" everywhere exerts over the young, as well as over so many grown-up readers. The secret of this spell is no doubt the fact that the poem narrates the doings of a childlike people in a land that is to us full of strange things. (Eric S. Robertson, *Life of Henry Wadsworth Longfellow* [London: Walter Scott, 1887], 140) Virginia Jackson has written fascinatingly on the questions raised by the popularity of Longfellow (albeit in an American context) in "Longfellow's Tradition." For the popularity of Longfellow in England generally—"a vast epic with a thousand and one episodes" (99)—see Gohdes, *American Literature*, 99–126.

57. [Davis], "Longfellow."

58. Boym, *The Future of Nostalgia,* xiv–xv.

59. Nathaniel Hawthorne to Henry Wadsworth Longfellow, 12 April 1856, (in *Life of Henry Wadsworth Longfellow,* by Longfellow), 2:276–77.

60. Newman, *Hiawatha,* vi–vii.

61. The poem opens as follows:

> Ye who love the haunts of Town-life,
> Love the kennel and the gutter,
> Love the doorway of the gin-shop,
> Love the mud about the kerb-stones,
> And the drippings from the houses,
> And the splashings of the rain-spouts
> Through their palisade of gratings,
> And the thunder of the coaches,
> Whose innumerable echoes,
> Roar like sea-waves on the shingle;—
> Listen to these wild traditions,
> To this song of Drop o'Wather!

> ([Clarke], *Song of Drop O'Wather,* 7)

62. Brassaï, "Carroll the Photographer," 188–98; reprinted in *Literature and Photography,* ed. Rabb, 51. "Hiawatha's Photographing" can be found in *Carroll's Complete Works* 768–772. First printed in the *Train* (December 1857), the poem was collected by Carroll in *Phantasmagoria* (London: Macmillan, 1869).

63. The notice in the *Athenaeum* was typical, despite its earlier enthusiasm for *Hiawatha.*

> He has acted upon his readers as a sort of male Mrs Hemans. He has constantly improved them, chastened and warmed their affections, nurtured their sense of the beautiful and the picturesque, mildly stimulated their minds, and contributed (it may be said) to fortify the bonds of union between the two great nations. All these good effects, however, have been produced in a comparatively tepid degree . . . . If we look from the direct to the indirect operation of Longfellow's poems, it may, without rashness, be said that the chief abiding sensation left by them upon the general body of his middle-class readers is a feeling of self-complacency. (Unsigned obituary, "Mr Longfellow," Athenaeum[1 April 1882], 388).

64. Ibid., 418.

65. Pisani, *Imagining Native America,* 135. Pisani offers an extended critique of this work on pp. 131–42.

66. See Green, "Requiem," 283–288.

67. Sir Hubert Parry, tribute to Coleridge-Taylor in the *Musical Times,* 1 October 1912, quoted in Tortolano, *Samuel Coleridge-Taylor,* 136. For Coleridge-Taylor, see also Sayers, *Samuel Coleridge-Taylor.*

68. Pisani, *Imagining Native America,* 157. For Coleridge-Taylor's oratorio, see 148–57.

69. Rossetti, *Lives of the Famous Poets,* 388.

70. Trachtenberg, *Shades of Hiawatha,* 92–3.

71. Subsequently, the rights to the play were transferred to the Grand Rapids and Indiana Railway, who moved the production to a location near Petoskey, Michigan, where it was performed every summer until 1914. For the history of Ojibwa and Odawa acting in *Hiawatha* pageants, see McNally, "Indian Passion Play."

CHAPTER SIX. SAVAGERY AND NATIONALISM: NATIVE AMERICANS AND POPULAR FICTION

1. Burnett, *The One I Knew the Best of All*, 60.
2. Hutcheson, "Young America," 41–42.
3. Berkhofer, *White Man's Indian*, 93.
4. Unsigned review article, "Indians of Western America," 441.
5. Unsigned obituary, *Athenaeum*, 4 October 1851, 1047.
6. Unsigned article, "Living Literary Characters, No. IV: James Fenimore Cooper," *New Monthly Magazine and Literary Journal* 31 (1831), 356–57.
7. Unsigned review (the Wellesley Index suggests Catherine E. Bagshawe as the probable author), "Cooper's Novels," *Dublin Review* 6 (1839), 491.
8. See, for example, Keningale Cook, "American Novelists," 387.
9. Kebbel, "Leather-Stocking," 191.
10. Maxwell, *Honourable Sir Charles Murray*, 195. As well as his account of his time among the Pawnee, Murray published an early British Western, *The Prairie Bird* (1844), based on his experiences. As his biographer notes, the book went through many editions and was to be found on railway bookstalls in the late nineteenth century, when it was "still a favourite with our schoolboys, and perhaps still more so with those of the United States. It is a romance of that kind which Fenimore Cooper succeeded in making so popular." Maxwell, *Murray*, 194–95.
11. For the way in which Cooper's Indians fed into domestic mythology, see Barker and Sabin, *Lasting of the Mohicans*. Barker and Sabin take a somewhat benevolent view of Cooper, perhaps underestimating the oversimplification of his types. Although Cooper's British receipts fell from £1,300 in 1831 to £100 in 1850 (see Patten, *Charles Dickens and His Publishers*), his works readily circulated in libraries and in cheap editions.
12. Baden-Powell, *Scouting for Boys*, 72.
13. Tompkins, *Sensational Designs*, 111.
14. Kebbel, "Leather-Stocking," 197. In this respect, the influence of not only Cooper's Magua was felt but also of the brutal, bellicose, and pidgin-English-speaking Indians of Robert Montgomery Bird's *Nick of the Woods* (1837). For the influence of Bird on the formation of "Indian" speech in fiction and later in film—the omission and confusion of pronouns and the addition of "-um" to a large number of words—see Stedman, *Shadows of the Indian*, 68. For Bird more generally, see Dahl, *Robert Montgomery Bird*.
15. Stocking, *Victorian Anthropology*, xii–xiii. See also "From Religion to Anthropology: The Genealogy of the Scientific Image of the Indian," part 2 of Berkhofer's *White Man's Indian*, 33–69, and Bieder, *Science Encounters the Indian*.

16. Beer, *Open Fields*, 25.

17. Pearce Stevenson, Esq. [Caroline Norton], *A Plain Letter to the Lord Chancellor on the Infant Custody Bill* (London: James Ridgway, 1839), 100.

18. Max Müller, "The Savage" (originally published in the *Nineteenth Century* [January 1885]), in *Last Essays*, 142–43.

19. Scheckel, *Insistence of the Indian*, 40.

20. Anderson, *Powers of Distance*, 87.

21. Bayly, *Birth of the Modern World*, 204.

22. Dickens wrote to Anna Maria Hall in December 1841. "He is an honest, hearty, famous fellow; and I shake hands with him in every page." Charles Dickens to Mrs. Samuel Carter Hall, 2 December 1841, in *Letters of Charles Dickens* 2:43. For Dickens and Native Americans, see Orestano, "Dickens on the Indians."

23. It is unclear whether Dickens had firsthand knowledge of the fiction of James Fenimore Cooper, although the 1854 inventory of contents of 1 Devonshire Terrace (completed by 27 May 1844) shows that Dickens owned a complete set of Cooper's *Novels and Tales*. See Dickens, *Letters of Charles Dickens* 4:719.

24. Charles Dickens to John Forster, 15, 16, and 17 April 1842, *Letters of Charles Dickens* 3:201.

25. Dickens to Daniel Maclise, 22 March 1842, *Letters* 3:154.

26. Dickens, *American Notes*, 160.

27. John Johnston, *Recollections of Sixty Years*, 47.

28. Dickens to John Forster, 24 and 26 April 1842, *Letters* 3:207.

29. Brooke, *History of Emily Montague*, 51.

30. Sir Walter Scott, *Guy Mannering*, 37. The comparison between Gypsies and Native Americans was not always thought to be a sustainable one, however. In his *History of the Gipsies* (1865), Walter Simson distinguishes them from North American Indians, since the latter are a race "which has ceased to exist, or is daily ceasing to exist. . . . The fact of these Indians, and the aboriginal races found in the countries colonized by Europeans, disappearing so rapidly, prevents our regarding them with any great degree of interest. This circumstance detracts from that idea of dignity which the perpetuity and civilization of their race would inspire in the minds of others" (446).

31. North, *Recollections of a Happy Life* 2:55.

32. Sigourney, *Pleasant Memories*, 116.

33. Matthew Arnold, "The Scholar-Gipsy," in *Poems of Matthew Arnold*, 366.

34. Nord, *Gypsies and the British Imagination*, 143.

35. Brine, *Travels amongst American Indians*, 116. He is describing the travels that he made in late 1869.

36. Kingston, *Western Wanderings* 2:179.

37. Marryat, *Diary in America*, 87.

38. Price, *The Two Americas*, 278.

39. Burton, *City of the Saints*, 101.

40. Peter Perkins Pitchlynn (1806–81) was a quarter native and the son of Sophia Folsom (a Choctaw/white woman) and Colonel John Pitchlynn. Although

his education was sporadic, he had attended both the Choctaw Academy, in Kentucky, and the University of Tennessee. A gifted orator, he had considerable influence over his tribe, eradicating polygamy and stopping the liquor traffic. He witnessed his tribe's removal from Mississippi in 1831–33 and subsequently became very engaged in land rights issues. See Baird, *Peter Pitchlynn*; Debo, *Rise and Fall.*

41. Nonetheless, the circulation figures for *American Notes* were disappointingly low; by the end of 1850, only eighty six copies had been sold. Patten, *Dickens and His Publishers*, 353.

42. [Head], "Red Man," 385. Despite his appreciation of native rights and culture, Head, however, believed strongly in the inevitable extinction of First Nations people; in considerable part, therefore, his libertarian attitude toward Indians was fueled by his belief that they "would be happiest if allowed to spend their last days free of white interference." John Webster Grant, *Moon of Wintertime*, 85. For more on Head, and the way in which the formulation and articulation of his policies were strongly influenced by Romantic perceptions of Indians, see Binnema and Hutchings, "The Emigrant and the Noble Savage."

43. [Head], "Red Man," 384.

44. Ibid.

45. Dickens, *American Notes*, 287. What Eve Kosofsky Sedgwick notes of Dickens in relation to slavery is also true, at this point of his career, of his treatment of Native Americans: "He was actually interested in American slavery as an institution and a lived experience, rather than just as a mother lode of rhetorical energy to be mined for British domestic use—though clearly, he was susceptible to the latter solicitation as well." *Touching Feeling*, 83.

46. Dickens, "The Noble Savage" (1853), in *Selected Journalism*, 560–61.

47. Wood, *East Lynne*, 477.

48. It is impossible to tell whether there is any deliberate irony here; until the twentieth century, the Choctaw were matrilineal by custom and laws.

49. Robbins, *Convert*, 58.

50. Dickens, *Bleak House*, 94. Although "Tockahoopo" is clearly a formation dependent on "cock-a-hoop," or wildly joyful and exuberant, one might well wonder whether Dickens was aware of the word's original meaning of "extremely drunk."

51. Altick, *Shows of London*, 283.

52. Charles Kingsley, *Alton Locke*, 37.

53. Dickens, *David Copperfield*, 80.

54. Dickens, *Little Dorrit*, Dickens's heavy-handed invention of "Indian" names calls to mind Jamaica Kincaid's comment that when she was about nine, and at school in Dominica, "my mind had already been firmly formed by the thing known as the 'British Empire,' and so I knew that people who lived in places near rivers with funny-sounding names like Zambezi or Amazon or Mississippi (and not proper-sounding names like Thames, for instance) were savages." Jamaica Kincaid, "The Little Revenge from the Periphery," *Transition* 73 (1998), 70.

55. Dickens, "Medicine Men of Civilization" (1863), in *Uncommercial Traveller*, 280.

56. Other writers, however, could be just as anxious to signal their *difference* from native peoples by mockingly indicating the strangeness, illogicality, and indeed unnaturalness of their beliefs and practices. Charles Alston Messiter, who over the course of thirteen years' hunting and traveling in the West had plenty of opportunities to get to know Indians at firsthand, nonetheless maintained an arch rhetorical distance from them, refusing thoughtful engagement with their "peculiarities." He describes staying among natives in Missouri and of the "pleasant surprises" that are in store for the visitor: "Some Indian often gets up and sings for an hour or more, beating an accompaniment on a tom-tom, and no one thinks of sending for a policeman or of shooting him, as would seem natural." *Sport and Adventures*, 25–26.

57. Head, "Red Man," 395.

58. Catlin, *Letters and Notes* 2:240.

59. Hunting wapiti on the plains in the early 1870s—with Buffalo Bill as one of his guides—the Earl of Dunraven "sat down on the trunk of a fallen cottonwood tree, and tried to realise that I was in the middle of those prairies that, thanks to Captain Mayne Reid, had haunted my boyish dreams. I cannot say that the realisation of my hopes fulfilled my expectation. I was oppressed with the vastness of the country." Dunraven, *Canadian Nights,* 60. On the other hand, Arthur Conan Doyle, traveling across Canada in 1914, exclaimed rhapsodically as mountains rose up before him: "Shades of Mayne Reid, they were the Rockies—my old familiar Rockies! Have I been here before? What an absurd question, when I lived here for about ten years of my life in all the hours of dreamland. What deeds have I not done among redskins and trappers and grizzlies within their wilds!" Conan Doyle, *Memoirs and Adventures*, 24, 340.

60. For Reid's life, see Joan Steele, *Captain Mayne Reid*. His widow, Elizabeth Reid, wrote two biographies of her husband: *Mayne Reid* and *Captain Mayne Reid*, although they are somewhat inaccurate in their details. Translations of Mayne Reid were published in at least twenty countries. He was especially popular in Eastern Europe and Russia. Vladimir Nabokov was an avid reader; for a discussion of Nabokov on Reid, see Lewis, *Unsettling the Literary West*, 227–31.

61. There is an extensive literature on the representation of the Indian in nineteenth-century American literature. Among the books I have found most useful on the topic is Barnett's *Ignoble Savage*. Barnett explains how the emphasis in the fiction of this period falls no longer on the problem of white survival, as was the case in captivity narratives, but on the inevitability of white domination of the continent. Also useful are Bold, *Selling the Wild West,* and Bellin, *Demon of the Continent*. James K. Folsom, in "English Westerns," discusses differences between British and American Westerns. For the formula of the Western in general—in both literature and film—see Mitchell, *Westerns.*

62. Krupat, *Ethnocriticism,* 135. The phenomenon of the Western was not limited to Britain and the United States, but was all over Europe. See Cracroft, "World Westerns."

63. Other writers who did, however, make considerable use of their personal experience (even if that was more limited than Reid's) when writing adventure

fiction include Charles Murray, Frederick Marryat, and Sir Frederick Charles Lascelles Wraxhall.

64. "The Skull Hunters," *Judy*, 22 May 1867.

65. [Probably Mayne Reid], "Catlin: A Name Too Little known and Too Slightingly Treated," *Onward* 2 (1869), 402.

66. Fiedler, *Return of the Vanishing American*, 50.

67. Mayne Reid, *Headless Horseman*, 83–84.

68. Mayne Reid, *English Family Robinson*, 296.

69. Joan Steele, *Captain Mayne Reid*, 66.

70. Streeby, *American Sensations*, 7–8.

71. Mayne Reid, *White Chief* 1:48–49.

72. Mayne Reid, *White Squaw*, 46. The novel is set some time after the conclusion of the second Seminole war in 1842. Admittedly, Wacora is half Spanish, but he identifies with the tribe of his father, loving them "as if he had been of their purest blood" (30). Alice, all the same, is made to voice an assimilationist agenda; not doubting that Wacora has "white blood in his veins," she wonders, "What might not a man of his intelligence, chivalric courage, and purity of thought have become in a society where civilisation would have developed all these mental qualities?" (118). However, the novella's conclusion does not enact the potential behind Alice's words, and Wacora's tribal loyalties are strong to the last—and shared by Alice.

73. *The Octoroon* includes an Indian character, Wahnotee, who was played by Boucicault himself in the original New York production. Prejudice against Indians leads the white characters to believe that he must have been the murderer of Paul, a young black boy, but a slow-exposed photographic plate provides the proof that the former white overseer, McClosky, was in fact responsible.

74. Moreover, Reid, on occasion, indicates that his interpretation of slavery reaches beyond its racial dynamics. In *The Quadroon*, he notes that the

> black man is a *slave*, and there are three millions of his race in the same condition. Painful thought! but less painful when accompanied by the reflection that the same broad land is trodden by *twenty millions of free and sovereign men*. Three millions of slaves to twenty millions of masters! In mine own land the proportion is exactly reversed! The truth may be obscure. For all that, I dare say there are some who will understand it. (Mayne Reid, *Quadroon*, 1:57–58).

75. Mayne Reid, *Headless Horseman*, 55–56.

76. Lott, *Love and Theft*, 194. This is not universally true of Reid's portrayal of slave owners, however; sometimes he presents "good" ones—like Eugénie in *The Quadroon*—who find their scope severely restricted by the economic and social system that surrounds them. But he sustains his hatred of slavery as an institution throughout his writing career.

77. Pearce, *Savagism and Civilization*, 202.

78. Mayne Reid, *Scalp Hunters* 3:289.

79. Mayne Reid, *No Quarter!* 3:17.

80. Mayne Reid, speech recorded in *American Thanksgiving Dinner,* 73.

81. Ibid., 74.

82. Mayne Reid, *White Gauntlet,* 270.

83. Mayne Reid, *No Quarter!* 1:242.

84. Here I am thinking particularly of Ebenezer Elliott's three-book poem "Withered Wild Flowers," in *Village Patriarch,* and his blank verse drama "Kerhonah," featuring Dixwell, the supposed executioner of Charles I.

85. Duane, "Boys' Literature," 106. See also Bristow's excellent *Empire Boys,* and Mackenzie, *Imperialism and Popular Culture.*

86. Other girls' novels featuring Indians were imported and published in England. Cynthia Westover's *Bushy* stars a particularly feisty heroine, who heads off with her geologist father to the Rockies, has her hair cut short, insists on being made a pair of pants, and is totally competent when she hears a horse galloping toward her: " 'Will father never get here! It is an Indian! Whizeration!' she exclaimed, as she ducked behind the bowlder. A Navajo rode into sight, bristling all over with weapons. He had two sets of bows and arrows, one revolver, two bowie-knives, and a tomahawk." She has no hesitation in shooting him dead. Yet this novel is distinguished from much of boys' fiction in one crucial respect: Bushy is far more sympathetic toward the Indian women whom she encounters than she is toward the men (and they, in turn, are kind to her). Westover, *Bushy,* 75.

87. Sally Mitchell, *New Girl,* 116.

88. Marchant, *Sisters of Silver Creek,* 100.

89. Kingston, *Adventures of Dick Onslow,* 9. For Kingston, see Kingsford, *Life, Work, and Influence.*

90. Suffling, *The Fur-Traders of the West,* viii.

91. Ballantyne, *Prairie Chief,* 2–3.

92. Ballantyne, *Golden Dream,* 188. For Ballantyne, see Hannabass, "Ballantyne's Message of Empire" Phillips, "Space for Boyish Men"; and chapters 3 and 4 of Quayle's *Ballantyne the Brave,* 29–78, which give a clear account of his time spent working for the Hudson's Bay Company and of his dealings with Indian fur traders, as does his own *Hudson's Bay.*

93. Henty, *Redskin and Cow-boy,* 228.

94. Lax, *Lax,* 92.

95. Ballantyne, *Red Rooney,* [iii].

96. Conrad, *Heart of Darkness,* 38.

97. Lang, *In the Wrong Paradise,* v.

98. The Riel Rebellion in Canada was put down in 1885; the massacre at Wounded Knee took place in late December 1890.

99. Torgovnick, *Gone Primitive,* 244. Brian V. Street's *Savage in Literature* barely mentions Native Americans.

CHAPTER SEVEN. INDIANS AND THE POLITICS OF GENDER

1. Campion, *On the Frontier* 1:2.

2. Bell, *New Tracks* 2:29. Bell was a fascinating figure, and his book well repays extensive study. He was a Cambridge graduate and a fellow of both the Royal Geographical and the Ethnological Society his account shows him to have been a keen observer and alert to the ethnological implications of his travels. He became progressively more sympathetic toward Indians, especially once he reached the Southwest and observed Pueblo, Moqui, Pima, and Papago Indians, and he took some important early photographs of native peoples. Eventually, Bell settled in Colorado, where he founded Manitou Springs; a significant number of travelers whose works are quoted in this chapter were early visitors to this resort.

3. Bell, *New Tracks* 1:63. Bell writes that he "had made the acquaintance of poor Sergeant Wylyams only the day before. He was an Englishman educated at Eton, and of good family, but while sowing his wild oats, he had made a fatal alliance in London, and gone to grief. Disowned by the family, he had emigrated to America, joined the Army, and was daily expecting promotion out of the ranks" (64). It seems likely that Wylyams had rewritten his life history somewhat; there are no records, for example, of his having attended Eton College. Coming from his particular background, however, Bell would surely have recognized whether or not the man's accent and general demeanor made his story a plausible one in terms of class and education, even if the specifics were invented.

4. Francis, *Saddle and Mocassin*, 202.

5. Vivian, *Wanderings in the Western Land*, 27–28.

6. For the relationship between international tourism based on hunting and an ethos of sportsmanship, and the values cherished by British imperialists, see Mackenzie, *Empire of Nature*. The hunting parties did not just consist of British visitors, of course; Joy Kasson notes: "As Americans began to prosper in the postwar years, and as prosperity brought nervous strain to the lives of successful city dwellers, the West was already identified with recreation, escapism, and renewed masculinity." *Buffalo Bill's Wild West*, 15.

7. Gillmore, *Hunter's Adventures*, 271.

8. Vivian, *Wanderings*, 213, 215, 215–16.

9. Kirkpatrick, "Literature of Travel," 256. Kirkpatrick's remarks are heavily gender inflected, but both travel narratives and adventure stories had considerable appeal for female readers.

10. Kingsley, *Notes on Sport and Travel*, 140.

11. Price, *The Two Americas*, 282.

12. Kingsley, *Notes on Sport and Travel*, 161, 159.

13. Ibid., 202. It should be noted, though, that Mary Kingsley goes on to acknowledge, despite her empathy with her father's desires, that she was "fully convinced his taking this view of life really caused the illness which killed my mother. For months at a time she was kept in an unbroken strain of nervous anxiety about him."

14. Cheyfitz, *Poetics of Imperialism*, 15.

15. Unsigned review article, "Savage Life," 446.

16. Berkhofer, *White Man's Indian*, 29.

17. Kebbel, "Leather-Stocking," 200.

18. Albers and James, "Illusion and Illumination," 35.

19. Hancock, *Emigrant's Five Years*, 241.

20. Rae, *Westward by Rail*, 216.

21. Donkin, *Trooper and Redskin*, 19–20.

22. Bell's point of reference is not unique; William Kingston observed of an elderly woman on Tomb Island, Lake Huron, that "she would have served a painter as an excellent model for a witch in Macbeth." Kingston, *Western Wanderings* 1:163.

23. [Campbell], *Short American Tramp*, 246.

24. Roscoe, *Changing Ones*, 209.

25. Jameson, *Winter Studies* 3:75.

26. *Bristol Press*, 21 July 1903. clipping, Buffalo Bill Collection, Denver Public Library.

27. Standing Bear, *My People the Sioux*, 268–69. While Standing Bear devotes an entire chapter (248–67) to his experiences with Buffalo Bill in England— paying particular attention to the difficulties of keeping some of the Indians from drinking alcohol—he has little to say about British social conditions, writing more about the foggy weather and muddy roads. He does, though, give a vivid sense of what life on the road was like for show Indians, the various ways in which they suffered discrimination within the entourage, and Cody's determination to counter any such treatment.

28. Maungwudaus, *Chippewa Indians*, 4.

29. Moodie, *Roughing It in the Bush*, 289–90. See further Gerson, "Nobler Savages."

30. Schoolcraft, *Personal Memoirs*, 566.

31. For Anna Jameson, see Judith Johnston's critical biography, *Anna Jameson*; Gerry, " 'I Am Translated' "; and Monkman, "Primitivism and a Parasol."

32. Gaskell, "Lois the Witch," 112.

33. Howitt, *Popular History* 2:404.

34. Uglow, *Elizabeth Gaskell*, 478.

35. George Egerton, *Keynotes and Discords*, 22.

36. There is a further crucial historical context in which "Lois the Witch" should be read. Gaskell had originally hoped that the story would appear in the *Atlantic Monthly*; instead, Dickens persuaded her to let him have it for his new weekly journal, *All the Year Round*. Had it been published in the American periodical, however, it would have been much easier to see it as a contribution to the abolitionist debate in its treatment of the damaging effects of intolerance and bigotry. Without setting any of the terms in a privileged relationship above the others, prejudice against women who did not fit an easy social mold, Indians, and African Americans would thus have been linked together, with Unitarian-informed humanitarian inclusiveness and Christian forgiveness occupying a mediating and unifying position.

37. Hale, *Lessons from Women's Lives*, 45.

38. Owen, *Heroines of Domestic Life*, 150 (Owen must have read an earlier version of Hale's account of Pocahontas).

39. *The Virginians* deserves the careful scrutiny of transatlantic scholars, even though it has traditionally been seen as among the very weakest of Thack-

eray's novels. Gordon Ray, for example, wrote: "In the past he had been typically careless about his plots, but he may be said to have reached an acme of formlessness in *The Virginians*." Ray, *Thackeray*, 373. Yet far from being formless, this novel depends on a series of tight parallelisms. Pocahontas had just been burlesqued in a much more exaggerated way in the Irish American John Brougham's *La Belle Sauvage: Burlesque in Five Scenes* (1855), which was roughly—very roughly—based on James Nelson Barker's *Indian Princess: or, La Belle Sauvage* (1808). Full of dreadful puns as well as topical allusions, including heavy-handed humor around women's rights, Brougham's drama was popular on both sides of the Atlantic for a couple of decades. Like Brougham's *Metamora; or, The Last of the Pollywoags* (a takeoff on John Augustus Stowe's *Metamora; or, The Last of the Wampanoags*, 1829), *La Belle Sauvage* satirized the American fashion for Indian dramas during the 1820s–40s. See Plotnicki, "John Brougham."

40. Tilton, *Pocahontas*, 1.

41. Howitt, *Popular History* 1:57.

42. Parker, *Works of Gilbert Parker* 7:7.

43. For Parker's life, see Adams, *Seated with the Mighty*; Fridén, *Canadian Novels*, which usefully gives a number of plot summaries of Parker's more historical novels; and Waterston, *Gilbert Parker*.

44. Lali is not a full-blood Indian herself; it is tacitly suggetsed that part of her refinement, her good looks, and even the degree to which she is drawn to Frank Armour in the first place might be a result of her miscegenated origins. As she is made to say, " ' I was only an Indian girl, but you must remember that I had also in my veins good white blood, Scotch blood. Perhaps it was that which drew me to you then.' " Parker, *Translation of a Savage*, 187. In his introduction to the Imperial Edition volume containing this novel, Parker notes: "The story had a basis of fact; the main incident was true. It happened, however, in Michigan rather than in Canada." Parker, Works 7:6.

45. Anzaldúa, *Borderlands/La Frontera*, 78.

46. Kaplan, *Anarchy of Empire*, 34.

47. Parker, *Works* 7:7.

CHAPTER EIGHT. INDIANS AND MISSIONARIES

1. William Howitt, *Colonization and Christianity*, vi, 7–8.

2. See especially Hall, *Civilising Subjects*.

3. *Report from the Select Committee on Aborigines*, 74–76.

4. Berkhofer, *Salvation and the Savage*, 14–15.

5. Fabian, "Religious and Secular Colonization," 339. For a challenge to the argument that missionary activity weakened non-Western societies to the point that they became more vulnerable to direct colonial rule, see Porter, " 'Cultural Imperialism.' " As Porter remarks in his later chapter, "Religion, Missionary Enthusiasm, and Empire," in volume 3 of the Oxford History of the British Empire, "the positive, liberating effect of much mission work is inescapable. . . . Evangelists could not control the use made of a Christian education" (239–40).

6. Anna Johnston, *Missionary Writing and Empire,* 3. She borrows the term "mutual imbrication" from Gikandi's *Maps of Englishness,* xviii.

7. Headland, *The Right Rev. John Horden,* 7, 14.

8. See, for example, Beaven, *Recreations of a Long Vacation,* and Bigsby, *Shoe and Canoe.*

9. Wilson, *Missionary Work,* 55.

10. Stocking, *Victorian Anthropology,* 87–88.

11. In her biography of William Duncan, Jean Usher notes that the Tsimshians at Metlakatla, in British Columbia, whom he had taught "were well versed in those mechanics of petitioning and letter-writing which characterize the relations of dissatisfied citizens with their government." Usher, *William Duncan of Metlakatla,* 128.

12. In drawing attention to the importance of missionary activity for a working-class conception of empire within Britain, I am in accord with Susan Thorne in her valuable book *Congregational Missions.*

13. Maclean, *Canadian Savage Folk,* 298.

14. John Webster Grant, *Moon of Wintertime,* 162. For details of Maclean's mission, he draws on J. E. Nix, "John Maclean's Mission to the Blood Indians, 1880–1889" (master's thesis, McGill University, 1977).

15. Egerton Ryerson Young, *Indian Trail,* 11.

16. Moodie, *Roughing It in the Bush,* 279.

17. Yonge, *Hopes and Fears* 1:4.

18. For the use of photography in disseminating visual information about First Nations people, see especially Williams, *Framing the West.*

19. For an excellent study of the history of missionary work in Canada, see John Webster Grant, *Moon of Wintertime.* For early missionary activity, see Kellaway *New England Company;* and Lyddeker, *Faithful Mohawks.* Other useful books include Duchaussois, *Mid Snow and Ice;* Gould, *Inasmuch;* and Graham, *Medicine Man to Missionary.* For a detailed study of this missionary work, the reports and papers of individual missionary societies are indispensable.

20. See Prochaska, "Little Vessels"; Brian Stanley, "Home Support for Overseas Missions in Early Victorian England, c. 1838–1873" (PhD diss., Cambridge University, 1979) and *Bible and Flag.*

21. A. C. Day, *Notes on Neepigon,* 16.

22. Headland *The Right Rev. John Horden,* 4. For more on Horden, see Batty, *Forty-two Years amongst the Indians and Eskimo.*

23. Caledonia, *A Grand Old Chief,* 9.

24. A. C. Day, *Notes on Neepigon,* 3. See also Burden, *Life in Algoma.*

25. Burden, *Manitoulin.*

26. Garrett, *Columbia Mission,* 19.

27. Egerton Ryerson Young, *On the Indian Trail,* 36.

28. Anna Johnston, *Missionary Writing,* 53.

29. Howse, *Grammar of the Cree Language,* vi, xii.

30. [Hood], "Folk-Lore of the Red Man," 275.

31. Porter, "Religion, Missionary Enthusiasm, and Empire," 241.

32. John Webster Grant offers a particularly helpful summary of such differences.

To the Christian the world as we know it is provisional, preparatory to a new order that will fully reveal the ultimate meaning of history. Religious belief and practice point to this culmination, preparing the individual for life in a new order of existence and calling for the social changes indicated by its imminence. For the Indian the meaning of existence was already given, the purpose of religious practice and even of prophetic movements being to maintain or restore the equilibrium inherent in nature. Christianity calls for repentance from conformity to the present age and for commitment to participation in God's intended transformation of life. The Indian sought alignment with the cosmos so that it might remain in place, so that the moose would appear in due season, the fish bit, and the body be maintained in health. For the Indian the ultimate religious symbol was the circle, represented in the campfire or the circuit of the heavens. For the Christian it might well be an arrow running from the creation of the world through God's redeeming acts in history to the final apocalypse. Misunderstandings were bound to arise from the imposition of one world-view on another. Such terms as "sin," "grace," and "faith," which derived their meaning from one, were not easily comprehended by those accustomed to the other. (*Moon of Wintertime*, 24)

33. Maclean, *Canadian Savage Folk*, 305.

34. Peter Jones, *Life and Journals*, 7. For the life of Jones, see Donald R. Smith, *Sacred Feathers*.

35. See especially Dresser, *Slavery Obscured,* and Kenneth Morgan, *Bristol and the Atlantic Trade.*

36. George Pocock, schoolmaster and inventor, was a pioneer in the use of kites for traction purposes and the inventor of an automatic machine for caning schoolboys.

37. Jones notes, too, that he has visited the following places, which gives some idea of the extent of his visibility: "Liverpool, London, Bristol, Birmingham, Chester, Manchester, Halifax, Huddersfield, Leeds, Hull, York, Stockton, Bradford, Sheffield, High Wycombe, Brighton, Lewes, Rochester, Reading, Windsor, Oxford, Lynn, Bury St. Edmond, Woolwich, Greenwich, Deptford, Lambeth, Norwood, Limehouse, Millhill, Pinner, Tottenham, &c., &c." (346).

38. Mahkoons, also known as Eshtonaquet, also known as Little Bear, toured England in 1834 with a dance troupe of six, including his wife, nephew, and one of his cousins. His wife, nephew, and one other member of the troupe died of smallpox while on the tour. Greg Curnoe, *Deeds/Nations: Directory of First Nations Individuals in South-Western Ontario, 1750–1850,* http://www.adamsheritage.com/deedsnations/m.htm.

39. Upton, *Micmacs and Colonists,* 188–92.

40. The formality of Jones and other Indian missionaries in their public utterances (whether the occasion was secular or spiritual) is unsurprising. Penny Petrone has described how native converts were mostly schooled along highly similar lines of sermon composition, their prose molded as "a typical blend of straightforward exposition and practical admonition, a mixture of spirituality and practicality expressed in balanced prose." As she puts it, they "produced

passionate sermons and lectures, as well as prose narratives that advocated the assimilation into the blessings and benefits of Christianity and progress." Petrone, *Native Literature in Canada,* 40, 69.

41. Peter Jones, 30 December 1831, letter to the editor, *Christian Guardian,* 22 February 1832.

42. Peter Jones, 15 August 1831, letter to the editor, *Christian Guardian,* 1 October 1831.

43. Peter Jones, "Farewell Sermon, at City Road Chapel [London], April 7, 1832," *Wesleyan Preacher* 2 (1832), 115.

44. Peter Jones, *History of the Ojebway Indians,* 29.

45. For more on Eliza Field, see Donald B. Smith, *Sacred Feathers,* 130–49.

46. *British Colonial Argus,* 28 September 1833, quoted in *Sacred Feathers,* by Donald B. Smith, 142.

47. See, in particular, Bellin, *Demon of the Continent,* 187–99; Ruoff, "Three Nineteenth-Century American Indian Autobiographers", Donald B. Smith, "Life of George Copway or Kah-ge-ga-gah-bowh"; and Walker, *Indian Nation.*

48. Peyer, *Tutor'd Mind,* 238–39.

49. The exception here is Peyer, "A Nineteenth-Century Ojibwa." See also Peyer, *Tutor'd Mind,* 224–77, for a longer discussion of Copway.

50. Walker, *Indian Nation,* 85.

51. Homi Bhabha, "Of Mimicry and Man: The Ambivalence of Colonial Discourse," in *Location of Culture,* 88.

52. Copway, *Running Sketches.*

53. "The Peace Congress," *Times,* 28 August 1850, 5.

54. Elihu Burritt, diary entry dated 24 August 1850, quoted by Donald B. Smith, "Life of George Copway," 24.

55. Berman, *All That Is Solid,* 17.

56. "Annual Meeting of the Society," *Wesleyan Missionary Notices,* n.s. 9 (June/July 1851), 110–12.

57. Peter Jacobs, *Journal of the Reverend Peter Jacobs,* 17.

58. See "An Indian Chief at the Mansion House," *Aborigines' Friend: A Journal of the Aborigines' Protection Society* (London), [4th] ser., 6 (1885), 255–56. Pahtahquahong was prepared for his role within the Methodist church from a young age and worked as a lecturer, interpreter, and accountant before becoming a preacher in the mid-1850s for a couple of years. After the death of Peter Jones and William Chase (the superintendent of Indian missions in the Canada Conference), the Methodist mission in Canada lost much of its impetus, and Pahtahquahong left the ministry and church in the late 1850s and worked as a merchant, before becoming an energetic member of the Anglican Church from 1863 (ordained in 1864) and taking a number of Ojibwa Methodists with him.

59. Wilson, *Missionary Work among the Ojebway Indians,* 100.

60. *Little Pine's Journal,* 17.

61. See Nock, "Chapter in the Amateur Period."

62. Freire, *Pedagogy of the Oppressed*; Fanon, *Black Skin.*

63. David Scott, *Conscripts of Modernity,* 19.

CHAPTER NINE. BUFFALO BILL'S WILD WEST AND ENGLISH IDENTITY

1. Stoker, "The Squaw," in *Midnight Tales*, 87. The story was first published in the Christmas number of the *Illustrated Sporting and Dramatic News*, 1893.

2. Spencer, "The Americans," 8. Spencer was being interviewed after he had been in the United States for less than two months, but he took the occasion to berate the Americans for paying too much attention to work, and too little attention to their health, both physical and mental; for living to work, rather than working to live better and fuller lives; for valuing wealth and honor above happiness; and for striving too hard for material gain and show.

3. Steele, "Reduced to Images," 45.

4. See Warren, "Buffalo Bill Meets Dracula."

5. "The American Exhibition," *Illustrated London News*, 16 April 1887, 440. For a detailed account of the American Exhibition and its planning and organization, see Lowe, *National Exhibitions*, 31–120. The thinking that led the instigator of the exhibition, John Whitley, to invite the participation of Buffalo Bill is explained:

> On the second occasion of his visiting Washington . . . a sudden thought struck Mr. Whitley. "Why not console ourselves," he asked, "for the defection of the Eastern States [many potential exhibitors had pulled out following the postponement of the exhibition by a year, to avoid clashing with the 1886 Colonial and Indian Exhibition] by enlisting on our side those of the West? Is not "Buffalo Bill," with his cowboys and his Indians, every bit as much a genuine product of American soil as Edison's telephones or Pullman's railway cars? And is it not even more unique and quite as interesting? Would not the people of England hail with delight an opportunity of seeing, at first hand almost, a phase of American life familiar to them only in the romances of Fenimore Cooper? (56–57).

For the culture of these large international exhibitions more generally, see Greenhalgh, *Ephemeral Vistas*.

6. *Daily Chronicle*, 10 May 1887, clipping in William F. Cody Collection Denver Public Library.

7. *Times*, 1 November 1887, clipping in Cody Collection.

8. William Ewart Gladstone, 29 April 1887, quoted by Lowe, *National Exhibitions*, 98.

9. For the history and context of Buffalo Bill's Wild West Show, see Blackstone, *Buckskins, Bullets, and Business;* Kasson, *Buffalo Bill's Wild West;* Moses, *Wild West Shows;* and Warren, *Buffalo Bill's America.* Buffalo Bill's British tours and reputation are chronicled in Gallop's *Buffalo Bill's British Wild West,* which is particularly rich in images of British shows, although, frustratingly, Gallop does not identify his numerous sources.

10. Quoted in Gallop's, *British Wild West*, 49.

11. Quoted ibid., 101.

12. Quoted ibid., 102.

13. Warren, *Buffalo Bill's America*, 199.

14. See the program cover from the 1891–92 British season, reproduced in Gallop, *British Wild West*, 168. The program neatly encapsulates the dual ethos of the presentation, announcing the Wild West as "America's National Entertainment: An Illustrated Treatise of Historical Facts and Sketches."

15. For the Ghost Dance movement, see Dee Brown, *Bury My Heart at Wounded Knee*, 389–412; DeMallie, "Lakota Ghost Dance"; Kehoe, *Ghost Dance*; and Osterreich, *American Indian Ghost Dance*.

16. For the Lakota who toured Britain with the Wild West, see Maddra, *Hostiles?* 122–75.

17. Blackstone, *Buckskins, Bullets, and Business*, 126.

18. Cody, *Story of the Wild West*, 730.

19. Advertisement in the *Manchester Evening News*, reproduced in Gallop's, *British Wild West*, 171.

20. See Maddra, *Hostiles?* 150–51.

21. *Morning Post*, 5 May 1887, clipping in Cody Collection.

22. Quoted in Gallop, *British Wild West*, 56.

23. *Sporting Life*, 15 April 1887, clipping in William F. Cody Collection, Denver Public Library.

24. *Liverpool Daily Post*, 7 July 1891, clipping in Cody Collection.

25. *London Evening News and Post*, 14 May 1892, clipping in Cody Collection.

26. *Manchester Guardian*, 29 April 1892, clipping in Cody Collection.

27. Newland, *Paving the Way*, 137.

28. *Daily Chronicle*, 6 May 1887, clipping in Cody Collection.

29. Waldrep, *Aesthetics of Self-Invention*, 70.

30. Warren, *Buffalo Bill's America*, 262.

31. *Illustrated Sporting and Dramatic News*, 16 July 1892, clipping in Cody Collection.

32. *Era*, 23 April 1887, clipping in Cody Collection.

33. *Sunday Chronicle*, 17 October 1886, clipping in Cody Collection.

34. *Field*, 14 May 1892, clipping in Cody Collection.

35. *Observer*, 24 April 1887, clipping in Cody Collection.

36. *London Gazette*, undated clipping from 1887, in Cody Collection.

37. *Sporting Life*, 2 July 1892, clipping in Cody Collection.

38. *Punch*, 7 May 1887, 217.

39. *Observer*, 8 May 1887, clipping in Cody Collection.

40. *Judy*, 11 May 1887, 228.

41. Traubel, *With Walt Whitman in Camden*, 423.

42. Gladstone introduced his first home rule bill after the 1885 election, which left the eighty-six members of Parnell's party holding the balance of power at Westminster. However, ninety-three of Gladstone's own Liberal MPs voted against it, leading to its defeat. He introduced a second bill in 1893, but it was defeated in the House of Lords; a third version became law in 1914, after the Liberal Party had become firmly committed to the issue, but took effect only in 1918.

43. *Truth*, 25 December 1887, clipping in Cody Collection.

44. *Pall Mall Gazette*, 26 April 1887, clipping in Cody Collection. Possibly, however, Cody had coached them in this rendition.

45. For Buffalo Bill in Europe, see Napier, "Across the Big Water"; Daniele Fiorentino, " 'Those Red-Brick Faces': European Press Reactions to the Indians of Buffalo Bill's Wild West Show," in Feest's, *Indians and Europe*, 403–14; Clerici, "Native Americans in Columbus's Home Land."

46. *Oracle*, 28 May 1892, clipping in Cody Collection.

47. *Daily Telegraph*, 21 April 1887, clipping in Cody Collection.

48. *Sheffield Leader* 5 May 1887, clipping in Cody Collection.

49. *Sheffield Leader*, 5 May 1887, clipping in Cody Collection.

50. Quoted in Gallop's *British Wild West*, 70.

51. *Globe*, undated clipping from 1887, in Cody Collection.

52. *Telegraph*, 12 May 1887, clipping in Cody Collection.

53. Black Elk, quoted in Raymond J. DeMallie's introduction to *The Sixth Grandfather: Black Elk's Teachings Given to John G. Neihardt*, by Black Elk (Lincoln: University of Nebraska Press, 1984), 8–9.

54. *Daily Mercury*, undated clipping from 1887, in Cody Collection.

55. Quoted in Gallop's, *British Wild West*, 167.

56. *Leeds Daily News*, 20 June 1891, clipping in Cody Collection.

57. For Buffalo Bill in Scotland, see, in addition to Maddra's *Hostiles?* Cunningham's *Diamond's Ace*, 87–118. The shirt was repatriated to the Wounded Knee Survivors' Association in 1999.

58. *Evening Express* (Cardiff), 26 September 1891, 4.

59. Maddra, *Hostiles?* 141.

60. R. B. Cunninghame Graham, "Long Wolf," in *Redeemed and Other Sketches* (London: William Heinemann, 1927), 71–72.

61. Graham concludes this piece—perhaps forcing the emotion somewhat—by speculating that Long Wolf's spirit

> still haunts hovering above the grave under the poplar-tree. I like to think, when all is hushed in the fine summer nights, and even London sleeps, that the wolf carved on the tomb takes life upon itself, and in the air resounds the melancholy wild cry from which the sleeper took his name.
>
> 'Twould be mere justice; but as justice is so scarce on earth, that it may well be rare even in heaven, 'twere better ears attuned to the light footfall of the unshod cayuse and the soft swishing of the lodge-poles through the grass behind the travois-pony should never open.
>
> The long-drawn cry would only break the sleeper's rest, and wake him to a world unknown and unfamiliar, where he would find no friends except the sculptured wolf.
>
> Let him sleep on. (Graham, "Long Wolf," 80–81)

But Long Wolf's grave did not stay undisturbed. His remains, and those of White Star Ghost Dog, the twenty-month-old girl who had been killed in a fall from a saddlebag in the Earl's Court arena in 1892, were repatriated to the Pine Ridge Indian Reservation in September 1997. See Gallop, *British Wild West*, 197–201, 260–61.

62. *Exeter Times*, 28 July 1903, clipping in Cody Collection. This also seems to have been a syndicated piece; it appears in a number of provincial newspapers.

63. "Buffalo Bill and the World's Changes," *Bristol Times*, 16 July 1903, clipping in Cody Collection.

64. *Leicester Mercury,* 11 September 1903, clipping in the Cody Collection.

65. *Cheltenham Mercury*, 27 June 1903, clipping in the Cody Collection.

66. *Daily Dispatch*, 14 April 1903, clipping in the Cody Collection.

67. *Leicester Mercury*, 11 September 1903, clipping in the Cody Collection.

68. *Swindon Advertiser*, 29 June 1903, clipping in the Cody Collection.

69. For the effort that Curtis made to present his Indians as inhabiting an anachronistic space and temporality, see Lyman, *Vanishing Race.*

70. Deloria, *Indians in Unexpected Places*, 145.

71. *Swindon Advertiser*, 29 June 1903, clipping in Cody Collection. There had been a foreshadowing of this "international fraternising," as Lowe terms it, toward the end of the 1887 exhibition, when Whitley arranged a meeting between the Indians and the troupe of Arabs from the Paris Hippodrome that was currently performing at Olympia; see Lowe, *National Exhibitions*, 115.

72. *Abergavenny Chronicle,* undated clipping in the Cody Collection.

73. Martin, "Grandest and Most Cosmopolitan Object Teacher," 107.

74. Moreover, the sense of familiarity with Cody's material must have been amplified by the fact that his were not the only Indians to be seen publicly. Other outfits whose English performances incorporated Indians included Mexican Joe's (joined in 1887 by Black Elk and the six other Lakota who had become detached from Cody's tour) and the Great Codys. Headed up by "Samuel Franklin Cody," who changed his name to claim a spurious connection with Buffalo Bill, this show incorporated such set pieces as the Klondyke Nugget. See Broomfield, *Pioneer of the Air.*

75. It was also based on the games Barrie played with the Llewellyn Davies boys. See Birkin, *J. M. Barrie;* Jack, *Road to the Never Land.*

76. Barrie, *Peter Pan*, 110.

77. Birkin, *J. M. Barrie*, 126. See also Mackail, *Barrie*, 379.

78. Slotkin, *Gunfighter Nation,* 349.

79. *Spare Moments*, 23 July 1892, clipping in Cody Collection.

CHAPTER TEN. INDIAN FRONTIERS

1. Kipling, *Kipling's America*, 98.

2. See Horsman, *Race and Manifest Destiny.*

3. Forester, *Beyond the Frontier*, 307.

4. Catlin, *Notes of Eight Years' Travel* 1:124, 126; 2:68.

5. Nesbit, *Story of the Treasure Seekers*, 186.

6. Nesbit makes much more extended play on the stereotypes of "Red Indians" and explores the influence of *The Last of the Mohicans* on children's play in chapter 10 of *Five Children and It* (1902), entitled "Scalps."

7. Turner, *Frontier in American History,* 11.

8. The literature of the American frontier is vast; my arguments in this chapter have been particularly influenced by Klein, *Frontiers of Historical Imagination,*

and two of Richard Slotkin's epic studies, *Fatal Environment* and *Gunfighter Nation*.

9. Roosevelt, "The Strenuous Life", quoted in Slotkin's *Gunfighter Nation*, 52.

10. Eliza Hamilton Dunlop, "The Aboriginal Mother (from Myall's Creek)," *Australasian*, 13 December 1838, quoted in Vickery's "'Lonely Crossing,' 33–34. Vickery sees Dunlop's longing for her native Ireland projected onto the fate of dispossessed Aborigines. See also O'Leary, "Giving the Indigenous a Voice."

11. Webb and Enstice, *Aliens and Savages*, 81.

12. Henry Kendall, "Aboriginal Death Song," in *Leaves from Australian Forests*, 349–50; Ettie A. Aycliffe, "Lubra," in *Original Poems*, reprinted in Jordan and Pierce's *Poet's Discovery*, 398.

13. Griffin, *Great Republic*, 167.

14. Bradley, "Red Man and White," 384.

15. Dilke, *Greater Britain*, 87.

16. H. M. Stanley, *My Early Travels*, 10.

17. Anthony Trollope *South Africa*, 45–46.

18. Seeley, *Expansion of England*, 49.

19. Warren, *Buffalo Bill's America*, 333.

20. Stoker, *Dracula*, 225.

21. Allen, *The Devil's Die*, 8.

22. Hofstadter, *Progressive Historians*, 103–4.

23. Kelly, *Excursion to California*, 1:46.

24. Indeed, Turner explicitly states that the project "of a kind of Roman wall" did not appeal to early frontiersmen. *Frontier in American History*, 40.

25. Fiedler, *Return of the Vanishing American*, 52.

26. Simon Pokagon, "The Red Man's Rebuke," reprinted in Walker's *Indian Nation*, 213. Pokagon himself is far from an unproblematic figure, however, since he was apparently much mistrusted by his tribe for his assimilationist outlook. For a synopsis of the debates concerning his ideological position, see Trachtenberg, *Shades of Hiawatha*, 47–48.

27. Deloria, *Indians in Unexpected Places*, 104.

28. Krupat, *Ethnocriticism*, 5, quoting James A. Clifton, ed., *Being and Becoming Indian* (Chicago: Dorsey Press, 1989), 24.

29. Owens, *Mixedblood Messages*, 26.

30. Limerick, *Legacy of Conquest*, 25.

31. Taylor, *Divided Ground*, 11.

32. Black Elk, *Sixth Grandfather*, 245.

33. Handley, *Marriage, Violence*, 62.

34. See Lucas, "Deerfoot in Britain."

35. Nahnee referred to Jones as her "uncle," but as Donald B. Smith notes, according to the European system of kinship terminology, he was most likely the first cousin of one of her parents. "Nahnebahwequay," 75.

36. Poem in Catherine Sutton's handwriting, William Sutton ledger, Grey County Museum Archives, Owen Sound, Ontario. My sense is that the poem is very likely by Sutton; it starts, as I quote, conventionally enough, but its meter soon breaks down, and its conclusion not only is full of the piety that

characterized both Suttons' journal and letter writing but suggests a work in progress:

> May God bless him with power from on high
> To proclaim liberty to the captive
> And Christ to all
> And with prudent foresight preparing for the future
> As God would have him be. amen

> Alone he came
> Yet not alone for God was with him.

37. For Nahnee's trip to London, see Haig-Brown, "Seeking Honest Justice." Haig-Brown has also written in more detail about her relationship with Quakers; see "'Friends' of Nahnebahwequa." For details of the Aborigines' Protection Society, see Bourne, *The Aborigines' Protection Society*.

38. Jameson, *Winter Studies* 3:263.

39. Extract from an entry for 19 June 1860 in Queen Victoria's Journal, Sutton materials, Grey County Museum, Owen Sound, Canada.

40. Catherine Sutton to C. A. Jones, 29 June 1860, published in the *Brantford Courier*, August 1860, cutting in Sutton materials.

41. Memoirs of Mary Wood Manley, as transcribed by Jane Miles; loose-leaf sheet in Grey County Records, Owen Sound, Canada.

42. "Aborigines' Protection Society," *Liverpool Courier*, 15 September 1860; cutting in Grey County Museum.

43. Ibid.

44. Catherine Sutton, ca. 1858, "For a Reference." Summary of her land claim attached to letter from chiefs supporting her claim, 1 (Record group 10, Indian Affairs, Public Archives of Canada, Ottawa, vol. 2877, file 177, 181); quoted in Haig-Brown's "Seeking Honest Justice," 158.

45. Catherine Sutton, draft of letter in William Sutton's Ledger [961.27.24], ca. 1862, Grey County Museum.

46. Monseigneur Henri Têtu, *Le R. P. Bouchard* (Quebec: Pruneau and Nirouac, 1897), 123–24. quoted in MacLaren, *Canadians on the Nile*, 65. Here is my translation: "What a weird collection of people! No uniforms—coats of every color—bronzed countenances, some of them bearing the marks of brutality and ferocity—here and there the sinister faces of the Caughnawaga Indians."

47. Louis Jackson, *Our Caughnawagas in Egypt*, 7.

48. Ibid., 34.

49. Pauline E. Johnson, "The Re-interment of Red Jacket," in *E. Pauline Johnson*, 11.

50. Pauline E. Johnson, "A Request," in *E. Pauline Johnson*, 23.

51. Pauline E. Johnson, "For Queen and Country: May 24th," in *E. Pauline Johnson*, 58.

52. [Watts-Dunton], *"Songs of the Great Dominion"* Watts-Dunton borrowed substantially from this review when he wrote the memorial introduction to *Flint and Feather* that appears in all editions of the volume published after Johnson's death.

53. Strong-Boag and Gerson, *Paddling Her Own Canoe*, 3. For Johnson's life, see also Gray, *Flint and Feather*. I have also learned much from Aigner-Varoz, "Suiting Herself."

54. Johnson's heyday as popular performer, it might be noted, coincided with the American "Hiawatha Revival" in turn-of-the-century America; see Trachtenberg, *Shades of Hiawatha*, 86–97.

55. Isabel Ecclestone Mackay, "Pauline Johnson: A Reminiscence," *Canadian Magazine*, July 1913, 274, quoted in Strong-Boag and Gerson's *Paddling Her Own Canoe*, 258. They note that the comment was made in connection to her writing but it may fairly be applied to her stage personae as well.

56. Pauline E. Johnson, "A Night with 'North Eagle,'" in *Shagganappi*, 93.

57. Pauline E. Johnson, interview in the *London Gazette*, summer 1894, reprinted in Sheila M. F. Johnston's. *Buckskin and Broadcloth*, 120. For the cultural scaremongering around reverse colonization, see Arata, "Occidental Tourist."

58. Strong-Boag and Gerson, *Paddling Her Own Canoe*, 4.

59. Pauline E. Johnson, *E. Pauline Johnson*, 105.

60. Pauline Johnson, *Moccasin Maker*, 8.

61. For this tradition, see Bissell, *American Indian*, esp. 37–77; Fairchild, *Noble Savage*, esp. 23–171; and Roach, *Cities of the Dead*, 170. Samuel Johnson, in *The Idler* of 3 November 1759 very effectively used an imaginary, naive Indian persona in order to indict British colonial policy toward North American natives.

62. Pauline E. Johnson, "Lodge of the Lawmakers."

63. Deloria, *Playing Indian*, 189.

64. "Appeal to the King: Indian Chiefs Coming to London," *Daily Express*, 19 July 1906, 1.

65. "Redskins to See the King: Chiefs Go to Buckingham Palace Today," *Daily Express*, 13 August 1906, 1.

66. "Redskins' Pilgrimage," *Daily Express*, 3 August 1906, 5.

67. Pauline E. Johnson, "Lodge of the Lawmakers," 4.

68. Pauline E. Johnson, "Origin of Lacrosse."

69. Pauline E. Johnson, "With Barry in the Bow."

70. Jean Stevinson, "Friends Pay Tribute to Indian Poetess on Anniversary of Death," *Calgary Herald*, 5 March 1932, quoted in Gray's *Flint and Feather*, 328–29.

71. George W. Bush, "'The Three Pillars of Peace and Security': The Whitehall Palace Address on Iraq Policy," delivered 19 November 2003 in Whitehall Palace, London. Transcript at http://www.mtholyoke.edu/acad/intrel/bush/whitehall.htm. Accessed 11 March 2008.

72. Slotkin, *Fatal Environment*, 37.

CONCLUSION. INDIANS, MODERNITY, AND HISTORY

1. For Brant-Sero and a comparison of his career with that of Pauline E. Johnson, see Cecilia Morgan, "'A Wigwam to Westminster.'"

2. "Adonises on the Pier," *Folkestone, Hythe, Sandgate, and Cheriton Herald*, 29 August 1908, 2.

3. "Stands Up for Redskin," *New York Times*, 1 July 1910, 1.

4. *Folkestone Express and Sandgate, Shorncliffe and Hythe Advertiser*, 29 August 1908, 8.

5. John Brant-Sero, "A Canadian Indian and the War," *Times*, 2 January 1901, **10.** Large numbers of Indians did, however, serve in the First World War (both the U.S. army and for Britain); as J. R. Miller remarks in relation to First Nations people, "After the Great War, traditional arguments that Indians had no grounds for complaint because they had made no recent contributions to the development of the country could hardly be sustained in the face of their recent sacrifice." *Skyscrapers Hide the Heavens*, 319.

6. See Gaonkar, "On Alternative Modernities."

7. My formulation here is indebted to Li, *Neo-primitivist Turn*. See also Torgovnick, *Gone Primitive*; Barkan and Bush, *Prehistories of the Future*; and Lincoln, *Sing with the Heart of a Bear,* to which I owe—among other things —my knowledge of T. S. Eliot's *Athenaeum* review.

8. Lears, *No Place of Grace, 57*. Huxley's version of native culture—strongly influenced by Lawrence's notions—is found primarily in the episode in *Brave New World* where Bernard Marx takes a young woman, Lenina, to New Mexico, where they visit a reservation containing some sixty thousand Indians. Although repelled by the Indian squalor (something that can be read as innate, a product of reservation life, or a combination of the two), Bernard is struck by their worship, deeply based on the idea of the land, and by the fact that women there bear children naturally; he takes a "half-breed," John, back to England, who in turn is horrified that the country bears no resemblance to the expectations he has derived from Shakespeare. John becomes a martyr, an ironic Christ figure, and, as Lois Palken Rudnick puts it, he "serves as Huxley's warning to his fellow humans to redeem themselves before they commit mass cultural suicide." *Utopian Vistas.* 151.

9. Lawrence, *Studies in Classic American Literature,* 34.

10. Lawrence, "New Mexico" (1931), in *Phoenix,* 145.

11. See Slotkin, *Gunfighter Nation*, esp. 231–312; Aleiss, *Making the White Man's Indian;* and Kilpatrick, *Celluloid Indians*.

12. "Red Wing's Gratitude," *Bioscope*, 9 December 1909, 48. For more on the part Indians played in the early film industry, see Deloria, *Indians in Unexpected Places*, 52–108.

13. Lawrence, *Lost Girl,* 150. The combination of the cinema and the genuine article, however, potently came together for Lawrence when, after his first visit to Taos, he saw the film *The Covered Wagon* in London—an event preceded by seven Indians walking onstage before the movie began. This all combined, according to Dorothy Brett, to make him acutely homesick for New Mexico. Brett, *Lawrence and Brett,* 26–27. Brett's own interest in Native Americans had been kindled when, at the age of five, she visited Buffalo Bill's Wild West, and, she believed, Sitting Bull made eye contact with her. For an account of Brett's life, see Hignett, *Brett*.

14. Lawrence, *Studies,* 56. Lawrence's portrayals of Native Americans (in "The Princess," "The Woman Who Rode Away"—topographically drawing on northern New Mexico, even if ostensibly set in Old Mexico—and *St Mawr,* as

well as in his nonfictional writings) are not without idealization, but this is always, and deliberately, accompanied by a sense of their ineffable otherness. For Lawrence in New Mexico, see Bachrach, *D. H. Lawrence in New Mexico*, as well, as Luhan, *Lorenzo in Taos*. For Luhan herself, see Rudnick, *Mabel Dodge Luhan*. Marianna Torgovnick, in *Primitive Passions,* 43–57, writes insightfully of the spiritual and sexual connections that Lawrence (and his heirs in the modern American men's movement) felt with the Indians he encountered.

15. See Roberts, *Fifty Years a Medium.*

16. Lawrence, *Studies,* 57.

17. Dunn, "Indian Children," 426, (quoted by Jacobs in Engendered Encounters, 155). For the conjunction of anthropology, tourism, and the Arts and Crafts movement in the Southwest, I am particularly indebted to Leah Dilworth, *Imagining Indians;* Margaret D. Jacobs, *Engendered Encounters;* and Sherry L. Smith, *Reimagining Indians.*

18. Priestley, *Midnight on the Desert,* 63.

19. Wendy Rose, "For the White Poets Who Would Be Indian,"in *Bone Dance,* 22.

20. See Black Elk, *The Sixth Grandfather,* 251–55.

21. Welch, *Heartsong of Charging Elk,* 59. Black Elk's own words were

"I wanted to see the great water, the great world and the ways of the white men; this is why I wanted to go. So far I looked back on the past and recalled the people's ways. They had a way of living, but it was not the way we had been living. I got disgusted with the wrong road that my people were doing now and I was trying to get them to go back on the good road; but it seemed as though I couldn't induce them, so I made up my mind I was going away from them to see the white man's ways. If the white man's ways were better, why I would like to see my people live that way." (Black Elk, *The Sixth Grandfather,* 245).

22. Ellen Arnold, "Listening to the Spirrits: An Interview with Leslie Marmon Silko," in *Conversations with Leslie Marmon Silko,* ed. Arnold, 179.

23. Peter Jones, *Life and Journals,* 398.

24. Silko, *Gardens in the Dunes,* 302. A. M. Regier provides an interesting reading of the novel in "Revolutionary Enunciatory Spaces" Ghost Dancing, Transatlantic Travel, and Modernist Arson in *Gardens in the Dunes,*" *Modern Fiction Studies* 51 (2005), 134–157.

25. Appadurai, "Sovereignty without Territoriality," 40–1.

26. Seeley, *Expansion of England,* 39.

27. This point has been well made by Michael A. Elliott in his review article "Indians, Incorporated," *American Literary History* 19 (2007), 141–159, esp. 159 n. 1.

Bibliography

Adams, John Coldwell. *Seated with the Mighty: A Biography of Sir Gilbert Parker.* Ottawa: Borealis Press, 1979.

Adye, General Sir John. *Indian Frontier Policy: An Historical Sketch.* London: Smith, Elder, 1897.

Aguirre, Robert D. *Informal Empire. Mexico and Central America in Victorian Culture.* Minneapolis: University of Minnesota Press, 2005.

Aigner-Varoz, Erika. "Suiting Herself: E. Pauline Johnson's Constructions of Indian Identity and Self." PhD diss., University of New Mexico, 2001.

Aitken, E. H. *The Tribes on My Frontier.* Calcutta: Thacker Spink, 1883.

Albers, Patricia C., and William R. James. "Illusion and Illumination: Visual Images of American Indian Women in the West." In *The Women's West,* edited by Susan Armitage and Elizabeth Jameson, 35–50. Norman: University of Oklahoma Press, 1987.

Aleiss, Angela. *Making the White Man's Indian: Native Americans and Hollywood Movies.* Westport, CT: Praeger, 2005.

Allen, Grant. *The Devil's Die.* New York: F. M. Lupton, 1888.

Allen, Paula Gunn. *Pocahontas: Medicine Woman, Spy, Entrepreneur, Diplomat.* New York: HarperSanFrancisco, 2003.

Allen, Robert S. *His Majesty's Indian Allies: British Indian Policy in the Defence of Canada, 1774–1815.* Toronto: Dundurn Press, 1992.

Altick, Richard D. *The Shows of London.* Cambridge, MA, Belknap Press of Harvard University Press, 1978.

———. *Deadly Encounters: Two Victorian Sensations*: Philadelphia: University of Pennsylvania Press, 1986.

American Thanksgiving Dinner. London: William Ridgway, 1863.

"Americus," *Where to Emigrate and Why.* London: American Emigration Agency, 1869.

Anderson, Amanda. *The Powers of Distance: Cosmopolitanism and the Cultivation of Detachment.* Princeton: Princeton University Press, 2001.

Anzaldúa, Gloria. *Borderlands/La Frontera.* San Francisco: Spinsters/Aunt Lute, 1987.

Appadurai, Arjun. "Sovereignty without Territoriality: Notes for a Postnational Geography," In *The Geography of Identity,* edited by Patricia Yaeger, 40–58. Ann Arbor: University of Michigan Press, 1996.

Arata, Stephen. "The Occidental Tourist: Dracula and the Anxiety of Reverse Colonization. *Victorian Studies* 33 (1990), 621–45.

Armstrong, Nancy. *How Novels Think: The Limits of Individualism from 1719–1900.* New York: Columbia University Press, 2005.

Arnold, Ellen, ed. *Conversations with Leslie Marmon Silko.* Jackson: University Press of Mississippi, 2000.

Arnold, Matthew. *The Poems of Matthew Arnold*. Edited by Kenneth Allott, 2nd ed. edited by Miriam Allott. London: Longman, 1979.

Ashcroft, Bill. *Post-Colonial Transformation*. London: Routledge, 2001.

Auerbach, Jeffrey A. *The Great Exhibition of 1851: A Nation on Display*. New Haven: Yale University Press, 1999.

Axelrad, Jacob. *Philip Freneau: Champion of Democracy*. Austin: University of Texas Press, 1967.

Axtell, James. *Beyond 1492: Encounters in Colonial North America*. New York: Oxford University Press, 1992.

———. "Through Another Glass Darkly: Early Indian Views of Europeans." In edited by Ken Coates and Robin Fisher, 17–29. *Out of the Background: Readings in Canadian Native History*, 2nd ed. Toronto: Copp Clark, 1996.

Bachrach, Arthur J. *D. H. Lawrence in New Mexico: "The Time Is Different There."* Albuquerque: University of New Mexico Press, 2006.

Baden-Powell, Robert. *Scouting for Boys: A Handbook for Instruction in Good Citizenship*. Edited with an introduction and notes by Elleke Boehmer. 1908. Reprint, Oxford: Oxford University Press, 2004.

Bage, Robert. *Hermsprong; or, Man as He Is Not*. 1796. Reprint, Oxford: Oxford University Press, 1985.

[Bagshawe, H. R., or Catherine E.]. "Cooper's Novels." *Dublin Review* 6 (1839): 490–529.

Baird, W. David. *Peter Pitchlynn: Chief of the Choctaws*. Norman: University of Oklahoma Press, 1972.

Ballantyne, Robert M. *Hudson's Bay; or, Every-Day Life in the Wilds of North America, during Six Years' Residence in the Territories of the Honourable Hudson's Bay Company*. Edinburgh: William Blackwood, 1848.

———. *The Golden Dream; or, Adventures in the Far West*. London: John F. Shaw, 1861.

———. *The Prairie Chief: A Tale*. London: James Nisbet, 1886.

———. *Red Rooney; or, The Last of the Crew*. London: James Nisbet, 1886.

Balsan, Consuelo Vanderbilt. *The Glitter and the Gold*. New York: Harper & Brothers, 1952.

Bannet, Eve Tavor. "The Theatre of Politeness in Charlotte Lennox's British-American Novels." *Novel* 33 (1999), 73–92.

Barkan, Elazar, and Ronald Bush, eds. *Prehistories of the Future: The Primitive Project and the Culture of Modernism*. Stanford: Stanford University Press. 1995.

Barker, Martin, and Roger Sabin. *The Lasting of the Mohicans: History of an American Myth*. Jackson: University Press of Mississippi, 1995.

Barnett, Louise. *The Ignoble Savage: American Literary Racism, 1790–1890*. Westport, CT: Greenwood Press, 1975.

Barrie, J. M. *Peter Pan*. In *Peter Pan and Other Plays*, edited by Peter Hollindale. 1904. Reprint Oxford: Oxford University Press, 1995.

Batten, Charles. *Pleasurable Instruction: Form and Convention in Eighteenth-Century Travel Literature*. Berkeley: University of California Press, 1978.

Batty, Beatrice. *Forty-Two Years amongst the Indians and Eskimo: Pictures from the Life of the Right Reverend John Horden, First Bishop of Moosonee.* London: Religious Tract Society, 1893.

Bayley, Stephen. *The Albert Memorial: The Monument in Its Social and Architectural Context.* London: Scolar Press, 1981.

Bayly, C. A. *The Birth of the Modern World, 1780–1914.* Oxford: Blackwell Publishing, 2004.

Beaven, James. *Recreations of a Long Vacation; or, A visit to Indian Missions in Upper Canada.* London: James Burns; Toronto: H. and W. Bowsell, 1846.

Beer, Gillian. *Open Fields: Science in Cultural Encounter.* Oxford: Oxford University Press, 1996.

Bell, William Abraham. *New Tracks in North America: A Journal of Travel and Adventure whilst Engaged in the Survey for a Southern Railroad to the Pacific Ocean during 1867–8.* 2 vols. London: Chapman and Hall, 1869.

Bellin, Joshua David. *The Demon of the Continent: Indians and the Shaping of American Literature.* Philadelphia: University of Philadelphia Press, 2001.

Berkhofer, Robert F., Jr. *Salvation and the Savage: An Analysis of Protestant Missions and American Indian Response, 1787–1862.* 1965. Reprint, New York: Athenaeum, 1976.

———. *The White Man's Indian: Images of the American Indian from Columbus to the Present.* New York: Random House, 1978.

Berlant, Lauren. *The Anatomy of National Fantasy: Hawthorne, Utopia, and Everyday Life.* Chicago: University of Chicago Press, 1991.

Berman, Marshall. *All That Is Solid Melts into Air: The Experience of Modernity.* New York: Simon and Schuster, 1981.

Bernadin, Susan. "The Authenticity Game: 'Getting Real' in Contemporary American Indian Literature." In *True West: Authenticity and the American West,* edited by William R. Handley and Nathaniel Lewis, 155–75. Lincoln University of Nebraska Press, 2004.

Bernhardt-Kabisch, Ernest. *Robert Southey.* Boston: G. K. Hall, 1977.

Marchant, Bessie. *Sisters of Silver Creek: A Story of Western Canada.* London: Blackie and Son, 1908.

Bhabha, Homi. "The Postcolonial Critic." *Arena* 96 (1991), 47–63.

———. *The Location of Culture.* London: Routledge, 1994.

Bickham, Troy. *Savages within the Empire: Representations of American Indians in Eighteenth-Century Britain.* Oxford: Oxford University Press, 2005.

Bieder, Robert E. *Science Encounters the Indian, 1820–1880.* Norman: University of Oklahoma Press, 1986.

[Bigg, John Stanyan]. "*The Song of Hiawatha.* By Henry Wadsworth Longfellow." *London Quarterly Review* 6 (1856), 333–345.

Bigsby, John J. *The Shoe and Canoe; or, Pictures of Travel in the Canadas. Illustrative of Their Scenery and of Colonial Life; With Facts and Opinions on Emigration, State Policy, and Other Points of Public Interest.* London: Chapman and Hall, 1850.

Binnema, Theodore, and Kevin Hutchings, "The Emigrant and the Noble Savage: Sir Francis Bond Head's Romantic Approach to Aboriginal Policy in

340 • Bibliography

Upper Canada, 1836–1838," *Journal of Canadian Studies* 39 (2005), 115–138.

Bird, Isabella Lucy. *The Englishwoman in America*. 1856. Reprint, Madison: University of Wisconsin Press, 1966.

Bird, S. Elizabeth, ed. *Dressing in Feathers: The Construction of the Indian in American Popular Culture*. Boulder, CD: Westview Press, 1996.

Birkin, Andrew. *J. M. Barrie and the Lost Boys*. London: Constable, 1979.

Bissell, Benjamin. *The American Indian in English Literature of the Eighteenth Century*. New Haven: Yale University Press: London: Oxford University Press, 1925

Black Elk. *The Sixth Grandfather: Black Elk's Teachings Given to John G. Neihardt*. Edited by Raymond J. DeMallie. Lincoln: University of Nebraska Press, 1984.

Blackstone, Sarah J. *Buckskins, Bullets, and Business: A History of Buffalo Bill's Wild West*. New York; Westport, CT: Greenwood Press, 1986.

Blair, Hugh. *Lectures on Rhetoric and Belles Lettres*. 1783. Reprint, London: T. Cadell, 1825.

[Blamire, Susanna]. *The Poetical Works of Miss Susanna Blamire, "The Muse of Cumberland."* Edinburgh: John Menzies, 1842.

Blodget, Harold. *Walt Whitman in England*. New York: Russell & Russell, 1934.

Bold, Christine. *Selling the Wild West: Popular Western Fiction, 1860 to 1960*. Bloomington: Indiana University Press, 1987.

Bolt, Christine. *The Anti-Slavery Movement and Reconstruction: A Study in Anglo-American Cooperation, 1833–77*. Oxford: Oxford University Press, 1969.

———. "The Anti-Slavery Origins of Concern for the American Indians." In *Anti-Slavery, Religion and Reform: Essays in Memory of Roger Anstey*, edited by Christine Bolt and Seymour Drescher, 233–253. Folkestone: Dawson: Hamden: Archon, 1980.

Bond, Richmond T. *Queen Anne's American Kings*. Oxford: Clarendon Press, 1952.

Bordewich, Fergus M. *Killing the White Man's Indian: Reinventing Native Americans at the End of the Twentieth Century*. New York: Anchor, 1997.

Bourne, H. R. Fox. *The Aborigines' Protection Society: Chapters in Its History*. London: P. S. King, 1899.

Boym, Svetlana. *The Future of Nostalgia*. New York: Basic Books, 2001.

Bradfield, Thomas. "William Cullen Bryant." *Westminster Review* 143 (1895), 84–91.

Bradley, A. G. "The Red Man and the White." *Macmillan's Magazine* 63 (1891), 381–91.

Brantlinger, Patrick. *Dark Vanishings: Discourse on the Extinction of Primitive Races, 1800–1930*. Ithaca: Cornell University Press, 2003.

Brassaï [Gyula Halász]. "Carroll the Photographer." Translated by Jeremy Fox. In *Lewis Carroll: Photos and Letters to His Child Friends*, edited by Guido Almansi, 188–98 Parma, Italy: Franco Maria Ricci, 1975.

Breen, T. H. "An Empire of Goods: The Anglicization of Colonial America, 1690–1776." *Journal of British Studies* 25 (1986), 467–99.

Brett, Dorothy. *Lawrence and Brett: A Friendship*. 1932. Reprint, Santa Fe: Sunstone Press, 2006.

Briggs, Charles, and Richard Bauman. "'The Foundation of All Future Researches': Franz Boas, George Hunt, Native American Texts, and the Construction of Modernity." *American Quarterly* 51 (1999), 479–528.

Brine, Lindesay. *Travels amongst American Indians*: London: S. Low, Marston, 1894.

Bristow, Joseph. *Empire Boys: Adventure in a Man's World*. Manchester: Manchester University Press, 1991.

Brontë, Charlotte. *Shirley*. 1849. Reprint, London: Penguin, 1974.

Brooke, Frances. *The History of Emily Montague*. Edited by Mary Jane Edwards. 1769. Reprint, Carleton: Carleton University Press, 1985.

Brooks, Chris. *The Albert Memorial: The Prince Consort National Memorial; Its History, Contests, and Conservation*. New Haven: Yale University Press, 2000.

Broomfield, G. A. *Pioneer of the Air: The Life and Times of Colonel S. F. Cody*. Aldershot: Gale and Polden, 1953.

Browder, Laura. *Slippery Characters: Ethnic Impersonators and American Identities*. Chapel Hill: University of North Carolina Press, 2000.

Brown, Charles H. *William Cullen Bryant*. New York: Charles Scribner's Sons, 1971.

Brown, Dee. *Bury My Heart at Wounded Knee: An Indian History of the American West*. New York: Henry Holt, 1970.

Browne, Ray B., Richard H. Crowder, Virgil L. Lokke, and William T. Stafford, eds. *Frontiers of American Culture*. Lafayette, IN: Purdue University Press, 1968.

Browning, Elizabeth Barrett. *The Letters of Elizabeth Barrett Browning to Mary Russell Mitford, 1836–1854*. Edited by Meredith B. Raymond and Mary Rose Sullivan. 3 vols. Winfield, KA: Wedgestone Press, 1983.

———. *Selected Poems*. Edited by Margaret Foster. Baltimore: Johns Hopkins University Press, 1988.

Bryant, William Cullen. *Poems of William Cullen Bryant*. New York: D. Appleton, 1871.

Burden, Harold Nelson. *Life in Algoma; or, Three Years of a Clergyman's Life and Church Work in That Diocese*. London: S.P.C.K., 1894.

———. *Manitoulin; or, Five Years of Church Work among Ojibway Indians and Lumbermen Resident upon That Island or in Its Vicinity, by H. N. B.* London: Simpkin, Marshall, Hamilton, Kent, 1895.

[Burke, Edmund]. "History of Europe." *Annual Register* (1778).

Burnett, Frances Hodgson. *The One I Knew the Best of All*. London: Frederick, Warne 1893.

Burnham, Michelle. *Captivity and Sentiment: Cultural Exchange in American Literature, 1682–1861*. Hanover, NH: University Press of New England, 1997.

Burton, Richard F. *The City of the Saints and across the Rocky Mountains to California*. London: Longman, Green, Longman, and Roberts, 1861.

Butler, Frances Anne [Fanny Kemble]. *Journal*, 2 vols. London: John Murray, 1835.

Butler, Frances Anne[Kemble], *Poems*, London: M. G. Clarke, 1844.

Caledonia, Bishop Ridley of. *A Grand Old Chief*. London: Church Missionary Society, n.d., ca. 1901.

Calloway, Colin G. *Crown and Calume: British Indian Relations, 1783–1815.* Norman: University of Oklahoma Press, 1987.

———. *The American Revolution in Indian Country: Crisis and Diversity in Native American Communities*. Cambridge: Cambridge University Press, 1995.

[Campbell, John Francis]. *A Short American Tramp in the Fall of 1864*. Edinburgh: Edmonston and Douglas, 1865.

Campbell, Thomas. *Gertrude of Wyoming: A Pennsylvanian Tale and Other Poems*. London: Longman, Hurst, Rees, and Orme, 1809.

———. "Letter to the Mohawk Chief Ahyonwaeghs, Commonly Called John Brant, Esq. of the Grand River, Upper Canada." *New Monthly Magazine* 4 (1822), 97–101.

Campion, J. S. *On the Frontier: Reminiscences of Wild Sports, Personal Adventure and Strange Scenes*. 2 vols. London: Chapman and Hall, 1878.

Carr, Helen. *Inventing the American Primitive: Politics, Gender, and the Reception of Native American Literature, 1790–1936*. Cork: Cork University Press, 1996.

Carroll, Lewis. *The Complete Works of Lewis Carroll*. London: Bracken Books, 1994.

Carter, Paul. *The Road to Botany Bay: An Essay in Spatial History*. London: Faber and Faber, 1987.

Carver, Jonathan. *Travels through the Interior Parts of North America, in the Years 1766, 1767, and 1768*. 3rd ed. 1781. Reprint, Minneapolis: Ross and Haines, 1856.

Castiglia, Christopher. *Bound and Determined: Captivity, Culture-Crossing, and White Womanhood from Mary Rowlandson to Patty Hearst*. Chicago: University of Chicago Press, 1996.

Castro, Michael. *Interpreting the Indian: Twentieth-Century Poets and the Native American*. Albuquerque: University of New Mexico Press, 1983.

Catlin, George. *Letters and Notes on the Manners, Customs, and Condition of the North American Indians*. 2 vols. London: published by the author, 1841.

———. *Catlin's Notes of Eight Years' Travels and Residence in Europe, with His North American Indian Collection*, 2 vols. London: published by the author, 1848.

———. *Life amongst the Indians*. 1861. Reprint London: Sampson Low, Son, & Marston, 1867.

Cheyfitz, Eric. *The Poetics of Imperialism: Translation and Colonization from "The Tempest" to "Tarzan."* New York: Oxford University Press, 1991.

Child, Lydia Maria. *"Hobomok" and Other Writings on Indians*. Edited by Carolyn L. Karcher. New Brunswick, NJ: Rutgers University Press, 1998.

Churchill, Lady Randolph. *The Reminiscences of Lady Randolph Churchill*. New York: Century, 1909.

Clarke, Mary Cowden, writing as "Harry Wandsworth Shortfellow." *The Song of Drop O'Wather*. London: G. Routledge, 1856.

Clerici, Naila. "Native Americans in Columbus's Home Land: A Show within the Show." In *Indians and Europe: An Interdisciplinary Collection of Essays*, edited by Christian Feest, 1989, 415–26. Reprint, Lincoln: University of Nebraska Press, 1999.

Cody, William F. *Story of the Wild West and Camp-fire Chats, by Buffalo Bill, (Hon. W. F. Cody). A Full and Complete History of the Renowned Pioneer Quartette, Boone, Crockett, Carson, and Buffalo Bill . . . Including a Description of Buffalo Bill's Conquests in England with His Wild West Exhibition, Where Royalty from All the European Nations Paid Him a Generous Homage and Made His Wonderful Show the Greatest Success of Modern Times*. Philadelphia: Historical Publishing, 1888.

Coleridge, S. T. *Lectures 1795 on Politics and Religion*, Edited by Lewis Patton and Peter Mann. London: Routledge; Princeton: Princeton University Press, 1971.

Colley, Linda. *Britons: Forging the Nation, 1707–1837*. New Haven: Yale University Press, 1992.

———. *Captives: Britain, Empire, and the World, 1600–1850*. London: Cape, 2002.

Collins, Paul. *Banvard's Folly: Tales of Reknowned Obscurity, Famous Anonymity and Rotten Luck*. New York: Picador USA, 2001.

Collins, Wilkie. *Hide and Seek*. 1854. Revised edition. London: Sampson Low, Son, 1861.

Conan Doyle, Arthur. *Memoirs and Adventures*. Crowborough edition. 24 vols. 1924. Reprint, Garden City, NY: Doubleday, Doran, 1930.

Conrad, Joseph. *Heart of Darkness*. 1899. Reprint, New York: W. W. Norton, 1988.

Cook, Eliza. *Jottings from My Journal*. London: Routledge, Warne and Routledge, 1860.

———. *The Poetical Works of Eliza Cook*. London: Frederick Warne, 1869.

Cook, Keningale. "American Novelists. I. James Fenimore Cooper." *Belgravia* 18, 379–87 (1872) .

Cooper, James Fenimore. *The Last of the Mohicans*. 1826, 1831. Reprint, New York: Modern Library, 2001.

Copway, George. (Kah-ge-ga-gah-Bowh),, *The Traditional History and Characteristic Sketches of the Ojibway Nation*. London: C. Gilpin, 1850.

———. *Running Sketches of Men and Places, in England, France, Germany, Belgium, and Scotland*. New York: J. C. Riker, 1851.

Costello, Louisa Stuart. *Songs of a Stranger*. London: Taylor and Hessey, 1825.

Cracroft, Richard H. "World Westerns: The European Writer and the American West." In *A Literary History of the American West*, 159–79. Sponsored by the Western Literature Association. Fort Worth: Texas Christian University Press, 1987.

Cunningham, Tom F. *The Diamond's Ace: Scotland and the Native Americans*. Edinburgh: Mainstream Publishing, 2001.

Cunninghame Graham, R. B. *Redeemed and Other Sketches*. London: William Heinemann, 1927.

Dafforne, James. *The Albert Memorial Description*. London: Virtue, 1878.

Dahl, Curtis. *Robert Montgomery Bird*. New York: Twayne, 1963.

[Davis, Theofilus]. "Longfellow." *National Review* 8 (1859), 198–209.

Day, A. C. *Notes on Neepigon and the Mission to the Red Indians at Negwenenang*. London: Colonial and Continental Church Society, 1892.

Day, Thomas. *The Dying Negro: A Poem*. 3rd ed. London: W. Flexney, 1775.

———. *The History of Sandford and Merton*. 1783–86. Reprint, New York: Derby & Jackson, 1857.

Debo, Angie. *The Rise and Fall of the Choctaw Republic*. Norman: University of Oklahoma Press, 1934.

Deloria, Philip J. *Playing Indian*. New Haven: Yale University Press, 1998.

———. *Indians in Unexpected Places*. Lawrence: University Press of Kansas, 2004.

DeMallie, Raymond J. "The Lakota Ghost Dance: An Ethnohistorical Account." *Pacific Historical Review* 51 (1982), 385–405.

Dickason, Olive Patricia. *Canada's First Nations: A History of Founding Peoples from Earliest Times*. Toronto: McClelland and Stewart, 1992.

Dickens, Charles. *The Uncommercial Traveller and Reprinted Pieces*. London: Oxford University Press, 1958.

———. *The Letters of Charles Dickens*, Vol. 2, *1840–41*, Edited by Madeline House and Graham Storey. Oxford: Clarendon Press, 1969.

———. *Little Dorrit*. 1857. Reprint, Harmondsworth: Penguin, 1969.

———. *The Letters of Charles Dickens*, Vol.3, *1842–43*, Edited by Madeline House, Graham Storey, and Kathleen Tillotson. Oxford: Clarendon Press, 1974.

———. *Bleak House*. 1853. Reprint, New York: W. W. Norton, 1977.

———. *The Letters of Charles Dickens*. Vol. 4, *1844–46*, Edited by Kathleen Tillotson. Oxford: Clarendon Press, 1977.

———. *The Dent Uniform Edition of Dickens' Journalism*. Vol. 2. *The Amusements of the People and Other Papers; Reports, Essays and Reviews, 1834–51*. Edited by Michael Slater. Columbus, Ohio: Ohio State University Press, 1996.

———. *Selected Journalism*. Edited by David Pascoe. London: Penguin, 1997.

———. *American Notes for General Circulation*. 1842. Reprint, London: Penguin, 2000.

Dilke, Charles. *Greater Britain: A Record of Travel in English-Speaking Countries during 1866 and 1867*. London: Macmillan, 1869.

Dilworth, Leah. *Imagining Indians in the Southwest: Persistent Visions of a Primitive Past*. Washington, DC: Smithsonian Institution Press, 1996.

Dippie, Brian W. *Catlin and His Contemporaries: The Politics of Patronage*. Lincoln: University of Nebraska Press, 1990.

———. *The Vanishing American: White Attitudes and U.S. Indian Policy*. Lawrence: University Press of Kansas, 1991.

Donkin, John G. *Trooper and Redskin in the Far North-West: Recollections of Life in the North-West Mounted Police, Canada, 1884–1888*. London: Sampson Low, Marston, Searle, & Rivington, 1889.

Douglas, David, ed. *Familiar Letters of Sir Walter Scott*, 2 vols. Edinburgh: David Douglas, 1894.

Dowd, Gregory Evans. *A Spirited Resistance: The North American Indian Struggle for Unity, 1745–1815.* Baltimore: Johns Hopkins University Press, 1992.

Dresser, Madge, and Sue Giles, eds. *Bristol and Transatlantic Slavery.* Bristol: Bristol Museums & Art Gallery, 2000.

Dresser, Madge. *Slavery Obscured: The Social History of the Slave Trade in an English Provincial Port.* London: Continuum, 2001.

Drinnon, Richard. *White Savage: The Case of John Dunn Hunter.* New York: Schocken Books, 1972.

Duane, Patrick A. "Boys' Literature and the Idea of Empire, 1870–1914" *Victorian Studies* 24 (1980), 105–121.

Dubinsky, Karen. *The Second Greatest Disappointment: Honeymooning and Tourism at Niagara Falls.* New Brunswick, NJ: Rutgers University Press, 1999.

Duchaussois, Pierre. *Mid Snow and Ice: The Apostles of the North-West.* London: Burns, Oates and Washbourne, 1923.

Duffy, Charles. "Thomas Campbell and America." *American Literature* 13 (1942), 346–55.

Duncan, Sara Jeannette. *A Social Departure: How Orthodocia and I Went round the World by Ourselves.* London: Chatto and Windus, 1890.

Dunn, Dorothy. "Indian Children Carry Forward Old Traditions," The School Arts Magazine 34 (1934–35), 426–35.

Dunraven, Earl of. *Canadian Nights: Being Sketches and Reminiscences of Life and Sport in the Rockies, the Prairies, and the Canadian Woods.* London: Smith, Elder, 1914.

Ebersole, Gary L. *Captured by Texts: Puritan to Postmodern Images of Indian Captivity.* Charlottesville: University Press of Virginia, 1995.

Egerton, George. *Keynotes and Discords. 1893, 1894.* Reprint. London: Virago, 1983.

Egerton, Judy. *Wright of Derby.* London: Tate Gallery, 1990.

Eliot, George. *Daniel Deronda.* 1876. Reprint, New York: Modern Library, 2002.

———. *Impressions of Theophrastus Such.* 1879. Reprint, Boston: Houghton Mifflin, 1908.

———. *The George Eliot Letters.* Edited by Gordon S. Haight, 9 vols. 1954–78. New Haven: Yale University Press.

Ellingson, Ter. *The Myth of the Noble Savage.* Berkeley: University of California Press, 2001.

Elliott, Ebenezer. *The Village Patriarch, Love, and Other Poems.* London: Benjamin Steill, 1834.

———. *Kerhonah, The Vernal Walk, Win Hill, and Other Poems.* London: Benjamin Steill, 1835.

Ellison, Julie. "Race and Sensibility in the Early Republic: Ann Elizabeth Bleecker and Sarah Wentworth Morton," *American Literature* 65 (1993), 445–48.

———. *Cato's Tears and the Making of Anglo-American Emotion.* Chicago: University of Chicago Press, 1999.

Emerson, Roger L. "American Indians, Frenchmen, and Scots Philosophers." *Studies in Eighteenth-Century Culture* 9 (1979), 211–36.

Engels, Friedrich. *The Condition of the Working Class in England.* Translated by F. K. Wischnewetzk. 1887. Reprint, London: Penguin, 1987.

Fabian, Johannes. *Time and the Other: How Anthropology Makes Its Object*. New York: Columbia University Press, 1983.

———. "Religious and Secular Colonization: Common Ground," *History and Anthropology* 4 (1990), 339–55.

Faery, Rebecca Blevins. *Cartographies of Desire: Captivity, Race, and Sex in the Shaping of an American Nation*. Norman: University of Oklahoma Press, 1999.

Fairchild, Hoxie Neale. *The Noble Savage: A Study in Romantic Naturalism*. New York: Columbia University Press, 1928.

Fanon, Frantz. *Black Skin, White Masks* [Peau noire, masques blancs, 1952]. New York: Grove, 1967.

Faragher, John Mack. "The Custom of the Country: Cross-Cultural Marriage in the Far Western Fur Trade." In *Western Women: Their Land, Their Lives*, edited by Lillian Schlissel, Vicki L. Ruiz, and Janice Monk, 199–215. Albuquerque: University of New Mexico Press, 1988.

Farley, Frank E. "The Dying Indian." In *Anniversary Papers by Colleagues and Pupils of George Lyman Kittredge, Presented on the Completion of His Twenty-fifth Year of Teaching in Harvard University, June, MCMXIII*. Boston: Ginn, 1913.

Feest, Christian F., ed. *Indians and Europe: An Interdisciplinary Collection of Essays*. 1989. Reprint, Lincoln: University of Nebraska Press, 1999.

Felsenstein, Frank, ed. *English Trader, Indian Maid: Representing Gender, Race, and Slavery in the New World; An Inkle and Yarico Reader*. Baltimore: John Hopkins University Press, 1999.

Ferguson, Moira. *Subject to Others: British Women Writers and Colonial Slavery, 1670–1834*. New York: Routledge, 1992.

Festa, Lynn. *Sentimental Figures of Empire in Eighteenth-Century Britain and France*. Baltimore: Johns Hopkins University Press, 2006.

Fiedler, Leslie A. *The Return of the Vanishing American*. London: Jonathan Cape, 1969.

Finson, Jon W. *The Voices That Are Gone: Themes in Nineteenth-Century American Popular Song*. New York: Oxford University Press, 1994.

Fiorentino, Daniele. " 'Those Red-Brick Faces': European Press Reactions to the Indians of Buffalo Bill's Wild West Show." In *Indians and Europe: An Interdisciplinary Collection of Essays*, edited by Christian Feest, 403–14. 1989, Reprint, Lincoln and London: University of Nebraska Press, 1999.

Fisher, Philip. *The Vehement Passions*. Princeton: Princeton University Press, 2002.

Fleming, E. McClung. "From Indian Princess to Greek Goddess: The American Image, 1783–1815." *Winterthur Portfolio* 3 (1967), 39–46.

Flint, Kate. "The American Girl and the New Woman," *Women's Writing* 3 (1996), 197–216.

Flores, Dan. *The Natural West: Environmental History in the Great Plains and Rocky Mountains*. Norman: University of Oklahoma Press, 2001.

Folsom, Ed. *Walt Whitman's Native Representations*. Cambridge: Cambridge University Press, 1994.

Folsom, James K. "English Westerns." *Western American Literature* 2 (1967), 3–13.

Foreman, Carolyn Thomas. *Indians Abroad, 1493–1938.* Norman: University of Oklahoma Press, 1943.

Forester, F. B. *Beyond the Frontier.* London: Pilgrim Press, 1914.

Forman, Ross G. "When Britons Brave Brazil: British Imperialism and the Adventure Tale in Latin America, 1850–1918." *Victorian Studies* (1999/2000), 455–87.

Foucault, Michel. "Of Other Spaces," *Diacritics* 16 (1986), 22–27.

Francis, Daniel. *The Imaginary Indian: The Image of the Indian in Canadian Culture.* Vancouver: Arsenal Pulp Press, 1992.

Francis, Jun. *Saddle and Mocassin.* London: Chapman and Hall, 1887.

Freire, Paulo. *Pedagogy of the Oppressed.* New York: Continuum Publishing, 1988.

Fridén, Georg. *The Canadian Novels of Sir Gilbert Parker: Historical Elements and Literary Technique.* Copenhagen: Ejnar Munksgaard and A.-B. Lundequistska Bokhandeln, 1953.

Froude, J. A. *Oceana.* 1885. New ed. London: Longmans, 1886.

Fryd, Vivien Green. *Art and Empire: The Politics of Ethnicity in the United States Capitol, 1815–1860.* New Haven: Yale University Press, 1992.

Fulford, Timothy. "Romantic Indians and Colonial Politics: The Case of Thomas Campbell," *Symbiosis: A Journal of Anglo-American Literary Relations.* 2 (1998), 203–24.

———. *Romantic Indians: Native Americans, British Literature, and Transatlantic Culture, 1756–1830.* Oxford: Oxford University Press, 2006.

Gaonkar, Dilip Parameshwar. "On Alternative Modernities." In *Alternative Modernities,* 1–23. Durham: Duke University Press, 2001.

Gallop, Alan. *Buffalo Bill's British Wild West.* Stroud: Sutton Publishing, 2001.

Garrett, John. *Columbia Mission: Dedicated by Permission to Miss Burdett Coutts; A Sermon Preached in St Stephen's, Westminster, on the Sunday before Advent, 1860.* London: Rivingtons, 1860.

Gaskell, Elizabeth. "Lois the Witch." 1859. In *Cousin Phillis and Other Tales.* Oxford: Oxford University Press, 1981.

Geist, Valerius. *Buffalo Nation: History and Legend of the North American Bison.* Stillwater, MN: Voyageur Press, 1996.

Gerry, Thomas M. F. " 'I Am Translated': Anna Jameson's Sketches and *Winter Studies and Summer Rambles in Canada.*" *Journal of Canadian Studies* 25 (1990–91), 34–49.

Gerson, Carole. "Nobler Savages: Representations of Native Women in the Writings of Susanna Moodie and Catharine Parr Traill." *Journal of Canadian Studies/Revue d'Etudes Canadiennes* 32 (1997), 5–21.

Gibbons, Luke. " 'Subtilized into Savages': Edmund Burke, Progress, and Primitivism. *South Atlantic Quarterly* 100 (2001), 83–109.

Gibson, Charles, ed. *The Black Legend: Anti-Spanish Attitudes in the Old World and the New.* New York: Knopf, 1971.

Gignilliat, George Warren, Jr. *The Author of Sandford and Merton: A Life of Thomas Day, Esq.* New York: Columbia University Press, 1932.

Gikandi, Simon. *Maps of Englishness: Writing Identity in the Culture of Colonialism.* New York: Columbia University Press, 1996.

Giles, Paul. *Virtual Americas: Transnational Fictions and the Transatlantic Imaginary.* Durham: Duke University Press, 2002.

Gillmore, Parker. *A Hunter's Adventures in the Great West.* London: Hurst and Blackett, 1871.

Gilroy, Paul. *The Black Atlantic: Modernity and Double Consciousness.* Cambridge, MA: Harvard University Press, 1993.

Girouard, Mark. *The Return to Camelot: Chivalry and the English Gentleman.* New Haven: Yale University Press, 1981.

Gisborne, Thomas. *Poems, Sacred and Moral.* London: T. Cadell jun. and W. Davies, 1799.

Gladstone, Thomas H. *The Englishman in Kansas.* New York: Miller, 1857.

Glenn, Cheryl. *Unspoken: A Rhetoric of Silence.* Carbondale: Southern Illinois University Press, 2004.

Gohdes, Clarence. *American Literature in Nineteenth-Century England.* New York: Columbia University Press, 1944.

Goldsmith, Oliver. *A History of the Earth, and Animated Nature.* 1774. 6 vols. Reprint, London: Richardson, 1822.

Goslee, Nancy Moore. "Hemans's 'Red Indians': Reading Stereotypes." In *Romanticism, Race, and Imperial Culture*, edited by Alan Richardson and Sonia Hofkosh, 237–61. Bloomington: Indiana University Press, 1966.

Gould, Sydney. *Inasmuch: Sketches of the Beginnings of the Church of England in Canada in Relation to the Indian and Eskimo Races.* Toronto: n.p., 1917.

Graham, Elizabeth. *Medicine Man to Missionary: Missionaries as Agents of Change among the Indians of Southern Ontario, 1784–1867.* Toronto: Peter Martin Associates, 1975.

Grant, Anne MacVicar. *Memoirs of an American Lady with Sketches of Manners and Scenery in America as They Existed Previous to the Revolution.* 2 vols. 2nd ed. London: Longman, Hurst, Ress, and Orme, 1808.

Grant, John Webster. *Moon of Wintertime: Missionaries and the Indians of Canada in Encounter since 1534.* Toronto: University of Toronto Press, 1984.

Gray, Charlotte. *Flint and Feather: The Life and Times of E. Pauline Johnson, Tekahionwake.* Toronto: HarperFlamingo Canada, 2002.

Green, Jeffrey. "Requiem: 'Hiawatha' in the 1920s and 1930s." *Black Music Research Journal* 21 (2001), 283–288.

Greenhalgh, Paul. *Ephemeral Vistas: The Expositions Universelles, Great Exhibitions, and World's Fairs, 1851–1939.* Manchester: Manchester University Press, 1988.

Greenwell, Dora. *The Soul's Legend.* London: Strahan, 1873.

Griffin, Sir Henry Lepel. *The Great Republic.* London: Chapman and Hall, 1884.

Gurney, George, and Therese Thau Heyman, eds. *George Catlin and His Indian Gallery.* Washington, DC: Smithsonian American Art Museum and W. W. Norton, 2002.

Haig-Brown, Celia. "Seeking Honest Justice in a Land of Strangers: Nahnebahwequa's Struggle for Land." *Journal of Canadian Studies* 36 (2001–2), 143–70.

———. "The 'Friends' of Nahnebahwequa." In *With Good Intentions: Euro-Canadian and Aboriginal Relations in Colonial Canada*, edited by Celia Haig-Brown and David A. Nock, Toronto: UBC Press, 2006.

Hakluyt, Richard. *Divers Voyages Touching the Discovery of America and the Islands Adjacent*. London: Hakluyt Society, 1850.

Hale, Sarah J. *Lessons from Women's Lives*. Edinburgh: William P. Nimmo, 1867.

Hall, Catherine. *Civilising Subjects: Metropole and Colony in the English Imagination 1830–1867*. Chicago: University of Chicago Press, 2002.

[Hall, Samuel Carter]. "Living Literary Characters, No. IV: James Fenimore Cooper." *New Monthly Magazine and Literary Journal* 31 (1831), 356–62.

Hancock, William. *An Emigrant's Five Years in the Free States of America*. London: T. Cautley Newby, 1860.

Handbook to the Prince Consort National Memorial. London: John Murray, 1872.

Handley, William R. *Marriage, Violence, and the Nation in the American Literary West*. Cambridge: Cambridge University Press, 2002.

Handley, William R., and Nathaniel Lewis. *True West Authenticity and the American West*. Lincoln; University of Nebraska Press, 2004.

Hannabass, Stuart. "Ballantyne's Message of Empire," In *Imperialism and Juvenile Literature*, edited by Jeffrey Richards, 53–71. Manchester: Manchester University Press, 1989.

Hayley, William. *An Essay on Epic Poetry*. 1782. A facsimile reproduction with an introduction by Sister M. Celeste Williamson, SSJ. Gainesville, FL: Scholars' Facsimiles & Reprints, 1968.

Hazlitt, William. *Lectures on the English Poets* [1818] *and The Spirit of the Age; Or, Contemporary Portraits* [1825]. London: J.M. Dent & Sons and E.P. Dutton, 1910.

[Head, Francis]. "The Red Man." *Quarterly Review* 66 (1840), 384–422.

Headland, Emily. *The Right Rev. John Horden, D.D.* London: James Nisbet, 1919.

Heckewelder, J. G. E. *An Account of the History, Manners, and Customs of the Indian Nations Who Once inhabited Pennsylvania and the Neighboring States*. 1818. Reprint, Philadelphia: Publication Fund of the Historical Society of Pennsylvania, 1876.

Hemans, Felicia. *Translations from Camoens, and Other Poets, with Original Poetry. By the Author of "Modern Greece," and The "Restoration of the Works of Art to Italy."* Oxford: Printed by S. and J. Collingwood for J. Murray, London, and J. Parker, Oxford, 1818.

———. *Songs of the Affections, with Other Poems*. Edinburgh: William Blackwood: London: T. Cadell, 1830.

———. *Felicia Hemans: Selected Poems, Letters, Reception Materials*. Edited by Susan J. Wolfson. Princeton: Princeton University Press, 2000.

Henry, Nancy. *George Eliot and the British Empire*. Cambridge: Cambridge University Press, 2002.

Henty, G.A. *Redskin and Cow-boy: A Tale of the Western Plains*. London: Blackie and Son, 1892.

Hignett, Sean. *Brett: From Bloomsbury to New Mexico*. London: Hodder and Stoughton, 1984.

Hinderaker, Eric. "The 'Four Indian Kings' and the Imaginative Construction of the First British Empire," *William & Mary Quarterly* 53 (1996), 487–526.

Hofstadter, Richard. *The Progressive Historians: Turner, Beard, Parrington*. New York: Alfred A. Knopf, 1968.

Honour, Hugh. *The European Vision of America*. Cleveland: Cleveland Museum of Art, 1975.

[Hood, Edwin Paxton]. "The Folk-Lore of the Red Man." *Eclectic Review* 126 (1867), 262–82.

Horsman, Reginald. *Race and Manifest Destiny: The Origins of American Racial Anglo-Saxonism*. Cambridge, MA: Harvard University Press, 1981.

Howard, Susan Kubica. "Seeing Colonial America and Writing Home About It: Charlotte Lennox's *Euphemia*, Epistolarity, and the Feminine Picturesque." *Studies in the Novel* 37 (2005), 273–91.

Howitt, Mary. *Ballads and Other Poems*. London: Longman, Green, Brown, and Longman, 1847.

———. *A Popular History of the United States of America: From the Discovery of the American Continent to the Present Time*, 2 vols. London: Longman, Brown, Green, Longmans, & Roberts, 1859.

Howitt, William. *Colonization and Christianity: A Popular History of the Treatment of the Natives by the Europeans in All Their Colonies*. London: Longman, Orme, Brown, Greene, & Longmans, 1838.

Howitt, William and Mary. *The Desolation of Eyam: The Emigrant, a Tale of the American Woods, and Other Poems*. London: Wightman and Cramp, 1827.

Howse, Joseph. *A Grammar of the Cree Language; With Which Is Combined an Analysis of the Chippeway Dialect*. London: J. G. F. & J. Rivington, 1844.

Hunter, John. *Memoirs of a Captivity among the Indians of North America, from Childhood to the Age of Nineteen*. Philadelphia, 1823.

Hutcheson, John C. "Young America." *Belgravia* 18 (1872), 38–45.

[Irving, Washington]. "A Biographical Sketch of Thomas Campbell," *Analectic Magazine*, n.s. 5 (1815), 234–59.

Isles, Duncan. "The Lennox Connection." *Harvard Library Bulletin* 18 (1970), 416–35.

Jack, R.D.S. *The Road to the Never Land*. Aberdeen: Aberdeen University Press, 1991.

Jackson, Louis. *Our Caughnawagas in Egypt: A Narrative of What Was Seen and Accomplished by the Contingent of North American Indian Voyageurs Who Led the British Boat Expedition for the Relief of Khartoum up the Cataracts of the Nile*. Montreal: Drysdale, 1885.

Jackson, Virginia. "Longfellow's Tradition; or, Picture-Writing a Nation", *Modern Language Quarterly* 59 (1998), 471–96.

Jacobs, Margaret D. *Engendered Encounters: Feminism and Pueblo Cultures, 1879–1934*. Lincoln: University of Nebraska Press, 1999.

Jacobs, Peter. *Journal of the Reverend Peter Jacobs, Indian Wesleyan Missionary, from Rice Lake to the Hudson's Bay Territory, and Returning, Commencing,*

May 1852, with a Brief Account of His Life, and a Short History of the Wesleyan Mission in that Country. Toronto: Anson Freen, 1853.

Jacobus, Mary. *Tradition and Experiment in Wordsworth's Lyrical Ballads (1798).* Oxford: Oxford University Press, 1976.

James, Henry. *The Portrait of a Lady.* 1881. Reprint, London: Penguin, 1986.

———. *The American Scene.* 1907. Reprint, New York: Penguin, 1994.

Jameson, Anna. *Winter Studies and Summer Rambles in Canada.* 3 vols. London: Saunders and Otley, 1838.

Jemison, Mary. *A Narrative of the Life of Mrs Mary Jemison.* In *Women's Indian Captivity Narratives,* edited by Kathryn Zabelle Derounian-Stodola. Harmondsworth: Penguin, 1998.

Johnson, Pauline E. "With Barry in the Bow: Interlude between Acts II and III." *The Rudder* (November 1896), 315–16.

———. "The Lodge of the Lawmakers: Contrasts between the Parliaments of the White Man and the Red," *Daily Express,* 13 August 1906, 4.

———. "The Origin of Lacrosse." [originally entitled "Witchcraft and the Winner"]. *Canada: An Illustrated Weekly Journal,* 1 December 1906, 303–4.

———. *The Moccasin Maker.* Introduction by Sir Gilbert Parker. Toronto: Briggs, 1913.

———. *The Shagganappi.* Toronto: Briggs, 1913.

———. *E. Pauline Johnson, Tekahionwake: Collected Poems and Selected Prose.* Edited by Carole Gerson and Veronica Strong-Boag. Toronto: University of Toronto Press, 2002.

Johnson, Samuel. *The Preface to Shakespeare: Johnson on Shakespeare,* Edited by Arthur Sherbo. In *The Yale Edition of the Works of Samuel Johnson.* New Haven: Yale University Press, 1958–.

Johnston, Anna. *Missionary Writing and Empire, 1800–1860.* Cambridge: Cambridge University Press, 2003.

Johnston, John. *Recollections of Sixty Years.* Dayton, OH: J.H. Patterson, 1915.

Johnston, Judith. *Anna Jameson: Victorian, Feminist, Woman of Letters.* Aldershot: Scolar Press, 1997.

Johnston, Sheila M. F. *Buckskin and Broadcloth.* Toronto: Natural Heritage Books, 1997.

Jones, Peter. *Life and Journals of Kah-Ke-Wa-Quo-Na-by: (Rev. Peter Jones).* Toronto: Anson Green, 1860.

———. *History of the Ojebway Indians.* London: A. W. Bennett, 1861.

Jones, Pip, and Rita Youseph. *The Black Population of Bristol in the 18th Century.* Bristol: Bristol Branch of the Historical Association, 1994.

Jordan, Richard D., and Peter Pierce. *The Poet's Discovery: Nineteenth-Century Australia in Verse.* Melbourne: Melbourne University Press, 1990.

Kaplan, Amy. *The Anarchy of Empire in the Making of U.S. Culture.* Cambridge, MA: Harvard University Press, 2002.

Kasson, Joy S. *Marble Queens and Captives: Women in Nineteenth-Century American Sculpture.* New Haven: Yale University Press, 1990.

———. *Buffalo Bill's Wild West: Celebrity, Memory, and Popular History.* New York: Hill and Wang, 2000.

Kebbel, T. E. "Leather-Stocking." *Macmillan's Magazine* 79 (1899), 191–201.

Kehoe, Alice B. *The Ghost Dance: Ethnohistory and Revitalization.* New York: Holt, Rinehart & Winston, 1989.

Kellaway, William. *The New England Company, 1649–1776: Missionary Society to the American Indians.* Westport, CT: Greenwood Press, 1961.

Kelly, William. *An Excursion to California over the Prairie; Rocky Mountains; and Great Sierra Nevada: With a Stroll through the Diggings and Ranches of that Country.* 2 vols. London: Chapman and Hall, 1851.

Kendall, Henry. *Leaves from Australian Forests: Poetical Works of Henry Kendall.* Sydney: Weldon Publishing, 1991.

Kestner, Joseph. *Masculinities in Victorian Painting.* Aldershot: Scolar Press, 1995.

Kilpatrick, Jacquelyn. *Celluloid Indians: Native Americans and Film.* Lincoln: University of Nebraska Press, 1999.

Kingsford, M. R. *The Life, Work, and Influence of William Henry Kingston.* Toronto: Ryerson Press, 1947.

Kingsley, Charles. *Alton Locke.* 1850. Reprint, London: Macmillan, 1908.

Kingsley, George Henry. *Notes on Sport and Travel, with a Memoir by His Daughter Mary Kingsley.* London: Macmillan, 1900.

Kingston, William H. G. *Western Wanderings: or, A Pleasure Tour in the Canadas.* 2 vols. London: Chapman and Hall, 1856.

———. *Adventures of Dick Onslow among the Red Indians.* London: Gall & Inglis, 1873.

Kipling, Rudyard. *Kipling's America: Travel Letters, 1889–1895.* Greensboro, NC: English Literature in Transition Press, 2003.

Kirkpatrick, F. A. "The Literature of Travel." In *The Cambridge History of English Literature. Vol. 14. The Nineteenth Century III*, edited by Sir A. W. Ward and A. R. Waller, Cambridge: Cambridge University Press, 1916. 240–56.

Klein, Kerwin Lee. *Frontiers of Historical Imagination: Narrating the European Conquest of Native America, 1890–1990.* Berkeley: University of California Press, 1997.

Krech, Shepherd, III. *The Ecological Indian: Myth and History.* New York: W. W. Norton, 1999.

Krupat, Arnold. *Ethnocriticism: Ethnography, History, Literature.* Berkeley: University of California Press, 1992.

Kupperman, Karen Ordahl. *Indians and English: Facing Off in Early America.* Ithaca: Cornell University Press, 2000.

Lang, Andrew. *In the Wrong Paradise and Other Stories.* London: Kegan Paul, Trench, 1886.

Lawrence, D. H. *Phoenix: The Posthumous Papers of D. H. Lawrence.* New York: Viking Press, 1968.

———. *Studies in Classic American Literature.* 1923. Reprint, London: Penguin, 1971.

———. *The Lost Girl.* 1920. Reprint, New York: Random House, 2003.

Lax, William. *Lax: His Book; The Autobiography of Lax of Poplar.* London: Epworth, 1937.

Lears, T. Jackson. *No Place of Grace: Anti-modernism and the Transformation of American Culture, 1880–1920*. 1981. Reprint, Chicago: University of Chicago Press, 1994.

Lennox, Charlotte. *Euphemia*. 4 vols. London: T. Cadell and J. Evans, 1790.

Lewis, Nathaniel. *Unsettling the Literary West: Authenticity and Authorship*. Lincoln: University of Nebraska Press, 2003.

Leyden, John. *The Poetical Remains of the Late Dr. John Leyden, with Memoirs of His Life, by the Rev. James Morton*. London: Strahan and Spottiswoode and A. Constable 1819.

Li, Victor. *The Neo-Primitivist Turn: Critical Reflections on Alterity, Culture, and Modernity*. Toronto: University of Toronto Press, 2006.

Liebersohn, Harry. *Aristocratic Encounters: European Travelers and North American Indians*. Cambridge: Cambridge University Press, 1998.

Limerick, Patricia. *The Legacy of Conquest: The Unbroken Past of the American West*. New York: W. W. Norton, 1988.

Lindfors, Bernth. "Ethnological Show Business: Footlighting the Dark Continent." In, *Freakery. Cultural Spectacles of the Extraordinary Body*, edited by Rosemarie Garland Thomson, 207–18. New York: New York University Press, 1996.

Little Pine's Journal: The Appeal of a Christian Chippeway Chief on Behalf of His People translated by the Reverend E. F. Wilson, of the Church Missionary Society. London: Grosvenor, 1872.

Longfellow, Henry Wadsworth. *The Poetical Works of Henry Wadsworth Longfellow: A New Complete Edition, Including the Song of Hiawatha*. London: George Routledge, 1856.

Longfellow, Samuel. *Life of Henry Wadsworth Longfellow: With Extracts from His Journals and Correspondence*. 2 vols. Boston: Ticknor, 1886.

Lootens, Tricia. "Hemans and Home: Victorianism, Feminine 'Internal Enemies,' and the Domestication of National Identity," *PMLA* 109 (1994), 238–53.

———. "Hemans and Her American Heirs: Nineteenth-Century Women's Poetry and National Identity." In *Women's Poetry, Late Romantic to Late Victorian; Gender and Genre, 1830–1900*, edited by Isobel Armstrong and Virginia Blain, London: Macmillan, 1999, 243–60.

Lott, Eric. *Love and Theft: Blackface Minstrelsy and the American Working Class*. New York: Oxford University Press, 1993.

Lowe, Charles. *National Exhibitions in London and Their Organizer*. London: T. Fisher Unwin, 1892.

Lucas, John. "Deerfoot in Britain: An Amazing American Long Distance Runner, 1861–1863." *Journal of American Culture* 6 (1983), 13–18.

Luhan, Mabel Dodge. *Lorenzo in Taos*. New York: Knopf, 1932.

Lyddeker, John Wolfe. *The Faithful Mohawks*. Cambridge: Cambridge University Press, 1938.

Lyman, Christopher M. *Vanishing Race and Other Illusions: Photographs of Indians by Edward S. Curtis*. New York: Pantheon Press, 1982.

Lyotard, Jean-François. *The Differend: Phrases in Dispute*. Translated by Georges Van Den Abbeele. Manchester: Manchester University Press, 1988.

Macaulay, Thomas Babington. *The Miscellaneous Works of Lord Macaulay*. 20 vols. New York: G. P. Putnam's Sons, 1898.

MacEwen, Grant. *Sitting Bull: The Years in Canada*. Edmonton: Hurtig Publishers, 1973.

Mackail, Denis G. *Barrie; The Story of J.M.B.* New York: C. Scribners Sons, 1941.

Mackenzie, John M. *The Empire of Nature: Hunting, Conservation, and British Imperialism*. Manchester: Manchester University Press, 1988.

———. ed. *Imperialism and Popular Culture*. Manchester: Manchester University Press, 1989.

MacLaren, Roy. *Canadians on the Nile, 1882–1898*. Vancouver: University of British Columbia Press, 1978.

Maclean, John. *Canadian Savage Folk: The Native Tribes of Canada*. Toronto: William Briggs, 1896.

Marchant, Bessie. *Sisters of Silver Creek: A Story of Western Canada*. London: Blackie and Son, 1908.

Maddox, Lucy. *Removals: Nineteenth-Century American Literature and the Politics of Indian Affairs*. New York: Oxford University Press, 1991.

———. *Citizen Indians: Native American Intellectuals, Race and Reform*. Ithaca: Cornell University Press, 2005.

Maddra, Sam A. *Hostiles? The Lakota Ghost Dance and Buffalo Bill's Wild West*. Norman: University of Oklahoma Press, 2006.

Malchow, H. L. *Gothic Images of Race in Nineteenth-Century Britain*. Stanford: Stanford University Press, 1996.

Manuel, F. E. *The Eighteenth Century Confronts the Gods*. Cambridge, MA: Harvard University Press, 1959.

Marryat, Frederick. *A Diary in America, with Remarks on Its Institutions*. Philadelphia: Carey & Hart, 1839.

Marsh, Peter, ed. *The Conscience of the Victorian State*. Syracuse, NY: Syracuse University Press, 1979.

Marshall, Peter. *The Anti-Slave Trade Movement in Bristol*. Bristol: Historical Association, Bristol Branch, 1968.

———. *Bristol and the Abolition of Slavery: The Politics of Emancipation*. Bristol: Historical Association, Bristol Branch, 1975.

Martin, Jonathan D. "'The Grandest and Most Cosmopolitan Object Teacher': *Buffalo Bill's Wild West* and the Politics of American Identity, 1883–1899." *Radical History Review* 66 (1996), 92–123.

Martineau, Harriet. *Society in America*. 3 vols. London: Saunders and Otley, 1837.

———. *Retrospect of Western Travel*. 2 vols. London: Saunders and Otley, 1838.

Maungwudaus. *An account of the Chippewa Indians, Who Have Been Travelling among the Whites, in the United States, England, Ireland, Scotland, France and Belgium. . . .* Boston: Published by the author, 1848.

Maxwell, Sir Herbert. *The Honourable Sir Charles Murray, K.C.B.* Edinburgh: William Blackwood and Sons, 1898.

McKay, Brenda. *George Eliot and Victorian Attitudes to Racial Diversity, Colonialism, Darwinism, Class, Gender, and Jewish Culture and Prophecy*. Lewiston: Edward Mellen Press, 2003.

McNally, Michael D. "The Indian Passion Play: Contesting the Real Indian in *Song of Hiawatha* Pageants, 1901–1965." *American Quarterly* 58 (2006), 105–36.

McNickle, D'Arcy. "American Indians Who Never Were," *Indian Historian* 3 (1970), 4–7.

Messiter, Charles Alston. *Sport and Adventures among the North-American Indians*. London: R. H. Porter, 1890.

Midgley, Clare. *Women against Slavery: The British Campaigns, 1780–1870*. London: Routledge, 1995.

Mignolo, Walter D. *Local Histories/Global Designs: Coloniality, Subaltern Knowledges, and Border Thinking*. Princeton: Princeton University Press, 2000.

Miller, J. R. *Skyscrapers Hide the Heavens: A History of Indian-White Relations in Canada*. 3rd ed. Toronto: University of Toronto Press, 2000.

Miller, Mary Ruth. *Thomas Campbell*. Boston: Twayne Publishers, 1978.

Mitchell, Lee Clark. *Westerns: Making the Men in Fiction and Film*. Chicago: University of Chicago Press, 1996.

Mitchell, Sally. *The New Girl: Girls' Culture in England, 1880–1915*. New York: Columbia University Press, 1995.

Monkman, Leslie. "Primitivism and a Parasol: Anna Jameson's Indians." *Essays on Canadian Writing* 29 (1984), 85–95.

Moodie, Susanna. *Roughing It in the Bush; or, Life in Canada*. 1852. Reprint, Toronto: McClelland and Stewart, 1989.

Moran, Rachel F. *Interracial Intimacy: The Regulation of Race and Romance*. Chicago: University of Chicago Press, 2001.

More, Hannah. *Works of Hannah More*. London: T. Cadell, 1788.

Morgan, Cecilia. " 'A Wigwam to Westminster': Performing Mohawk Identity in Imperial Britain, 1890s–1990s." *Gender & History* 15 (2003), 319–41.

Morgan, Kenneth. *Bristol and the Atlantic Trade in the Eighteenth Century*. Cambridge: Cambridge University Press, 1993.

Morrison, Toni. *Playing in the Dark: Whiteness and the Literary Imagination*. Cambridge, MA: Harvard University Press, 1992.

Moses, L. G. *Wild West Shows and the Images of American Indians, 1883–1933*. Albuquerque: University of New Mexico Press, 1996.

Mossiker, Frances. *Pocahontas: The Life and the Legend*. New York: Da Capo, 1976.

Moyles, R. G., and Douglas Owram, *Imperial Dreams and Colonial Realities: British Views of Canada, 1880–1914*. Toronto: University of Toronto Press, 1988.

Müller, Max. *Last Essays. First Series. Essays on Language, Folklore and Other Subjects*. London: Longmans, Green, 1901.

Murray, Amelia M. *Letters from the United States, Cuba and Canada*. 2 vols. London: John W. Parker and Son, 1856.

Murray, Charles Augustus. *Travels in North America, Including a Summer Residence with the Pawnee Tribe of Indians, in the Remote Plains of the Missouri, and a Visit to Cuba and the Azore Islands.* 2 vols. 1839. 3rd edition revised, with a new introduction. Reprint, London: Richard Bentley, 1854.

Murray, David. *Forked Tongues: Speech, Writings, and Representation in North American Indian Texts.* Bloomington: Indiana University Press, 1991.

Nabokov, Peter. *Native American Testimony: A Chronicle of Indian-White Relations from Prophecy to the Present, 1492–2000.* Rev. ed. New York: Penguin, 1999.

Nadal, E.S. "William Cullen Bryant." *Macmillan's Magazine* 38 (1878), 369–75.

Namias, June. *White Captives: Gender and Ethnicity on the American Frontier.* Chapel Hill: University of North Carolina Press, 1993.

Napier, Rita G. "Across the Big Water: American Indians' Perceptions of Europe and Europeans, 1887–1906." In *Indians and Europe: An Interdisciplinary Collection of Essays,* edited by Christian Feest, 383–401. 1989. Reprint, Lincoln: University of Nebraska Press, 1999.

Nesbit, E. *The Story of the Treasure Seekers.* London: Ernst Benn, 1899.

Newland, Simpson. *Paving the Way: A Romance of the Australian Bush.* 1893. Reprint, Adelaide: Rigby, 1954.

Newman, Francis William. *Hiawatha: Rendered into Latin, with Abridgment.* London: Walton and Maberly, 1862.

Nock, David A. "A Chapter in the Amateur Period of Canadian Anthropology: A Missionary Case Study." *Canadian Journal of Native Studies* 2 (1982), 249–67.

Nord, Deborah. *Gypsies and the British Imagination, 1807–1930.* New York: Columbia University Press, 2006.

North, Marianne. *Recollections of a Happy Life.* Edited by Mrs. John Addington Symonds. 2 vols. London: Macmillan, 1892.

Norton, Anne. *Reflections on Political Identity.* Baltimore: Johns Hopkins University Press, 1988.

O'Leary, John. "Giving the Indigenous a Voice: Further Throughts on the Poetry of Eliza Hamilton Dunlop." *Journal of Australian Studies* 82 (2004), 85–96.

Oliphant, Laurence. *Minnesota and the Far West.* Edinburgh: William Blackwood and Sons, 1855.

[Oliphant, Margaret]. "Modern Light Literature—Poetry," *Blackwood's Edinburgh Magazine,* 79 (1856).

Olson, Lester C. *Emblems of American Community in the Revolutionary Era: A Study in Rhetorical Iconology.* Washington, DC: Smithsonian Institution Press, 1991.

Orde, Anne. *The Eclipse of Great Britain: The United States and British Imperial Decline, 1895–1956.* New York: St. Martin's Press, 1996.

Orestano, Francesca. "Dickens on the Indians." In *Indians and Europe: An Interdisciplinary Collection of Essays* edited by Christian F. Feest, 277–86. 1989, Reprint, Lincoln: University of Nebraska Press, 1999.

Osterreich, Shelley Anne. *The American Indian Ghost Dance, 1870 and 1890: An Annotated Bibliography.* New York: Greenwood Press, 1991.

Owen, Mrs. Octavius Freire. *The Heroines of Domestic Life*. London: Routledge, Warne, & Routledge, 1861.

Owens, Louis. *Mixedblood Messages: Literature, Film, Family, Place*. Norman: University of Oklahoma Press, 1998.

Oxley, J. Macdonald. "The Indian in Canada," *Macmillan's Magazine* 59 (1889), 194–201.

Parker, Gilbert. *The Translation of a Savage*. London: Methuen, 1894.

———. *The Works of Gilbert Parker*. Imperial Edi. 20 vols. London: Macmillan, 1913.

Pascoe, Peggy. "Race, Gender and Intercultural Relations: The Case of Interracial Marriage." In *Writing the Range. Race, Class, and Culture in the Women's West*, edited by Elizabeth Jameson and Susan Armitage, 69–80. Norman: University of Oklahoma Press, 1997.

Pattee, Fred Lewis, ed. *The Poems of Philip Freneau*. 3 vols. Princeton: Princeton University Library, 1903.

Patten, Robert L. *Charles Dickens and His Publishers*. Oxford: Oxford University Press, 1978.

Pearce, Roy Harvey. *Savagism and Civilization: A Study of the Indian and the American*. Baltimore: Johns Hopkins University Press, 1967.

Petrone, Penny. *Native Literature in Canada: From the Oral Tradition to the Present*. Toronto: University of Toronto Press, 1990.

Peyer, Bernd C. *The Tutor'd Mind: Indian Missionary-Writers in Antebellum America*. Amherst: University of Massachusetts Press, 1997.

———. "A Nineteenth-Century Ojibwa Conquers Germany." In *Germans and Indians: Fantasies, Encounters, Projections*, edited by Colin G. Calloway, Gerd Gemünden, and Susanne Zantop, 141–64. Lincoln: University of Nebraska Press, 2002.

Pfeiffer, Emily. *Flying Leaves from East and West*. London: Field and Tuer, 1885.

———. *Flowers of the Night*. London: Trübner, 1889.

Phillips, R. S. "Space for Boyish Men and Manly Boys: The Canadian Northwest in Robert Ballantyne's Adventure Stories." *Essays on Canadian Writing* 59 (1996), 46–64.

Phillips, Ruth B., and Christopher B. Steiner, eds. *Unpacking Culture: Art and Commodity in Colonial and Postcolonial Worlds*. Berkeley: University of California Press, 1999.

Pisani, Michael V. *Imagining Native America in Music*. New Haven: Yale University Press, 2005.

Plotnicki, Rita M. "John Brougham: The Aristophanes of American Burlesque." *Journal of Popular Culture* 12 (1978), 422–431.

Porter, Andrew. "'Cultural Imperialism' and Protestant Missionary Enterprise, 1780–1914." *Journal of Imperial and Commonwealth History* 25 (1997), 367–91.

———. "Trusteeship, Anti-Slavery and Humanitarianism" and "Religion, Missionary Enthusiasm, and Empire." In vol. 3 of *The Oxford History of the British Empire*, edited by Andrew Porter, 198–246. Oxford: Oxford University Press, 1999.

Pratt, Stephanie. *American Indians in British Art, 1700–1840.* Norman: University of Oklahoma Press, 2005.

Price, Major Sir Rose Lambart. *The Two Americas: An Account of Sport and Travel; With Notes on Men and Manners in North and South America.* London: Sampson Low, Marston, Searle, and Rivington, 1877.

———. *A Summer on the Rockies.* London: Sampson Low, Marston, 1898.

Prichard, James Cowles. "On the Extinction of the Human Races." *Edinburgh New Philosophical Journal* 28 (1839), 166–70.

Priestley, J. B. *Midnight on the Desert: Being an Excursion into Autobiography during a Winter in America, 1935–6.* London: William Heinemann, 1937.

Prochaska, F. K. "Little Vessels: Children in the Nineteenth-Century English Missionary Movement." *Journal of Imperial and Commonwealth History* 6 (1978), 103–18.

Psomiades, Kathy Alexis. "Heterosexual Exchange and Other Victorian Fictions: *The Eustace Diamonds* and Victorian Anthropology." *Novel* 33 (1999), 93–118.

Quayle, Eric. *Ballantyne the Brave: A Victorian Writer and His Family.* London: Rupert Hart-Davis, 1967.

Rabb, Jane, ed. *Literature and Photography: Interactions, 1840–1990.* Albuquerque: University of New Maxico Press, 1955.

Rae, William Fraser. *Westward by Rail: A Journey to San Francisco and Back and a Visit to the Mormons.* 2nd ed. London: Longmans, Green, 1871.

[Rankin, Arthur]. *A Short History and Description of the Ojibbeway Indians Now on a Visit to England.* London: Vizetelly Brothers, 1844.

Ray, Gordon. *Thackeray: The Age of Wisdom.* New York: McGraw-Hill, m.d., ca. 1958.

Reddin, Paul. *Wild West Shows.* Urbana: University of Illinois Press, 1999.

Regier, A. M. " 'Revolutionary Enunciatory Spaces': Ghost Dancing, Transatlantic Travel, and Modernist Arson in *Gardens in the Dunes.*" *Modern Fiction Studies* 51 (2005), 134–57.

Reid, Elizabeth. *Mayne Reid: A Memoir of His Life.* London: Ward & Downey, 1890.

———. *Captain Mayne Reid: His Life and Adventures.* London: Greening, 1900.

Reid, Mayne. *The Scalp Hunters; or, Romantic: Adventures in Northern Mexico.* 3 vols. London: Charles J. Skeet, 1851.

———. *The English Family Robinson. The Desert Home; or, The Adventures of a Lost Family in the Wilderness.* London: David Bogue, 1852.

———. *A White Chief: A Legend of Northern Mexico.* 3 vols. London: David Bogue, 1855.

———. *The Quadroon; or, A Lover's Adventures in Louisiana.* 3 vols. London: Hyde, 1856.

———. *The White Gauntlet: A Romance.* 1864. Reprint, London: Charles H. Clarke, 1865.

———. *The Headless Horseman: A Strange Tale of Texas.* London: Charles A. Clarke, n.d. [1866].

———. *The White Squaw, and the Yellow Chief.* London: Charles H. Clarke, 1871.

———. *No Quarter!* 3 vols. London: Sonnenschein, 1888.

Report from the Select Committee on Aborigines (British Settlements), Parliamentary Papers (1837).

Retamar, Roberto Fernández. *Caliban and Other Essays.* Translated by Edward Baker. Minneapolis: University of Minnesota Press, 1989.

Rich, E. E. *The History of the Hudson's Bay Company, 1670–1870.* 3 vols. London: Hudson's Bay Record Society, 1958.

Richter, Daniel K. "Native Peoples of North America and the Eighteenth-Century British Empire." In *Oxford History of the British Empire: The Eighteenth Century*, edited by P. J. Marshall, 347–71. Oxford: Oxford University Press, 1998.

Roach, Joseph. *Cities of the Dead: Circum-Atlantic Performance.* New York: Columbia University Press, 1996.

Robbins, Elizabeth. *The Convert.* 1907. Reprint, London: Women's Press, 1980.

Roberts, Estelle. *Fifty Years a Medium.* New York: Avon, 1972.

Robertson, Bruce. "The Portraits: An Iconographical Study." In *The Four Indian Kings/Les Quatre Rois Indiens*, edited by John G. Garratt, 139–49. Ottawa: Canadian Government Printing Centre, 1985.

Robertson, Eric S. *Life of Henry Wadsworth Longfellow.* London: Walter Scott, 1887.

Robertson, William, and W. F. Robertson. *Our American Tour: Being a Run of Ten Thousand Miles from the Atlantic to the Golden Gate, in the Autumn of 1869.* Edinburgh: W. Burness [for private circulation], 1871.

Roehm, Marjorie Catlin, ed. *The Letters of George Catlin and His Family: A Chronicle of the American West.* Berkeley: University of California Press, 1966.

Romero, Laura. "Vanishing Americans: Gender, Empire, and New Historicism." *American Literature* 63 (1991), 385–404.

Rosaldo, Renato. *Culture and Truth: The Remaking of Social Analysis.* Boston: Beacon Press, 1989.

Roscoe, Will. *Changing Ones: Third and Fourth Genders in Native North America.* New York: St. Martin's Griffin, 1998.

Rose, Jonathan. *The Intellectual Life of the British Working Classes.* New Haven: Yale University Press, 2001.

Rose, Wendy. *Bone Dance: New and Selected Poems, 1965–1993.* Tucson: University of Arizona Press, 1994.

Rossetti, William Michael. *Lives of the Famous Poets.* London: Moxon, 1878.

Rudnick, Lois Palken. *Mabel Dodge Luhan: New Woman, New Worlds.* Albuquerque: University of New Mexico Press, 1999.

———. *Utopian Vistas: The Mabel Dodge Luhan House and the American Counterculture.* Albuquerque: University of New Mexico Press, 1999.

Ruoff, A. LaVonne Brown. "Three Nineteenth-Century American Indian Autobiographers." In *Redefining American Literary History*, edited by Ruoff and Jerry W. Ward, 251–269. New York: MLA, 1990.

Russell, Henry. *Cheer! Boys, Cheer! Memories of Men and Music.* London: John MacQueen, 1895.

Saldívar, José David. *The Dialectics of Our America: Genealogy, Cultural Critique, and Literary History.* Durham: Duke University Press, 1991.

Sanjek, Russell. *American Popular Music and Its Business.* 3 vols. Oxford: Oxford University Press, 1988.

Saum, Lewis O. *The Fur Trader and the Indian.* Seattle: University of Washington Press, 1965.

Sayers, W. C. Berwick. *Samuel Coleridge-Taylor, Musician: His Life and Letters.* London: Cassell, 1915.

Scheckel, Susan. *The Insistence of the Indian: Race and Nationalism in Nineteenth-Century American Culture.* Princeton: Princeton University Press, 1998.

Schoolcraft, Henry. *Personal Memoirs of a Residence of Thirty Years on the American Frontier.* Philadelphia: Lippincott, 1851.

Schramm, Walter. "*Hiawatha* and Its Predecessors." *Philological Quarterly* 11 (1932), 321–43.

Scott, David. *Conscripts of Modernity: The Tragedy of Colonial Enlightenment.* Durham: Duke University Press, 2004.

[Scott, Sir Walter]. "Gertrude of Wyoming, a Pensylvanian [*sic*] Tale, and Other Poems." *Quarterly Review* 1 (1809), 241–58.

Scott, Sir Walter. *Guy Mannering.* Edited by P. D. Garside. 1815. Reprint, Edinburgh: Edinburgh University Press, 1999.

Sedgwick, Eve Kosofsky. *Touching Feeling: Affect, Pedagogy, Performativity.* Durham: Duke University Press, 2003.

Seeley, J. P. *The Expansion of England.* London: Macmillan, 1883.

Shebbeare, John. *Lydia; or, Filial Piety.* 4 vols. 1755. Reprint, New York: Garland Publishing, 1974.

Shelley, Mary. *Frankenstein.* 1818, 1831. London: Penguin, 1992.

Shnookal, Deborah, and Mirta Muñiz, eds. *José Martí Reader: Writings on the Americas.* Melbourne: Ocean Press, 1999.

Sigourney, Mrs. L. H. *Pocahontas, and Other Poems.* London: Robert Tyas, 1841.

———. *Pleasant Memories of Pleasant Lands.* London: Tilt and Bogue, 1843.

Silko, Leslie Marmon. *Gardens in the Dunes.* New York: Simon and Schuster, 1999.

Simms, William Gilmore. *Views and Reviews in American Literature: History and Fiction, First Ser.* Edited by C. Hugh Holman. Cambridge, MA: Harvard University Press, 1962.

Simson, Walter. *A History of the Gipsies: With Specimens of the Gipsy Language.* London: Sampson Low, Son, and Marston, 1865.

Slotkin, Richard. *The Fatal Environment: The Myth of the Frontier in the Age of Industrialization, 1800–1890.* 1985. Reprint, Norman: University of Oklahoma Press, 1994.

———. *Gunfighter Nation: The Myth of the Frontier in Twentieth-Century America.* 1992. Reprint, Norman: University of Oklahoma Press, 1998.

Smith, Charlotte. *Elegiac Sonnets, the Seventh Edition, with Additional Sonnets and Other Poems.* London: T. Cadell, 1795.

Smith, Donald B. "Maungwudaus Goes Abroad, 1845." *Beaver* 22 (1976), 4–9.

———. *Sacred Feathers: The Reverend Peter Jones (Kahkewaquonaby) and the Mississauga Indians*. Toronto: University of Toronto Press, n.d. ca. 1987.

———. "The Life of George Copway or Kah-ge-ga-gah-bowh (1818–1869)— and a Review of His Writings." *Journal of Canadian Studies* 23 (1988), 5–38.

———. "Nahnebahwequay (1824–1865) 'Upright Woman.' " *Canadian Methodist Historical Society Papers* 13 (2001).

Smith, Sherry L. *Reimagining Indians: Native Americans through Anglo Eyes, 1880–1940*. New York: Oxford University Press, 2000.

Smith-Rosenberg, Carroll. "Subject Female: Authorizing American Identity." *American Literary History* 5 (1993), 481–511.

Sollors, Werner. *Beyond Ethnicity: Consent and Dissent in American Culture*. New York: Oxford University Press, 1986.

Southey, Robert. *The Complete Poetical Works of Robert Southey*. New ed. New York: D. Appleton, 1851.

Spencer, Herbert. "The Americans: A Conversation and a Speech, with an Addition." *Contemporary Review* 43 (1883), 1–15.

Sproat, Gilbert Malcolm. *Scenes and Studies of Savage Life*. London: Smith, Elder, 1868.

Stafford, Fiona J. *The Last of the Race: The Growth of a Myth from Milton to Darwin*. Oxford: Clarendon Press, 1994.

Standing Bear, Luther. *My People the Sioux*. 1928. Reprint, Lincoln: University of Nebraska Press, 1975.

Stanley, Brian. *The Bible and the Flag: Protestant Missions and British Imperialism in the Nineteenth and Twentieth Centuries*. Trowbridge, England: Apollos, 1990.

Stanley, H. M. *My Early Travels and Adventures in America and Asia*. 1895. Reprint, London: Gerald Duckworth, 2001.

Stedman, Raymond William. *Shadows of the Indian: Stereotypes in American Culture*. Norman: University of Oklahoma Press, 1982.

Steele, Jeffrey. "Reduced to Images: American Indians in Nineteenth-Century Advertising." In *Dressing in Feathers: The Construction of the Indian in American Popular Culture*, edited by S. Elizabeth Bird, 45–64. Boulder, CO: Westview Press, 1996.

Steele, Joan. *Captain Mayne Reid*. Boston: Twayne Publishers, 1978.

Stevens, Laura. "The Christian Origins of the Vanishing Indian." In *Mortal Remains: Death and Mourning in Early America*, edited by Andrew Burstein and Nancy Isenberg, 17–30. Philadelphia: University of Pennsylvania Press, 2002. 17–30.

Stevenson, Robert Louis. *The Travels and Essays of Robert Louis Stevenson: The Amateur Emigrant, Across the Plains, The Silverado Squatters*. New York: Charles Scribner's Sons, 1897.

Stevenson, Winona. "Beggars, Chickabobbooags, and Prisons: Paxoche (Ioway) Views of English Society, 1844–45." *American Indian Culture and Research Journal* 17 (1993), 1–23.

Stewart, T. D., and Marshall T. Newman. "A Historical Résumé of the Concept of Differences in Indian Types." *American Anthropologist* 53 (1951), 19–36.

Stocking, George W., Jr. *Victorian Anthropology*. New York: Free Press, 1987.

Stoker, Bram. *Midnight Tales*. London: Peter Owen, 1990.

———. *Dracula*. 1897. Reprint, London: Penguin, 1993.

Storey, Mark. *Robert Southey: A Life*. Oxford: Oxford University Press, 1997.

Streeby, Shelley. *American Sensations: Class, Empire, and the Production of Popular Culture*. Berkeley: University of California Press, 2002.

Street, Brian V. *The Savage in Literature: Representations of "Primitive" Society in English Fiction*. London: Routledge and Kegan Paul, 1975.

Strettell, Alma. "An Indian Festival." *Macmillan's Magazine* 47 (1882), 21–38.

Strong-Boag, Veronica, and Carole Gerson. *Paddling Her Own Canoe: The Times and Texts of E. Pauline Johnson (Tekahionwake)*. Toronto: University of Toronto Press, 2000.

Suffling, Ernest R. *The fur-traders of the West; or, Adventures among the Redskins*. London: Frederick Warne, 1896.

Swagerty, William R. "Marriage and Settlement Patterns of Rocky Mountain Trappers and Traders." *Western Historical Quarterly* 11 (1980), 159–80.

Sweet, Nanora. "History, Imperialism, and the Aesthetics of the Beautiful: Hemans and the Post-Napoleonic Moment." In *At the Limits of Romanticism*, edited by M. A. Favret and N. J. Watson, 170–84. Bloomington: Indiana University Press, 1994.

Taylor, Alan. *The Divided Ground: Indians, Settlers, and the Northern Borderland of the American Revolution*. New York: Alfred A. Knopf, 2006.

Thackeray, William Makepeace. *The Virginians: A Tale of the Last Century*. 1858–59. Reprint, London: Macmillan, 1911.

Thompson, Isabel. *Joseph Brant, 1743–1807: Man of Two Worlds*. Syracuse: Syracuse University Press, 1984.

Thorne, Susan. *Congregational Missions and the Making of an Imperial Culture in Nineteenth-Century England*. Stanford: Stanford University Press, 1999.

Tilton, Robert S. *Pocahontas: The Evolution of an American Narrative*. Cambridge: Cambridge University Press, 1994.

Tobin, Beth Fowkes. *Picturing Imperial Power: Colonial Subjects in Eighteenth-Century British Painting*. Durham: Duke University Press, 1999.

Tocqueville, Alexis de. *Democracy in America*. Edited by J. P. Mayer, translted by George Lawrence. 1835, 1840. Reprint, Garden City, NY: Doubleday/Anchor, 1969.

Tompkins, Jane. *Sensational Designs: The Cultural Work of American Fiction, 1790–1860*. New York: Oxford University Press, 1985.

Torgovnick, Marianna. *Gone Primitive: Savage Intellects, Modern Lives*. Chicago: University of Chicago Press, 1990.

———. *Primitive Passions: Men, Women, and the Quest for Ecstasy*. 1996. Reprint, Chicago: University of Chicago Press, 1998.

Tortolano, William. *Samuel Coleridge-Taylor: Anglo-Black Composer, 1875–1912*. Metuchen, NJ: Scarecrow Press, 1977.

Trachtenberg, Alan. *Shades of Hiawatha: Staging Indians, Making Americans, 1880–1930*. New York: Hill and Wang, 2004.

Trant, William. "The Treatment of the Canadian Indians." *Westminster Review* 144 (1895), 506–27.

Traubel, Horace. *With Walt Whitman in Camden*. 7 vols. 1906–1992. Vol. 6, edited by Gertrude Traubel and William White. Carbondale: University of Southern Illinois Press, 1982.

Treuttner, William H. *The Natural Man Observed: A Study of Catlin's Indian Gallery*. Washington, DC: Smithsonian Institution Press, 1979.

Trollope, Anthony. *South Africa*. Edited by J. H. Davidson. 1878. Reprint, Cape Town: A. A. Balkema, 1973.

———. *He Knew He Was Right*. 1869. Reprint, Oxford: Oxford University Press, 1985.

Trollope, Frances. *The Refugee in America: A Novel*. 3 vols. London: Whittaker, Treacher, 1832.

———. *The Life and Adventures of Jonathan Jefferson Whitlaw*. 3 vols. London: Richard Bentley, 1836.

———. *The Old World and the New*. 3 vols. London: Henry Colburn, 1849.

———. *Domestic Manners of the Americans*. Edited by Donald Smalley. 1832. Reprint, New York: Alfred A. Knopf, 1949.

Turner, C. Frank. *Across the Medicine Line*. Toronto: McClelland and Stewart, 1973.

Turner, Frederick Jackson. *The Frontier in American History*. 1920. Reprint, Mineola: Dover Publications, 1996.

Uglow, Jenny. *Elizabeth Gaskell*. London: Faber and Faber, 1993.

Unsigned article. "An Indian Chief at the Mansion House." *Aborigines' Friend: A Journal of the Aborigines' Protection Society* (London), [4th] ser., 6 (1885), 255–56.

Unsigned obituary. "H. W. Longfellow: In Memoriam." *Athenaeum*, 1 April 1882, 411–12.

Unsigned review. "The Poetical Works of Henry W. Longfellow." *Illustrated London News*. 24 November 1855, 630.

Unsigned review. "The Mystic, and the Song of Hiawatha." *Saturday Review*, 10 November 1855, 34–35.

Unsigned review. "*The Song of Hiawatha*. By H. W. Longfellow." *Athenaeum*, 10 November 1855, 1295–96.

Unsigned review. "Longfellow's Song of Hiawatha." *Spectator* 17 November 1855, 1200–1201.

Unsigned review. "Poetry of the Past Year." *Christian Remembrancer* 31 (1856), 264–308.

Unsigned review. "Longfellow's Song of Hiawatha." *Dublin University Magazine* 47 (1856), 90–99.

Unsigned poem. "The Song of Hiawatha (Author's Protective Edition)." *Punch*, 12 January 1856, 17.

Unsigned review. "The Song of Hiawatha." *New Quarterly Review* 5 (1856).

Unsigned review article. "The Indians of Western America: Glimpses of California and Texas." *Ainsworth's Magazine* 4 (1843), 441–48.

Unsigned review article. "Savage Life: The Western Tribes of North America." *Westminster Review* o.s. 103, n.s. 47 (1876), 416–51.

Upton, L.F.S. *Micmacs and Colonists: Indian-White Relations in the Maritimes, 1713–1867*. Vancouver: University of British Columbia Press, 1979.

Usher, Jean. *William Duncan of Metlakatla: A Victorian Missionary in British Columbia*. Ottawa: National Museums of Canada, 1974.

Van Kirk, Sylvia. *Many Tender Ties: Women in Fur Trade Society in Western Canada, 1670–1870*. Winnipeg: Watson and Dwyer, 1981.

Vickery, Ann. "A 'Lonely Crossing': Approaching Nineteenth-Century Australian Women's Poetry." *Victorian Poetry* 40 (2002), 33–53.

Vivian, Arthur Pendarves. *Wanderings in the Western Land*. London: Sampson Low, Marston, Searle, & Rivington, 1879.

Vizenor, Gerald. "Edward Curtis: Pictorialist and Ethnographic Adventurist." In *True West: Authenticity and the American West*, edited by William R. Handley and Nathaniel Lewis, 179–93. Lincoln: University of Nebraska Press, 2004.

Waldrep, Shelton. *The Aesthetics of Self-Invention: Oscar Wilde to David Bowie*. Minneapolis: University of Minnesota Press, 2004.

Walker, Cheryl. *Indian Nation: Native American Literature and Nineteenth-Century Nationalisms*. Durham, NC: Duke University Press, 1997.

Warburton, T. A. "Pocahontas, the Indian Heroine." *Bentley's Magazine*, 24 July 1848, 41–52.

Warren, Louis S. "Buffalo Bill Meets Dracula: William F. Cody, Bram Stoker, and the Frontiers of Racial Decay." *American Historical Review* 107 (2002), 1124–57.

———. *Buffalo Bill's America: William Cody and the Wild West Show*. New York: Random House, 2005.

Warton, Joseph. "The Dying Indian." In *The British Poets. Including Translations*. 100 vols. Vol. 58. T. Warton and J. Warton. Chiswick, England: Whittingham, 1822.

Waterston, Elizabeth. *Gilbert Parker and His Works*. Toronto: ECW Press, 1994.

[Watts-Dunton, Theodore]. "*Songs of the Great Dominion.*" *Athenaeum*, 28 September 1889, 412.

Webb, Janeen, and Andrew Enstice. *Aliens & Savages: Fiction, Politics and Prejudice in Australia*. Sydney: HarperCollins, 1998.

Weierman, Karen Woods. *One Nation, One Blood: Interracial Marriage in American Fiction, Scandal, and Law, 1820–1870*. Amherst: University of Massachusetts Press, 2005.

Welch, James. *The Heartsong of Charging Elk*. New York: Doubleday, 2000.

Westover, Cynthia M. *Bushy: A Romance Founded on Fact*. London: George Routledge and Sons, 1896.

White, Richard. *The Middle Ground: Indians, Empires, and Republics in the Great Lakes Region, 1650–1815*. Cambridge: Cambridge University Press, 1991.

Whitman, Walt. *Leaves of Grass*. Edited by Sculley Bradley, Harold W. Blodgett, Arthur Golden, and William White. 1855. Reprint, New York: Norton, 1980.

Wild, Isaac. *Travels through the States of North America and the Provinces of Upper and Lower Canada during the Years 1795, 1796, and 1797.* London: J. Stockdale, 1799.

Williams, Carol J. *Framing the West: Race, Gender, and the Photographic Frontier in the Pacific Northwest.* Oxford: Oxford University Press, 2005.

Williams, Daniel E. "Until They Are Contaminated by Their More Refined Neighbors: The Images of the Native American in Carver's *Travels through the Interior* and Its Influence on the Euro-American Imagination." In *Indians and Europe: An Interdisciplinary Collection of Essays,* edited by Christian F. Feest, 195–214. Reprint, Lincoln: University of Nebraska Press, 1999.

Williams, Samuel Cole. ed. *Adair's History of the American Indians.* 1775. Reprint, New York: Argonaut Press, 1966.

Wilson, Edward F. *Missionary Work among the Ojebway Indians.* London: Society for Promoting Christian Knowledge, 1886.

Wind, Astrid. "'Adieu to All': The Dying Indian at the Turn of the Eighteenth Century." *Symbiosis: A Journal of Anglo-American Literary Relations* 2 (1998), 39–55.

Wolfson, Susan. "'Domestic Affections' and 'the Spear of Minerva': Felicia Hemans and the Dilemma of Gender." In *Re-Visioning Romanticism: British Women Writers, 1776–1837,* edited by Carol Shiner Wilson and Joel Hafner, 128–66. Philadelphia: University of Pennsylvania Press, 1994.

———. "Gendering the Soul." In *Romantic Women Writers: Voices and Countervoices,* edited by Paula R. Feldman and Theresa M. Kelley, 33–68. Hanover, NH: University Press of New England, 1995.

———. *Borderlines: The Shiftings of Gender in British Romanticism.* Stanford: Stanford University Press, 2006.

Wood, Ellen. *East Lynne.* 1861. Reprint, London: Dent, 1984.

Wordsworth, William. *The Letters of William and Dorothy Wordsworth.* Arranged and edited by the late Ernest de Selincourt. 2nd ed. 8 vols. Oxford: Clarendon Press, 1867–1993.

———. *Lyrical Ballads.* Edited by Michael Mason. London: Longman, 1992.

Wright, Frances. *Views of Society and Manners in America.* 1821. Edited by Paul R. Baker. 1821. Reprint, Cambridge, MA: Belknap Press of Harvard University Press, 1963.

[Young, Arthur]. *The Adventures of Emmera, or the Fair American, Exemplifying the Peculiar Advantages of Society and Retirement.* 2 vols. London: W. Nicoll, 1767.

Yonge, Charlotte M. *Hopes and Fears; or, Scenes from the Life of a Spinster.* 2 vols.

Young, Egerton Ryerson. *On the Indian Trail, and Other Stories of Missionary Work among the Cree and Saulteaux Indians.* London: Religious Tract Society, 1897.

Young, Robert J. C. *Colonial Desire: Hybridity in Theory, Culture and Race.* London: Routledge, 1995.

Index